RAGE + HOPE

COUNTERPOINTS

Studies in the Postmodern Theory of Education

Joe L. Kincheloe and Shirley R. Steinberg
General Editors

Vol. 295

PETER LANG
New York • Washington, D.C./Baltimore • Bern
Frankfurt am Main • Berlin • Brussels • Vienna • Oxford

RAGE + HOPE

Interviews with Peter McLaren on War, Imperialism, + Critical Pedagogy

EDITED BY
Peter McLaren

PETER LANG
New York • Washington, D.C./Baltimore • Bern
Frankfurt am Main • Berlin • Brussels • Vienna • Oxford

Library of Congress Cataloging-in-Publication Data

McLaren, Peter.
Rage and hope: interviews with Peter McLaren on war, imperialism,
and critical pedagogy / edited by Peter McLaren.
p. cm. — (Counterpoints: studies in the postmodern theory of education; v. 295)
Some interviews previously published.
Includes bibliographical references and index.
1. Critical pedagogy. 2. Education—Political aspects. 3. McLaren,
Peter, 1948– —Interviews. 4. Educators—Canada—Interviews. I. Title. II. Series:
Counterpoints (New York, N.Y.); v. 295.
LC196.M353 370.11'5—dc22 2005035584
ISBN 0-8204-7917-9
ISSN 1058-1634

Bibliographic information published by **Die Deutsche Bibliothek**.
Die Deutsche Bibliothek lists this publication in the "Deutsche
Nationalbibliografie"; detailed bibliographic data is available
on the Internet at http://dnb.ddb.de/.

Cover photo by Laura McLaren-Layera

Cover design by Lisa Barfield

The paper in this book meets the guidelines for permanence and durability
of the Committee on Production Guidelines for Book Longevity
of the Council of Library Resources.

29 Broadway, New York, NY 10006
www.peterlang.com

Printed in the United States of America

Contents

Preface

For over a decade I have recognized and tried to put some flesh and muscle on my conviction that interviews can be liberatory social tools for students, teachers, and activists alike. I learned about the advantage of interviews as a graduate student when I was trying to delve into the arcane and labyrinthine depths of critical theory. I always was delighted when I was able to locate an interview with a philosopher or critical theorist whose work I was studying. Of course, interviewing the theorist firsthand is always the best strategy but opportunities to do so are rare indeed. Interviews generally seem not only more humanizing, but they usually contain the germs, or nuggets of a theorist's ideas. I still enjoy reading interviews, just to see if I am on track with an author's work.

Every week I receive a dozen or more questions from students, seasoned scholars, and activists around the world in which I am asked to kindly (and sometimes not-so-kindly) clarify, synthesize, or expand upon some aspect of my work. And in such cases I usually recommend to them that they read some of my interviews. Students who have difficulty with my books and articles, or who simply enjoy my work—or in some cases, both enjoy and curse them in one breath—have often told me how much my interviews help them navigate my ideas. That is one of the reasons that I decided to put together this book, which contains what I believe to be some of the more interesting and reflective interviews with me that have been published in journals and magazines over the last fifteen years. The majority of these interviews were done over email, which afforded me the opportunity to refer back to my own written work (which is always better than going on sheer memory) and occasionally, when the answer to an interviewer's question demanded some very in-depth theorizing, to borrow or modify selected paragraphs from some of my published articles. My advice to readers is to skip over sections that repeat the same material. From time to time I have taken sections of interviews and later on developed them into articles. In the main, however, the interviews are an attempt to summarize some of the major currents of my thinking. Certainly, they contain the ideas that most readily come to mind—and which I believe to be the most salient—when I am asked to share the more protean and robust developments in my recent work.

However, the reader should be warned that some sections of these interviews can be demanding, and in some cases it would be wise to read them alongside longer, more in-depth treatments that I have undertaken in my articles and books. Of course, the purpose of this book is not to navigate theory for its own sake or for academic jollification, but to help in a modest way to create the conditions for a social revolution in the tradition of socialist revolutionaries of the past and present—from the footloose rebels, soapboxers, hobos, shop stewards, union organizers and other working class militants that used to fill the Wobbly tent camps and fight against the bosses and the scabs, to the Magonistas and the Bolsheviks, to the present day Zapatistas, Chavistas of the Bolivarian revolution and Landless Peasant's Movement activists.

All of these interviews are wide-ranging, and usually I am given lots of latitude to reflect upon issues that are most pressing to my political work at the time. Because of this, there will be a great deal of overlap in the questions and answers but I hope that each interview will be helpful in some unique way.

Peter McLaren
Los Angeles, California
October 2005

global capitalism, imperialism and development in the age of empire

Introduction

I cannot feign some distanced objectivity in writing this profile of Peter McLaren. Our relationship dates back to 1989, when Philip Stedman, one of my professors at the University of Cincinnati, invited me to accompany him on a visit to Peter at nearby Miami University of Ohio. I had read some of Peter's work, particularly some of his early collaborations with Henry Giroux, who had helped bring Peter to Miami from Canada. No amount of reading, however, could have prepared me for meeting him face-to-face.

At the time, Peter and his wife Jenny, a beautiful woman possessed of equally great intelligence and compassion, lived an hour's drive from Cincinnati in the small town of Oxford, which is situated in the middle of southwest Ohio farm country. After we parked the car in front of their modest house, Jenny welcomed us warmly at the door before we ever had the chance to knock. She invited us in and we exchanged introductions for what seemed like a long time. Being so new to academia, I was anxious to meet Peter who was, even then, an important figure in critical educational studies. When he did appear, he too welcomed us warmly, receiving us like we had known each other for years and like our arrival was as much of an event for him as it was for us. As I've grown to know Peter over the past fifteen years, I've learned to trust and appreciate his immediacy as part of the more general passion with which he lives his life. It's the same passion unmistakably reflected in his writings, and the same passion that generates such tremendous shared loyalty and bonds of solidarity between himself, his students, and others of us who work with him.

As Alipio Casali & Ana Maria Araújo Freire so accurately describe him in a chapter from Marc Pruyn and Luis Huerta-Charles's new book, *Teaching Peter McLaren: Paths of Dissent* (2005), "it is impossible not to notice Peter McLaren in the middle of a crowd, much as it is impossible not to be completely drawn in by his image: the extravagance of his mode of dress, his disheveled hair, his tattoos, his quick, sudden gestures, his attentive manner and luminous aura. At first, he seems a caricature, a remnant of the counterculture of the 1960s" (21). Though the tattoos came after our Cincinnati years, I, too, was "drawn in" by Peter, but not as much by his appearance and demeanor as by the energy and the commitment that he brings to his work. Over a career that, to date, spans just two and a half decades, he has authored or co-authored more than 25 books, edited or co-edited 15 others, authored or coauthored over 100 chapters and more than 150 articles in scholarly journals.

Writing this profile of Peter has been a liberating catharsis for me. As much as I have always been drawn to his work, and as many times as he has come through for me when I've asked him to contribute to various projects (he has never rejected an invitation), my own stupid insecurities have prevented me from being totally comfortable in his presence. Antonia Darder shares similar feelings in her preface to *Teaching Peter McLaren* when she writes that "in all honesty, I must confess that although I appreciated his rhetorical gift, unusual language and powerful writings, I did not easily warm up to *the man* [emphasis added]. In fact, it took years for me to recognize the biases and prejudices that sharply colored my impressions." Though Darder doesn't discuss the nature of those "biases and prejudices," I have to wonder if they relate to what I've identified as the academy-induced feelings of insecurity that has inhibited me from feeling closer to him. Partially because of the passion of his presence described by Casali & Freire above, and partially because of his stature as perhaps the most internationally renowned figure in critical educational theory alive today, it is too easy to feel awestruck by Peter. It's also easy, I think, for some to feel jealous of his achievements. There are those, after all, who seem resentful of him. We can't deny the power of academia's hidden curriculum to socialize us into heavily narcissistic patterns wherein we learn to gaze upon our selves in the mirror pools of our curriculum vitas. We can, however, recognize it for the bourgeois ideology that it is and, therefore, strive to resist its counterrevolutionary effects by framing our relationships less in terms of career aspirations and more in terms of a common struggle.

Naming the Common Struggle

Peter McLaren's name may be new to many readers of mainstream left-leaning publications.The reasons for this are tragic. The Left has simply failed to mobilize any significant movement in recognition of the central importance that public education holds for the great historic struggle for democracy. For many reasons beyond its control, the political left in the United States has always been fragmented and reactionary. It simply lacks the resources to create and sustain the organizational structures necessary to compete with corporate-financed structures developed by the Right to inhibit the advancement of democracy. In contrast, since the populist movements of the 1960s that witnessed the potential of democratic movements to impact public institutions by harnessing the power of the state to serve public interests, the corporate sector of private wealth and privilege has subsidized the formation of a vast network of foundations, institutes, and think-tanks through which to bludgeon the mass-mind of government into complicity with their campaign of class warfare. The tight connections between these structures and the corporate-media have also given rise to such rightwing media celebrities as Rush Limbaugh, Ann Coulter, Bill O'Reilly and others. That same network also has very close ties to televangelists like Pat Robertson and Jerry Falwell, again using the media to generate religious fervor in support of their neo-liberal economic and neo-conservative political agendas. Those connections, of course, were most crudely revealed to us by Reverend Pat Robertson's recent call for the assassination of Hugo Chavez in which he expressed overt support for state terrorism in the name of U.S. imperialism.

Those who operate within elite planning circles that now include the likes of Reverend Robertson and other proto-fascists understand perfectly well the importance of maintaining the illusion of democracy. They also understand that combating democratic populism through military or police violence, as in a totalitarian state, would destroy that illusion. Therefore, they have invested heavily in developing these various structures dedicated to what Edward Herman and Noam Chomsky famously labeled "manufacturing consent." In order to maintain the illusion of democracy, they must control what people think, and they have made major inroads over the past thirty years toward turning the entire information system of our society into one huge propaganda machine.

Against this background, we can best understand their assault on public education and Peter McLaren's position as a leading figure in the resistance against capital's ruthless campaign against democracy domestically as well as globally.

Life in Schools?

For those of us who recognize public schools as legitimate sites for democratic advancement and for the contestation of capital's domination, Peter's work has always held central importance. Though he finds it impossible to identify a single moment in his life as sparking his politicization, Peter does recall a formative "series of events that began when my dad was fired from an electronics firm that was headquartered in Toronto. All the managers over fifty were fired so new managers could take over. I grew to hate corporations after watching my dad suffer. His emphysema grew worse. He refused to accept welfare, and got part-time work in various electronics stores. He died bitter and unhappy. I was bitter, too, and joined the counterculture."

This was around 1968, and joining the counterculture, for Peter, meant leaving Canada and going to the U.S. where he became involved in antiwar efforts. After a brief period in Los Angeles and San Francisco, he returned to Ontario, entered Waterloo University and earned his Bachelor of Arts in English Literature in 1973. Soon after, he began teaching at a middle school where he worked with inner-city students from Canada's largest public-housing project in the Jane-Finch area of Toronto. He would later write a book, *Cries from the Corridor,* on these experiences that, to his later horror, became a best-seller in Canada.

> I didn't offer any critical analysis in that first book, just stories of about my frustrations in trying to reach these inner-city kids who brought the violence of their lives outside the schools into the school itself. The book was shocking to Canadians. By not providing any critical analysis of the situation faced by these kids and their families, I left the door open for a lot of people to blame them for their own plight. That's when I became involved in critical theory, so I could get the story right the next time. That's what I tried to do

> with *Life in Schools: An Introduction to Critical Pedagogy and the Foundations of Education*. It's not a bestseller like *Cries from the Corridor,* but I've never had a bestseller since that first book, and I never will. But I don't care. As long as I can provide an analysis, I'll keep writing. (personal communication, 2005)

Internationally recognized as one of the leading architects of critical pedagogy, Peter was a close friend and associate of Paulo Freire, the late Brazilian theorist and activist whose famous book *Pedagogy of the Oppressed* helped to reawaken democratic energies around educational issues in North America and the rest of the world beginning in the 1970s. In a recent interview with Michael Shaughnessy (included in this volume, Interview Fifteen), Peter described Freire's work as being "about establishing the critical relationship between pedagogy and politics, highlighting the political aspects of the pedagogical and drawing attention to the implicit and explicit domain of the pedagogical inscribed in the political." While he could have well described his own work in those same terms, Peter's recognition of capital as the overwhelmingly dominant social relation of our times has led him to infuse his writings on critical pedagogy with his own brand of Marxist humanism, which he identifies as the "cornerstone" of his work. Capital, as a social relation, negates democracy by denying us our humanity, alienating us from our ability to autonomously act in community with others to create and recreate the world by reducing human beings to dead labor—strapped down and fed into the same system that produces and reproduces the private property that subjugates us in the first place. The aim of revolutionary critical pedagogy, for Peter, lies not with the abolition of private property, but with the abolition of the alienated labor on which it depends. For critical pedagogy to transcend its own domination under the social relations of capital, it must help those engaged in the pedagogical encounter to transcend their own alienation. To do so, Peter has written, critical pedagogy must brush

> against the grain of textual foundationalism, ocular fetishism, and the monumentalist abstraction of theory that characterizes most critical practice within teacher education classrooms. I am calling for a pedagogy in which a revolutionary multicultural ethics is performed—is lived in the streets—rather than simply reduced to the practice of reading texts (although the reading of texts with other texts, against other texts, and upon other texts is decidedly an important exercise). Teachers need to build upon the textual politics that dominate most multicultural classrooms by engaging in a politics of

> bodily and affective investment, which means "walking the talk" and working in those very communities one purports to serve. A critical pedagogy for multicultural education should quicken the affective analysis of students as well as provide them with a language of social analysis, cultural critique, and social activism in the service of cutting the power and practice of capital at its joints. (McLaren, 2005, p. 92)

With his open embrace of Marxist humanism, of course, Peter has become the target of the rightwing attack machine described above. One element of the rightwing network of ideological enforcement, the *Washington Times*, published an article by Kenneth Lloyd Billingsley attacking critical pedagogues in general, and Peter in particular. In another article appearing in the ominously titled magazine *Education Next*, published by the Hoover Institute (a neo-conservative think-tank that has become home to rightwing demagogue David Horowitz), J. Martin Rochester laughably accuses Peter of "intellectual flabbiness" while attacking critical pedagogy, first, for

> its emphasis on the affective-normative domain at the expense of the cognitive-empirical domain [This is simply not true and reflects either Rochester's ignorance of critical pedagogy or his willingness to lie about it.]—it is more interested in engaging students in understanding the world as it ought to be than in how it is [Again, this is another falsehood.]—and, second, [for] its acceptance of the hierarchical, judgmental classroom, where the teacher's role is not to facilitate value-free inquiry but instead to use the bully pulpit to preach doctrinaire gospel [The opposite is true, and critical pedagogues have always been especially self-conscious about guarding against such behavior], with schools performing the function not of political socialization but of counter-socialization. The school is to be, if not a ministry, at least a political party.

In criticizing critical pedagogy for politicizing education, both Billingsley and Rochester falsely portray traditional patterns in American schooling as benevolently apolitical and ideologically neutral, just as they would present their own arguments as being independent of the neo-conservative agendas of the publications in which they appeared. Both the *Washington Times*, owned by billionaire neo-conservative Reverend Sun Myung Moon, and *Education Next* support the No Child Left Behind law which pressures teachers to teach in manner deemed most efficient toward maximizing students' scores on standardized tests. Under these pressures, teachers do not approach student learning as a process of "value-free inquiry" as Rochester mischaracterizes the traditional patterns. Rather, they approach student learning in the most vulgar of didactic terms—drilling and killing the kids to score well on the tests. Under these prevailing conditions in public schools today, Billingsley and Rochester hardly need to worry themselves, however, over the prevalence of critical pedagogy. Education in the United States is as far away from revolutionary critical pedagogy as the American political system is from democracy.

Just Rewards

For those of us writing from the left, being attacked in popular rightwing publications comes as an honor. It is a signal to us of our success. The Right attacks only those whom it fears, and it fears only those whose work threatens to awaken the public to seek the truth about their own realities and to transform those realities in accordance with alternative possibilities of their own imagining. The more the Right attacks us, the more energized we become, because we know our efforts are making a difference in people's lives.

In Peter's case, the difference his work is making has spilled over our own borders to attract international attention and honors. In 2004, an international panel of experts organized by The Moscow School of Social and Economic Sciences, a Russian-British University, named *Life in Schools* one of the 12 most significant education books ever written. In that same year, he received an honorary doctorate from the University of Lapland in Finland and, most notably, a group of scholars in northern Mexico established an institute in his name—La Fundación McLaren de Pedagogía Crítica (The McLaren Foundation of Critical Pedagogy).

In spite of the international and national awards and honors that he has received over the years, those of us who know Peter realize that he derives the greatest honor from the privilege of working with his students and his colleagues. As Antonia Darder reported earlier, she remained aloof from Peter for many years. Eventually, however, she expressed her gratitude to him for "his patience and perseverance" with her. "For what I learned over time," she writes, "was that Peter McLaren is one of the kindest and generous souls that I have met in the world of academia. Yes, like so many of us pitiful humans, he forever struggles with personal questions of insecurity and self-doubt—but like few, he is ever willing to extend a hand and create opportunities for comrades and struggling young scholars who seek his support."

As previously mentioned, two of those young scholars, former students, and comrades—Marc Pruyn and Luis Huerta-Charles—have recently honored Peter by publishing a book (*Teaching Peter McLaren: Paths of Dissent*) of essays written by colleagues and other former students. Nathalia Jaramillo, one of his current students recently wrote to me that

> I consider Peter not only my mentor but my camarada, a dear and special friend. Working with Peter has changed my life completely, and it is not only because he serves as my academic mentor who has taught me a great deal about the ins and outs of the academy and of producing scholarship. I've learned the most from Peter because of who he is inside. It's his spirit, his heart, his loyalty, imagination for and fearless defense of revolutionary praxis that has taught me the most. I've had the opportunity to work closely with Peter for the past three years and I'm blessed. I'm blessed to be in his company and in that of people around the world who are striving to make this a better place for us all.

Even before the neoconservative revolution intensified the horrifying effects of neoliberalism at home and abroad, Peter's work has always reminded us how far we are from the democratic ideals our governing elites profess to emulate here in the United States. In this sense, Peter's words provoke our rage. At the same time, he also empowers us with hope. Through his words and his comradeship, Peter inspires us to solidarity, to action, and to a critical-socialist pedagogy that is so much sorely needed in these dark times.

References

McLaren, Peter. (2005). *Capitalists and Conquerors: Critical Pedagogy Against Empire*. Lanham, Maryland: Rowman and Littlefield.

Pruyn, Marc and Huerta-Charles, Luis. (Editors) (2005). *Teaching Peter McLaren: Paths of Dissent*. New York: Peter Lang Publishing.

Interview 1

toward a critical revolutionary pedagogy

Michael Pozo

Mike Pozo had done interviews with Henry Giroux and E. San Juan for his university journal, and I was highly impressed with his knowledge and politics. After doing this interview with me, I invited Mike to give a talk at the opening of La Fundación McLaren de Pedagogía Crítica at the Universidad de Tijuana. He was a hit at the opening. Mike is a doctoral student in English literature, and while he is not in education, he appreciates the transdisciplinary importance of critical pedagogy. I always look forward to doing interviews in journals that are outside of my official field of education. It helps get debates going in other fields. And these debates are absolutely urgent, especially when the country is in such a mess with the current Bush administration. This is important for the social revolution through knowledge and dialogue that practitioners of critical pedagogy try to initiate.

MICHAEL POZO: Can you give us some background to your most well known book of critical pedagogy?

PETER MCLAREN: I started out in the world of pedagogy as an elementary school teacher in the mid-seventies and when I published my school diary, *Cries from the Corridor: The New Suburban Ghettoes*, in 1980, I was as heart-thumpingly surprised as everyone else that it became a national best-seller, even provoking a national debate on the state of Canada's inner-city schools. I eventually grew to dislike the book—disgusted perhaps is a better term—but felt it would be useful to publish it here in the U.S. on condition that it be accompanied by an extended self-critique. The problem that I had with the original book is that it was a journalistic description of my experience with little analysis so that it could have been, and was, read as blaming the students and their families for the violence that permeated their lives both inside and outside of the school context. That all changed when I republished the book as *Life in Schools*, with an extended leftist analysis, and the book gradually became more politically radical and more theoretically nuanced with each edition (there have been four so far). I was fortunate indeed to have had a left-wing editor who took a chance on the book when most publishers felt it was too radical to be taken up in colleges of education for any purpose other than mockery.

MICHAEL: Can you describe your initial steps into critical pedagogy as a student and then as a professor?

PETER: When I entered graduate school, I was seen as a "hands on" veteran inner-city teacher who, having paid his dues, understandably emphasized the everyday pedagogical dilemmas and concerns of the classroom teaching. The more that I had time to read in the fields of critical theory, Marxist revolutionary theory, cultural studies, and feminist studies, the more that I realized that teachers could benefit from being grounded theoretically and politically (that they refracted their experiences through both practical/informal/tacit knowledge and normal theoretical constructs)—and this meant the difficult work of developing a coherent "philosophy of praxis."

After I finished publishing a number of subsequent books, the descriptions that followed me through the field changed from a hands-on practitioner to that of: "a theorist whose vocabulary is a definite challenge for many teachers." My work became less directed at the classroom per se, and more focused on issues such as political, cultural and racial identity, anti-racist/multicultural education, the politics of white supremacy, resistance and popular culture, rituals of the school as vehicles for both resistance and conformity, the formation of subjectivity, and liberation theology. I was becoming focused on the larger relevance of critical pedagogy.

In other words, I felt that critical pedagogy was habitually elusive when it came to hands-on solutions but fiercely relevant when addressing life's permanent conditions of exploitation. I realized that there were teachers who could write about the classroom and in doing so provide more practical insights than I could but that I could make a contribution in rethinking the conceptual and political terrain of critical pedagogy in the educational literature. When Henry Giroux graciously invited me to come to the U.S. to start a cultural studies center with him (after my first year as a professor in Canada ended with the Dean refusing to renew my contract because of the controversy over my politics and pedagogy), I left for the mid-western U.S. This was the mid-1980s. Around that time Paulo Freire had invited me to a conference in Cuba, where I met a lot of Brazilians and Mexicans in attendance. I began spending time in Latin America and becoming more interested in Marxist critique of political economy. Subsequently, I began to realize that postmodern theory could be quite a reactionary approach in so far as it failed to challenge with the verve and sustained effort that was demanded of the times the social relations of capitalist production and reproduction. While I still adopted the term, critical postmodernism, or resistance postmodernism, to describe my work, I was haunted by the realization that I had not sufficiently engaged the work of Marx and Marxist thinkers.

The more I began engaging in the work of Marx, and meeting social activists driven by Marxist anti-imperialist projects throughout the Americas, I no longer felt that the work on "radical democracy" convincingly demonstrated that it was superior to the Marxist problematic. It appeared to me that, in the main, it had despairingly capitulated to the inevitability of the rule of capital and the regime of the commodity. That work, along with much of the work in post-colonialist criticism, appeared too detached from historical specificities and basic determinations. Marxist critique to my mind more adequately addressed the differentiated totalities of contemporary society and their historical imbrications in the world system of global capitalism.

MICHAEL: So in your book *Life in Schools* we read of your personal growth as an inner-city elementary school teacher to a future practitioner of critical pedagogy. In 2000 your book, *Che Guevara, Paulo Freire and the Pedagogy of Revolution* seemed like yet another step in your life as an educator. Can you then describe the differences/similarities between the critical pedagogy you began with and the pedagogy of revolution you now practice?

PETER: Rather than employ the term critical pedagogy, I often use the term that British educator Paula Allman has christened "revolutionary critical pedagogy." I do so because it raises issues and unleashes the kind of uncompromising critique that more domesticated currents of critical pedagogy do not. It draws attention to the key concepts of imperialism (both economic and military) and neo-liberalism and, by tacking around the work of Karl Marx, Paulo Freire, and Antonio Gramsci (not to mention Amilcar Cabral, Frantz Fanon, C.L.R. James, and Walter Rodney), it brings some desperately needed theoretical ballast to the teetering critical educational tradition. Such theoretical infrastructure is absolutely necessary for the construction of concrete pedagogical spaces in schools and in other sites where people struggle for educational change and social and political transformation.

I will say that I am more comfortable having my work described as Marxist humanist, a term developed by Raya Dunayevskaya, who once served as Trotsky's secretary in Mexico, and who developed the tradition of Marxist humanism in the U.S. Let me also say that critical revolutionary pedagogy, as I am trying to develop it, offers a counterpoint to many educational programs that describe themselves under the heading of "social justice." As I see it, the term "social justice" often operates as a cover for legitimizing capitalism or for tacitly admitting to or resigning oneself to its brute intractability. I try to develop a counterpoint to the way social justice is used in progressive education by inviting students to examine critically the epistemological and axiological dimensions of democracy.

I reject the idea of evaluating a society primarily on the basis of maximizing minimal well-being for the poor and the powerless. I do this because the concept of social justice often serves an ideological smokescreen for reproducing ruling-class interests when it is used to refer to resource redistribution. Programs centering on the concept of education and social justice—and this is the case in many colleges of education, as far as I am concerned—draw inspiration from a liberal, Rawlsian or Habermasian conception of social justice. Such conceptions are premised on the idea of a democratic society preoccupied by the logic of reformism. This is at odds with the idea of a socialist society actively engaged in revolutionary transformation.

When the production of inequalities begins to affect the weakest, only then does capitalist society consider an injustice to have occurred. Marx's critique of political economy and the theories of social justice propounded by Rawls and Habermas are fundamentally at odds; in fact, they are virtually irreconcilable. Liberal theories of justice attempt to harmonize individual interests in the private sphere. But as Daniel Bensaid points out, correctly in my view, you can't allocate the collective productivity of social labor individually; the concept of cooperation and mutual agreement between individuals is a formalist fiction. Nor can you reduce social relations of exploitation to intersubjective relations.

I agree with Bensaid's critique of the Rawlsian conception of the social contract—that its conclusions are built into its premises. For Rawls, it is possible for inequality to exist only so long as such inequalities make a functional contribution to the expectations of the least advantaged. It is okay for the capitalist pie to get bigger for the captains of industry as long as the narrow piece carved out for the poor grows a sliver in return.

But the political conception of justice, be it Rawls or Habermas, starts to break down in the face of real, existing inequality premised on the reproduction of capitalist social relations of exploitation. In a world devoid of class conflict, one that is fundamentally driven by intersubjectivity and communicative rationality, the political conception of social justice makes sense, but we don't inhabit such a world. We don't live in a world where class relations and property relations are dissolved in a formal world of inter-individual juridical relations. I can't accept the social justice position because it accepts a priori the despotism of the market; it egregiously ignores questions of production and in my mind all theories of justice are relative to the mode of production. As long as you focus one-sidedly on the distribution of wealth, and issues of fairness and justice in this regard, you intentionally or not camouflage the social relations of production, the execrable systemic exploitation of workers by capitalists, and the exploitative nature of capitalism (the subsumption of living labor by abstract labor) at its very roots. To what extent, then, do schools that are underwritten by a theory of social justice function as NGOs (see Michael Parenti on this) that help to provide "self-help" projects, "popular education," and job training, to temporarily absorb small groups of poor, to co-opt critical efforts to contest capitalist exploitation, and to undermine anti-imperialist struggles? To what extent do social justice programs give the impression that capitalism is fundamental to democracy?

So, in effect, this is a position that I take within revolutionary critical pedagogy, a position that is highly critical of most social justice agendas as they are put into practice in schools and colleges of education. Let me make clear, however, that the emphasis on redistribution of wealth is not rejected tout court, but its inner contradictions are exposed and opportunities are created for discussing the possibility, the necessity, of creating a world outside the social universe of capital. We start to ask ourselves: What might a transition to socialism mean at this precise time in world history, and especially in terms of what is happening here in the United States, in what has been called the belly of the beast.

Remember, Mike, that whereas it was a difficult struggle for popular movements of poor and working people to pressure states to intervene in the capitalist economy—in the processes of production and circulation—in order to redistribute wealth and provide some kind of social protection from unchecked market forces during the time of Keynesianism or social capitalism, it is much more difficult today. As Bill Robinson points out, during the days of Keynesianism the state intervened under pressure by the working class by means of taxes on capital, government regulation of corporate activities, minimum wages, strong labor and other social protection laws, public spending on the social wage in health, education, public housing, job creation programs, and public provision of essential services such as water, sanitation, and electricity. But these constraints on profit-making can be eradicated by neoliberalism—which is what is happening at present—by means of unfettered global transnationally oriented capital.

There are two processes at work here. One is worldwide market liberalization and the construction of a new legal and regulatory superstructure for the global economy. The other is the internal restructuring and global integration of each national economy. Robinson underscores correctly that the goal of this twin-engine juggernaut of capitalist globalization is to break down all national barriers to the free movement of transnational capital across borders, and to institute the free operation of capital within borders, which has the combined effect of opening up all areas of society to what he calls "the logic of profit-making unhindered by the logic of social need." Robinson calls this "global apartheid"—a very appropriate term, in my view.

I am not against attempts to redistribute the wealth from the tiny minority who exercise political power over the poor (due to the fact that they control most of the wealth) to the vast armies of the poor, but rather to challenge the very social relations and social logic of capital and resist it. Of course, redistribution with a democratic socialist initiative could indeed be a first step.

MICHAEL: Most students are taught under a skills-oriented type of education that basically prepares them to be workers and not, say, revolutionaries. What would you say differentiates a student taught by critical pedagogy as she enters the same world after graduation?

PETER: I teach in the doctoral program at UCLA, but my classes are often a collection of doctoral, masters, and undergraduate students. Most of my doctoral student advisees are getting their PhDs so that they can become professors and transform teacher education institutions. They were radical teachers and/or social activists who now want to help to transform institutions of "higher" learning. So my own classroom teaching focuses on the philosophical, theoretical, and political debates among the left progressives and the more revolutionary left and how this could apply to critical pedagogy.

My main task has been to develop a coherent philosophy of praxis in which critical pedagogy can be located. This has meant for me de-domesticating critical pedagogy, which has, in many cases, been limited to putting students in a circle and having discussions on contemporary themes, so that everyone is encouraged to speak. Or else it has been confined to creating versions of a student-centered curriculum, etc.

My particular task is to transform teacher and student practice into a far-reaching political praxis linked to social movements to contribute to creating a multi-racial, gender-balanced, anti-imperialist, anti-capitalist movement that is internationalist in scope. The process whereby labor-power is transformed into human capital and concrete living labor is subsumed by abstract labor requires a dialectical understanding that historical materialist critique can best provide. Historical materialism provides critical pedagogy with a theory of the material basis of social life rooted in historical social relations and assumes paramount importance in uncovering the structure of class conflict as well as unraveling the effects produced by the social division of labor.

I have set my work up to critique mainstream liberal versions of critical pedagogy—which attempts to reconcile social change to the imperatives of capital's law of value—by using an historical materialist approach.

MICHAEL: How does your classroom environment prepare students for a world that is often like a harsh wake-up call from life in a university where different groups mix together and academic success is said to be equally accessible to all?

PETER: For teachers working in teacher preparation programs, critical pedagogy has been a way of introducing students—often white, middle-class students—to revolutionary figures such as Paulo Freire and Malcolm X, for example. When teachers read the works of Freire, or other critical educators, often they are introduced conceptually for the first time to the irrepressible conflict-ridden nature of the capital/labor dialectic and are given the rare opportunity—rare within colleges and schools of education that are traditionally conservative—to explore various theoretical languages with which to unpack this intractable antagonism and open it up for scrutiny.

Many students claim that their courses in critical pedagogy apprised them for the first time with the opportunity to explore the relationship between ideology and pedagogical practice. By the end of the course they were able to participate actively and creatively in a critique of the manifold mediations of social forces and social relations of exploitation that shaped the historical specificity of their social being. They were able to explore their own self and social formation in a language that uncovered the role of capital and class in their everyday lives and helped to explain how class relations have been racialized and linked to patriarchy and heterosexism.

It is not that critical pedagogy helped to bring this knowledge and insight all about. But critical pedagogy helped many to clarify some aspects of these processes and relations and assisted in providing a more revealing sociological language in which to discuss them. Many had already come to recognize that the inequality, racism, and sexism that is rife in civil society is indeed historically alterable. They had already come to acknowledge, as well, the profound fecundity of their own social agency. But critical pedagogy enabled them to clarify their tacit knowledge about these issues and locate their understanding in a wider theoretical framework that enabled them to make connections that they didn't make beforehand.

In the end, some would ally themselves with Freire's practice of critical literacy, for example. Others would want to focus on anti-racism. Still others made the decision to contribute to the development of feminist pedagogy. In some cases, students decided that revolutionary critical pedagogy makes much more sense than the liberal variants of critical pedagogy in addressing issues such as the globalization of capital, U.S. imperialism, and the privatization, corporatization, and businessification of schooling, and its links to the military industrial complex. But the important issue is that the seeds of critique and transformation have been planted as soon as students are afforded the opportunity to become—and treated as—agents of their own history rather than passive recipients of a history written for them by the ambassadors of empire and their corporate quislings.

It takes human beings to recreate the revolutionary dialectic. And as Raya Dunayevskaya notes, it is not enough to meet this challenge from practice, or from one's experience, but also from the self-development of the Idea (Hegel's term) so that theory can be deepened to the point where it can engage the Marxian notion of the philosophy of revolution in permanence. Here, the work of Marx becomes the quilting point between theory and practice, where ideas can be made concrete in the specificity of human struggle. A philosophically driven revolutionary critical pedagogy—one that aspires towards a coherent philosophy of praxis—can help teachers and students grasp the specificity of the concrete within the totality of the universal—for instance, the laws of motion of capital as they operate out of sight of our everyday lives and thus escape our common-sense understanding.

Revolutionary critical pedagogy can assist us in understanding history as a process in which human beings make their own society, although in conditions most often not of their own choosing and therefore populated with the intentions of others. And further, the practice of double negation can help us understand the movement of both thought and action by means of praxis, or what Dunayevskaya called the "philosophy of history." The philosophy of history proceeds from the messy web of everyday social reality—from the arena of facticity and tissues of empirical life—and not from lofty abstractions or idealistic concepts gasping for air in the lofty heights of Mount Olympus (the later being an example of the bourgeois mode of thought).

Critical revolutionary educators engage students in a dialectical reading of social life in which "the labor of the negative" helps them to understand human development from the perspective of the wider social totality. By examining Marx's specific appropriation of the Hegelian dialectic, students are able to grasp how the positive is always contained in the negative. In this way, every new society can be grasped as the negation of the preceding one, conditioned by the forces of production—which gives us an opportunity for a new beginning. I think it is certainly a truism that ideas often correspond to the economic structure of society, but at the same time we need to remember that history is in no way unconditional. In other words, not everything can be reduced to the sum total of economic conditions.

The actions of human beings are what shapes history. History is not given form and substance by abstract categories. Both Freire and Dunayevskaya stress here that the educator must be educated. The idea that a future society comes into being as a negation of the existing one (whose habits and ideas continue to populate it) finds its strongest expression in class struggle. Here we note that dialectical movement is a characteristic not only of thought but also of life and history itself.

But at this current historical moment it seems to many of us that we are being overtaken by history, it appears to be moving too fast, we feel that we are powerless to stop it from leaving us behind, flailing wildly in its wake as it rushes towards a globalized future.

Globalization has meant worldwide empowerment of the rich and devastation for the ranks of the poor as oligopolistic corporations swallow the globe and industry becomes dominated by new technologies. The transnational private sphere has been empowered by globalization, as corporations, financial institutions, and wealthy individuals seize more and more control. The creation of conditions favorable to private investment becomes the cardinal function of the government. Deregulation, privatization of public service, and cutbacks in public spending for social welfare are the natural outcomes of this process.

The signal goal here is competitive return on investment capital. In effect, financial markets controlled by foreign investors regulate government policy and not the other way around since investment capital is for the most part outside all political control. Citizens can no longer be protected by nation-states and offered any assurance that they will be able to find affordable housing, education for their children, or medical assistance. And it is the International Monetary Fund and the World Trade Organization who oversee regulatory functions outside the purview of democratic decision-making processes.

It is these bureaucratic institutions that set the rules and arbitrate between the dominant economic powers, severely diminishing the power of governments to protect their citizens, and crippling the democratic public sphere in the process. We are now in the midst of an "epidemic of overproduction," and a massive explosion in the industrial reserve army of the dispossessed that now live in tent cities—or casas de carton—in the heart of many of our metropolitan centers. At this moment we are witnessing a re-feudalisation of capitalism, as it refuels itself with the more barbarous characteristics of its robber baron and McKinley-era past. We are not talking here about lemonade stand capitalism on steroids, but the most vicious form of deregulated exploitation of the poor that history has witnessed during the last century.

MICHAEL: I draw certain parallels from Paulo Freire's comments on the responsibility of the oppressed to that of some students who believe the sole purpose of an education is to provide the means to achieve material gains. In *Pedagogy of the Oppressed* Freire describes the dual task of the oppressed as self and social liberation. He writes, "In order for this struggle to have meaning the oppressed must not in seeking to regain their humanity (which is a way to create it) become in turn oppressors of the oppressors but rather restorers of the humanity of both"(26). Have you encountered resistance from students to your ideas? And if so, how do teachers with similar concerns use critical pedagogy to convince students of such a heavy responsibility to not only their needs but those of the community?

PETER: Yes, I have encountered resistance indeed. The first reaction I get to the critique of political economy from many students in my classes is either plumping for free enterprise capitalism out of a Panglossian conviction that it represents the best of all possible arrangements or a "pragmatic" desire to "fix" capitalism so that resources are more evenly distributed—the latter is not a bad sentiment in and of itself, of course—and these same students often stubbornly express the view that revolutionary praxis is but an abstract ideal—a thin red membrane in the metaphysical body of the social—that can serve as little more than a moral corrective to capitalism by making capitalism a bit more "humane" and "people friendly." They point to what they perceive as the abysmal "failure" of revolutions of the past and the historical defeat of revolutionary movements worldwide. Many defensively—if not triumphantly—embrace the view that capitalist democracy, while admittedly imperfect, is still by far the least oppressive social arrangement available to humankind and that it has brought freedom and human rights to many nations around the world.

So as you can see, Mike, there is a great deal of work to do in class in terms of mounting a trenchant, uncompromising and convincing challenge to these perspectives that are very commonly (although sometimes cautiously and occasionally reluctantly) held by U.S. students entering graduate programs in education. This is not to dismiss their views tout court but to tease out the contradictions in their perspectives. We begin by examining the intrinsically exploitative nature of capitalist society, using some introductory texts and essays by Bertell Ollman, and then tackle the difficult task of reading *Capital*, Volume 1, and the labor theory of value.

We look at this issue from the perspective from a number of Marxist orientations and I try to present the case that capitalism can't be sufficiently reformed and still remain capitalism. This provokes lively debates, as you can well imagine. Students also anguish about the fact that, as future professors of education, they will be co-opted by the system. Some want tangible evidence that critical pedagogy can be effective in transforming the system. And it does happen that some opt out of the doctoral program to engage in grassroots political activism. Others resign themselves to a left liberalism that works on the basis of making slow, step-by-step, incremental changes.

Still others approach their work from the perspective of the dialectic between reformism and revolution: they work in the arena of policy, curriculum and pedagogical reform, while keeping in mind the wider goal of revolutionary social change which stipulates an eventual transition to socialism. I would put myself in this category, although I certainly lean heavily on the side of a Marxist revolutionary politics. All kinds of dynamics occur and perspectives are raised in my classrooms. We try to work through them, name them for what they are, raise issues, pose difficult questions that are dangerous to the system, and develop strategies.

I can say that I am proud, for instance, of the way that many students in our graduate school of education took action against the imperialist war on Iraq, how they organized protests, challenged professors who supported the war, and made links with social movements inside and outside of the university. Not all students were active on this front. Some students feel that upon graduation they won't be hired by schools of education if they work in the field of critical pedagogy and if they are perceived as outspoken critics of the system. I've heard from students who attend Ivy League schools of education that critical pedagogy is decried in many of their courses as "unscientific" and its more revolutionary variants are deemed an example of left-wing, anti-American political propaganda. A few students have told me that references to critical pedagogy have to be expunged from their dissertations.

But your question raises an important issue: How do the oppressed avoid becoming the oppressor? As I have mentioned, one of the ways to approach this with students is through Raya Dunayevskaya's work on the negation of the negation—which uses a left Hegelian and Marxist approach to the concept of absolute negativity. One of the questions raised within the Marxist humanist tradition becomes: Why have so many revolutions in the past transformed into their opposite? Here Dunayevskaya's protean concept of absolute negativity comes in play in the sense that it represents both totality and a new beginning. She noted that without a philosophy of revolution, activism focuses on anti-imperialism and anti-capitalism without ever revealing what it stands for, without ever describing what a society outside of the value form of labor or social universe of capital might look like. For a new beginning to occur, the separation between mass activity and the activity of thinking must be broken down. But to do this, students and teachers need to grasp the vantage point of critique and transformation for themselves.

MICHAEL: How does critical pedagogy address the more standard pedagogy practiced so widely in most schools? How do you see critical pedagogy surviving and growing in an atmosphere of rampant conservativism from school administrators?

PETER: Speaking about the current atmosphere of rampant conservatism, I just read an attack on critical pedagogy by The Hoover Institute's education journal, *Education Next*, that demonstrates the type of overt attempts by conservative attack-dogs to harmonize the purpose and function of schooling with the current reign of capital and the contemporary dynamics of advanced capitalism—not necessarily in the gratingly familiar mode of conservative denunciations and sound-byte Viagraizations associated with FOX TV editorializing—but in the reasoned tone of conservative academics who routinely dismiss attempts on the part of radical educators to "politicize" classroom subject-matter. For instance, the author attacks me for failing to mention the "normal stuff of schooling" which he characterizes as "alphabets," "algorithms," and "lab experiments," and he condemns, among many things, my remark that the "U.S. is fascist" and the point I make that "the greed of the U.S. ruling class is seemingly unparalleled in history." Offering no arguments to counter my statements, he sets forth his own vision of education—promoting "the discipline and furniture of the mind"—which he takes, astonishingly, from an 1830 Yale University report (about as enfeebling a vision of education that you could find anywhere).

The ideology driving this creed evades the systemic totality of capitalism, and the determinative force of capitalism, capturing one reason why critical pedagogy is under intense scrutiny in schools or why it comes under attack by conservative forces in schools of education. Dare I say that critical pedagogy comes under similar attacks among critics in the humanities?

In schools of education, critical pedagogy has always been a marginal approach and continues to be so, although panels on critical pedagogy continue to attract interest at some of the national education conferences. It is at the same time in a process of transition; while critical pedagogy is becoming more visible in certain venues, it nevertheless remains in danger of political domestication through its dalliance with conservative postmodern theories and in approaches that define themselves as post-Marxist. The type of curricula and pedagogies practiced widely in schools of education do not, for instance, address the concept of labor. For me, the concept of labor is axiomatic—the Archimedean fulcrum—for theorizing the school/society relationship and thus for developing radical pedagogical imperatives, strategies, and practices for overcoming the constitutive contradictions that such a coupling generates, such as educating students to play a role in the privatization of surplus extraction. The larger goal that revolutionary critical pedagogy stipulates for radical educationalists involves direct participation of students in thinking critically about what a socialist reconstruction and alternative to capitalism might look like.

However, without a critical lexicon and interpretative framework that can unpack the labor/capital relationship in all of its capillary detail, critical pedagogy is likely to remain at the level of what I have called "the democracy of empty forms." By that term I refer to formal changes in the structure of classroom discourse—sitting in a circle, student-centered curricula, matching teaching styles to learning styles, etc.—something that I mentioned in my answer to one of your previous questions. Of course, any improvements in these directions are to be welcomed, but they can't be a substitute for critical pedagogy. Today, as has been the case throughout the history of capitalism, labor-power is capitalized and commodified and education plays a tragic role in this cruel history. But—and here is a fundamental point—in so far as schooling is premised upon generating the living commodity of labor-power, upon which the entire social universe of capital depends, it can become a foundation for human resistance. There are constitutive and defining limits to how far labor-power can be commodified. After, all, workers are the sources of labor-power, and as such can potentially engage in acts of refusing alienation. Capital, a relation of general commodification predicated on the wage relation, needs labor. But labor does not depend upon capital. Labor can dispense with the wage, and with capitalism, and it is potentially autonomous in the sense that it can potentially organize its creative energies in a different way outside of the value form of labor. One of the goals of revolutionary critical pedagogy is to discover socialist alternatives to the current value form of labor that drives capitalist society. In so far as education and training socially produce labor-power, this process can be resisted.

The most stalwart radical educators push this resistance to the extreme in their pedagogical praxis centered around an anti-imperialist, anti-capitalist agenda. The overall goal of revolutionary critical pedagogy, in my view, is to help students discover how the use-value of working-class labor-power is being exploited by ruling class capital but also to learn that working-class initiative and power can destroy this type of determination and force a recomposition of class relations. Sure, it's unreasonable to expect a working-class revolution at this particular historical moment. But it is possible down the line with an increase in the creation of critical consciousness among workers, and the likelihood that the current crisis of capital will worsen.

Critical pedagogy can help students in their efforts to break down capital's control of the creation of new labor-power and to resist the endless subordination of life to work in the social factory we call everyday life. Critical pedagogy is necessary but insufficient. In the ongoing struggle, it is not a panacea for bringing about the social revolution we all very much desire. But it can play a formidable role. As a critical educator, I follow Glenn Rikowski's work and encourage students to ask themselves the following question: What is the maximum damage we can do to the rule of capital, to the dominance of capital's value form? The answer to this is not simple. It might include organizing against sweatshops; working with aggrieved communities in the area of media literacy; assisting grassroots activist organizations in developing pedagogical projects directed at unpacking the links among capitalism, imperialism, and war; joining forces with anti-globalization groups; increasing public awareness about the dangers of educational privatization; fighting racism and sexism in the workplace; and the list goes on.

MICHAEL: Again, in *Che Guevara, Paulo Freire and the Pedagogy of Revolution* you quote an important passage from Freire. "Hoping that the teaching of content in and of itself will generate tomorrow a radical intelligence of reality is to take on a controlled position rather than a critical one. It means to fall for a magical comprehension of content which attributes to it a criticizing power of its own. The more we deposit content in the learners' heads and the more diversified the content is, the more possible it will be for them to, sooner or later experience a critical awakening, decide and break away" (157). Do you feel places like English or history departments or even composition courses are viable sites for sustainable dissent and/or critical pedagogy?

PETER: If they are not already viable sites, then they must be made into viable sites. One indication that they are not becoming sites of sustainable dissent is the way in which the work of Paulo Freire has become—in many instances—reconciled to capitalism through political vulgarization and pedagogical domestication. The work of Freire is often used in the field of critical literacy in a way that alarmingly disconnects literacy and pedagogy from capitalist exploitation and class struggle: in short, in a way that side-steps revolutionary praxis. It is not enough to put Freire on the reading lists, or Fanon, or Malcolm X, or Menchú, and others, for that matter. It is essential that they be read against, alongside and upon the daily struggles that envelope us, both here and elsewhere around the world.

As universities become more privatized, or corporatized, this task becomes more difficult. It is also more difficult post-9/11. Here, at UCLA, progressive faculty are currently resisting an attempt by the senate to weaken academic freedom by placing it in the hand of the university's governing body, rather than leaving it—as it currently exists—linked to an individual professor's constitutional rights.

MICHAEL: How would you describe the roles teachers, students and workers play after 9/11?

PETER: I am writing this interview in a café in West Hollywood that currently displays a big ugly banner surrounded by American flags that says: "We Will Never Forget." Rather than focus on the horrible tragedy of 9/11 in the context of the murder of thousands of innocent civilians, I think it would be better for the political soul of the United States if it decided not to forget its complicity in the murder of millions of innocent victims over the last century alone. We should not forget that Bush's permanent war on terrorism is sacrificing the lives of the poor who serve in the military to enforce the profit-making capacities of the rich CEOs of companies like Halliburton. More than ever, teachers need to educate their students about U.S. imperialism, militarism, war crimes, and U.S. support for right-wing dictatorships throughout the world. Of course, we should remember 9/11 and mourn the victims and honor their lives, but we should not let this act of infamy contribute further to our egregious historical amnesia surrounding the destructive role that the U.S. has played in the history of other nations.

I am not simply referring to the practice of surveying the brute, incontrovertible historical facts, those that Michael Parenti, Noam Chomsky, Bill Blum, and others have courageously made available to the American public (but which remain relatively unknown among teacher educators as well as education students because they get little, if any, mainstream media exposure): over the last five decades the U.S. national security state funded and advised right-wing forces in the overthrow of reformist governments in Argentina, Bolivia, Chile, Brazil, Indonesia, Uruguay, Haiti, the Congo, the Dominican Republic, Guyana, Syria, Greece, etc.; the U.S. has participated in proxy mercenary wars against Nicaragua, Angola, Mozambique, Ethiopia, Portugal, Cambodia, East Timor, Peru, Iran, Syria, Jamaica, South Yemen, the Fiji Islands, Afghanistan, Lebanon, etc.; the U.S. government has supported ruthless right-wing governments who have tortured and murdered opposition movements such as in the case of Turkey, Zaire, Chad, Pakistan, Morocco,

Indonesia, Guatemala, El Salvador, Honduras, Peru, etc.; or, since World War II, the U.S. military has invaded or bombed Vietnam, North Korea, Cambodia, Grenada, Panama, Somalia, Yugoslavia, Libya, Iraq, Lebanon, Afghanistan, Laos, etc.

My emphasis is on linking these acts of barbarism to the political history of capitalism. This will involve examining critically the recent invasion and occupation of Iraq, the counter-insurgency war the U.S. has launched against Colombian guerrilla movements, the attempt to overthrow Venezuela's Hugo Chavez, as well as the continuing U.S. support for death squads linked to reactionary ruling oligarchies throughout the world who are served by neoliberal globalized capitalism and imperialism. What Parenti, Chomsky, and others have made clear is that the U.S. will oppose any country unwilling to become integrated into the capitalist marketplace. Those that refuse to open themselves up to transnational investors will be in serious trouble.

The U.S. will oppose—ruthlessly, and militarily if need be—countries where economic reformist movements and labor unions, peasant insurgencies, etc., threaten to destabilize unequal distributive policies that favor the ruling class. Democracies must be market-based, or they are not considered democracies at all. If they are not market-based, they must be reoriented into the world market—by force, if necessary. Publicly owned or worker-controlled companies might set an example for the rest of the world that a successful alternative to capitalism exists—and could exist—for the betterment of humankind.

Successful radical change, such as under Allende in Chile, was threatening to the U.S. because this was seen as possibly fomenting similar changes throughout Latin America. Successful socialist agendas in one country could be alluring to other countries whose impoverished populations faced daily suffering and misery under brutal political regimes. For the U.S. ruling class, rising expectations on the part of the suffering masses had to be obliterated. Joel Kovel points out in his Foreword to *Marxism and Freedom* by Dunayevskaya, that during the McCarthy era, even university courses that were blatantly anti-Marxist were banned simply for exposing Marx's name to a generation of growing minds. We don't ban discussions of Marx today, largely because the corporate media in the U.S. has done such a good job of rendering him a relic of the past—an imbrutement of the old bearded devil that we are told gave birth to the gulags of Stalin. Yet we still can't afford to give socialism even the slightest degree of attention that isn't already dipped in acrimony and derision.

If a few countries, by some circumstance of history, manage to survive outside the rules of the marketplace laid down by the IMF, World Bank, and other organizations who work on behalf of U.S. and dominant Western capital, despite all attempts by the U.S. to destabilize them, then it becomes necessary to demonize the leaders, as in the case of Cuba's Fidel Castro. This history of convincing the citizenry—largely through the channels of the corporate media—that no alternative to free-market capitalism can work—needs to be understood in the context of U.S. capitalist elites and their opposition—vis-à-vis the military industrial complex—to progressive forces in the Middle East, East Asia, Africa, and Latin America, both in the past and in the present. Parenti recently raised an important point with respect to the history of U.S. imperialism: Why, after the end of World War II, didn't the U.S. and its capitalist allies eradicate fascism from Europe? Clearly because fascist governments were the lesser evil when compared to the rising up of masses of popular democratic struggles which at that time were vociferously demanding public ownership of the means of production and an eradication of class society.

One of the goals of revolutionary critical pedagogy is to develop hope and possibility through the creation of "critical subjectivity." Critical subjectivity operates out of a practical, sensuous engagement within social formations that enable rather than constrain human capacities. Here critical pedagogy reflects the multiplicity and creativity of human engagement itself: the identification of shared experiences and common interests; the unraveling of the threads that connect social process to individual experience; rendering transparent the concealed obviousness of daily life; the recognition of a shared class interests; the unhinging of the door that separates practical engagement from theoretical reflection; the changing of the world by changing one's nature, and changing one's nature by changing the social relations in which individual and collective subjectivity is formed. Here, revolutionary critical pedagogy seeks to make the division of labor coincident with the free vocation of each individual and the association of free producers.

At first blush this may seem a paradisiac notion in that it posits a radically eschatological and incomparably "other" endpoint for society as we know it. Yet this is not a blueprint but a contingent utopian vision that offers direction not only in unpicking the apparatus of bourgeois illusion but also in diversifying the theoretical itinerary of the critical educator so that new questions can be generated along with new perspectives in which to raise them. Here, the emphasis is on posing new questions rather than on providing blueprints for social change.

Historical changes in the forces of production have reached the point where the fundamental needs of people can be met—but the existing social relations of production prevent this because the logic of access to "need" is "profit" based on the value of people's labor for capital. Consequently, critical revolutionary pedagogy argues that without an accompanying class struggle, critical pedagogy is impeded from effecting praxiological changes (changes in social relations).

Revolutionary critical pedagogy supports a totalizing reflection upon the historical-practical constitution of the world, our ideological formation within it, and the reproduction of everyday life practices. The core of capitalism can thus be undressed by exploring the contradictory nature of the use-value and exchange value of labor-power. In Los Angeles, this challenge can be made concrete through comparative analysis: by looking at labor conditions in West Los Angeles and comparing them to East Los Angeles, the Pico-Union district, and South Central or Watts. A number of my students have grown up in these areas, and can revisit their experiences in light of the vocabulary of critique they are helping to create in class.

MICHAEL: Let's address the postmodernist "legacy" in academe. Your critique of postmodernism runs throughout your work and is an important yet often neglected argument against the hype of postmodernist theories. Can you elaborate on your definition of postmodernism and where you locate its shortcomings?

PETER: I have just finished editing a book on this very topic with some British colleagues in which I perforce admit a certain generalizing sweep that for the most part avoided mentioning particular authors, which is decidedly a weakness, not one I would attribute to the book itself, but to some of my own arguments in that book. In a nutshell, my critique of postmodernism from a nonsectarian and broadly defined Marxist humanist perspective takes the position that postmodernism is more inclined to locate power in discourse and "representations" rather than in social relations. The issue of mediation has been replaced by that of representation. Contradictions between labor and capital are ignored or omitted and issues dealing with conflicting epistemologies put in their place.

The problem with understanding discourses as epistemologies of oppression is that too often they are stripped of their historical specificity by bourgeois, postmodern theorists. What is of singular importance to the critical educator is not, say, their formal link to Eurocentrism, but the way in which these discourses have been used by capitalists to exploit the objective world (as opposed to the lexical universe) of the working classes. Just as I would not reject my former work, which was informed by a critical postmodernist perspective, neither do I want to denigrate the work of other postmodernists unfairly.

To be sure, postmodern theory enabled me to transcend the limitations of some inherited frameworks and think through the prolix and variegated issues of identity construction within the context of contemporary U.S. culture. But over the years I became increasingly concerned that political agency was—and here I would like to borrow the terminology from an interview I did recently when I was asked a similar question—being reduced to little more than the part that we play in some unending signifying chain that descends from the sky in the middle of nowhere, like Jacob's Ladder. Reading postmodern theory, political agency seems locked into the role of affirming our right to difference as a call for dignity and respect (which is a good thing in itself), without addressing issues of how the very concept of difference—racial, gender, etc.—is defined in relation to existing social relations of capitalist production and subjected to their interests.

Postmodernism fails in my mind to reveal how class exploitation impacts on all identities and social relations. In postmodernism's rejection of grand historical narratives, of central struggles that teleologically define history, of the pure historical subject, and in its argument that knowledge is constituted in diffuse power relations, that is, in discourse (which is for postmodernists the sole constitutive element in social relations) has helped to pave the way for important discussions of the role of language in the ordering and regulation and reproduction of power. But many of these contributions by postmodern theory and its perfumed vocabulary of "difference" haven't been up to the task of exploring adequately how differences are shaped by the historical shifts within the globalization of capitalism that are currently devastating the entire globe.

Nor have they adequately explained how identity formations are implicated in the coercive structures and homogenizing tendencies of capital's value form. In my view postmodernists too often detach cultural production from its basis in economic and political processes. Culture is spoken about as a signifying system that is all but sundered from its constitutive embeddedness in the materiality of social life or, at the most, that is tenuously connected to the production of value. Exploitation is not primarily a linguistic process; it takes place in the materiality of social life, in the bowels of everyday economic contradictions, which expel relations of equality.

I don't want to deny, of course, that there are some postmodernists who have written with great sensitivity and erudition about issues of globalization, but many have been unwilling to make the connection between globalization and imperialism, which I think is a major weakness. For me, it is important to operate from a critique of political economy within an international framework of opposition to U.S. imperialism, an imperialism that is grounded in super-exploitation (especially of colonial and female labor) through economic, military and political aggression in the context of protecting United States interests.

Postmodern educationalists, as I saw them, were championing a diversity of identities, but they failed in important ways—in my view, at least—to situate identity within the totality of capitalism, the international division of labor, and within the politics of class differences. Difference was rendered opaque in that it was often unhinged from its historical embeddedness in colonial/imperialist relations. And for me, opposition to U.S. imperialism—especially in the grip of Bush's hair-trigger, flash-point mentality—is crucial if we want to fully challenge structural racism, white supremacy, patriarchy, homophobia, oppressed nationalities, xenophobia and other injustices that are part and parcel of the cruel legacy of transnational capitalism that is centered here in the United States. Capitalism needs to be investigated for its negative propensity to create social divisions and in this way we can, for instance, view racism as the product of distinctive tendencies brought about by the capitalist mode of production and capitalist social relations of production.

There is no question that to raise the issue of class exploitation is to demand that we understand that such exploitation includes forms of racialized and gendered class production. Signification doesn't take place in some structural vacuum, frozen in some textual netherworld, de-fanged of capitalist alienation. Anyway, I found that the work by many postmodernists devalued or downgraded and in some instances scuppered altogether the material basis of cultural production, and instead embraced the fabulously entrenched pessimism advanced by Foucault and other post-structuralists in their assertion that articulating a vision of the future—however contingent—only reinforces the tyranny of the present.

As Peter Hudis has noted, contrary to Derrida and others, the fetish is opposable. We can do more than engage in an endless critique of the forms of thought defined by commodity fetishism. We can accomplish a great deal more than an enjoyment of our symptoms in a world where the subjects of capitalism have been endlessly disappearing into the vortex of history. I believe that the value form of mediation within capitalism is indeed permeable and that another world outside of the social universe of capital can be achieved. We are in need of an overall philosophy of praxis—and I would argue this struggle must be rooted in class struggle.

MICHAEL: As a student of critical theory it's easy to feel the sway of post-structuralist "bohemia" and academic celebrities. But it seems so much of their "discoveries" of inadequacies or biased social structures have never been lost on those who lived through them. Do you think it has been a question of not having the "language" to adequately express such ideas from the perspectives of "minorities" or marginalized groups?

PETER: I don't think it would be appropriate for me to speak on behalf of people of color, I would prefer for them to answer, but let me address this in a more general way. Among many middle-class, Euro-Americans—white folks—it is not just a question of lacking a language of analysis—via, say, the counter-canon of Third World literature or anti-imperialist critique—that can lead to obstacles on the path to revolutionary praxis. Sometimes it is a question of never being a victim of racist, sexist, and homophobic violence, as well as other types of violence, and therefore not being able to connect one's lived experiences of this violence to the variegated and specific histories of racism, sexism and homophobia and to their local and wider determinations. Being hit over the head with a police baton in a demonstration can give you a more convincing understanding of the power of the state than any book on critical theory. Where critical social theory can help—both minorities and marginalized groups, including working-class white folks, is in the development of a coherent philosophy of revolution that can approach the question of resisting and transforming capitalist exploitation and the racialization of class relations (and other forms of oppression) dialectically and not from a presumed position of unequivocal transhistorical continuity.

MICHAEL: How has your implementation and study of people like Ernesto Guevara, Malcolm X and Rosa Luxemburg returned the lived experiences back to students taught under "detached" theories?

PETER: It is impossible to return experiences to the oppressed without, in some way, first taking them away, and once they are taken away, and returned, categories are invariably imposed upon them. It is not that there exists as recoverable some kind of pristine, unmediated, untainted or unsoiled experiences—which would be a romantic, nativist pursuit or else a blind concession to solipsism—but that experiences read through external theories are always necessarily counterfeit, although they might be airbrushed to appear as though they have been redeemed by the philosopher's pen so as to make their return appear as a gift that has been detoxified and perfumed. The question is not one of providing the correct political language—revolutionary critical pedagogy, critical theory, historical materialism, analytical or dialectical Marxism, or what have you—but to create pedagogical spaces and contexts for the oppressed to fashion their own understandings out of their shared history of struggle.

If they want to borrow from the aforementioned theoretical approaches, yes, that could be extremely valuable, but there is always the danger of dissolving one's own historicity in the process. Theories—especially those grounded in post-Cartesian philosophy—often set up an opposition—an irreconcilable dualism or un-transcendable antimony or incontestable contradiction between the subject and the object or nature of knowledge where the ontological structure of subjective agency supposedly corresponds to the actual dualisms of the mode of production, albeit in its alienated and reified formations. In this process, the concrete historical subject is obliterated, abstracted away, so that it is made to feel as if it were at one with the madness of capital into which it has been insinuated, so that the subject resigns itself to an inevitable complicity with the processes of its own formation.

The outcome is that what is contingent about subjectivity has been eternalized; what is concrete and material has been made supra-historical. The antagonisms of the empirical world are eviscerated; dependent hierarchies are "flattened out" and transformed into a metaphysical unity of oppositions—as part of the universe of natural law. What gets lost is the notion of social determinateness, or structurally enforced domination, or what István Mészáros identifies as the hierarchical structural determinations of domination and subordination within the antagonistic class parameters of the social totality of existing capitalist society. We can reconcile the antimonies of labor/capital, for instance, in the heady discourses of bourgeois ethics and their ought-ridden, impervertible ethical propositions, or within bourgeois conceptions of morality but what we are left with is precisely what Mészáros calls an "impotent counter-image of the real world" that is condensed in idealistic exhortations addressed to the individual, in moral approbation and disapprobation, and the like.

Isn't this what most schools of education do in their teacher education classes—reduce structural contradictions to moral a priorism, to appeal to the individual consciousness to exercise goodness not to dismantle the world of facticity, the existing social order and its fundamental structures of exploitation and instead impotently occupy vertical spaces of power and privilege, armed to the teeth with private decision-making criteria that emanate from subjective and arbitrary world views? This leads to a radicalism that extols transformation in the very act of repudiating it. The challenge of what to do about the dehumanizing public world of oppression and exploitation then becomes a dialogue between irreconcilable private and public values.

According to Mészáros, this process works to reproduce the overall relationship between capital and labor as a form of structural dependency in which the rule of capital is intrinsically exploitative, and this antagonism can never be transcended as long as they are part of a system that reproduces the unvarnished and brute antimonies of real life, which give rise to these philosophical conceptualizations in the first place. So a key pedagogical task for me is to invite students to analyze the philosophical ground out of which the languages of political economy and ethics emerge—i.e., their limited ethico-political parameters.

Of course, this is part of a far-reaching—indeed, a never-ending—task of developing a philosophy of praxis. As revolutionary educators, we need to understand how philosophy and political economy end up being articulated from the standpoint of capital in which practical dualisms are reproduced in actuality, while attempts are made to resolve them at some metaphysical level. We need to be able to fathom how rigid asymmetrical relations of power and privilege are reproduced within post-Cartesian philosophy so that they a priori reject the possibility of mediation and transformation of these relations of domination and capitalist exploitation. Mészáros is helpful here; Bertell Ollman is excellent, as well. There are many good sources available.

We read philosophers and social theorists, but do so critically. We also read the lives and ideas of social activists and political revolutionaries. The key for me is to break out of philosophical dualism by means of a dialectical approach, and this requires presenting students with various vocabularies of struggle—those of Malcolm, Che, Luxemburg, Raya Dunayevskaya—and then inviting students to connect these dialectically to the circumstances in which they are making sense of the world around them. It is not to re-tread student experiences with theory, or to read experiences back to students through these various analyses and vocabularies of critique, but to invite students to engage them for their usefulness in understanding the forces and relations in which they, the students, are enmeshed—but more importantly, for overcoming them. The goal, of course, is to become associated producers, working under conditions that will advance humankind, where the measure of wealth is not labor time but solidarity, creativity, and the full and creative development of human capacities.

MICHAEL: Henry Giroux has always called for teachers to be at the forefront of social/political issues. But do you think we see so very few "public" or "notable" radicals of color today because they are under pressure to curb their ideas on race, class or the war on "terror" in order to be perceived as non-threatening or loyal patriots?

PETER: I would think that this is the case, yes, Mike. Look at the racialization of individuals and group affiliations that has filled the air with ideological toxins and soiled civil society with practices of political repression—it has been intensified dramatically post-9/11, especially the demonization of Muslims and their Islamic communities. Whereas Dante cast the prophet Muhammad into the eighth of the nine circles of hell, in his *Inferno*, where Muhammad's body was eternally being severed from groin to brain, Bush has followed Reagan in casting entire nations into the pit of hell through his denunciation that they are evil. What makes this any different from religious positions taken towards the United States by the Taliban?

The Israeli newspaper *Haaretz* was given transcripts of a negotiating session between (former) Palestinian Prime Minister Mahmoud Abbas and faction leaders from Hamas and other militant groups. In these transcripts, Abbas described his recent summit with Ariel Sharon and Bush hijo. During the summit, Bush allegedly told Abbas: "God told me to strike at al Qaida and I struck them, and then He instructed me to strike at Saddam, which I did, and now I am determined to solve the problem in the Middle East. If you help me I will act, and if not, the elections will come and I will have to focus on them." This reminds me of the same kind of social Darwinist millenarianism that I felt in 1982 when Admiral Rickover implied that nuclear war was inevitable and said that a better species might follow, and that getting rid of the Defense Department might be the best way to increase our security.

Bush does little to assuage the current sordid atmosphere of mutual fear, and actually takes the current climate of hate and instability to cosmic proportions. To exercise political agency as educators and speak out against the madness of U.S. imperialism, and the eschatological aspect of U.S. foreign policy, is to go directly against the White House consensus and risk being (symbolically) burned as a heretic in the corporate media. Bush has established a global nursery for nurturing such dangerous perspectives among Western democracies. In his subordinated partnership with the Jesus of the right-wing Christian fundamentalists, Bush and his deacon of the faith, John Ashcroft, have created a theocratic climate of fear surrounding the politics of dissent that gives many people pause before challenging the guardians of the Homeland. It is very likely that the Bush gang will make more concerted efforts to root out dissention in the universities, especially if there are further attacks on U.S. soil. Once they feel they have public support for such a measure, they won't hesitate.

MICHAEL: Finally, do you feel class/race issues in the United States are often upstaged by the more "global" events and concerns? Of course, such events are important yet at times they seem more tolerable topics of discussion and protest from dissidents, radicals and the Left solely because of their distance?

PETER: I agree. Yesterday I went to see Chris Marker's, *One Day in the Life of Andrei Arsenevich,* which is a wonderful documentary film about Russian filmmaker, Andrei Tarkovsky, and also Marker's film, *The Last Bolshevik,* which examines the work of the Russian filmmaker Alexander Medvedkin. I couldn't help but see these films in terms of critical pedagogy. Especially in the case of Marker's discussion of Medvedkin, I could see both a critique and embrace of Soviet Communism, but I could also apply a similar critique to the increasingly authoritarian aspects of U.S. society, especially after 9/11, but especially the ruthless totalizing aspect of capitalism itself. On the one hand you have a form of bureaucratic Soviet state capitalism, and on the other, a form of decentralized, free-market capitalism.

It always seems as though we are more comfortable criticizing another country, another time, or another type of outcome of capital's value form. We are prone in the U.S. to criticize Cuba, for instance, but we never talk in the corporate media about the Cuban Five held in prison here in the United States—imprisoned because they were trying to infiltrate U.S. terrorist groups plotting attacks on Cuba. We rarely talk about the war against the poor by the rich and the odious practices of the state to keep the poor in a condition of powerlessness. Here in the U.S. there exists an implosive reduction of the central antagonism of labor and capital to a single, uniform, denial of structural class conflict. The mirror of capitalist production reflects back images that so sharply contradict the generalized image that has been manufactured for us of the defining virtues upon which this country rests, that it must always be held outwards, away from us, and towards the empty horizon of the "other."

"Toward a Critical Revolutionary Pedagogy: An Interview with Peter McLaren" was published by Michael Alexander Pozo in the *St. John's University Humanities Review, volume 2*, issue 1, Fall, 2003, 58–77. The interview has been reprinted in two internet journals, *Axis of Logic* and *Dissident Voices*.

Interview 2

rage and hope: the revolutionary pedagogy of Peter McLaren

Mitja Sardoc

I was invited by Mitja Sardoc to publish an article in his influential European journal, The School Field. *At the time, I was eager to share with my international readers the shift that I had made over the last several years from a post-structuralist, or critical post-modernist, approach to social analysis to a historical materialist approach grounded in Marxist humanism. I decided that an interview was the best format to do this. Fortunately, Mitja agreed with me. While important, the postmodernist school of "radical democracy" basically ignores the mode of production and the social relations of production in its strategies of social transformation. Instead, this school favors focusing on theories of social justice and cultural identity. This was an opportunity for me to signal my move away from the radical democracy school and toward a socialist alternative to capitalism by way of a re-engagement with Marx's writings and the Marxist humanist school of interpreting his work.*

MITJA SARDOC: I first became aware of your work through *Schooling as a Ritual Performance*, which combined a structuralist, post-structuralist, and Marxist analysis of Catholic schooling. Since that time your work (I am thinking of the third edition of *Life in Schools*, *Critical Pedagogy and Predatory*

Culture, *Revolutionary Multiculturalism*, and *Che Guevara, Paulo Freire, and the Pedagogy of Revolution*) has become much more informed by postmodern theory but also has been moving—quite noticeably in your last book, *Che Guevara, Paulo Freire, and the Pedagogy of Revolution*—toward a reengagement with historical materialist analysis, a critique of the globalization of capitalism, and a preoccupation with class struggle. Class struggle and other Marxist ideas seem to be outdated with the fall of the Berlin Wall and what Francis Fukuyama called the "end of history" or the "end of ideology." But if we read, for example, *The Communist Manifesto*, we find some parts of it even more relevant today that when *The Communist Manifesto* was originally published in 1848. Why are Marxist ideas still haunting mainstream western educational discourse despite the apparent closure of the Marxist legacy in history's cabinet of lost revolutionary dreams?

PETER MCLAREN: I agree with you, Mitja, that Marx's ideas are still haunting Western educational discourses, but I don't agree that educationalists in North America have been affected by these ideas to any substantive degree. Postmodern theory seems to be holding sway—at least it has become the most fashionable form of educational criticism. While many of my erstwhile Marxist colleagues are embracing postmodern theory and its post-Marxist variants, and the work of Foucault, Lyotard, Virilio, Baudrillard, Kristeva, Butler, Derrida, Deleuze, Guattari, and the like, my work is becoming more centered in Marxist critique. A number of my colleagues have said to me: "Why, when postmodern theory is at the cutting edge of critical social theory, would you want to re-join the dinosaurs of historical materialism?" My answer is that one does not have to be a postmodernist to work on the cutting edge of social theory. Perry Anderson, Ellen Meiksins Wood, Claus Offe, Raymond Williams, Eric Hobsbawm, Robert Brenner, and Alex Callinicos—who work in a Marxist tradition—are hardly theoretical slackers. If one follows the trajectory of my work over the last several decades one will quickly discover a constant motion. Sometimes it is a steady march, perhaps even militant; sometimes a swaying motion from idea to idea, as in my dalliance with left-postmodern theory; more often than not lumbering gestures towards a definitive line of reasoning; and on too many occasions recently I find myself staggering across the intellectual firmament like a drunken sailor after a night out on the town. I become, in other words, intoxicated by the possibilities of linking revolutionary theory to political praxis. The motion, however direct, purposeful, or erratic, is always towards Marx and the Marxist tradition. The work of Marx is continually being revisited in my work. For instance, in the new edition of *Schooling as a Ritual Performance*, I updated my work on the ethnography of symbols, with a short discussion of Marx. Basically I argued that class exploitation within capitalist societies occupies a strategic centrality in organizing those very activities that make us human, including our sign and symbol systems. Volosinov and others have maintained—rightly in my view—that speech genres themselves are determined by production relations and the machinations of the socio-political order. This is an important assertion especially in view of the fact that, as John McMurtry notes, the market system is being applied to democracy itself, where democracy is seen as occurring at the sites where market intervention occurs the least, where abstract law overrides concrete determinations and abstracts real existence into nothingness, where distributive principles overrule concrete struggles for new freedoms, where a successful democracy is defined in terms of its ability to become self-legitimating and self-justificatory, where the market is permitted to remain impersonal and omnipresent and is encouraged and facilitated in its efforts to totalize the field of social relations in which it has become a central force. Surplus extraction occurs through processes that are dialogical and simultaneously economic, political, and ideological. These are not ontologically privileged processes but rather become central in the way that they organize the constitutive processes of everyday life. In other words, the class struggle is also a language game. And one that in some fundamental way co-ordinates all the other language games. All language games and symbol systems are accented by class power. If this is the case, then living in a capitalist social order demands the continual affirmation of a working-class struggle not only against capitalism, but against capital itself. Marx, after all, held that capital was a social relation: the abolition of capital, then, requires us to abolish a particular form of social relation. Volosinov goes so far as to argue that the sign becomes the very arena of class struggle because the continual accumulation of capital can only continue through an unequal exchange between social agents—an exchange that favors one social agent while the other is reduced to scrounging out of mere necessity. So I have tried to amend some of my earlier insights in *Schooling as a Ritual Performance*, with an engagement—however brief—with Marx.

MITJA: Some scholars and researchers have remarked that Marx is returning with a vengeance to the social sciences? Why, in your opinion, isn't this the case, as you claim, among educationalists in the United States?

PETER: You could say that Marx is returning with a vengeance; yes, Mitja, I would agree. To a certain extent you are correct. While anti-capitalist struggle and Marxist analysis has an indistinct and relatively undigested place in the field of educational theory, there is some movement towards Marx in the social sciences here in North America. With one glaring exception being the educational left in the United States, I would say that Marx is being revisited by social scientists of all disciplinary shapes and sizes—even, and perhaps most especially and urgently today, when capitalism is in a state of severe crisis. While hardly on their way to becoming entrenched and pervasive, Marx's ideas are taking their significance most strikingly from the particular and varied contexts in which his ideas are being engaged. In the face of the cultivated arrogance and pitilessness of the post-Marxists, the unabashed triumphalism of the apostates of neo-liberalism, and the tight-lipped solemnizers of bourgeois democracy as they choose to ignore the precariousness of the current triumph of capitalism over communism—not to mention the unprecedented gravity of the crisis of neo-liberalism's death-squad capitalism—it is not easy to recover the soiled mantle of Marx from the gravesite where it had been derisively and capriciously flung in those ecstatic moments of bourgeois revelry and spiteful, tongue-wagging glee, when the ruling classes watched from their princely Western heights the "popular democracies" of Eastern Europe trembling alongside the wobbling pillars of communism that were collapsing across that crimson space of historical memory we know as the Soviet Union. There have been times when I have coquetted with postmodern theory, with the voguish apostasy of post-structuralist brigandry, or deconstructionist outlawry—even to the point where I have been identified as the first to introduce the term "postmodernism" into the lexicon of educational criticism (a dubious claim, but one made of my work nonetheless)—but I have found there to be insuperable limitations to the work, not to mention a growing confederacy of academic sycophants who these days appear to overpopulate North American and European critical studies. As Callinicos has noted, much of what we find in French post-structuralism in many ways is a continuation of the thought of Nietzsche, reformulating it by way of Saussure's theory of language and Heidegger's philosophy of Being. And he also notes that much of the critique of the Enlightenment undertaken by Foucault and other postmodern theorists had already been anticipated by the Frankfurt School theorists—Adorno, Horkheimer, Benjamin, and others. This is not to disparage their work—I think it is immensely important—although I also think that, for the most part, postmodern theorists and critical theorists (in the tradition of the

Frankfurt School) are too pessimistic about the possibilities of social revolution. I have found that there exists a strategic centrality in Marx's work—the work that, as Callinicos puts it, "survived the debacle of Stalinism."

MITJA: Strategic centrality?

PETER: Yes, in terms of linking educational theory to a political project that can address the onslaught of globalization, in particular, the globalization of capital. However, "disorganized" capitalism has become, I don't believe that we live in an era of capitalism without classes.

MITJA: There is some irony, living in the United States—in Hollywood no less!—and working as a Marxist.

PETER: Yes, many people outside the United States find it a bit—how should I put it?—strange. But it might surprise you how many Marxists I've met in Hollywood. More than you might think. But we are certainly outnumbered by the postmodernists! Though many criticalists in education are reluctant to descend from the topgallant of postmodern theory into the heated "red" engine room of social analysis, I find that practicing sociology below-the-water line, in the "hatch," so to speak, has its distinct advantages. Marx's work enables me to explore with fewer theoretical constraints, in more capillary detail, and with more socio-analytical ballast, the dynamic complexity of the social totality. Marxism provides me with the conceptual tools necessary to navigate between the Scylla of positivism and the Charybdis of relativism. It also provides an approach to praxis that, in these world-historical times of the epochal dominance of capital and the reworking of forms of global capitalist imperialism, is fundamentally necessary.

MITJA: What theorists have influenced your recent turn towards historical materialism?

PETER: Well, I could extend the list I gave earlier to include Marx, Gramsci, Lukács, Althusser, Trotsky, Malcolm X, István Mészáros, Boris Kalgarlitsky, Terry Eagleton, Aijaz Ahmad, Frantz Fanon, Albert Memmi, Paulo Freire, Stuart Hall, Rosa Luxemburg, Epifinio San Juan, Slavoj Žižek, and a host of others too numerous to mention. Of course, I have learned much from Foucault, whose lectures I was able to attend (in Canada) a few years before he died. And Lyotard, certainly, and Baudrillard. I can't deny that there was a time when the postmodern thinkers played a central role in my work. Not to mention the important work of Mauss, Victor Turner, and Pierre Bourdieu

(I still follow Bourdieu's work), to cite but three examples from the anthropological literature. Through my current reengagement with Marx, and the tradition of historical materialism, I have enjoyed the company of British colleagues—Glenn Rikowski, Mike Cole, and Dave Hill—whose work is paving the way for new generations of educationalists to encounter Marx. I have also been influenced by the Marxist humanism of Peter Hudis and Raya Dunayevskaya, the "red feminism" of Teresa Ebert, and Rosemary Hennessey, the Marxist-Leninism of Mas'ud Zavarzadeh, and Donald Morton, and the work of Canadian philosopher, John McMurtry, and others. Ramin Farahmandpur and I have been working together on a number of projects related to rethinking Marxist educational praxis.

To repeat my previous comment, Marx is being reevaluated on numerous fronts today: sociology, political science, philosophy, economics, ethics, history, and the like. It is perhaps more difficult for such a reevaluation to take place in education here in North America, mainly because his work was never very important in the education debates here to begin with.

MITJA: What about the early 1980s? Wasn't there interest in Marxist analysis among critical educators in the United States during that time?

PETER: Yes, that's true, there were a handful of educationalists who incorporated some Marxist insights into their work—I am thinking of the important contributions of Henry Giroux, Mike Apple, Phil Wexler, and Jean Anyon (who are still turning out splendid work)—but the influence of Marxist and quasi-Marxist analysis (mostly influenced by British educationalists) lasted about five years. Then postmodern theory started to be taken up. And . . .

MITJA: And?

PETER: And . . . well . . . for the most part this has led to a stress on identity politics—a proliferation of issues dealing with race, ethnic, and sexual identities and a waning and supersession of discussion around social class. The interest in identity politics is understandable enough—especially given the burgeoning migration to the United States over the last several decades.

MITJA: So I take it that you are a dyed-in-the-wool Marxist.

PETER: Let me make this qualification before I continue. I am not one of those die-hard leftists who regard Marxism as a religion that explains everything that needs to be known about humanity. Marxism is not a faith; it is not a sibylline discourse. I have no truck with solifidianism—Marxist or ecclesiastic. In fact, Marxism puts its stock in good works rather than in faith. It puts an emphasis in denouncing and transforming the world, not wrapping doctrinal tentacles around its major texts, or clinging steadfastly to historical materialism as if it admitted a pristine purity or sacerdotal truth. There is a denunciatory aspect to Marxism that is crucial here. If the language of analysis that informs your work does not enable you and encourage you to denounce the world, then you would be wise to reconsider the language that you are using. Even Pope John Paul II, in his encyclical, *Centesimus Annus*, admits to at least some "seeds of truth" in Marxism.

MITJA: Please, Peter, you're not saying the Pope is a Marxist, are you?

PETER: I believe in the power of salvation, but this, I fear, is asking too much of God, and of Marx, I am afraid!

MITJA: What about the post-Marxist movement? You mentioned identity politics—isn't that part of it?

PETER: As I said previously, I find the efflorescence of identity politics problematic but it is never the less understandable. The problem is that identities are often framed within a discourse of militant particularism, and there are ways that a stress on identity politics can sabotage class struggle, especially when it is uncoupled from the larger social totality of advanced capitalism. In a class I taught this summer, the students didn't want to discuss class. They thought that issues of race and gender were more important. And while all identities are racialized, sexualized, and gendered, and located in class relations—in a non-synchronous way, as Cameron McCarthy has pointed out—I think we have forgotten how social class works in our everyday lives. I think that recovering class struggle is essential in creating wider political solidarities necessary in the current movement against global capitalism. Class exploitation is not to be "privileged" over racism or sexism or homophobia—please let me underscore that point again—but I feel that capitalist social formations often co-ordinate and organize and reify these other, equally important, forms of oppression. It's a more central form of oppression, but that doesn't mean it is more important. I hope that I am making myself clear.

MITJA: It's clear to me.

PETER: Let's move away from identity politics specifically for a moment and return to your question about post-Marxism. I find much about post-Marxist theory—and postmodern theory—to be functionally advantageous to the status quo. In fact, I find a thunderous resonance in the work of the postmodernists with that of the New Right. The work of Laclau and Mouffe is a case in point. I have great respect for their scholarship, but they tend to look at social contradictions as semantic problems whereas I see social contradictions as anchored in the objective nature of things; they are part of the structural determinations of the social. For the most part Laclau and Mouffe reject dialectical thought and have abandoned the notion that capitalist exploitation is linked to the law of value and the extraction of surplus value. Exploitation is not a linguistic process only—it takes place objectively, in the bowels of everyday contradictions which expel relations of equality, and I do not believe that resistance has to be conscious on the part of workers in order for exploitation to take place. As the Argentine scholar, Atilio Boron provocatively notes, relations of subordination are antagonistic in relation to an ideology (a logic of capital) that rationalizes this relationship. Boron has revealed how the work of Laclau and Mouffe, far from constituting a supersession of Marxism, is, in effect, reproductive of some of the fundamental expressions of United States sociology of the 1950s, as found in the work of Talcott Parsons, for instance. Unlike Laclau and Mouffe, I do not believe hegemony is purely an articulatory device, but a politico-ideological process that is grounded in class relations.

MITJA: But how feasible is class struggle today?

PETER: That is a point of real contestation among social theorists and political activists. On the one hand I agree, Mitja, that there is no guarantee that a class *in itself* will be transformed into a class *for itself*; there is no metaphysical guarantee hovering over the outcome of class struggle. There is no secret structure of predestination, no teleological certainty. On the other hand, Mitja, I agree that there is today the necessity of class struggle. It is a concrete necessity. Look at what happened in Seattle. Forty-thousand young people protesting the World Bank and the global economic interests of the ruling class! I think that a new generation of young people is waking up to the injuries of globalized capitalist relations. Making politics practical is what is driving my work these days. I am not so much interested (as are many postmodern educators) in decentering capitalist social relations, relations of exchange, or consumer culture, although I do think it is important to analyze the objective determinations that have given rise to the complex ensemble of dislocated and dispersed identities that we find in contemporary postmodern necropolises—hybridized and creolized identities that have resulted from the unequal and combined character of capitalist development. I am more interested at this point in time in how education can play a fundamental role in developing new forms of non-alienated labor through the dismantling of capitalist social relations and capital itself. I am trying to develop ways of encouraging students to think of such a possibility through the creation of what I have called a "revolutionary pedagogy." By extension, I am interested in the role that education can play in the wider society by dismantling capital's law of value as a central form of mediation between human beings.

MITJA: While you have made it clear in recent work that you are not a postmodernist theorist, or a postmodern Marxist . . .

PETER: How about a classical Marxist!

MITJA: Okay, a classical Marxist. You have, nevertheless, mentioned that postmodernism has helped deepen our understanding of the way that ethnic and racial identities have been constructed. Traditionally excluded "social groups" such as Blacks, women and other minority social groups, generally defined as "others" in opposition to the mainstream discourse, were traditionally excluded from the curriculum. How productive do you find their inclusion in the curriculum, thus making it multicultural? Following that, do you think that multiculturalism's replacing of universalism with the call for diversity and tolerance has contested the conservative agenda that disempowered and depoliticized the powerless and the marginalized? And one final question related to this issue: What do you think is the difference between "inclusion"—the integration of previously marginalized groups into the mainstream culture on terms that secure their freedom and equality—and "assimilation" which can be associated as its negation? How does those two practices differ in educational policy?

PETER: These are important questions, Mitja, that have to do with what has been called "the politics of difference." I have tried to address such a politics in a number of books that I have co-edited with Christine Sleeter, Carlos Ovando, and Henry Giroux. You are correct when you note that postmodern theory has helped educators to understand how identity formations are constructed within various social and institutional formations within capitalist consumer society. Yet much of this work locates power in discourse and "representations" rather than social relations. The issue of mediation has been replaced by representation. Contradictions between labor and capital are replaced by issues of conflicting epistemologies. The problem with understanding discourses as epistemologies of oppression is that too often they are stripped of their historical specificity by bourgeois/postmodern theorists—what is of singular importance to the critical educator is not their formal link to Eurocentrism, but the way that they have been used by capitalists to exploit the objective world (as opposed to the lexical universe) of the working classes. The fascism of the Third Reich has been defeated, and the communism of the Soviet Union has been brought to its knees, it seems, mainly so that transnational identities can be constructed by developed nations with the promise of a thousand years of uninterrupted shopping and watching re-run episodes of *Baywatch*. Our subjectivities are being created out of the detritus of productive forces, the expelled vomit of overaccumulation, and the bloated promise of globalized capitalist relations. The economies of desire linked to capitalist social relations are myriad, and complex, and it would take too much time to explore them here. Suffice it to say that identity construction is a process that cannot be ignored by those of us in education. In fact, it is a key challenge. But the challenge has to be greater than surfing for identities within hybridity, and among spaces opened up by the furious clashes in the *Fight Clubs* of culture. For me, such identity construction must take into account the relationship between subjective formation and the larger totality of globalized capitalist social relations. Capitalism here must not be perceived as anodyne, but rather as a brakeless train that is smashing all that is in its path, continuing to savage the possibility of constructing free associative forms of labor and the flourishing of human capacities. But now let me move on to the other issues that you have raised about multiculturalism.

Let me address your comment on universalism. Yes, the general critique of the post-colonial theorists is that asserting universal claims is tantamount to exercising disciplinary power in putting forward a hidden particularism. There is much to be said for this criticism. But Callinicos argues, and I agree with him, that abjuring appeals to universal principles on the basis of a particular standpoint, of, say, the community, ignores the asymmetrical relations of power and privilege in local situations and in the end truncates the form of social criticism you are able to muster. Rather than dismissing universalisms as masked particularisms (which leaves you the choice of ranking your particularisms on some scale of preference), I would side with Callinicos, Eagleton, and others, in arguing that what is needed is a genuine universality in which everyone is included and there are no "others." In this way, the Enlightenment project is called upon to live up to its name. This is ultimately what I believe the project of Habermas is all about. My position is that if we are to deepen the project of the Enlightenment rather than jettison it, we need to decide if capitalism has a place—central or peripheral. In my opinion, it doesn't have a place. I do not believe it is justifiable on ethical grounds or political grounds. Here we need to replace analyses by neo-classical economists with that of Marx. And we need to develop a coherent political and pedagogical theory that takes this factor into account. But I could go on. . . .

MITJA: Let me ask you how what you have been saying fits with your ideas on multiculturalism.

PETER: Let me try. Calls for diversity by politicians and educators and social reformers have brought historically marginalized groups—Latino/as, African Americans, Asians, indigenous populations—to the center of society in terms, at least, of addressing the importance of addressing their needs, rather than *actually* addressing their needs, or addressing their *actual* needs. In other words, this call for diversity has been little more than Enlightenment rhetoric, certainly not practice. However, motivated by a lack of opposition to capitalist exploitation that has been fostered by neo-liberal policies worldwide, multicultural education continues to defang its most emancipatory possibilities by initiating what I believe are, for the most part, politically "empty" calls for diversity—calls for diversity carried out in antiseptic isolation from an interrogation of capitalism's center. This center is what gives ballast to the production of sameness that I call the *eternal recurrance of whiteness*. This sameness constitutes the distillate of colonialism, imperialism, and the ether of white lies that spikes the very air we breathe. It means that pluralism is secretly aligned with assimilation. To be brought "into the center" without being permitted to critique that center is tantamount to internalizing the codes of whiteness (without being granted the benefits of actually assuming the "social position" of whiteness). There is a parallel here with some of the debates on social exclusion in the European Union. Eurocapitalist states advance a rhetoric of social inclusion—of the unemployed, of adults who can't read, of the disabled and other groups—that simultaneously stigmatizes the "excluded" as either victims or lacking in certain skills or attitudes, whilst claiming to want to include them as *equals* (with the whole question of equality left up in the air). But this is a cruel fantasy. In a sense, there are no "socially excluded": everyone is included into capital's social universe—but differentially, on obscenely unequal grounds. Possession of capital in its money form excludes people—to vastly differing degrees—from buying all manner of goods, real human need going by the board. On the other hand, capital includes us all, only to generate incredible differences between us on the basis of money. Gender, "race" and other social and cultural differences are grounds within bourgeois metaphysics and "ethics" for differentiating and fragmenting us on the basis of money. Capital drives us, therefore, against ourselves. Going back to postmodernism, postmodernists given over to identity politics frequently overlook the centrality of social class as an overarching identity that inscribes individuals and groups within social relations of exploitation. What identity politics and pluralism fail to address is the fact that diversity and difference are allowed to proliferate and flourish, provided that they remain within the prevailing forms of capitalist social arrangements, including hierarchical property arrangements. Of course, I agree that class relations are most certainly racialized and gendered. I do not want to subordinate race, gender, or sexuality to that of social class; rather I want to emphasize that without overcoming capitalism, anti-racist, anti-sexist and anti-homophobic struggles will have little chance at succeeding. Slavoj Žižek has said that in the Left's call for new multiple political subjectivities (e.g., race, class, feminist, religious), the Left in actuality asserts a type of all-pervasive sameness—a non-antagonistic society in which room is made for all manner of cultural communities, lifestyles, religions, and sexual orientations. Žižek reveals that this Sameness relies on an antagonistic split. As far as this split goes, I believe that it results, at least to a large degree, from the labor-capital relation sustained and promoted by white supremacist capitalist patriarchy. In other words, I do not see the central tension as one between the autochthonous and the foreign—but between labor and capital. As you might be aware, I am very sympathetic to the movement here in the United States known as the "new abolitionists."

MITJA: Tell me about this movement—it relates to the politics of whiteness, correct?

PETER: Correct. Scholar-activists such as Noel Ignatiev, David Roediger, and others are calling for the abolition of whiteness, or the abolition of the white race. What they mean by this is that there is no positive value that can be given to the social position known as whiteness. The term cannot be recovered, or given a positive spin. White people need to disidentify entirely with the white race since it is constitutively premised on the demonization of all that is not-white. To seek any kind of positive identity with a white race—or political détente—is ill-conceived at best. This is because the white race was an historical invention born in the ovens of racial superiority and European caste. We have to un-invent the white race, and not re-invent it!

Theodore Allen and other scholars have noted, and rightly so, that the social function of whiteness is social control, a practice which has colonial origins that can be traced back to the assault upon tribal affinities, customs, laws, and institutions of Africans, Native Americans, and Irish by English/British and Anglo-American colonialism. Such insidious practices of social control reduce all members of oppressed groups to one undifferentiated social status beneath that of any member of the colonizing population. With the rise of the abolitionist movement, racial typologies, classification systems, and criteriologies favoring whiteness and demonizing Blackness as the lowest status within humanity's "great chain of being" spread throughout the United States. These typologies or myths (in Barthes' sense) were used to justify and legitimize the slavery of Africans and ensure the continuation of lifetime chattel bond-servitude. Today "whiteness" has become naturalized as part of our "commonsense" reality. Ignatiev has noted that whiteness is not a culture. There is Irish culture and Italian culture and American culture; there is youth culture and drug culture but, he asserts, there is no such thing as white culture. He points out that Shakespeare was *not* white; he was English. Mozart was not white; he was Austrian. According to the new abolitionists, whiteness has nothing to do with culture and everything to do with social position. Ignatiev notes that without the privileges attached to it, there would be no white race, and fair skin would have the same significance as big feet.

Ignatiev further notes that identification with white privilege reconnects whites to relations of exploitation. The answer to this plight, is, of course, for whites to cease to exist as whites. He claims that the most challenging task is to make it impossible for anyone to be white. This entails breaking the laws of whiteness so flagrantly as to destroy the myth of white unanimity.

What is also needed—and here the work of Marx becomes crucial—is an acute recognition of how the ideology of whiteness contributes to the reproduction of class divisions—particularly divisions between working-class Anglo-Americans and ethnic minorities—in order to reinforce existing property relations and reproduce the law of value as a mediatory device *par excellence* in reifying and fetishizing social relations in general.

Along with efforts to abolish the white race (not white people, there is, of course, a distinct difference) we must mobilize efforts to abolish capital. Capital is a social relation, as I noted earlier—not a "thing." It is a relation between all of us (not just those in work, at work) and value, which is the substance of capital, its lifeblood. The very existence of the capitalist class rests on surplus value, unrequited labor-time, our sweat, our mental processes, and our domestic labor (to bring up and maintain the next batch of laborers), our education (as generator of the attributes of labor-power or the capacity to labor) and every other sphere of social life. Capital is a global virus that finds its way (mediated by our labor—that is the tragedy) into all areas of contemporary human life. It is nurtured by the New Right and all those who stand to gain millions, billions of dollars from the expansion of this demon seed. We need to reclaim human life from capital.

MITJA: What about the politics of globalization? How does that feature in your work?

PETER: The richest tenth of households in the United States own 83 percent of the country's financial assets, while the bottom four-fifths own about 8 percent. As Cuban Foreign Minister Felipe Roque exclaimed recently: Are the 4.5 billion human beings from underdeveloped countries who consume only 14 percent of the world's total production really as free and equal as the 1.5 million living in the developed world that consume the other 86 percent? What are we to think of the globalization of capitalism when the combined assets of the three richest people in the world exceed the combined GDP of the 48 poorest nations; and when the combined assets of the 225 richest people are roughly equal to the annual incomes of the poorest 47 percent of the world's population? What indeed! I link globalization—or what has been described as "capitalism with the gloves off"—to its governmental bed-fellow, neo-liberalism. We have seen neo-liberalism at work in the oppression by the state of nonmarket forces, in the dismantling of social programs, in the enthronement of a neo-mercantilist public policy agenda, in the encouragement of social life—almost every inch of it!—to be controlled by private interests, in the scrapping of environmental regulation, and in its interminable concessions to transnational corporations. While globalization has been used to describe social, political and economic shifts in late capitalism, such as the deregulation of the labor market and the globalization of liquid capital, I prefer a more close-to-the-bone definition that links it to a form of imperialism. This might seem a rebarbative exaggeration, but I see it as a recomposition of the labor and capital relationship that subordinates social reproduction to the reproduction of capital.

MITJA: How would you assess the politics of resistance in opposition to the conservative obviousness of predatory culture?

PETER: Mitja, I like the way that you framed that question. The obviousness of conservative culture is precisely why it is so hidden from view. Much like those who controlled the *paradis articificels* of everyday life in the film, *The Truman Show*. I am struck each day by the manner in which predatory capitalism anticipates forgetfulness, nourishes social amnesia, smoothes the pillows of finality, and paves the world with a sense of inevitability and sameness. I am depressingly impressed by what a formidable opponent it has proven to be, how it fatally denies the full development of our human capacities, and inures us to the immutability of social life. In other words, it naturalizes us to the idea that capital is the best of all possible worlds, that it may not be perfect, but it certainly is preferable to socialism and communism. Many leftists have unwittingly become apologists for capitalist relations of domination because they are overburdened by the seeming inability of North Americans to imagine a world in which capital did not reign supreme. To address this situation, I have turned to critical pedagogy.

MITJA: You are very much identified with the field of critical pedagogy. How would you define critical pedagogy? What is your position within this field today?

PETER: As you know, Mitja, critical pedagogy has been a central liberatory current in education of the last two decades. Critical pedagogy has served as a form of struggle within and against the social norms and forces that structure the schooling process. Most approaches to critical pedagogy are limited to disturbing the foundations upon which bourgeois knowledge is built, placing the term "schooling" itself under scrutiny. Questions that arise in critical pedagogy often have to do with the relationship among schooling and the broader array of publics constructed by the marketplace and brought about by the secularization and the internationalization of the politics of consumption. In other words, critical pedagogy most often deals with cultural manifestations of capital, and the norms and formations that are engendered by means of relations of exchange. This is a good strategy as far as it goes. However, the revolutionary pedagogy that I advocate, that I have built from the roots of Freire's and Marx's work and the work of many others, such as the great revolutionary Che Guevara, involves the uprooting of these seeds of naturalization—planted through the reification of social relations and the subsumption of difference to identity by means of the law of value—and this means undressing the exploitative, sexist, racist, and homophobic dimensions of contemporary capitalist society. But it also means more than simply "uncovering" these relations, or laying them bare in all of their ideological nakedness. It stipulates—and here it is important not to mince words—the total uprooting of class society in all of its disabling manifestations. Revolutionary pedagogy refers to taking an active part in a total social revolution, one in which acting and knowing are indelibly fused such that the object of knowledge is irrevocably shaped by the very act of its being contemplated. That is, the very act of contemplation (I need to emphasize that this act of contemplation is collective and dialogical) shapes—and is shaped by—the object under investigation. The knowers are shaped—through dialogue—by the known. Revolutionary pedagogy attempts to produce an excess of consciousness over and above our conditional or naturalized consciousness, to create, as it were, an overflow that outruns the historical conditions that enframe it and that seek to anchor it, so that we might free our thought and, by extension, our everyday social practices from its rootedness in the very material conditions that enable thinking and social activity to occur in the first place. In other words, revolutionary pedagogy teaches us that we need not accommodate ourselves to the permanence of the capitalist law of value. In fact, it reveals to us how we can begin to think of continuing Marx's struggle for a revolution in permanence. A number of thinkers have helped to unchain the revolutionary implications of Freire's thought in this regard—Donaldo Macedo, Henry Giroux, Ira Shor, Peter Mayo, among others. I have attempted to do this by iterating the protean potential of his work for social revolution and not just the democratizing of capitalist social relations. So much contemporary work on Freire has inflated its coinage for transforming classroom practices but devalued its potential for revolutionary social change outside of the classroom in the wider society. Revolutionary pedagogy requires a dialectical understanding of global capitalist exploitation. Freire is often brought in to illuminate debates over school reform that are generally structured around the conceit of a dialogue over equality of opportunity, which rarely go beyond momentous renunciations of corporatism or teeth-rattling denunciations of privatization. But such debates studiously ignore the key contradictions to which history has given rise—those between labor and capital. Such debates are engineered in the United States to avoid addressing these contradictions.

MITJA: What do you see as the most important challenge in the future for educational researchers?

PETER: The key to see beyond the choir of invisibilities that envelope us, and to identify how current calls for establishing democracy are little more than half-way house policies, a smokescreen for neo-liberalism and for making capitalism governable and regulated—a "stakeholder" capitalism if you will. I do not believe such a capitalism will work, nor am I in favor of market socialism. We need to chart out a type of positive humanism that can ground a genuine socialist democracy without market relations, a Marxist humanism that can lead to a transcendence of alienated labor. Following Marx, Eagleton claims that we are free when, like artists, we produce without the goad of physical necessity; it is this nature which for Marx is the essence of all individuals. Transforming the rituals of schooling can only go so far, since these rituals are embedded in capitalist social relations and the law of value. There are signs that research in the social sciences might be going through a sea-shift of transformation. I think we need to take the focus away from how individual identities are commodified in postmodern consumer spaces, and put more emphasis on creating possibilities for a radical reconstitution of society. I like the new public role of Pierre Bourdieu—a role that sees him taking his politics into the streets and factories of France, fighting the structural injustices and economic instabilities brought about by capitalism and neo-liberalism—fighting what, in effect, are nothing short of totalitarian practices that are facilitating the exploitation of the world's workers. Bourdieu realizes that we haven't exhausted all the alternatives to capitalism. If that is the case, we need, as researchers, to bring our work to bear on the seeking out of new social relations around which everyday life can be productively and creatively organized. In my view, this is social science—and politics—the way it should be practiced.

"Rage and Hope: The Revolutionary Pedagogy of Peter McLaren" was first published by Mitja Sardoc in *Educational Philosophy and Theory*, Vol. 33, No. 3 & 4, August & November 2001, pp. 411–439. It was reprinted in *Casopis za Kritiko Znanosti*, XXXIX, 2001 (202–203) pages 11–21. (Slovenia). It was also published in *Herramienta* (Argentina, in Spanish).

Interview 3

the globalization of capital, critical pedagogy, and the aftermath of September 11

Lucía Coral Aguirre Muñoz

I spend considerable time lecturing and offering seminars throughout Latin American, particularly in Mexico. Although my Spanish is weak, I manage to get by with a good translator. Lucia teaches at a university not far from where I was giving some seminars, and I received a message from her that she would like to interview me for her journal. After our interview was published, I decided to expand on it bit, and reprint it in Multicultural Education, *published by Alan Jones. It gave me an opportunity to have this interview reach a wider audience in the United States at a time when neo-liberal capitalism was being celebrated in the mainstream press for plans to "uplift" the peoples of the so-called Third World. That myth needed to be punctured.*

LUCÍA CORAL AGUIRRE MUÑOZ: Postmodern theorists have argued that the working class has largely disappeared in the United States and that what faces the U.S. today is a new information economy in a new era of globalization. What would you say to this?

PETER MCLAREN: If the postmodernists—those voguish brigands of the bourgeois salons and English department seminar rooms—want to brag about the disappearance of the U.S. working class and celebrate the new culture of lifestyle consumption, then they need to acknowledge that the so-called disappearing working class in the U.S. is reappearing again in the assembly lines of China, Brazil, Indonesia, and elsewhere, where there exist fewer impediments to U.S. profit-making. Of course, this observation actually confuses the issue somewhat, because there is a working class in the United States. It has not disappeared, but has been reconfigured and resignified somewhat.

Back to your question about globalization, I think that globalization can be better understood as a form of imperialism and intensification of older forms of imperialism. But I think it is important to recognize that we need to refigure the term "imperialism" somewhat so that it does not come across as too economistic, so that we recognize along with William Robinson and others that while we do still have inter-state rivalries, we also have more and more consensual transactions among the global capitalist transnational elite.

Globalization represents an ideological façade that camouflages the manifold operations of imperialism. In fact, the concept of globalization has effectively replaced the term imperialism in the lexicon of the ruling elite for the purpose of exaggerating the global character of capitalism as an all-encompassing and indefatigable power that apparently no nation-state has the means to resist or oppose. It further confuses the issue that capitalism no longer needs the protection of the nation-state.

LUCÍA: Does this position hide the fact that state power still works mainly on behalf of the transnational corporations?

PETER: Yes, it does. Moreover, the globalization thesis maintains that whereas state power can be used in the interests of the large multinational corporations, it cannot be employed in the interest of the working class. I am using the term imperialism here after Lenin, to refer to the merging of industrial capital via cartels, syndicates, and trusts, with banking capital, the result of which is finance capital. I agree with William Robinson that transnational capital has become hegemonic and that transnationalized fractions have gained a powerful hold over most nation states worldwide. The global capitalist historical bloc is attempting to consolidate its social compact but is riven with contradictions and competing forces.

This is not the same thing as arguing that a global capitalism is free-floating. Because capitalism was formerly organized in geographically bound national circuits, and today these circuits are less anchored to the nation state, does not mean that nation states are irrelevant sites for commandeering capital, or, for that matter, sites for resisting the "capitalization" of the lifeworld. I do agree with the insight of Robinson, that the social configuration of space within transnationalized circuits of capital can no longer be conceived solely or mainly in national state terms. We have to think more in terms of what Robinson describes as uneven accumulation denoted for the most part by social group rather than differentiation by national territory. Nation states and national production systems no longer mediate local, regional, and global configurations of space the way that they used to before the move towards a transnationalization of the productive forces.

LUCÍA: So, globalization is not about the standardization of commodities? The same designer clothes appearing in shopping plazas throughout the world?

PETER: It is really really much more than this. It is tied to the politics of neo-liberalism, in which violence asserts itself through a recomposition of the capital-labor relationship. Such a recomposition entails the subordination of social reproduction to the reproduction of capital, the deregulation of the labor market, the globalization of liquid capital, the outsourcing of production to cheap labor markets, and the transfer of local capital intended for social services into finance capital for global investment. Teresa Ebert has provided a lucid and incisive "materialist" critique of two approaches to globalization: what she calls the globalization-as-transnationalism argument and the political theory of globalization. The former representation of globalization refers to the putative emergence of a new world community based on a shared cosmopolitanism and culture of consumption.

This perspective shares a culture and a state orientation. The cultural orientation emphasizes global symbolic exchanges relating to values, preferences, and tastes rather than material inequality and class relations. It is essentially a form of cultural logic. The focus on the state explores the relationship between the local and the global and whether globalization means the reorganization or disappearance of the nation-state. The political theories of globalization generally argue about the sovereign status of the nation-state. They argue that local legal codes, local currencies, and local habits and customs that enable the rise of capitalism now serve as constraints on capital, so that now the new transnational institutions more suitable to the new phase of capitalism are developing. Ebert rightly stresses the importance of production and highlights what the politics of globalization is really about: the continuous privatization of the means of production; the creation of expanding markets for capital and the creation of a limitless market of highly skilled and very cheap labor in order for capitalists to maintain their competitive rate of profit. In short, this process is all about the internationalization of capitalist relations of exploitation.

LUCÍA: When you come to think about it, this new imperialism is not really so new after all.

PETER: That's correct. As Ramin Farahmandpur and I have argued repeatedly, it's really a combination of old-style military and financial practices as well as recent attempts by developed nations to impose the law of the market on the whole of humanity itself. The global aristocracy's new world order has set out to expand the free market in the interest of quick profits (just think here of Enron!), to increase global production, to raise the level of exports in the manufacturing sector, and to intensify competition among transnational corporations. It has also benefited from part-time and contingent work, reduced the pool of full-time employment, and accelerated immigration from Third World and developing countries to industrial nations.

I very much agree with the thesis of James Petras and Henry Veltmeyer here. Capital and goods moving across national boundaries were always centered in specific nation states. The results of the expansion of capital and goods across national boundaries has always benefited classes in an unequal fashion, even when you consider the contemporary presence of transnational capitalists from former colonial countries who are engaged in capital export. Here Petras and Veltmeyer give the examples of China, Hong Kong, Mexico, Chile, South Korea, Taiwan, and Saudi Arabia. Even though the world is seeing more new billionaires from ex-colonial countries, and the expansion of new centers of accumulation, the qualitative class relations remain the same. The capitalist class—the transnational capitalist elite—benefits, while the working classes continue to be exploited with unprecedented brutality.

LUCÍA: Could you summarize some more of their recent observations?

PETER: I will try but I believe they are well worth examining in more detail than I can do here. Petras and Veltmeyer maintain that the idea of globalization as a sharing of economies whose national interdependence will lead to shared benefits is obfuscating. It is more accurate to use the concept of imperialism, which emphasizes the domination and exploitation by imperial states and multinational corporations and banks of less developed states and laboring classes.

The notion of imperialism fits the reality of the situation much better. As Petras and Veltmeyer make clear, it is the dominated, primarily Third World countries that are the low wage areas, the interest and profit-exporters (not importers), and that they are prisoners of international financial institutions and dependent on limited overseas markets and export products. There is a strong relationship between the growth of international flows of capital and an increase in inequalities between states, and a difference in salaries between CEOs (Chief Executive Officers of corporations) and workers.

LUCÍA: Let us return to the concept of social class. Would you please elaborate on this? How do you understand the concept of social class and education in what some people are calling a postmodern, globalized world?

PETER: Let me try to answer that as best as I can. Ken Moody points out that the number of industrial workers in the global South has increased from 285 million in 1980 to 407 million in 1994. The ranks of the industrial working class are rising. And in places in the more industrialized countries like Brazil, South Korea, and South Africa, union membership is on the rise. However, the composition of the working class is changing. There is more temporary employment, informal employment, as well as increased unemployment, and together these are occurring at a faster rate than the creation of permanent, formal jobs.

So we largely have in the current working class a new reserve army of labor, as Marx put it. Given the increasing scale of capitalist development and the separation of direct producers from their means of production, there has never been a more important time to rethink the notion of social class. The ruling class has deflected attention from the reality of class-based inequality within the globalization of capitalism by taking advantage of intra—and cross—class conflicts. Of course, the situation in Argentina now has revealed just how serious the crisis of global capitalism has become.

LUCÍA: Do we need to remember that not all classes in developed nation-states benefit from the globalization of capitalism?

PETER: Correct. It is mostly the large dominant enterprises that prosper. I believe that especially at this particular juncture in history, it is important to approach the question of social class from a Marxist perspective. I would emphasize this even further, considering the fact that in the universities in Britain, the U.S. and elsewhere, a new-Weberian view of social class, along with its technicist tendency to line the idea of social class to occupation still predominates. Here I follow the lead of some of my British colleagues Paula Allman, Dave Hill, Mike Cole, and Glenn Rikowski, to be specific—who have written a great deal on this subject. They have roundly criticized conventional neo-Weberian social "class" categories based not only on income but also on notions of status and associated consumption patterns and lifestyles because such notions ignore, indeed hide, the existence of the capitalist class—that class which dominates society economically and politically. This class owns the means of production, and the means of distribution and exchange, i.e., they are the owners of factories, transport companies, industry, finance, the media.

In other words, these consumption-based patterns mask the existence of capitalists, including the super rich and the super powerful: the ruling class. In addition, consumption-based classifications of social class mask the fundamentally antagonistic relationship between the two main classes in society, the working class and the capitalist class. Of course, Marxist analysis is being linked to "anti-Americanism." The Cold War basically drove Marxism out of mainstream intellectual life in the U.S. Some Marxist scholars inhabit the universities, but they are under close scrutiny, especially after September 11. Nevertheless, we need to analyze class using a Marxist approach. It is more important now than ever, especially given the influence of "postmodernism" among the U.S. educational left.

LUCÍA: How do you see it through a Marxist analysis?

PETER: Okay, now let me further explain what I mean by the concept of class. The working class includes not only manual workers but also millions of white-collar workers, such as bank clerks and supermarket check-out operators, whose conditions of work are similar to those of manual workers. Hill, Cole, Allman, Rikowski, Peter Mayo and other Marxists have long argued that neo-Weberian and technicist conceptions of "class" function to segment the working class, covering up the very presence of the working class. By segmenting different groups of workers, for example white-collar and blue-collar workers, and workers in managerial roles and the so-called underclass workers, they divide the working class against itself—this is the familiar "divide and rule" tactic.

By creating subdivisions of the working class—often termed class fractions or segments—it is easier to disguise the common interests of these different groups comprising the working class. This fundamentally inhibits the development of a common (class) consciousness against the exploiting capitalist class. Hill and Cole's powerful Marxist critique of the mainstream neo-Weberian perspective on social "class" reveals its inherently ideological nature. Their latest book, *Schooling and Equality: Fact, Concept and Policy*, expands on this point, as well as providing significant insights into the education impact on gender, race, and other forms of inequality that haunt contemporary life.

LUCÍA: The United States has been successful in its propaganda campaign in favor of free trade. What is your opinion?

PETER: The United States ruling class has made a powerful argument here that wealth depletion among developing nations is rescued by capital from the globalized activities of advanced capitalist countries. This, of course, is a boldfaced lie, but this lie has been hidden from the public by the mass media. In actual fact, transnational corporations drain the local capital from poor countries rather than bring in new capital. Because their savings are often low, banks in developing countries would rather lend to their own subsidiary corporations (who send their profits back to advanced nations) than to struggling local businesses in Third World countries. Faced with low prices for exports, high tariffs on processed goods, and a lack of capital and rising prices, local businesses are locked into entrenched impoverishment because of what have been euphemistically described as "structural adjustment measures" to balance the budget.

LUCÍA: How are such measures financed?

PETER: Mainly through cuts in spending for human development. The World Trade Organization does not permit poor countries to prioritize fighting poverty over increasing exports or to choose a development path that will advance the interests of the countries' own populations. Big business is in control of the government here in the United States (well, big business and the military industrial complex, I should say) and the U.S. basically is dedicated to serve profits rather than its citizens. The Enron scandal has shown us this and Bush and Cheney mirror in frightening ways the corporate mentality of the Enron CEO. And many corporations have more income-generating power than entire countries. For instance, General Motors is bigger than Denmark in wealth; Daimler Chrysler is bigger than Poland; Royal Dutch/Shell is bigger than Venezuela. We need to stand back and take a deep breath, asking ourselves to whom—as citizens in the world's poster-child democracy—we really serve and for whose benefit. In 1990, the sales of each of the top five corporations (General Motors, Wal-Mart, Exxon, Mobil, and Daimler Chrysler) were bigger than the GDPs (Gross Domestic Product) of 182 countries.

But as Leo Panitch and others have suggested, we must avoid a false polarity between corporations and nation-states in so far as we need to recognize that the power of transnational corporations is still largely conditional upon and mediated by state apparatuses.

Let's take a closer look at the situation here in the United States. We are currently witnessing a right-wing backlash against the civil rights of working class minority groups, immigrants, women, and children. What we are essentially seeing is increasing rights for business owners' worldwide—privatization, budget cuts and labor "flexibility"—due to the engineered absence of government constraint on the production, distribution, and consumption of goods and services brought about by global neo-liberal economic policies. Within the United States' Wall Street democracy, the tyranny of the market that ruthlessly subjects labor to its regulatory and homogenizing forces of social and cultural reproduction, is laid bare. The entrails of the eviscerated poor serve as the defining mechanisms for the soothsayers of the investment corporations. It comes as no surprise that the privatization of health care, drastic reduction of social services for the poor, and rumors of Social Security in connivance with Wall Street have coincided with the stagnation of wage growth and declining economic prosperity for most working-class men, women, and children. These recent trends are also associated with the shrinking middle class in the United States.

LUCÍA: Given such a daunting scenario, does democracy seem unreachable?

PETER: Very much so. We witness the frontiers of human freedom being pushed back as "free" market forces are being pushed forward by the ruling class. Astonishingly, even given this shocking state of expanding social and economic inequality in the United States, capitalism has never been so blindly infatuated with its own myth of success. Corporate leaders in the United States and dominant media have inured us into accepting the capitalist marketplace as the only possible social reality. Contemporary pro-capitalist ideology "betrays a remarkable amnesia about capitalism itself." It forgets that its success is dependent upon the blood, sweat, and tears of the poor. It effectively naturalizes the exploitation of the world's poor and powerless, reducing workers to the market price of their labor-power. If U.S. capitalists could have their own way, they would market for sale the tears of the poor.

The buying and selling of human lives as commodities, the creation of what Marx called "wage slaves," must be guaranteed as a constitutive factor of our democracy, so this condition is carefully disguised as a "voluntary contractual agreement," even though the only alternatives to shaking the sweaty palm of the market's invisible hand of indifference to human needs are starvation, disease, and death. Liberals and conservatives alike love to heap fulsome praise on the United States as the world's bastion of freedom, while ignoring the fact that its grandiloquent dream for saving the world has been a dismal failure. The backwardness of the economies of the so-called Third World has become a necessary condition for the flourishing of the economies of the so-called First World.

LUCÍA: Despite all the fanfare surrounding the promises of free trade, does it remain the case that both advanced and developed countries have been hurt by globalization?

PETER: Only a few metropolitan centers and select social strata have benefited, and it is no secret who these select occupants are. The functional integration among production, trade, global financial markets, and transport and speed technologies that make financial transactions instantaneous, have facilitated the re-deployment of capital to "least-cost" locations that enable exploitation on the basis of advantages it will bring to those wishing to become part of the "Millionaires Club."

As global assembly lines increase, and as speculative and financial capital strikes across national borders in commando-like assaults ("move in, take the goods, and move out"), the state continues to experience difficulty in managing economic transactions, but has not yet detached itself from the infrastructure of corporate imperialism. Transnational corporations and private financial institutions—Gold Card members of the leading worldwide bourgeoisie—have formed what Robinson and Harris call a "transnational capitalist clan." And while the emergent global capitalist historic bloc is marked by contradictions in terms of how to achieve regulatory order in the current global economy, national capitals and nation states continue to reproduce themselves. Home markets have not disappeared from the scene since they continue to provide ballast for the imperialist state through ensuring the general conditions for international production and exchange.[1]

The globalization of capital has dramatically occasioned what Mészáros (1999) describes as the "downward equalization of the differential rate of exploitation," where workers all over the world—including those in advanced capitalist countries such as the United States—are facing a steady deterioration of working conditions, due to the structural crisis of the capitalist system, a crisis of monetarist capitalism and the aggressive marketization of social relations.

Capitalism is predicated on the over-accumulation of capital and the super-exploitation of rank-and-file wage laborers. The irreversible contradictions inherent within capitalist social and economic relations—those between capital and labor—are taking us further away from democratic accountability and steering us closer to what Rosa Luxemburg (1919) referred to as an age of "barbarism."[2]

LUCÍA: Do you consider that the nature of capitalism is hidden?

PETER: It is hidden because it is everywhere. In another sense, capital's cheerleaders have hidden its diabolical nature and refusal to be accountable to democratic interests behind the non-sequitur claim that the free market promotes democracy. In fact, self-determining governments only get in the way of the goal of transnational corporations, which is, as Canadian philosopher John McMurtry argues, to open all domestic markets, natural resources, built infrastructures, and labor pools of all societies of the world to foreign transnational control without the barrier of self-determining government and people getting in the way.

McMurtry asserts that a free market democracy is a self-certifying term premised on the most odious of lies. Corporations steward us in the direction of market doctrine, a doctrine legitimized by its baptism in the fire of commodity production. He asks: Who are the producers? They are, after all, owners of private capital who purchase the labor of those that produce, including, notes McMurtry, the labor of white-collar managerial and technical workers. While some investing owners may also be producers—paying themselves as managers in addition to the remuneration they receive as owners—most corporate "producers" do not actually produce goods. These owners have no roles in the production process and are constituted as fictitious legal entities or "corporate persons." The real producers—the workers—are reduced to faceless "factors of production" employed by the owners of production.

As McMurtry argues, there is not freedom for the actual producers within the "free market economy." This is because the real producers belong to the employer, where they serve as the instruments of the employer's will. What little freedom exists is located at the top levels of management, but even here freedom exists only so far as it conforms to the ruling command of maximizing profitability for stockholders and owners. Obedience to the market god has been perceived as the only path to freedom and fulfillment.

LUCÍA: Can you be more specific on how would you evaluate the success of globalized capitalism?

PETER: The economic performance of industrial countries under globalization in the 1980s and 1990s is much poorer than during the 1950s and 1960s, when they operated under a more regulated social-market economy. Economic growth as well as GDP growth has been lowered and productivity has been cut in half; in addition, unemployment has risen dramatically in the OECD countries.

Latin American countries that have liberalized their trading and external capital regimes have suffered from fallouts and from severe financial crises, including the "peso crisis" of 1994–95 in Mexico and the "Samba effect" of 1999 in Brazil. Latin American countries following the Washington Consensus have, since the late-1980s, experienced a long-term growth rate reduction from 6 percent per annum to 3 percent per annum. And now, of course, we have the complete breakdown of the Argentine economy.

Globalization has been a dismal failure for the vast majority of the world's capitalist nations. And yet the corporate elite refuses to concede defeat. In fact, they are boldly claiming victory and, furthermore, that history is on their side. In a sense, they are correct. But we have to understand that they are claiming history for themselves. They have been victorious. In fact, they've made millions.

LUCÍA: At whose expense?

PETER: On the other hand, Lucia, as I have pointed out in my work with Ramin Farahmandpur, the growing bipolarization and the over-accumulation of capital by the new breed of opulent gangster capitalists and global carpetbaggers from reigning global mafiacracies, has reduced the odds of surviving hunger, poverty, malnutrition, famine, and disease for a growing segment of working-class men, women, and children who are now joining the ranks of the urban ghettos and global slum dwellers in their *casas de carton* all over the world. We are not talking only about Calcutta and Rio de Janeiro, but our own urban communities from New York to Los Angeles.

Whether by increasing the extortion of absolute surplus-value through the proliferation of maquiladoras along the U.S.-Mexican *frontera*, or increasing relative surplus value extortion through increasing the productivity of labor and reducing the value of labor-power, capitalism continues to hold living human labor hostage, fetishizing its own commodity logic and valorization process, and recasting the world into its own image. Valuing the medium and the outcome of abstract labor binds individuals to its law of motion. James Petras makes it astonishingly clear that one quarter of the capitalist world cannot prosper when three quarters are in deep crisis. The laws of capitalist accumulation cannot operate in such restricted circumstances.

LUCÍA: Do you think we have entered into a post-industrial economy?

PETER: I am not persuaded that we have entered into a post-industrial economy where production can be moved easily from advanced capitalist countries in the North to developing countries in the South. As Kim Moody has noted, most production still occurs in the North and most foreign direct investment is still controlled by the North. In fact, 80 percent of this investment is invested in the North itself. While it is true that northern industries are being transplanted to the south to take advantage of the cheaper labor markets, the North merely modernizes its economic base while making it more technologically sophisticated.

Sure, as Charlie Post points out, industry has declined worldwide, but the number of industrial workers in the most industrialized societies has remained relatively stable or has grown somewhat. However, the total output produced by industrial workers has greatly increased over the past fifty years. Something else to remember is that most service sector investment is related to business services such as legal and financial operations. Industrial investment is still dominant. Furthermore, the deskilling, flexible specialization and outsourcing that we are seeing mostly has to do with lean production and regional production chains eliminating excess materials, activities, and workers. Most of the key centers of advanced capitalism are still in Western Europe, the U.S. and Japan.

LUCÍA: Many of us in Latin America have been criticizing the policies of neo-liberalism for decades. Now we see criticisms appearing from U.S. educators.

PETER: That is true, and it is a good sign. Neo-liberalism, "capitalism with the gloves off" or "socialism for the rich," as I employ the term, refers to a corporate domination of society that supports state enforcement of the unregulated market, engages in the oppression of non-market forces and anti-market policies, guts-free public services, eliminates social subsidies, offers limitless concessions to transnational corporations, enthrones a neo-mercantilist public policy agenda, establishes the market as the patron of educational reform and permits private interests to control most of social life in the pursuit of profits for the few (i.e., through lowering taxes on the wealthy, scrapping environmental regulations, and dismantling public education and social welfare programs). It is undeniably one of the most dangerous politics that we face today.

LUCÍA: I have heard that some scholars in North America have compared Osama bin Laden to Che Guevara. Since you are a great admirer of Che, and have written about him, what is your reaction?

PETER: Yes, I will provide you here with my response that I have made public in the United States. Any comparison of Osama bin Laden to Che Guevara is grossly misleading. In fact, it is a dangerous comparison. One man, whose terrorist practices most Muslims worldwide find to be repugnant, wages a religious war (jihad) against Judaism and secularism under the cry of "Nasr min Allah, wa fathun qarib" ("Victory is from God, and conquest is near"); the other, an atheist, refused to persecute anyone on the basis of religious beliefs, as he fought against brutal dictatorships, economic and military imperialism, and the oppression of the poor in Latin America, the Caribbean, and Africa.

One struggles for the installation of a repressive authoritarian theocracy where women are subjugated, prevented from working and receiving an education, where minorities are extirpated as "infidels" (witness the Taliban's persecution of the Shiite minority in Afghanistan). The other struggled for a socialist and democratic society where women work alongside men in a relation of equality, where racism of all kinds is condemned and abolished, where illiteracy is virtually unknown and where each and every person has access to an education and adequate medical care.

Che's *guerrilleros* did not throw acid in the faces of unveiled women or assassinate tourists with automatic weapons. (We know that Ronald Reagan was a great admirer of the Mujahedin leader, Gulbuddin Hekmatyar, who, along with associates at Kabul University, threw acid in the faces of women who were not veiled [see Elich, 2001].) Unlike members of bin Laden's International Islamic Front for Jihad Against Jews and Crusaders, Che would never have purposely attacked innocent civilians. The beret-clad Che and bin Laden in the white robe and Kaffiyeh of a Saudi preacher have little more in common than facial hair.

To compare Che and his *foco* in Bolivia or the Sierra Maestro to Osama bin Laden and al-Qa'eda is a fatuous move. The recent attacks in Washington and New York City were reactionary acts of mindless terrorism with no explicit and anti-capitalist or anti-imperialist agenda. They had nothing to do with "class struggle" or the fight for human liberation and everything to do with human cruelty.

So far nobody has presented demands or clarified the purpose of this horrendous act, and at best we can speculate that they were motivated by a hatred of U.S. secular society, the support of Israel by the U.S. government, and for what bin Laden sees as a violation of the Koran and the Hadith (the sayings of the Prophet Muhammad), the continuing U.S. military presence in Saudi Arabia that pollutes the land of the Al Aksa Mosque and the holy mosque. They were also fostered by the U.S. invasion of Iraq and the continuing U.S. sanctions. Bin Laden exhorts his followers to pursue a hegira (a religious journey) to places such as Afghanistan and enlist in a jihad. It is said that bin Laden issued a *fatwa* in 1998 that called on Muslims to kill Americans wherever they are found.

A statement from the National Editorial Board of News and Letters, an international Marxist-humanist organization cites: "The September 11 attacks have nothing to do with any struggle against capitalism, injustice, or U.S. imperialism. They were a brutal act of violence against U.S. workers that has no rational cause, legitimacy, or justification. They were simply geared to kill as many people as possible, without any regard for class, race, or background." Nothing could be further from what Che stood for, and died for.

It is true that in order to understand the actions of bin Laden one cannot decouple them from the innocent Muslim victims of U.S. imperialist military interventions, both overt and covert. And I would argue that the broader issue is to link the climate of and context for terrorism to the global division of labor created by world capitalism. But I want to make clear that understanding this relationship is not the same as condoning acts of terrorism or providing a rationale for it. Terrorism is to be condemned. Period.

LUCÍA: So, would you say there is a difference between Che's utilization of the guerrilla and the terrorism of bin Laden?

PETER: There is a profound difference between Che's utilization of guerilla warfare tactics and bin Laden's acts of terrorism such as the world witnessed in horror on September 11. In fact, President Bush recently described the current commando actions by the U.S. military in Afghanistan as "guerrilla warfare." Even Bush appears to note the distinction, which is saying a lot. To compare guerrilla campaigns against federal troops in wars of liberation with bin Laden's criminal and morally abhorrent terrorism against the innocent is facile and pernicious. It is clear that the U.S. media will continue to make this connection in order to distort and damage the legacy of Che and that of anti-capitalist liberation struggles in general.

Che was certainly not a perfect human being, but his thoughts and actions have inspired everyone from Catholic priests to landless peasants. Next thing you know, some U.S. academics will be comparing Osama bin Laden to Subcomandante Marcos, who has used guerrilla tactics and is also an international icon, which would be an insult to the ongoing struggle of indigenous communities throughout the Americas.

One can only hope that the U.S. ceases its military action that will only bring about yet more civilian casualties and direct more hatred against the U.S. and seeks instead diplomatic efforts to resolve the current crisis. It is clear that the U.S. military actions in Afghanistan will only increase the cycle of violence and bring about more terrorist attacks in the U.S. I fear the U.S. and Britain will only provoke more intense social upheaval around the world.

First of all, think about the global alliance they are creating with despotic regimes in order to unleash the most sophisticated weapons of death on the poorest nation on the planet. Think of the pressure they are putting on protest groups and trade unions to abandon or de-emphasize their struggles, legitimate struggles for better working conditions. A more dangerous threat than acts of terror are the contradictions internal to the system of world capitalism. Throughout its history, capitalism has tried to survive in time of crisis by eliminating production and jobs and forcing those in work to accept worse conditions of labor, and seizing opportunities that might arise in which the public would support military action in order to protect markets or create new ones.

LUCÍA: How do you regard President Bush's call to fight terrorism as a fight for freedom and democracy?

PETER: As I have mentioned in some recent articles, this is a particularly difficult time to call for rethinking the role that the United States plays in the global division of labor. Let me repeat what I have written elsewhere on this topic. The recent events of mind-shattering apocalyptic dimensions, the sudden unfolding nightmare that saw death and destruction unleashed upon thousands of innocent and unsuspecting victims in Washington and New York City such that the gates of hell appeared to have been blown open, have made it difficult for many U.S. citizens to comprehend why their familiar world has suddenly turned upside-down.

Critical or revolutionary pedagogy takes a strong position against terrorism. Acts of terrorism are as backward and horrific as acts of capitalist-driven imperialism and in no circumstances can they be justified. It is clear to me that today world capitalism is trying to re-establish itself, since its current forms are unsustainable. In other words, it seizes opportunities to use military force to protect its markets and create new ones. However, it is important here that critics of U.S. capitalism—and world capitalism, for that matter—and I count myself as one of them, cannot simply list all the horrible acts of imperialism engaged in historically by the United States—a long and bloody list, to be sure—as evidence of or a rationale for why these terrorist acts occurred. To do so is irresponsible. The terrorist attacks occurred without reason, demand, or proclamation.

These acts were not acts against U.S. capitalism, imperialism, or injustice, but were demonic crimes against working people and crimes against humanity as a whole. For instance, hundreds of Latinos/as were killed in the attack on the World Trade Center, more victims than from any other nation outside of the United States. They worked at Windows on the World, in the office cafeterias, cleaning services, and delivery companies and little media attention has so far been paid to them. And while we can gain a deeper understanding of those events by recognizing how the Unites States is implicated in a long history of crimes against the oppressed throughout the world—including interventions in post-Cold War theaters—this history in no way justifies the terrorist attacks. These attacks were, in the words of Peter Hudis, "the reverse mirror image of capitalism and imperialism" and not the opposite of capitalism and imperialism. I think this is a good description.

Such attacks have been propelled by reactionary religious fundamentalist ideology—what could more accurately be called Islamism—that in no way represents all followers of Islam. As Edward Said remarks: "No cause, no God, no abstract idea can justify the mass slaughter of innocents, most particularly when only a small group of people are in charge of such actions and feel themselves to represent the cause without having a real mandate to do so." Terrorism is one of the most repulsive acts imaginable and the recent attacks of September 11 certainly qualify as a crime against humanity. These attacks follow the terrorist killing of 239 U.S. servicemen and 58 French paratroopers in Beirut in 1983; the 1998 bombings of U.S. embassies in Kenya and Tanzania in which hundreds were killed; the 1996 car-bomb attack on a U.S.

barracks in Dhahran, Saudi Arabia, that a killed 19 Americans; the 1995 car-bomb attack on an American National Guard Training Center in Riyadh, Saudi Arabia, that took four lives and, of course, the 1993 World Trade Center truck-bombing that killed six people and injured over a thousand others. And there was the more recent attack on the *U.S. Cole* in Aden that killed 17 sailors.

Terrorism is always abhorrent, and on September 11, 2001 it was captured by the media in Washington and New York City in such a fashion that the images of New York City during and after the attack will permanently be fixed in the structural unconscious of U.S. citizens. As a nation, we are still in shock. We are trying our best to heal. As Peter Hudis noted, even in the midst of this anti-human destruction the light of humanism did shine, in the hundreds of workers and citizens who flocked to "ground zero" in New York to help clear rubble, save victims, and provide medical aid to those who had been bloodied and battered in the attack. Construction workers rushed to save office workers; Black youth assisted elderly Jewish people to get out of the area—events like these became commonplace. Hudis reports on new forms of solidarity that emerged that included prisoners at Folsom Prison, most of them Black, who collected $1,000 to aid victims of the disaster. However, as Hudis further notes, these humanist expressions of solidarity are being quickly silenced by Bush's effort to use the attacks as an excuse to militarize America, restrict civil liberties, and prepare for what the rulers have long aspired for—permanent military intervention overseas. Hudis remarks that in just one single day the terrorists succeeded in totally shifting the ideological ground and handed the far right one of its greatest victories.

Another point worth making is this: What would be the response if CNN and the major U.S. television networks had covered in great detail the civilians killed by U.S. bombs in Afghanistan—the so-called "collateral damage" which some have estimated to be over three thousand men, women, children and infants? Why didn't the U.S. networks cover civilian casualties of U.S. bombings—well, they did cover some of this, but superficially. We can only truly heal if we attempt to uncover the complex and multistranded history of multinational capital and U.S. imperialism, accounts that have been barnacled by popular media representations. We must refuse to let history be characterized by the corporate media.

I think critical educators across the country must oppose what we are now seeing throughout the United States—a senseless xenophobic statism, militarism, erosion of civil liberties, and a quest for permanent military interventions overseas within the fracture zones of geo-political instability that have followed in the wake of the attacks, all of which can only have unsalutary consequences for world peace. This is particularly crucial, especially in light of the history of U.S. imperialism, and in light of another of Said's trenchant observations—that that "bombing senseless civilians with F-16s and helicopter gunships has the same structure and effect as more conventional nationalistic terror."

As critical educators we are faced with a new sense of urgency in our fight to create social justice on a global scale, establishing what Karl Marx called a "positive humanism." At a time when Marxist social theory seems destined for the political dustbin, it is needed more than ever to help us understand the forces and relations that now shape our national and international destinies. It is interesting, isn't it, that Marxist theory is now considered primordial and irrelevant when Christian Dior is marketing a $6,740.00 camouflage ball gown. War doesn't only generate profits for the arms manufacturers!

I am committed to the belief that critical/revolutionary pedagogy can help to bring about a global society where events like September 11, 2001, are less likely to occur. Critical pedagogy is a politics of understanding, an act of knowing that attempts to situate everyday life in a larger geo-political context, with the goal of fostering regional collective self-responsibility, large scale ecumene, and multiracial and international worker solidarity. It will require the courage to examine social and political contradictions, even, and perhaps especially, those that govern mainstream United States social policies and practices. It also requires a re-examination of some of the failures of the Left, as well.

I take the position that capitalist social relations constitute the material basis of racism and that therefore anti-racist struggles need to be situated in the larger context of anti-capitalist struggles. This means that the central target of anti-racists should be white supremacy. In making this assertion, I am not taking a class-first position. Rather, I am arguing that within Western capitalist democracies the exploitation of human labor comprises the "substratum" that enables institutionalized racist formations and practices, although admittedly racism often takes on a life of its own. Racism is capitalism's most odious and powerful weapon. We need to do more, of course, than just attack the rule of capital. It is an imperative that we resist racism in all of its hydra-headed incarnations. That is, we need to resist racism in its cultural, ideological, and symbolic manifestations on a daily basis.

Additionally, we need to deal racism a fatal blow by transforming the social relations of production and moving in the direction of a socialist alternative. A racially oppressed society is built upon the social relations of a class-defending state. Social class undergirds a state apparatus that creates races and shapes relations of gender. I do not have a dogmatic blueprint for a socialist alternative because the kind of socialism that needs to be fought for will depend upon the wishes of the people. I have discovered that merely mentioning the word "socialism" in the United States is tantamount to conjuring up images of Satanic forces bent on devouring democracy. The whole point of showing how capitalist social relations constitute the bedrock of racism is to deepen anti-racist struggle through anti-capitalist initiatives and at the same time deepen anti-capitalist initiatives through anti-racist practices (and those of anti-sexism and anti-homophobia). However, many anti-racist projects don't even mention capitalism. Either people see no problem with it, or else they haven't made the connection between capitalism and racism. Remember, capital is not a thing; it is a social relation. It is also moving like a brakeless train throughout the world. Who knows ultimately what destruction it will wreak?

Given this daunting global scenario, it is important that educators ask the following: Is there a viable socialist alternative to capitalism? What would a world without wage labor be like? Without living labor being subsumed by dead labor? Without the extraction of surplus value and the exploitation that accompanies it?

The practices of U.S.-backed regimes in the Middle East—such as Egypt, Algeria, Jordan, and Saudi Arabia who are waging brutal campaigns of violence against their Islamic opposition—certainly provide a backdrop against which we can begin to analyze the events of September 11. However, I think bin Laden's recent comments that the attacks were a retaliation for the U.S. sanctions on Iraq and for the U.S. support of Israel in its attacks on Palestinians is to a great extent a form of political opportunism on bin Laden's part. I'm not so sure that he really cares much about the Iraqi or Palestinian people.

I have a description by Edward Said of the attacks of September 11. In a recent interview with David Barsamian in *The Progressive*, Said wrote:

> At bottom, it was an implacable desire to do harm to innocent people. It was aimed at symbols: the World Trade Center, the heart of American capitalism, and the Pentagon, the headquarters of the American military

> establishment. But it was not meant to be argued with. It wasn't part of any negotiation. No message was intended with it. It spoke for itself, which is unusual. It transcended the political and moved into the metaphysical. There was a kind of cosmic, demonic quality of mind at work here, which refused to have any interest in dialogue and political organization and persuasion. This was bloody-minded destruction for no other reasons than to do it. Note that there was no claim for these attacks. There were no demands. There were no statements. It was a silent piece of terror. This was part of nothing. It was a leap into another realm—the realm of crazy abstractions and mythological generalities, involving people who have hijacked Islam for their own purposes. It's important not to fall into that trap and to try to respond with a metaphysical retaliation of some sort.

Unfortunately, George W. Bush has fallen into the baleful trap of a metaphysical retaliation of apocalyptic proportions. Bush himself early on described the war on terrorism as a "holy war" but dropped that description at the urging of his advisors. And while the terrorist attacks were indeed from another realm, another planet, an understanding of the recent history of *this planet*—particularly U.S. relations in the Middle East—could go a long way in understanding the attacks of September 11. U.S. actions in the geopolitical arena of the Islamic world certainly can help provide an historical and explanatory framework for probing the events of September 11.

Said notes that the root causes of terrorism can be traced to "a long dialectic of U.S. involvement in the affairs of the Islamic world, the oil producing world, the Arab world, the Middle East—those areas that are considered to be essential to U.S. interests and security. And in this relentlessly unfolding series of interactions, the U.S. has played a very distinctive role, which most Americans have been either shielded from or simply unaware of." For instance, one contradiction springs to mind. One of the pretexts given by the Clinton administration for bombing Yugoslavia was to enforce the right of return for ethnic Albanian refugees from Kosovo. But, as Ibish Hussein and Ali Abunimah point out, if refugee rights are so inviolable, why does the U.S. continue to insist that Palestinians drop their right to return, a return attached to specific homes and parcels of land to which many Palestinians hold the legal deed? Indeed, the Universal Declaration of Human Rights, specifically Article 13 and the Fourth Geneva Convention, guarantees the right of return to all refugees.

I think the word "dialectic" is important in understanding the relationship between U.S. foreign policy and economic imperialism and the events of September 11. I don't think we should say that U.S. actions were the direct cause of the attacks, because such a position is undialectical. As Peter Hudis has pointed out, the North Vietnamese, who suffered the tragic loss of millions of dead at the hands of the U.S., did not attack the U.S. populace in retaliation. But it is surely the case that U.S. involvement in the Islamic world created the geopolitical seedbed in which terrorism can grow.

I agree with my colleague Doug Kellner that the terrorist attacks can best be understood by using Chalmers Johnson's model of "blowback" (i.e., a term first used by the Central Intelligence Agency but adopted by some leftists to refer to actions that result from unintended consequences of U.S. policies kept secret from the American public). More specifically, as Johnson notes, what the mainstream media reports as the malign acts of "terrorists" or "drug lords" or "rogue states" or "illegal arms merchants" often turn out to be blowback from earlier covert U.S. operations. Blowback related to U.S. foreign policy occurred when the U.S. became associated with the support of terrorist groups or authoritarian regimes in Asia, Latin America, or the Middle East, and when its clients turned on their sponsor.

In Johnson's sense, September 11 is a classic example of blowback, in which U.S. policies generated unintended consequences that had catastrophic effects on U.S. citizens and the American and indeed global economy. As Kellner points out, the events of September 11 can be seen as blowback since bin Laden and the radical Islamic forces associated with the al Qaeda network were supported, funded, trained, and armed by several U.S. administrations and by the CIA.

In Kellner's astute reading, the CIA's catastrophic failure was not only to have not detected the danger of the event and taken action to prevent it but to have actively contributed to producing those very groups who are implicated in the terrorist attacks on the U.S. on September 11. The book, *White-out: The CIA, Drugs and the Press* by Cockburn and St. Clair reveals how the CIA assisted the opium lords who took over Afghanistan and helped to usher the Taliban into power, eventually helping in the financing of Osama bin Laden's al Qaeda network. More broadly speaking, I think we need to see the events of September 11 in the context of the crisis of world capitalism. I would like to share with you a quotation by Manuel Salgado Tamayo of Ecuador that viscerally captures what global capitalism is all about in terms of the current U.S. "war on terrorism."

> Now that the "evil empire" as Reagan called the U.S.S.R. has disappeared, the battle against narco-trafficking, the "defense" of human rights, expansion of market democracies, and the war on terrorism serve as smokescreens for advancing a world order that for the first time in the history of capitalism has the world's population by the scruff of its neck. This order, or world disorder, is neo-liberal globalization, whose postmodern philosophy expounds the death of reason and humanism, the total imposition of capital over labor, a "free" market for the South vs. protectionism for the North, and a type of financial freedom that allows the rich to steal the savings of the poor. The powerful have at last built a world in which only two slogans reign: "Everything for us, nothing for the rest" and "Enrich yourself and think only of yourself."

It is capital that guarantees regimes of injustice, as Aijaz Ahmad argues. But capital does not emanate only from the World Trade Towers or the Pentagon. The problem, in the larger sense, is capitalism as a world system and the array of injustices that historically proceed from it. The larger problem is the global division of labor that is created. Of course, the Unites States is certainly a major, if not the major, player in this system. U.S. policies—driven by capitalist accumulation—play a factor in the attacks, but the attacks are not a direct outcome of U.S. policies and practices. The U.S., along with other countries in the capitalist West, certainly helps to create the global culture that nourishes and helps to sustain the virus of terrorism—such as the horror of a bin Laden, whom the CIA originally helped to fund when he was fighting the Soviets.

It is no secret that Reagan's "secret" war in Afghanistan totaled $3.8 billion and was the largest covert action undertaken in U.S. history. Reagan wanted to bring down the socialist government in Afghanistan and to draw the Soviets into a "Vietnam" situation. The mujahedin troops that the U.S. supported liked to burn down schools and they frequently massacred teachers who dared to offer an education to women. Reagan celebrated the mujahedin 'freedom fighters,' but when they started to murder Americans, then they became terrorists (see Elich, 2001).

In other words, U.S. policies and odious covert operations as well as military interventions constitute some of the key environmental factors that produce a hatred for the United States. I have heard it said that the 1996 interview of Madeline Albright (when she was U.S. Ambassador to the United Nations) by U.S. journalist Lesley Stahl was distributed throughout the Middle East. Stahl compared the number of children who have died as a result of U.S. sanctions on Iraq—half a million—to the number of children who died in Hiroshima and Albright replied that "the price is worth it." Albright blamed Saddam Hussein for their deaths since he has built 48 presidential palaces since the Gulf War at a cost of 1.5 billion and has made the choice to let Iraqi children starve. This is of course partly true—Saddam Hussein is using the sanctions to keep certain sectors of his population starving and sick.

But, as Steve Niva and others have pointed out, Saddam could not do so without the sanctions—the U.S. has given him this tool to begin with. Secondly, the sanctions have been disastrous even without Saddam using them in certain ways and the U.S. equally bears responsibility. Surely these sanctions should be part of the context when we discuss the causes of Islamism and terrorism. Other issues should be discussed too, but you won't see the mass media discussing them. You won't hear much about the former U.S. support of the Taliban in return for pipeline agreements throughout the Caspian Sea region with companies like Unocal. You won't hear much about the Northern Alliance's history of extreme brutality, as documented by Human Rights Watch. You won't hear much about which industries the U.S. government is willing to bailout financially, and the thousands of Americans who have lost their jobs because of the terrorist attacks, workers who are apparently expendable.

And while there is plenty of news about Enron, chances are that the inquiries implicating Bush and Cheney will fall short, although we'll have to see. You won't hear much about how the U.S. helped create the Taliban movement with the assistance of Pakistan's intelligence agencies. You won't hear much about how the CIA was the former paymaster of Osama bin Laden. You won't see replays of newscaster Dan Rather broadcasting in the 1980s about the "freedom fighters" in Afghanistan—those very same people we are now seeking out with cruise missiles. For these connections, we need to turn to Arundhati Roy, who writes:

> In 1979, after the Soviet invasion of Afghanistan, the CIA and Pakistan's ISI (Inter Services Intelligence) launched the largest covert operation in the history of the CIA. Their purpose was to harness the energy of Afghan resistance to the Soviets and expand it into a holy war, an Islamic jihad, which would turn Muslim countries within the Soviet Union against the communist regime and eventually destabilize it. When it began, it was meant to be the Soviet Union's Vietnam. It turned out to be much more than that. Over the years, through the ISI, the CIA funded and recruited almost 100,000 radical mojahedin from 40 Islamic countries as soldiers for

> America's proxy war. The rank and file of the mojahedin were unaware that their jihad was actually being fought on behalf of Uncle Sam. (The irony is that America was equally unaware that it was financing a future war against itself.)

I think Bush's characterization of the U.S. as good and every country who does not support the U.S. war in Afghanistan as evil is wrong-headed. The same can be said for Bush's description of Iraq, Iran, and North Korea as the "axis of evil." The U.S. has to acknowledge how its own political and military actions—the bombing of civilians, sanctions that are responsible for hundreds of thousands of deaths, covert and overt military operations and interventions over the years—have created great misery and destruction.

There might be some who defend such actions as necessary in order to avoid even greater misery (although I generally don't buy this argument), but it is foolish to deny or to avoid the arguments of those throughout the world (arguments backed by empirical evidence) who are convinced that the U.S. is responsible for a great deal of oppression and exploitation throughout the world, usually in the so-called Third World.

On the other hand, as I have mentioned earlier, I think it is misleading to explain the horror of September 11 mainly as a mechanical reflex of specific U.S. policies overseas, as if it were an incontrovertibly causal, one-to-one correspondence. U.S. policies and practices are certainly a factor, however, and we do have to emphasize how the U.S. has helped create the terrain of suffering that gives rise to horrors like bin Laden, either directly through CIA funding or indirectly through support for Israel's policies against the Palestinians, U.S. bases in Saudi Arabia, etc. However, it is clear that other factors are involved, like anti-Semitism, anti-Americanism, as against genuine anti-Imperialism as a reaction against the dimensions of "Western society" that every leftist should support: workers rights, feminism, gay rights, etc.

As Peter Hudis and others have noted, it is wrong to believe that bin Laden was simply responding to the same injustices as radical leftists, except that he used a method leftists would never condone and would find utterly abhorrent. Steve Niva has pointed out, for instance, that bin Laden's small, violent, and socially reactionary network—influenced by the socially reactionary Wahhabi school of Islam practiced in Saudi Arabia and the conservative Pakistani Islamist Party, Jamaat-i Islami—is antagonistic to social justice and differs in important ways with the wider current of Islamic activism in Arab world and more globally.

The wider current of Islamic activism does have a social justice agenda on behalf of the poor and dispossessed, is more involved in party building and mass mobilization, and largely rejects the simplistic Islamic doctrines promoted by bin Laden's network. Moreover, Niva stresses that bin Laden's organization is disconnected from wider Islamic activist movements in that they do not locate their struggle in a national context, but rather in a global war on behalf of Muslims worldwide. The political Islam of bin Laden is opportunistic and its project only pretends to speak for oppressed people. As Samir Amin notes, political Islam is not a liberation theology but is "the adversary of liberation theology. It advocates submission, not emancipation." Amin notes that in the case of political Islam, its spokespersons are in general harmony with liberal capitalism. Amin notes the case of the Egyptian parliament that grants "absolute freedom of maneuver to landowners and nothing whatsoever to the peasant farmers who work their land." It is problematic therefore to locate the attacks on September 11 to a natural reflex reaction to U.S. policies and practices. It is much more complicated than that.

LUCÍA: Is viewing the attack of September 11 as mainly a reaction to U.S. foreign policies and military interventions an irresponsible position to take?

PETER: Again, one has to view U.S. policies and interventions as part of the overall context for understanding these events because they contribute to the environmental backdrop against which these acts of terrorism occurred. However, the context in which Islamic fundamentalism or Islamism (or what Samir Amin refers to as "political Islam") arises is a lot broader than simply a reaction against U.S. foreign policy, although as I mention once again, this is surely one among several other factors that creates a climate of hate against the U.S. and the problem of understanding the attacks of September 11 is certainly greater than attributing it to bin Laden's hatred of modernity.

Again, we can't look at bin Laden's puritanical Islamism and ignore the actions of the U.S. on the stage of world history. Our approach needs to be a dialectical one. According to Tariq Ali, after the Afghan Communist Party carried out a coup against the corrupt regime of Daoud and established improved medical care and free education and schools for girls, there was factional fighting that led to the victory of Hafizullah Amin, a repressive organization. The Red Army was sent in by the Soviet Union to topple Amin and to sustain the Afghan Communist Party. The U.S. decided to destabilize the regime by arming the ultra-religious tribes and employing the Pakistan Army to coordinate the efforts of the religious extremists against the Soviet Union.

When the Saudi regime suggested that bin Laden could help in this effort, the U.S. recruited and trained him and sent him to Afghanistan where in one strike he is reported to have attacked a co-educational school and killed the teachers. After the Soviet Union withdrew its forces from Afghanistan, a coalition government was formed consisting of groups loyal to Iran, Tajikistan and Pakistan but a civil war broke out among these groups. Pakistan had been training a student militia (the Taliban, who were influenced by Wahhabism and believed in permanent jihad against infidels and other Muslims such as the Shias) in special seminary schools and these were sent into the civil war in Afghanistan.

The Taliban eventually captured Kabul and most of the country and until about June, 2001, some U.S. think tanks were even thinking about using the Taliban to destabilize the Central Asian Republics. Shouldn't teachers in the U.S. be encouraged to study this part of U.S. history linked to the Cold War? Or will this history be "off limits" in our high schools? But in describing the context of events leading up to September 11, I think it is also important to criticize the lack of success of the secular left. After all, part of the problem also has been the retreat—and the defeat—of the revolutionary left worldwide.

A case can be made that the rise of Islamism, for instance, is related to the defeat of the secular left by U.S./Western imperialism. Aijaz Ahmad has pointed out that in Iran and other countries, the "defeat" of the socialist and anti-colonial nationalist movements enabled the Islamic fundamentalists to take over. It could be said, for instance, that Islamism arose to fill that space in Iran which had been left vacant with the elimination of secular anti-imperialist nationalism. Let's cite one example. In the 1970s there was a massive secular anti-imperialist movement in Iran—many of the 250,000 Iranian students in exile considered themselves Marxists. In 1979 the "Marxist" (semi-Stalinist) Fedayeen group had a large following. Peter Hudis notes, however, that part of the problem was with the Left itself—that, for instance, that Iranian left was dominated by a unilinear revolutionist political perspective which led it to support Khomeini on the grounds that he would lead the country to the necessary stage of the bourgeois democratic revolution.

Islamic movements that might have been able to offer a more anti-colonialist alternative were defeated. There were contradictions within the Iranian left's revolutionary politics—and also within Arab socialism in general—that could not be overcome. Steve Niva points out that much of the lead up to the Iranian revolution was actually secular left but that the revolution was hijacked by the reactionary wing of the Islamic camp. The issue isn't only secular versus religious ideology. There was also a non-secular Islamic group that was also against imperialism that was caught between the secular left and the right wing of Islamic revolutionism.

Well, this is a discussion for another time. But there is another important point here to be made from the perspective of Marxist Humanism. Peter Hudis notes, and I agree, that while we surely have to expose the actions of the U.S. military and its leaders in the government, for their role in shaping history towards violence against oppressed peoples, and while we need to oppose Bush's war drive, we also can't ignore how the internal contradictions in radical politics that was defined by "first negation" also contributed to this situation.

Marxist humanists do not stop at the first negation, but rather move forward to negate the negation. They don't, in other words, just want to defeat capitalism, but raise the issue of what society will be like after the revolution. Here, revolutionary praxis is defined by absolute negativity as the seedbed of liberation. As Marx once put it, "the correct formulation of the problem already indicates its solution."

Something that is very evident now in the U.S. is that public discourse has been hijacked by the popular media. Will the culpability of our acts of imperialist aggression continue to be covered up by the mass media? The mainstream media have helped to whip up a climate of revenge across the country under a spectacle of patriotism.

I think it was H. L. Mencken, playing on Samuel Johnson's famous description of patriotism (as the last refuge of a scoundrel), who referred to patriotism as the great nursery of scoundrels. So much about patriotism is nourished by the distortion of history and false claims about a nation's past. Many students across the country know little about the efforts of the U.S. to secure economic and military world hegemony, often through supporting dictatorships and autocratic regimes in the so-called Third World.

It is easy to convince the U.S. public that the "new war" that we are waging is a fight between good and evil, when that same public is kept in the dark by the mainstream media with respect to the history—past and present—of U.S. foreign policy. Students in United States colleges and universities don't really comprehend why so many in developing countries dislike the U.S. They are not, for the most part, aware of this history.

LUCÍA: Would you say it is a virtually hidden history?

PETER: It is virtually a hidden history, yes. The facts are available, of course, but they are rarely discussed in the mainstream media. To unscroll these facts in public would be participate in a ritual that challenges the very sanctity of patriotism. It is difficult for students to comprehend, for example, why Third World peoples blame the U.S. government for the deaths of half a million children and thousands of adult civilians as a result of U.S. sanctions on Iraq. Or why the U.S. is blamed for killing thousands of Sudanese and then blocking a UN investigation into the killing. Or blamed for the thousands who died in Nicaragua at the hands of Oliver North's murderous Contras. Or blamed for the suffering in Cuba due to a U.S.-imposed embargo. Or blamed for an event that occurred on a different September 11, 28 years ago, when the Chilean Air Force, with support from the U.S. (including Henry Kissinger) bombed its own Presidential Palace in downtown Santiago, causing the death, among others, of socialist President Salvador Allende.

I should note here that renowned Chilean author, Ariel Dorfman, wrote recently that the notion that we have lost our innocence and that the word will never be the same again that was uttered by the people of Chile in the context of Chilean terror that began on September 11 in 1973 is now being heard in the streets throughout the U.S. Dorfman rejects the demonization of the U.S. even though he has been the victim of U.S. arrogance and intervention, and he hopes that "the new Americans forged in pain and resurrection" will be "ready and open and willing to participate in the arduous process of repairing our shared, our damaged humanity."

U.S. students can't comprehend why the U.S. is blamed for its terror and toruture campaigns against the North Vietnamese or why it is blamed for bringing four million people to the brink of starvation in Afghanistan because of U.S. sanctions; or blamed for supporting dictatorships in places like El Salvador and Guatemala that murdered hundreds of thousands of indigenous peoples with Apache helicopter gunships. Or blamed for killing thousands of civilians in Yugoslavia with cruise missiles, smart bombs, F-16s, and depleted uranium ordinances.

According to Canadian philosopher, John McMurtry, over 90 percent of military-wrought deaths in the world have been on unarmed people since the fall of the Berlin Wall in 1989. There are more examples. The U.S. installed the Shah in Iran in 1953, who ran a regime of terror, including the torture of dissidents. Later on, in 1983, the U.S. gave the Khomeini government in Iran a list of members of the communist Tudeh Party, claiming these members were Soviet agents. This led to the torture and imprisonment, and execution of thousands of people (see Elich, 2001). The U.S. helped to support the Indonesian invasion of 1975 where over 200,000 East Timorese were slaughtered and the U.S. reportedly supplied General Suharto of Indonesia with assassination lists. In 1965, a CIA-backed coup had forced out President Sukarno and replaced him with General Suharto. The U.S. government had given Suharto a list of members of the Indonesian Communist Party. Thousands were imprisoned and killed. Suharto's butchering of communists was supported and funded by the U.S. Between 500,000 to one million trade unionists, peasants, ethnic Chinese and communists were savagely slaughtered by Suharto and his military (see Elich, 2001).

The U.S. continues to support the Colombian government where paramilitaries slaughter 3,000 citizens a year with U.S. military aid. In fact, the Bush administration's multibillion dollar aid to Colombia (the 3rd largest recipient of U.S. military aid in the world) is supposed to help to suppress cocaine production, but that money—as the Bush administration well knows—is used by right-wing paramilitary groups to target trade union leaders who are organizing in the coal mines. Coal is being encouraged for use in U.S. power plants and some coal mines in Colombia are owned by U.S. multinational corporations based in places like Birmingham, Alabama. Not only have hundreds of mine workers been murdered, who were trying to organize unions, but hundreds of teacher union leaders have been murdered as well.

As Tamayo notes, Plan Colombia and the Andean Initiative are really all about U.S. control over strategic natural resources—it is about U.S. domination of the American continents, especially the Bolivian triangle (the Venezuela of Hugo Chavez; the activities of the FARC (Fuerzas Armadas Revolucionarias de Colombia) and the ELN (the Ejército de Liberación Nacional); and the indigenous rebels of Ecuador and Panama. Venezuela is the most important provider of petroleum for the U.S. on the continent. Yet President Chavez sells petroleum to Cuba and has diplomatic ties with Iraq and is helping to rebuild OPEC. No wonder the U.S. helped orchestrate a coup against Chavez! As imperialist alpha-males, how could they not? The FARC is attempting to resist the imperialism of the United States. The FARC is certainly to be held accountable for its killings, but by far the greatest purveyor of violence in Colombia is the Colombian military. The FARC have been criticized for their treatment of indigenous peoples and Afro-Colombians and for their lack of cooperation with broad-based grassroots coalitions whereas the ELN has galvanized a broad social base and both are the target of para-military forces.

The Ecuadorian indigenous community is fighting neo-liberal policies and the elite bankers who run the country. And, well, if we want to talk about Argentina we could be here for weeks. According to the Health Education

Trust in London, 200,000 Iraqis died during and in the immediate aftermath of the Gulf War. We are the world's largest seller of weapons. For a time we were close allies with Saddam Hussein, Noriega, bin Laden, Duvalier, and Marcos of the Philippines. Look, in the past 20 years we've bombed Libya, Panama, Grenada, Somalia, Haiti, Afghanistan, Sudan, Iraq, and Yugoslavia. Let me share with you, Lucia, another quotation by Arundhati Roy:

> The September 11 attacks were a monstrous calling card from a world gone horribly wrong. The message may have been written by bin Laden (who knows?) and delivered by his couriers, but it could well have been signed by the ghosts of the victims of America's old wars. The millions killed in Korea, Vietnam and Cambodia, the 17,500 killed when Israel—backed by the U.S.—invaded Lebanon in 1982, the 200,000 Iraqis killed in Operation Desert Storm, the thousands of Palestinians who have died fighting Israel's occupation of the West Bank. And the millions who died in Yugoslavia, Somalia, Haiti, Chile, Nicaragua, El Salvador, the Dominican Republic, Panama, at the hands of all the terrorists, dictators and genocidists whom the American government supported, trained, bankrolled and supplied with arms. And this is far from being a comprehensive list.

Edward Herman and David Peterson have made a distinction between the wholesale terrorism of nation states and the retail terrorism of non-state terrorists. They describe the U.S. policy against Iraq, for instance, as wholesale terrorism. They recall that "the United States is the only country that has used nuclear weapons and has threatened their further use many times. Its employment of chemical weapons more than competes with Saddam Hussein's use in the 1980s, one of the U.S. legacies being some 500,000 Vietnamese children with serious birth abnormalities left from a decade of U.S. chemical warfare in the 1960s." We seem fearful of raising questions today that were raised by activists decades ago—activists who are today revered as heroes.

For instance, how much different are we now as a country than when Martin Luther King described the United States on April 4, 1967, at the Riverside Church in New York, where he said: "my government is the world's leading purveyor of violence?" We should be allowed to raise this question in our schools. There will surely be many different answers and arguments. But we should be allowed to debate this question with the best rational, analytical, and dialectical means at our disposal. Lynne Cheney can call us "enemies of civilization" for criticizing U.S. imperialism; she can call us the "hate America" crowd if she wants. But there are some of us who believe that patriotism should be more than mindless flag-waving. Patriotism that is not at the same time conjugated with introspection and critical self-reflexivity is a patriotism that does injustice to the word. To be self-reflective, to think critically is one of the markers of a true democracy.

Of course, there are many academics who are not prepared to question seriously the material basis of exploitation in U.S. capitalist society because they benefit from it. All of us benefit from it, to some extent, if we teach at universities, but the point that I am making is that there are a lot of academics who won't listen to arguments *against* capitalism or *for* socialist alternatives because they presume that if you are a Marxist or a socialist you must be dogmatic and totalitarian and militantly prepared to push your vision of social justice down people's throats, or else you support a vanguard party of select intellectuals, or you are already preparing the gulags for recalcitrant socialists.

Many of the postmodernists with whom I come into contact frankly know very little about the Marxist tradition. It is not surprising that Tamayo calls postmodernism the philosophy of neo-liberal globalization. My perspective on the transition to socialism does not follow the dictates of the Second International. It is, for instance not focused on the seizure of state power. I think John Holloway has made some excellent points when he argues that the world cannot be changed through the state in the sense of capturing positions of power; rather, the revolution should be directed not at the conquest of power but at dissolving relations of power.

The struggle we should be waging is based on the recognition of people's dignity, as the Zapatistas would put it. As Holloway notes, the struggle for the dissolution of power is at one and the same time a struggle for the emancipation of power to (potentia) from power-over (potestas). We need to practice the mutual recognition of dignity as a way of bringing about anti-power (not counter-power, because the notion of counter-power assumes it has a symmetry with power). Because as workers we produce the capital that subordinates us, our struggle should involve among other things, a fight against fetishism, reification, and identification—all aspects of alienation. Here Holloway notes that struggles may take the form of open rebellion, control of the labor process, or control over the processes of health and education. (However, I disagree with Holloway's position that we do not need to take control of the state.)

We are not talking here about the politics of certainty but of continuous struggle. While Marxists are often caricatured as dogmatic, totalizing, and lacking in tolerance, I must confess, here, quite honestly, that the most intolerant, overbearing, and dogmatic academics that I have met are those who identify themselves as progressive postmodernists. They are usually the ones who try to silence me at conferences on the basis that I must be intolerant and dogmatic because I identify myself as a Marxist. (This is not the case for all postmodernists, let's be clear on that.) The point I am trying to make is that it is difficult to engage in the politics of criticism without first establishing the context for dialogical relationships with those with whom one disagrees. I remember attending classes taught by Michel Foucault in the late-1970s. (I cannot recall the exact date) and he was very generous and open to critique. I wish more people would follow his example.

Self-criticism is what deep democracy is about. A democracy that lives up to its name. We don't ask this question to assist the enemies of the U.S. We ask this question because it is the type of question that must define us as a democracy since democracy is never fully achievable but always in the process of creating itself through analyzing both its weaknesses and its strengths. If we shut down this question—and there are many U.S. religious, political, and cultural leaders who say that we should—then at some level we are capitulating to the terrorists. We then create the type of closed society that we accuse our detractors of supporting. Then we take a big step towards fascism.

Speaking of fascism, I think that at this moment we are living in a de facto military dictatorship, and we are seeing signs of totalitarian leadership all around us. After September 11, a climate of mutual suspicion has been created, which James Petras argues is one of the hallmarks of a totalitarian regime. Let me read you what he says:

> The Federal Bureau of Investigation (FBI) soon after September 11 exhorted every U.S. citizen to report any suspicious behavior by friends, neighbors, relatives, acquaintances, and strangers. Between September and the end of November almost 700,000 denunciations were registered. Thousands of Middle Eastern neighbors, local shop owners, and employees were denounced, as were numerous other U.S. citizens. None of these denunciations led to any arrests or even information related to September 11. Yet hundreds of thousands of innocent persons were investigated and harassed by federal police.

I believe Petras makes an important point about dictators. He notes that in totalitarian states, the supreme leader seizes dictatorial powers, that he suspends constitutional guarantees, and gives special powers to the secret police forces. So, by that definition we are living now in a police state in the U.S. In fact, as far as the tribunals go, the government can arrest any non-citizen that it suspects might be a terrorist. The trial can be held in secret, the prosecutors do not have to present evidence if it is in the interests of national security, and those who are condemned by the tribunal can be executed even if one third of the military judges disagree. And the Patriot Act, well, it defines terrorism so broadly that, as Petras notes, even any anti-globalization protest such as the one that occurred in Seattle can now be called a "terrorist act."

Let me share with you a profound contradiction. President Bush argues that we're fighting for democracy, pluralism, and civil liberties. In a recent speech before Congress he said that terrorists "hate what they see right here in this chamber: a democratically elected government." He went on to say: "They hate our freedoms: our freedom of religion, our freedom of speech, our freedom to vote and assemble and disagree with each other. They want to overthrow existing governments in many Muslim countries such as Egypt, Saudi Arabia, and Jordan." He ended his speech by saying: "This is the fight of all who believe in progress and pluralism, tolerance and freedom."

But how could this be true, since any coalition that includes Egypt, Saudi Arabia, or Jordan cannot include the principles stated by Bush in his speech. After all, each of these countries restricts freedom of speech, the press, assembly, association, religion, and movement. Jordan is a monarchy whose security forces have engaged in "extra judicial" killings. The establishment of political parties are prohibited in Saudi Arabia. In fact, they have a religious police force to enforce a very conservative form of Islam. Egyptian security forces regularly arrest and torture people under the banner of fighting terrorism.

You know, it strikes me as disingenuous that Bush now seeks global/international cooperation to fight terrorism, especially after abrogating the ABM (Anti-Ballistic Missile) treaty and abandoning other multilateral treaty frameworks such as the Kyoto Protocol and the Biological Weapons Convention, walking out of the UN conference against racism held in South Africa, and extending NATO into Eastern Europe. And in order to fight terrorism, the U.S. is even willing to go to bed with Pakistan's General Musharraf, offering American Aid and shedding the sanctions that it had imposed after Pakistan's nuclear build-up. When the mujahedin were fighting the Soviets, the United States provided three billion dollars to bolster radical Islamic groups, and the CIA worked with Pakistani intelligence to help create the Taliban.

Within the Bush administration there are those, like Deputy Secretary of Defense, Paul Wolfowitz, who in 1992 wrote a Pentagon memo arguing for a frontal U.S. assault on Russia in order to liberate the Baltic states, who want to go to war not only with Afghanistan but also Iran and Iraq. And we continue to support Israel, which some have described as a vassal state of the global American empire that we have bankrolled during its 34-year illegal occupation of the West Bank and Gaza, and where Palestinians are treated much like indigenous peoples were treated in the U.S. by the U.S. government during the "western expansion" or much like the South African government treated its Black population forced into Bantusans during the days of apartheid. Israel has a policy of state-sponsored terrorism, gives the Palestinians the choice between resistance or surrender, and is led by Ariel Sharon, whose invasion of Lebanon claimed the lives of 17,000 civilians. We continue to protect Israel from international sanction when they clearly have violated the rights of the Palestinian people. (Thank goodness some Israeli military officers are now refusing to serve in the Gaza Strip because they recognize that they are working to humiliate and brutalize the Palestinian people.) By the same token, we need to take a strong stand against Palestinian terrorism as well, which includes suicide bombing attacks on innocent Israeli citizens.

And what about the U.S. claim that it stands for freedom against evil? Human rights against anarchy? What about this metaphysical Manichean divide conjured up by George Bush? I am sure that the U.S. wants to be always on the side of freedom and human rights. Or actually believes it is always on the side of freedom and human rights. But the historical record tells us a somewhat different story. The United States has indeed supported the political and civil rights aspect of the Universal Declaration of Human Rights, to its credit, but it conspicuously avoids that aspect of the Declaration that deals with economic rights and freedoms. This is troubling, but we can see the connection here in our discussion of globalization as a form of imperialism.

Well, there are many more issues to discuss. I am worried about the newly established Office of Homeland Security and the possible consequences of new national security measures on civil liberties. I am referring here to wiretaps, secret searches of citizens' residences, the imprisonment or deportation of immigrants without supporting evidence, and I fear that checks against the FBI's domestic surveillance will disappear. Well, they are already disappearing. Non-citizens can be put under suspicion of terrorism, tried in secret by a military tribunal, and executed even if one third of the members of the tribunal disagree. I am worried about an increase in racial profiling. I am also worried about academic freedom, about the freedom of scholars to assess U.S. foreign and domestic policy without fear of retribution or censorship.

Edward Said puts it this way: "What terrifies me is that we're entering a phase where if you start to speak about this as something that can be understood historically—without any sympathy—you are going to be thought of as unpatriotic, and you are going to be forbidden. It's very dangerous. It is precisely incumbent on every citizen to quite understand the world we're living in and the history we are a part of and we are forming as a superpower."

I couldn't agree more. And outside of the academy we have serious concerns as well. I worry that George W. Bush will now have more power to use political and economic repression to squash democratic protests by the working class against an economic crisis that was beginning to lurch out of control long before September 11.[3]

LUCÍA: What are the implications of all of this for educators?

PETER: It is to think about the pedagogical implications for understanding the role of imperialism and the globalization of capital on the world scene today. The question is not to argue that U.S. military actions and U.S. support for brutal dictatorships in the past—and I could include Vietnam and Cambodia as well—but rather somehow to provide a justification for terrorism. [Speaking of Cambodia, how can the U.S. forget its support of the Khmer Rouge in its guerrilla war against the socialist government of Hun Sen. This was when the Khmer Rouge was part of the Coalition Government of Democratic Kampuchea. Prince Norodom Sihanouk and Son Sann of the coalition carried out joint operations with the Khmer Rouge. The Khmer Rouge are famous for their genocide in Cambodia (see Elich, 2001).]

Only a monster like bin Laden could make such a case for terrorism. There is no justification for terrorism. Absolutely none. The point I am making is a pedagogical one: Can we learn from capitalism's role in world history? Can we explore the relationship between capitalism and nationalism, between capitalism and nation-building? Can students in the U.S. learn from the role of the U.S. in world history? Can we seek a world where terrorism and oppression in all of its forms cease to exist? What would a world look like in which terrorism would not be a choice? Some would say that the U.S. has a responsibility as an empire. Others, such as myself, would say that we have a responsibility to create a social universe without empires. For me, the whole question of why so many in the world hate the U.S. is an important pedagogical question. Of the 50 million students in U.S. schools, how many will learn about the dirty wars conducted by or at least supported by the U.S.?

LUCÍA: Is blaming only the U.S. a simplistic point of view?

PETER: It is not only simplistic but wrong-headed. Here I need to sound a caution to my leftist compañeros. It is not useful or correct—in fact it is repugnant—to argue that we are now repaying in blood what we have done to other countries. Because this skips over the notion that some forces, like the terrorist factions of Osama bin Laden, are as regressive as anything done in the service of U.S. imperialism. There is a great array of crimes that can be linked to world capitalism, that go beyond the participation of the U.S. I have listed above acts of U.S. imperialism not in order to create an excuse or rationale for the terrorist acts, but to provide a context for discussing world history in light of the globalization of capitalism and contemporary geo-politics. On the other hand, we in the U.S. must share the burden of history. Our actions on the world scene are related to September 11. We are not morally or politically above the fray.

To share the burden of history we need to become critically self-reflexive about our political system, its economic, domestic, and foreign policies in the context of the globalization of capitalism or what I have called the new imperialism. The problem is that students in the U.S. rarely are given the opportunity to discuss the above events because the media mostly avoid discussing them in depth. How many U.S. citizens know that George Bush senior got anti-Castro terrorist, Orlando Bosch, out of jail in the U.S. (see Bortfeld & Naureckas, 2001)? Bosch had been arrested in 1988 for illegally entering the U.S. Even though Bosch was accused of masterminding the bombing of a Cuban civilian airliner that killed 73 people, and though he was linked by the Justice Department to 30 acts of sabotage, he was released in 1990 after Bush's son, Jeb, lobbied for his release so that he could win the approval and support of the Miami anti-Castro Cubans.

And it is possible in the present climate to be branded a traitor if you do discuss events such as these. The point is that we need to be self-reflective as a citizenry—we owe it not only to ourselves as U.S. citizens, but as world citizens—and provide spaces for critical dialogue about these events. This is where critical pedagogy can be extremely important. The present generation has been sacrificed in advance to the globalization of capital. This poses a major dilemma for the future of the globe. And pedagogically, it places a heavy challenge in the hands of teachers and cultural and political workers worldwide.

LUCÍA: Why try to help young people adapt to a system that is designed to exclude them?

PETER: The idea here is not to adapt students to globalization, but make them critically maladaptive, so that they can become change agents in anti-capitalist struggles. In the face of such an intensification of global capitalist relations, rather than a shift in the nature of capital itself, we need to develop a critical pedagogy capable of engaging everyday life as lived in the midst of global capital's tendency towards empire, a pedagogy that we have called revolutionary critical pedagogy.

LUCÍA: How would you recommend that critical educators examine the concept of class?

PETER: My answer to this question draws substantially on the work of a group of Marxist theorists and writers on Marxist educational theory, researchers and activists working in the U.K.: Paula Allman, Mike Cole, Ana Dinerstein, Dave Hill, Mike Neary and Glenn Rikowski. Helen Raduntz in Australia has also contributed to this work. In particular, Paula Allman's groundbreaking book, *Critical Education Against Global Capitalism: Karl Marx and Revolutionary Critical Education*, encapsulates much of what I wish to say on the issue of class and education.

It follows from the writings of these comrades that theorizing class is fundamental in critical pedagogy. It is the heart and soul of critical pedagogy. This is because capitalism constitutes the material basis of institutionalized racism in the United States. Critical pedagogy must be exercised as an aspect of the overall critique of political economy, and, in the process, provide a critique of class. Class theory is a theory against class society, that is, an aspect of the exploration of the constitution of capitalism that is premised upon a project for its abolition. Let me emphasize. It is a theory against capitalist society, and not just a theory of it, as John Holloway and Glenn Rikowski have indicated. Class theory is therefore concerned with the abolition of class (Marx's position) and the opening up of human history from the desolation of its prehistory, as Ana Dinerstein, Paula Allman, and Mike Neary have emphasized. Some critical educators think that the so-called Third World is the only location in which the "true" working class can still be found in any abundance.

In taking this position, they fundamentally ignore the most essential component of Marx's class analysis: his dialectical concept, or conceptualization, of class (as Paula Allman notes in her latest book). The concept of internal relations is crucial here as a way of understanding Marx's thought. Marx explains capitalism in terms of internal relations—the type of relations that are central to his dialectical conceptualization of capitalism—because he found this type of relation in the real world of capitalism. Of course this was not the world of capitalism that we experience daily but the reality of capitalism that Marx was able to reveal through his penetrating analysis of the surface phenomenon—which constitutes our immediate and illusory experience—of capitalism. As Paula Allman and Glenn Rikowski have noted, when we apply a philosophy of internal relations to our subject of study, we focus on the relation and how it is responsible for the past and present existence of the related entities—the opposites in the relation—as well as the ongoing internal development within the related entities.

According to Marx's analysis of capitalism, the dialectical contradiction that lies in the heart of capitalism is the relation between labor and capital. This relation together with the internal relation between capitalist production and circulation/exchange constitutes the essence of capitalism, as Paula Allman has noted. The labor-capital relation, however, is our focus. It is the relation that produces a historically specific form of wealth. As Ramin Farahmandpur and I have argued, it is important to engage the issue of educational reform from the perspective of Marx's value theory of labor. Marx's value theory of labor does not attempt to reduce labor to an economic category alone but is illustrative of how labor as a value form constitutes our very social universe, one that has been underwritten by the logic of capital. Value is not some hollow formality, neutral precinct, or barren hinterland emptied of power and politics, but the very matter and anti-matter of Marx's social universe. It is important to keep in mind that the production of value is not the same as the production of wealth.

The production of value is historically specific and emerges whenever labor assumes its dual character. Rikowski and Dussel have made this clear, and so has the philosopher Denys Turner. This is most clearly explicated in Marx's discussion of the contradictory nature of the commodity form and the expansive capacity of the commodity known as labor-power. For Marx, the commodity is highly unstable, and non-identical. Its concrete particularity (use-value) is subsumed by its existence as value-in-motion or by what we have come to know as "capital" (value is always in motion because of the increase in capital's productivity that is required to maintain expansion). The issue here is not simply that workers are exploited for their surplus value but that all forms of human sociability are constituted by the logic of capitalist work.

Labor, therefore, cannot be seen as the negation of capital or the antithesis of capital, but the human form through and against which capitalist work exists, as Glenn Rikowski has pointed out. Capitalist relations of production become hegemonic precisely when the process of the production of abstraction conquers the concrete processes of production, resulting in the expansion of the logic of capitalist work. At the risk of getting into a theoretical discussion, let me expand on Marx's dialectical approach to exploitation because I want to make sure I am clear on this. To approach the concept of class from a dialectical Marxist conception stipulates a grasp of Marx's philosophy of internal relations.

As adumbrated in the work of Paula Allman, Glenn Rikowski, and other Marxist educationalists, the philosophy of internal relations underscores the importance of relational thinking (relational thinking is not the same thing as relativism!). Relational thinking is distinct from categorical thinking. Whereas the former examines entities in interaction with each other, the latter looks at phenomena in isolation from each other. Relational thinking can refer both to external relations or internal relations. Marx was interested in internal relations. External relations are those that produce a synthesis of various phenomena or entities that can exist outside of or independent of this relation. Internal relations are those in which opposite entities are historically mediated so that they do not obtain independent results. In fact, once the internal relationship ceases to exist, the results of their interaction also cease to exist.

A dialectical concept of class examines the internal relations between labor and capital in terms of their dialectical contradictions. A dialectical contradiction is an internal relation consisting of opposites in interaction that would not be able to exist in the absence of their internal relationship to each other. When this internal relationship is abolished, so are the entities. All dialectical contradictions are internal relations. However, not all internal relations are dialectical contradictions. Dialectical contradictions—or the "unity of opposites"—are those that could not exist or continue to exist or have come into existence in the absence of their internal relation to one another. The very nature (external and internal) of each of the opposites is shaped within its relation to the other opposite.

The antagonistic relation between labor and capital or the relation between production and circulation and exchange, constitutes the essence of capitalism. The labor of workers is utilized within the capital-labor relation. Workers may be said to constitute the dialectical opposite of capital and within a capitalist society enter into a value creation process. The basis of the rift or split within capitalist labor is the relation internal to labor: labor as a value producer and labor as a labor-power developer. One of the oppositions always benefits from this antagonistic internal relationship. Capital (the positive relation) structurally benefits from its relation to labor (the negative relation). To free itself from its subordinate position, labor must abolish this internal relation through the negation of the negation.

To understand class society in this way offers a more profound analytical lens than Weberian notions of class that reduce it to skill, occupational status, social inequality, or stratification. This is because what is at stake in understanding class as a dynamic and dialectical social relation is undressing the forces that generate social inequality. (Dave Hill and Mike Cole make this clear in their work on class.) This can only be accomplished by analyzing the value form of labor within the entire social universe of capital, including the way that capital has commodified our very subjectivities. This mandates that we grasp the complex dialects of the generation of the capital-labor relation that produces all value.

The labor-capital contradiction constitutes the key dialectical contradiction that produces the historically specific form of capitalist wealth or the value form of capitalist wealth. It is important to remember that the worker does not sell to the capitalist the living active labor which she performs during the hours of her work but rather sells her labor-power or her capacity to work for a certain number of hours per week. In exchanging her labor-power for wages, the worker receives in return not wages but what Marx called wage goods (see Turner, 1983). That is, the worker gets what is determined in amount by what is required for her maintenance and her reproduction as a worker. Thus, she gets no general or abstract form of power over commodities in exchanging her labor-power for a wage. She only gets power over those particular commodities which are needed for her maintenance and for the reproduction of other workers. It is the capitalist who has the power to consume the labor-power which he has bought (see Turner, 1983).

Labor-power purchases for the worker only exchanges with values. Labor, as distinct from labor-power, is the exercise of labor-power and it is labor that produces value. The worker is paid for the availability of her labor-power even before commodities have been produced. A certain proportion of the values produced by the worker by means of her labor are over and above the value that she has received as equivalent to the availability of her labor-power. When the capitalist consumes what he has paid for, he therefore receives a higher value than that which is represented in the wages paid out to the worker. The capitalist receives a surplus value created by the worker's labor.

The wages the worker receives are therefore not the equivalent of her labor, or her value-producing activity.

It is important to realize that the money equivalent of labor-power is not the same as the money equivalent of labor. This point is made (after Marx) by Glenn Rikowski, Denys Turner, and others. The surplus value extracted by the capitalist is actually the unpaid labor of the worker. Labor-power exchanges with value whereas labor produces value. The capitalist exchanges wages for the worker's labor-power (her power and skills) for a certain number of hours per week. Because the capitalist owns the worker's labor-power, he can sell that labor-power as a commodity for a money-equivalent of the value of that labor-power. The worker's labor-power does not create value but the worker's labor does. Labor-power (the potential to labor), when it is exercised concretely by the worker in the very concrete act of laboring, is what creates capital or the value-relation of exploitation. Concrete labor exercised by the worker constitutes value produced over and above what she gets paid for her labor-power. The worker thus creates the very relation that exploits her.

What appears to be an equal exchange—the social transaction of wages for work done as equivalents—is actually a relation of exploitation. It is a relation between persons reduced to a relation between things. The labor/wage relationship as one of equal exchange is only equal from the perspective of its relationship to the market. But what appears to be the exchange of equivalents is actually an exploitative extraction of surplus value by the capitalist. What we are dealing with here, in other words, is the fetishized appearance of a relation of equality. The value produced by labor is "fetishistically" represented equivalently by wages. The dialectical contradiction or internal relation inheres in the fact that the capitalist mode of production of wealth premised on an exchange of equivalents is in essence a relation of exploitation through the extraction of surplus value on the part of the capitalist.

There is no way to approach the analysis of class within the social universe of capital without addressing the central relation of class struggle that permeates all of social life within capitalist societies. Enrique Dussel, who has done an extensive analysis of Marx's manuscripts of 1861–1863, makes some similar points to Turner, Rikowski, and others, although he seems to be using the term "labor capacity" the way that Rikowski uses the term "labor-power." Labor is sold to the capitalist not as labor per se, but as a capacity, whose real manifestation of power takes place after its alienation of the use-value. Labor capacity has a use-value and an exchange-value. The price of labor capacity is the wage, as it is exchangeable for the money of the capitalist. After this transaction is completed (which becomes the valorization moment for capital), this money becomes transformed into capital. Here, living labor is incorporated and subsumed by this process of formal alienation.

When the laborer actually sells her capacity to labor, the exchange with money assimilates and totalizes living labor. This, according to Dussel, is an ontological act that denies the "exteriority" of living labor. The transformation of living labor into wage labor constitutes the negation of the Other, of all that is non-capital. Labor capacity is available as potency and when it is exchanged for wages, it becomes an act wherein capacity is transformed into power through the effective actualization of labor, the act of laboring. When the physical-biological force of the laborer is exchanged for wages, then concrete labor becomes social labor. The individual becomes "socialized" thanks to capital. Only when money is exchanged with the commodity, with living labor, only when it intra-totalizes the living exteriority of the laborer, only when it pays for her labor capacity with the means of subsistence required to reproduce the live of the laborer does money become capital, and labor capacity become productive force. As Dussel notes, living labor as non-capital is transformed into capital; whole nothingness is transformed into absolute nothingness.

Dussel maintains that the capital-labor social relation is a vertical relation of exploitation. Here, labor creates new value, surplus value. The international social relation of a national bourgeoisie that is in possession of a more developed total national capital in competition with the bourgeoisie of the less developed total national capital is a horizontal relation of international domination where surplus value is not created but transferred. More developed capital, however, tends to destroy all of the protectionist barriers of the less developed capital and shoves it into competition wherein, as Dussel remarks, the more developed capital will extract surplus value from the less developed capital.

For Marx, the law of value continues to operate within international relations and there can be profit in exchange between nations. Dussel notes that even though the commodity of the more developed capital will have a lower value, competition will equalize the price of both commodities in a single average price, so that the commodity with the lower value gains a price greater than its value, which is realized by extracting surplus value from the commodity with a higher value. Heaven help those countries who want to escape competition. Remember Guatemala? Remember Nicaragua? What do you think Plan Colombia is all about? The U.S. will coerce it via its vast military power to return to what Dussel calls "the system of 'freedom in competition.'" It is what the dominant power refers to as "democracy." We have to remember, too, that labor-power, or labor capacity (as Dussel would use the term) is capital's weak point. The key is to disrupt the process of labor-power production (i.e., via education and training).

After all, as Rikowski notes, it is labor-power that generates the substance of the social universe of capital. The social form assumed by labor-power in a capitalist society is human capital. Schools, for instance, serve as production sites for human capital. We need to struggle against capitalist social relations and capital's value-form of labor. Capitalist society needs the expenditure of our labor-power. We can resist this manipulation, this forced exploitation. We need to terminate the value-form of labor, of capitalism, of capital. My own particular task has been to find ways of resisting capital's social form in school sites and community sites as well as trying to build transnational multiracial dialogues. Schools are but one site of possible resistance, but an important site.

LUCÍA: When we look at the issue of educational reform, is it important to address the issue of teachers' work within a capitalist society as a form of alienated labor, that is, as the specific production of the value form of labor?

PETER: Yes. Absolutely. This becomes clearer when we begin to understand that one of the fundamental functions of schooling is to traffic in labor-power; it has to do with the engineering and enhancement of the capacity to labor so that such labor-power can be harnessed in the interests of capital. Glenn Rikowski's premise is provocative yet compelling and perhaps deceptively simple: education is involved in the direct production of the one commodity that generates the entire social universe of capital in all of its dynamic and multiform existence: labor-power (these points will be repeated in my later interviews with Rikowski).

Within the social universe of capital, individuals sell their capacity to labor for a wage. Because we are included in this social universe on a differential and unequal basis, people can get paid above or below the value of their labor-power. Because labor-power is implicated in human will or agency, and because it is impossible for capital to exist without it, education can be re-designed within a social justice agenda that will reclaim labor-power for socialist alternatives to human capital formation.

LUCÍA: What can be done to defeat globalization as you have described it?

PETER: Well I think Petras and Veltmeyer have done a good job of giving some direction for moving towards a socialist transition. They don't think it is a good idea to de-link from world production, and I agree. We would be giving up too many necessary products for consumption and production. We can't go the way of market socialism, because this opens the door for plundering the state for private gain, and here the market will direct socialism and not the other way around.

I agree with Petras and Veltmeyer that a good place to start would be to increase local capacity to advance the forces of production and democratize its relations. However, any external linkage must help create the conditions for increasing the internal capacity to deepen the domestic market and serve popular needs. Market relations must be subordinated to a democratic regime based on direct popular representation in territorial and in productive units. Direct producers must make basic decisions. Exchanges between regions, sectors and classes must be integrated. Petras and Veltmeyer advocate an assembly-style democracy (not to be confused with Clinton's "town hall meetings"!) to control the content and direction of market exchanges. The focus must be on the creation and reconstruction of essential links between domestic economic sectors, and the creation of socio-economic linkages among domestic needs, latent demands, and the reorganization of the productive system.

There needs to be a focus as well on the ideological and cultural education of working people in values of cooperation, solidarity, and equality. If it is true that the transition from the nation-state to a new global phase of capitalism involves the necessary transnational integration of national production systems, as Robinson argues, this means that we need to organize the transnational working class. This doesn't mean, however, that competition and conflict among capitalists is coming to an end. But, as Robinson notes, inter-capitalist conflict is no longer coterminous with inter-state conflict. We need a global struggle, a counterhegemonic struggle against transnational capital, and a struggle for a socialist alternative.

The key point here is to smash the myths about sustainable economic growth and control of allocation by the market winners. This is where critical pedagogy can play an important role in environmental education. In this regard I admire the work of the Coalition for Educational Justice and the Labor/Community Strategy Center in Los Angeles who really walk the talk. David Korten has recently challenged the prevailing assumptions about economic growth and globalization that I believe are worth summarizing. For instance, the assumption that sustained economic growth is necessary to meet human needs, improve living standards, and to provide the financial resources necessary to implement environmental protection is highly suspect.

It needs to be read against the fact that little of the economic growth of the past twenty years has done anything to improve the quality of human life. Only the wealthy have really benefited. Any benefits to growth outside of lining the pockets of the rich and powerful capitalist class have been offset by the costs of resource depletion, social stress, and environmental health hazards caused by economic growth.

As to the notion that apparent limits to growth will be eliminated by technological innovation and the market, this misguided logic flies in the face of the fact that consumption of environmental resources already exceeds sustainable limits. The primary initiative for production must be to reallocate the use of sustainable resource flows and to ensure that large consumers significantly reduce their per capita resource consumption. Critical educators need to address the relationship between capitalism, ecosystem destruction, and sustainable forms of development.

Production systems absolutely must be transformed in order to maximize the recycling of materials and to eliminate nonessential forms of consumption. In response to the prevailing idea that achieving sustainable growth in the South depends upon accelerating economic growth in the North to increase demand for Southern exports, Korten argues that environmental problems are in large part a consequence of Northern countries exporting their ecological deficits to the South through both trade and investment. Northern overconsumption limits the per capita shares of available resources in Latin American countries and prevents them from meeting domestic needs and pushes the economically weak to marginal ecological areas.

Latin American countries that depend upon foreign aid, loans and investment remain in a cycle of debt and dependence upon the North, especially in terms of a dependence on Northern technology and products. So we need to create greater access to sustainable natural resource flows so that the basic needs of the poor can be met. Political conditions must be created for resources to be distributed equitably and used efficiently.

In response to the misguided but often repeated assertion that environmental problems are caused by poverty, Korten explains the overconsumption by Northern countries is the big problem. The poor consume very little. Population growth is a concern, but mainly in the North. Poverty is not the key problem, Korten argues. Inequality is the key problem. The wealthy are able to pass on the social and ecological costs of their overconsumption to the poorer nations. Sure, poverty does cause some people to over-exploit environmentally fragile land, but this happens out of desperation and because the poor have no other way to survive. This is especially true in the export-processing zones on the U.S.-Mexican border, where there exists a barbaric hyperextraction of surplus value by the capitalists.

The epidemic of overproduction is one of the biggest culprits in this global drama of free trade. What is stabilizing the population of the world somewhere between 12 to 15 billion people is not some "natural" force endemic to capitalism, as some people claim, but mass starvation and violence brought about by the lack of radical economic reforms addressing social security, investment in female education, family planning, and health. We need to remember, too, that jobs are not created through economic growth, since, as Korten notes, technology and reorganizations are eliminating good jobs faster than growth is creating them. What jobs are being created are those that are mainly temporary, those that provide workers with few benefits, and that are based in unsustainable rates of resource extraction.

Free trade is not the answer. Free trade, as Korten explains, leads to competition between localities in need of jobs to reduce costs of local production by suppressing wages and allowing maximum externalization of environment, social, and production costs. The marketplace is not a level playing field. In fact, it reflects the preferences for the private goods of those who belong to the capitalist class. It does not consider the needs of the poor. It tends towards monopoly control of allocation decisions by the market winners. Korten is very perceptive in making these observations.

LUCÍA: Is this where critical pedagogy can play a powerful role?

PETER: Yes, in creating a society where real equality exists on an everyday basis. Challenging the causes of racism, class oppression, ecosystem degradation, and sexism and their deep entanglement in the exploitation of labor demands that critical teachers and cultural workers re-examine capitalist schooling in the contextual specificity of global capitalist relations. Critical educators recognize that schools as social sites are linked to wider social and political struggles in society and that such struggles have a global reach. Here the development of a critical consciousness enables students to theorize and critically reflect upon their social experiences, and also to translate critical knowledge into political activism.

A socialist pedagogy or revolutionary critical pedagogy actively involves students in the construction of working-class social movements. We acknowledge that building cross-ethnic/racial alliances among the working class has not been an easy task to undertake in recent years. Critical educators encourage the practice of community activism and grassroots organization among students, teachers, and workers. They are committed to the idea that the task of overcoming existing social antagonisms can only be accomplished through class struggle, the road map out of the messy gridlock of historical amnesia.

I support a socialist pedagogy that follows Marx's life-long struggle of liberating labor from its commodity form within relations of exchange and working towards its valorization as a use-value for workers' self-development and self-realization. It strikes me that there is so much talent and brilliance among the educational left, but the vision is often too narrow, and frequently small-minded, and occasionally pernicious. If ever there was a time to take our role in the world of global politics seriously, it is now. A good example of social activism is the Labor/Community Strategy Center in downtown Los Angeles. The Left has many new challenges to face today, and many questions have been placed before us that need to be addressed with a new urgency. One can only hope that we treat these questions seriously.

As Marx has said: "Frequently the only possible answer is a critique of the question and the only solution is to negate the question." I believe that the socialist revolution can be brought about by democratic struggle, by infusing formal democracy (focusing on political rights) and substantive democracy (focusing on economic/material rights). There can, in my view, be no substantive democracy without formal democracy. We need both.

To embrace a Marxist-humanism is indispensable in the context of the concrete particularity of our struggle against capital, in the objective situation of our struggle against the hydra-headed forms of imperialism facing us: bin Laden, Bush, Islamic fundamentalism, Christian fundamentalism, neoliberalism and the like. We have great challenges to face amidst Bush's step in creating a permanent war. However, as Peter Hudis (2001) notes, we need to move beyond a narrow anti-U.S. imperialism and get back to the principled anti-imperialism of Lenin during World War I. We need to move beyond an anti-Westernism and get on with the task of supporting class struggle and creating a new, human society.

Remaining critical of U.S. foreign and economic policies is important but we must avoid falling into a reactionary anti-Americanism. Instead, let's set our struggle against monopoly capitalism, which is at the root of imperialism. As Hudis notes, imperialism is an outgrowth of state-monopoly capitalism as it exists on a world stage. Today, when the stakes are so high, I hope that we can move beyond ad hominem and mean-spirited criticism of each other (often carried out in the name of love and affirming diverse voices!) in order to embrace a new political imaginary dedicated to the struggle for human liberation. This imaginary will emerge from the working class not as a master narrative but rather as guiding principles, or what I have elsewhere referred to as a contingent metanarrative of hope and solidarity.

While it is true that Marx described human beings as ensembles of social relations, Marx's value system was based on an inherent or internal criterion and not on imposed, external criteria. In his *Theses on Feuerbach*, Marx affirmed certain common attributes shared by all human beings and the existence of a common human nature in the sense that human beings are all social, economic, political, and moral beings. As Ferraro notes, Marx's humanism made possible Marx's science. We need to be joined by that which we all share, our common humanity. And we need to draw upon such a common humanity to deepen our scientific and philosophical understanding of the world—not in order to interpret the world, but as Marx argued, in order to change it.

Notes

1. The globalization of capital has new features that some argue constitute a new stage of capitalist formation. These include but are not limited to the following internally related developments: the rise in influence of financial capital; a glamorous new role for banks and treasury ministries; a massive increase in personal debt that serves as a catapult for increased consumption; a restructuring and downsizing of the labor force and a fluid relocation of industries to developing countries in order to secure lower labor costs; the weakening of independent organs of the working class; the rapid flows of advertising, public relations and infotainment; the replacement of real goods as the main targets of investment with "financial instruments," such as national currencies, insurance, debts, and commodity futures; an increase in outsourcing and contract labor following the replacement of full time jobs with temporary and part-time jobs; the privatization of public institutions and attacks on economic welfare and security reforms of the past century (Ollman, 2001).
2. For an expanded discussion of the role of the proletariat in the contemporary context of the globalization of capital, see my exchange with Slavoj Žižek. Peter McLaren, "Slavoj Žižek's Naked Politics: Opting for the Impossible, a Secondary Elaboration," *Journal of Advanced Composition, vol. 21*, no. 3 (Summer, 2001), 613–647. See also Slavoj Žižek, "Our Daily Fantasies and Fetishes," *Journal of Advanced Composition, vol. 21*, no. 3 (Summer, 2001), 647–653. Also see my exchange with Gregor McLennan, "Can There be a 'Critical' Multiculturalism," *Ethnicities, vol. 1*, no. 3 (December 2001), 389–408. See also Peter McLaren, "Wayward Multiculturalists," *Ethnicities, vol. 1*, no. 3 (December 2001), 389–408, and Gregor McLennan, "Not Multiculturalism: A rejoinder to Peter McLaren," *Ethnicities, vol. 1*, no. 3 (December, 2001), 420–422.

3. I wish to note that much of the discussions about September 11 and its aftermath are from larger works that will appear in *Cultural Studies/Critical Methodologies*.

References

Amin, Samir. (2001). Political Islam. *Covert Action Quarterly*, no. 71 (Winter), 3–6.

Anderson, Karen. (2001). Immigrant victims of the WTC attack. *NACLA Report on the Americas. vol. XXXV*, no. 3, 1–2, 4.

Arendt, Hannah. (1955). *The origins of totalitarianism*. London: George Allen and Unwin.

Baker, Dean. (2001). From new economy to war economy. *Dollars & Sense* (November/December), no. 238, 7, 39.

Bamford, James. (2001). *Body of secrets: Anatomy of the ultra-secret National Security Agency. From the Cold War through the dawn of a new century*. New York and London: Doubleday.

Barber, Benjamin. (2002). Beyond jihad vs. mcworld: On terrorism and the new democratic realism. *The Nation, vol. 274*, no. 2 (January 21), 11–18.

Barsamian, David. (2001). Arundhati Roy Interview. *The Progressive, vol. 65*, no. 4.

Barsamian, David. (2001a). Edward Said interview. *The Progressive, vol. 65*, no. 11.

Barsamian, David. (2001b). What they want is my silence: Edward Said interview. *International Socialist Review*, issue 18, June-July.

Bauman, Zygmunt. (2002). Global solidarity. *Tikkun, vol. 17*, no. 1 (January/February), 12–14, 62.

Beccaria, Cesare. (1963). *On crimes and punishment*. Translated and with an Introduction by Henry Paolucci. New York: Macmillan Publishing Company, and London: Collier Macmillan Publishers. (Originally published in 1764)

Bortfeld, Joey, & Naureckas, Jim. (2001). Unpardonable disparities. *Extra!, vol. 14*, no. 3 (June), 14.

Boyle, Francis. (2001). Speech at Illinois Disciples. Oct. 18, 2001. Retrieved from http://msanews.mynet.net/Scholars/Boyle/nowar.html

Brown, Matthew Hay. (2001). Bioterrorism nothing new to native Americans. *Hartford Courant*, November 1.

Carson, Trevor. The race to bomb. *The Nation, vol. 273*, no. 13, October 29, 25–30.

Castro, Fidel. (2001). Televised presentation by Commander-in-Chief Fidel Castro Ruz, President of the Republic of Cuba, on the present international situation, the economic and world crisis and its impact on Cuba. Havana, (November 2).

Chomsky, Noam. (2001). *9–11*. New York: Seven Stories Press.

Chomsky, Noam. (2001a). The new war against terror. *Counterpunch*, October 24.

Cockburn, Alexander. (2001). The wide world of torture. *The Nation, vol. 273*, no. 17 (November 26), 10.

Cockburn, Alexander. (2001). Sharon or Arafat: Which is the sponsor of terror? *The Nation, vol. 273*, no. 21 (December 24), 10.

Cockburn, Alexander. (2002). Forbidden Truth? *The nation, vol. 274*, no. 3, 9.

Congressional Statement. Federal Bureau of Investigation. May 10, 2001. Retrieved from http://www.fbi.gov/congress/congress01/freeh051001.htm.

Cypher, James M. (2002). Return of the iron triangle: The new military buildup. *Dollars & Sense*, no. 239 (January/February), 16–19, 37–38.

Dorfman, Ariel. (2001). Unique no more. *Counterpunch*, October 3.

Dussel, Enrique. (2001). *Towards an unknown Marx: A commentary on the manuscripts of 1861–1863*. Translated by Yolanda Angulo. Edited by Fred Mosley. London and New York: Routledge.

Eco, Umberto. (2001). The roots of conflict. *The Guardian*, October 13.

Elich, Gregory. (2001). War criminals, read and imagined. *Covert Action Quarterly*, no. 71 (winter), 19–24.

El-Sayed Sae'ed Mohammad. (2001). Osama bin Laden: A primitive rebel. *Islam Online*, October 28.

Galeano, Eduardo. (2000). *Upside down: A primer for the looking-glass world*. New York: Metropolitan Books.

Galeano, Eduardo. (2001). The theatre of good and evil. Translated by Justin Podur. *La Jornada*, September 21.

Glendinning, Chellis. (2002). Remembering decolonization. *Tikkun, vol. 17*,no. 1 (January/February), 41–43.

Goering, Hermann. (2001). Cited in *The Canadian Defence of Liberty Committee Newsletter*, November 18.

Hart, Peter, & Ackerman, Seth. (2001). Patriotism & censorship. *Extra!, vol. 14*, no. 6 (December), 6–9.

Hart, Peter. (2001). No spin zone? *Extra!, vol. 14*, no. 6 (December), 8.

Herman, Edward S., & Peterson, David. (2002). The threat of global state terrorism: Retail vs. wholesale terror. *Z Magazine, vol. 15*, no. 1 (January), 30–34.

Hill, D. (2001). State theory and the neo-liberal reconstruction of schooling and teacher education: A structuralist neo-Marxist critique of postmodernist, quasi-postmodernist, and culturalist neo-Marxist Theory. *British Journal of Sociology of Education, vol.* 22, (1) 137–157.

Hill, D., & Cole, M. (2001). Social class. In D. Hill & M. Cole (Eds.), *Schooling and equality: Fact concept and policy*. London: Kogan Page.

Holloway, John. (2002). Twelve theses for changing the world without taking power. *The Commoner*, no. 4 (May).

Hudis, Peter. (2001). Terrorism, Bush's retaliation show inhumanity of class society. *News & Letters, vol.* 46, no. 8 (October), 1, 10–11.

Huntington, Samuel. (1996). *The clash of civilizations and the remaking of world order*. New York: Touchstone Books.

Hussein, Ibish, & Abunimah, Ali. (2001). Palestinian diaspora and the right of return. *Covert Action Quarterly*, no.71 (Winter), 30–32.

Johnson, Chalmers. (2000). *Blowback: The costs and consequences of American empire*. New York: Owl Books.

Johnson, Chalmers. (2001). Blowback. *The Nation, vol. 273*, no. 11, October 15, 13–15.

Kawell, Joann. (2001). Terror's Latin American profile. *NACLA Report on the Americas, vol. XXXV*, no. 3, 50–53.

Kellner, Douglas. (2002). September 11, terror, war, and blowback. *Cultural Studies <=> Critical Methodologies*, vol. 2, no. 2, 27–39.

Klare, Michael T. (2001). *Resource wars: The new landscape of global conflict*. New York: Metropolitan Books.

Klare, Michael T. (2001a). The geopolitics of war. *The Nation, vol. 273*, no. 14 (November 5), 11–15.

Klare, Michael T. (2001b). Asking "why." *Foreign Policy in Focus*, September.

Korten, David. (2002). Sustainable development: Conventional versus emergent alternative wisdom. *Educate!, vol. 1*, no. 3, 50–53.

Kovel, Joel. (2002). Ground work. *Tikkun, vol. 17*, no. 1 (January/February), 17, 20.

Lapham, Lewis. (2001). Drums along the Potomac. *Harper's Magazine, vol. 303*, no. 1818 (November), 35–41.

Le Carre, John. (2001). A war we cannot win. *The Nation, vol. 273*, no. 16 (November 19), 15–17.

Los Angeles Times. (2001) Response to terror: In brief. Tuesday, November 16, A10.

Luxemburg, R. (1919). *The crisis in German social democracy: The Junius Pamphlet*. New York: The Socialist Publication Society.

Marable, Manning. (2001). Terrorism and the struggle for peace. *Along the color line*. Retrieved from www.manningmarable.net

Marable, Manning. (2001a). The failure of U.S. foreign policies. *Along the color line*. Retrieved in November from www.manningmarable.net.

Maresca, John. (1998). Testimony by John J. Maresca, vice president, international relations, Unocal Corporation to House Committee on International Relations, Subcommittee on Asia and the Pacific, February 12, 1998, Washington, D.C.

Marlowe, Lara. (2001). U.S. efforts to make peace summed up by oil. *The Irish Times*, Monday, November 19.

Marx, K. (1973). *Grundrisse: Foundations of the critique of political economy*. Translated by M. Nicolaus. London: Penguin Books.

McLaren, Peter, & Pinkney-Pastrana, Jill. (2001). Cuba, Yanquizacion, and the cult of Elian Gonzales: A view from the 'enlightened' states. *International Journal of Qualitative Studies in Education, vol.14*, no. 2, (March/April), 201–219.

McMurtry, John. (2001). Bombs away: The unseen war in America. Unpublished manuscript.

McMurtry, John. (2001). Why is there a war in Afghanistan? Opening Address, Science for Peace Forum and Teach-in, University of Toronto, Canada, December 9.

Mészáros, I. (1999). Marxism, the capital system, and the social revolution: An interview with István Mészáros. *Science and Society*, 63(3), 338–361.

Monbiot, George. (2001). Backyard terrorism. The *Guardian*, October 30.

Monbiot, George. (2001). The Taliban of the West. *The Guardian*, Tuesday, December 18.

Monchinski, Tony. (2001). Capitalist schooling: An interview with Bertell Ollman. Retrieved from *Cultural Logic: An Electronic Journal of Marxist Theory and Practice* from http://eserver.org/clogic/4–1/monchinski.html.

Niva, Steven. (2001). Addressing the sources of Middle Eastern violence against the United States. *Common Dreams News Center*, Friday, September 14.

Niva, Steven. (2001). Fight the roots of terrorism. *Common Dreams News Center*, Friday, September 21.

O'Brien, Bill. (2001). Say anything. *Slate Magazine*, Saturday, December 1.

Ollman, Bertell. (2001). *How to take an exam and remake the world*. Montreal: Black Rose Books.

Petras, James. (2002). Signs of a police state are everywhere. *Z Magazine*, *vol. 15*, no. 1 (January), 10–12.

Petras, James, & Veltmeyer, Henry. (2001). *Globalization unmasked: Imperialism in the 21st century*. London and New York: Zed Books and Halifax, Canada: Fernwood Publishing.

Pilger, John. (2001). There is no war on terrorism. If there was, the SAS would be storming the beaches of Florida. *New Statesman*, *vol. 14*, issue 680 (October 29), 16–18.

Pilger, John. (2001a). This war is a farce. *The Mirror*, October 29.

Pilger, John. (1999). *Hidden agendas*. London: Vintage Press

Post, Charlie. (2002). Empire and revolution. *Fourth international press list*.

Powers, John. (2001). Wyatt Earp and the Witchfinder General. *LA Weekly*, *vol. 24*, no. 4, December 14–20, 18.

Powers, John. (2002). Rank and yank at Enron, or, the fine art of bankruptcy. *LA Weekly*, *vol. 24*, no. 3 (January), 11–17.

Rikowski, G. (2001). Fuel for the living fire: Labor-power! In Ana C. Dinerstein & Michael Neary (Eds.), *The labor debate: An investigation into the theory and reality of capitalist work*. Aldershot, England: Ashgate.

Rikowski, G. (2000). Messing with the explosive commodity: School improvement, educational research and labor-power in the era of global capitalism. A paper prepared for the symposium If We Aren't Pursuing Improvement, What Are We Doing? at the British Educational Research Association Conference 2000, Cardiff University, Wales, Session 3.4, September 7.

Rikowski, G. (2001a). *The battle in Seattle: Its significance for education*. London: Tufnell Press.

Rikowski, G. (2001b). After the manuscript broke off: Thoughts on Marx, social class and education. A paper prepared for the British Sociological Association, Education Study Group Meeting, King's College, London, June 23.

Robinson, William. (2001). Global capitalism and nation-state-centric thinking—What we *don't* see when we *do* see nation-states: Response to critics. *Science & Society, vol.* 65, no. 1 (Winter), 500–508.

Robinson, William. (2001). Social theory and globalization: The rise of a transnational state. *Theory and Society, 30,* 157–200.

Robinson, William. (2001a). Response to McMichael, Block, and Goldfrank. *Theory and Society,* 30, 223–236.

Robinson, William. (2001b). The debate on globalization, the transnational capitalist class, and the rise of a transnational state. Paper delivered at the meeting of the American Sociological Association, Anaheim Hilton, Los Angeles, August 18–21.

Robinson, William, & Harris, Jerry. (2000). Towards a global ruling class? Globalization and the transnational capitalist class. *Science & Society,* 64, no. 1 (Spring), 11–54.

Roy, Arundhati. (2001). Brutality smeared in peanut butter. *The Guardian,* October 23.

Roy, Arundhati. (2001a). The algebra of infinite justice. *The Guardian,* September 29.

Roy, Arundhati. (2001b). War is peace. *Z Magazine.*

Said, Edward. (2001). *The Observer.* September 16.

Schell, Jonathan. (2001). A chain reaction. *The Nation, vol. 273,* no. 21, 9.

Scigliano, Eric. (2001). Naming—and unnaming—names. *The Nation, vol. 273,* no. 22 (December 31), 16.

Shami, Salah. (2001). A review of *Walimath li-A'shab al-Bahr (Banquet for seaweed)* by Haydar Haydar. *Workers Vanguard,* no. 770 (December 7), 6–7, 11.

Statement of the emergency committee against U.S. intervention in Afghanistan. *Fight Back!*, vol. 4, no. 4 (Fall), 11–12.

Tamayo, Manuel Salgado. (2001). The geo-strategy of Plan Colombia. *Covert Action Quarterly, no. 71* (Winter), 37–40.

Tryferis, Alfredo. (2001). Bill's blather. *New Times,* December 6–12, 7.

Turner, Denys. (1983). *Marxism and Christianity.* Oxford: Basil Blackwell.

Wolcott, James. (2001). Terror on the dotted line. *Vanity Fair,* January, 50–55.

Zinn, Howard. (2001). Beyond the fame. In Media Education Foundation. http://mediaed.sitepassport.not/btf/Zinn/index_ .

This article was first published in *Multicultural Education,* Fall, 2002, volume 10, no. 1, 7–17. It is a revised version of an interview conducted by Lucia Coral Aguirre Munoz of the Instituto de Investigacion y Desarrallo Educative of the Universidad Autonoma de Baja California that first appeared in *Revista Electronica de Investigacion Educativa,* 3, no. 2, and subsequently appeared in *The School Field* (Slovenia), *XII,* no. 516 (Winter 2001), 109–156.

Interview 4

the path of dissent

Marcia Moraes

Marcia and I have been close friends for years. She met me at a reception for Paulo Freire in Chicago over a decade ago, and shortly thereafter became my doctoral student when I was teaching at Miami University of Ohio. I was recruited by UCLA a year before Marcia graduated, and when I returned to Ohio for her dissertation defense, I brought her some Antarctica (cans of Guarana). If you are Brazilian, you'll be able to appreciate my gesture. Marcia is a brilliant feminist scholar who now teaches in Rio de Janiero.

MARCIA MORAES: In Brazil, despite the brilliant contributions of Paulo Freire, it is quite difficult to say that teacher education programs are totally related to the philosophy of critical pedagogy. On the other hand, teacher education programs in the United States have been dealing with critical pedagogy for several decades now. What progress has been made on the critical pedagogy front?

PETER MCLAREN: This is an excellent question to begin our conversation. Let me begin by challenging the term "critical pedagogy." I much prefer the term that British educator Paula Allman has christened "revolutionary critical pedagogy." It raises important issues that more domesticated currents of critical pedagogy do not. For example, it draws attention to the key concepts of imperialism (both economic and military) and the value form that labor assumes within capitalist society. It also posits history as the mediator of value production within capitalist society. In political partnership with educationalists such as Paula Allman, Glenn Rikowski, Dave Hill, Ramin Farahmandpur, and Mike Cole, and in comradely conversations with Peter Mayo, Rich Gibson, Wayne Ross, and others, I have made some modest efforts to revive the fecundity of Marxist critique in the field of education, since I believe Marxist theory, in all of its heteronomous manifestations and theoretical gestation for well over a century, performs an irreplaceable analytical and political function of positing history as the mediator of human value production. By pivoting around the work of Karl Marx, Paulo Freire, and Antonio Gramsci, and by maneuvering and tacking around the work of contemporary continental philosophers and critical theorists, critical revolutionary pedagogy brings some desperately needed theoretical ballast to the teetering critical educational tradition. Such theoretical infrastructure is absolutely necessary if we are to create concrete pedagogical spaces in schools and in other sites where people struggle for educational change and transformation. The critical revolutionary pedagogy I am envisioning here operates from the premise that capital in its current organizational structure provides the context for working-class struggle. My approach to understanding the relationship between capitalism and schooling and the struggle for socialism is premised upon Marx's value theory of labor as developed by British Marxist educationalist Glenn Rikowski and others, including scholars such as Enrique Dussel (especially his commentary on Marx's manuscripts of 1861–1863). In developing further the concept of revolutionary critical pedagogy and its specific relationship to class struggle, it is necessary, I believe, to focus on labor's value form. This focus will unlock a path towards a Marxist-humanist approach to educational struggle. There are many approaches to Marxist humanism, and here I look to the writings of Raya Dunayevskaya, the works of Erich Fromm, C.L.R. James, and various and varied works within the Marxist-Hegelian tradition. Critical revolutionary educators follow the premise that value is the substance of capital. Value, it should be understood, is not a thing. It is the dominant form that capitalism as a determinate social relation takes. Within the expansive scope of revolutionary critical pedagogy, the concept of labor is fundamental for theorizing the school/society relationship and thus for developing radical pedagogical imperatives, strategies, and practices for overcoming the constitutive contradictions that such a coupling generates. The larger goal that revolutionary critical pedagogy stipulates for radical educationalists involves direct participation with the masses in the discovery and charting of a socialist reconstruction and alternative to capitalism. However, without a critical lexicon and interpretative framework that can unpack the labor/capital relationship in all of its capillary detail, critical pedagogy is doomed to remain trapped in domesticated currents and vulgarized formations. That's precisely why it is important to bring the various languages of Marxist analysis into schools of education. Why? Because the process whereby labor-power is transformed into human capital and concrete living labor is subsumed by abstract labor is one that eludes the interpretative capacity of rational communicative action and requires a dialectical understanding that historical materialist critique can best provide. Historical materialism provides critical pedagogy with a theory of the material basis of social life rooted in historical social relations and assumes paramount importance in uncovering the structure of class conflict as well as unraveling the effects produced by the social division of labor. Today, labor-power is capitalized and commodified, and education plays a tragic role in these processes. According to Rikowski, schools therefore act as vital supports for, and developers of, the class relation, at the core of capitalist society and development.

Here is a crucial point. Insofar as schooling is premised upon generating the living commodity of labor-power, upon which the entire social universe of capital depends, it can become a foundation for human resistance. In other words, labor-power can be incorporated by the forces of capital only so far. Workers, as the sources of labor-power, can engage in acts of refusing alienating work and delinking labor from capital's value form. As a relation of general commodification predicated on the wage relation, capital needs labor. But I emphasize labor does not need capital. Labor can dispense with the wage and with capitalism and find different and more autonomous ways to organize its productive relations. I am thinking of social forms and human relations that draw from, but are not limited to, the rich tradition of socialism.

Inasmuch as education and training socially produce labor-power, this process can be resisted. This is because labor-power is never completely controllable. Glenn Rikowski has made the important point that people can learn something other than that which capital intends them to learn. Critical educators push this "something other" to the extreme in their pedagogical praxis centered around a social justice, anticapitalist, antiracist, and anti-imperialist agenda. One key—and I am not suggesting it is in any way sufficient—is to develop a critical pedagogy that will enable the working class to discover how the use-value of their labor-power is being exploited by capital but also how working-class initiative and power can destroy this type of determination and force a recomposition of class relations by directly confronting capital in all of its hydra-headed dimensions. Here I am talking of an anti-imperialist, internationalist, gender-balanced, and multiracial social movement that addresses issues related to education, but not limited to education. Efforts can be made to break down capital's control of the creation of new labor-power and to resist the endless subordination of life to work in the social factory of everyday life. Students and education workers can ask themselves, to borrow from Glenn Rikowski: What is the maximum damage they can do to the rule of capital, to the dominance of capital's value form? Ultimately, to which we need to respond: Do we, as radical educators, help capital find its way out of crisis, or do we help students and educational workers find their way out of capital? And as I have phrased this in a number of my recent writings, the success of the former challenge will only buy further time for the capitalists to adapt both their victims and their critics; the success of the latter will determine the future of civilization, or whether or not we will have one.

As Glenn Rikowski has noted, possibility often hides its liberating force within contradictions. The struggle related to what Marx called our "vital powers," our dispositions, our inner selves and our objective outside, our human capacities and competencies and the social formations within which they are produced, ensures the production of a form of human agency that reflects the contradictions within capitalist social life. Yet these contradictions also provide openness regarding social being. They point towards the possibility of collectively resolving contradictions of "everyday life" through what Allman has called revolutionary/transformative praxis or, if we prefer, "critical subjectivity." Critical subjectivity operates out of practical, sensuous engagement within social formations that enable rather than constrain human capacities. Here, critical revolutionary pedagogy reflects the multiplicity and creativity of human engagement itself: the identification of shared experiences and common interests; the unraveling of the threads that connect social process to individual experience; the rendering as transparent the concealed obviousness of daily life; the recognition of ourselves as both free and conditioned; an understanding of the future as both open and necessary; the recognition of a shared social positionality; the unhinging of the door that separates practical engagement from theoretical reflection; the changing of the world by changing one's social nature, one's social subjectivity. It achieves this through an understanding of Marx's dialectical approach. While

I don't have space to go into these, I would like to point to Bertell Ollman's analysis of Marx's dialectical approach and repeat Ollman's warning here that the laws of dialectics do not in themselves explain, prove, or predict anything in themselves or cause anything to happen. What they do is organize the most common forms of change and interaction that exist on any level of generality so that we might be able to study and intervene into the world of which they are a part.

The crucially important work of Bertell Ollman has proved valuable in explaining how Marx's dialectical analysis can bring out the differences between two or more aspects of an interactive system in order to highlight the asymmetry in their reciprocal effect. For instance, take Marx's example of abstracting social reality into objective and subjective conditions. By abstracting a vantage point first in objective conditions, and then in subjective conditions, Marx can see these conditions as two distinct forms of the same essential conditions, and thus he can uncover the objective aspects of what is generally assumed to be subjective and vice versa.

Critical revolutionary educators seek to realize in their classrooms democratic social values and to believe in their possibilities—consequently, we argue that they need to go outside of the protected precincts of their classrooms and analyze and explore the workings of capital there as well, to workplaces, to neighborhoods, to urban zones, to rural communities, and so forth. Critical revolutionary pedagogy thus sets as its goal the reclamation of public life—what has been called by Canadian philosopher John McMurtry the "civil commons." It seeks to make the division of labor coincident with the free vocation of each individual and the association of free producers. At first blush, this may seem a paradisiac or radically utopian notion in that it posits a radically eschatological and incomparably "other" endpoint for society as we know it. Yet this is not a blueprint but a contingent utopian vision that offers direction not only in unpicking the apparatus of bourgeois illusion but also in diversifying the theoretical itinerary of the critical educator so that new questions can be generated along with new perspectives in which to raise them (I emphasize this point because it is precisely here that the postmodern pundits argue that, as a Marxist, I must be trying to impose some kind of totalitarian vision on unsuspecting educators). Here, the emphasis is not only on denouncing the manifest injustices of neo-liberal capitalism and serving as a counterforce to neo-liberal ideological hegemony but also on establishing the conditions for new social arrangements that transcend the false opposition between the market and the state.

In contrast to a number of incarnations of postmodern education, critical revolutionary pedagogy emphasizes the material dimensions of its own constitutive possibility and recognizes knowledge as implicated within the social relations of production (i.e., the relations between labor and capital). I use the term materialism here not in its postmodernist sense as a resistance to conceptuality, a refusal of the closure of meaning, or whatever "excess" cannot be subsumed within the symbol or cannot be absorbed by tropes; rather, materialism is being used, after Teresa Ebert, in the context of material social relations, a structure of class conflict, and an effect of the social division of labor. Historical changes in the forces of production have reached the point where the fundamental needs of people can be met—but the existing social relations of production prevent this because the logic of access to "need" is "profit" based on the value of people's labor for capital. Consequently, critical revolutionary pedagogy argues that without a class analysis, critical pedagogy is impeded from effecting praxiological changes (changes in social relations).

As I often discuss the term, critical revolutionary pedagogy includes what might be perceived as a three-pronged approach: I have called the first moment a pedagogy of demystification centering around a semiotics of recognition, where dominant sign systems, tropes, conceits, discourses, and representations are recognized and de-naturalized, where commonsense understandings of social and institutionalized spheres of everyday life are historicized, and where signification is understood as a political practice that refracts rather than reflects reality, where cultural formations are understood and analyzed in relation to the larger social factory of the school and the global universe of capital. The second moment could be called a pedagogy of opposition, where students engage in analyzing various political systems, ideologies, and histories, but with the emphasis on students developing their own political positions that, in time, they are able to extend, deepen, and refine. They are also able to defend their political positions, perspectives, and philosophies within, alongside, and in opposition to other positions. Inspired by a sense of ever-imminent hope, students move to a third moment, which includes developing a philosophy of praxis, where deliberative practices for transforming the social universe of capital into noncapitalist alternatives are developed and tested, where theories are mobilized to make sense of and to deepen these practices, and simultaneously where everyday practices help to challenge, deepen, and transform critical theories. How this occurs within the classroom will vary from individual to individual, from group to group, depending upon the sociopolitical context and the historical and the geopolitical spaces in which such pedagogies are played out. Revolutionary critical pedagogy supports a totalizing reflection upon the historical-practical constitution of the world, our ideological formation within it, and the reproduction of everyday life practices. It is a pedagogy with an emancipatory intent. It looks towards the horizon of the future from the vantage point of the present while simultaneously analyzing the past, refusing all the while to form a specific blueprint for change. Practicing revolutionary critical pedagogy is not the same as preaching it.

Repeating some of my recent work, I would argue that revolutionary critical pedagogy is not born in the crucible of the imagination as much as it is given birth in its own practice. That is, revolutionary critical education is decidedly more praxiological than prescored. The path is made by walking, as it were. Revolutionary educators need to challenge the notion implicit in mainstream education that ideas related to citizenship have to travel through predestined contours of the mind, falling into step with the cadences of common sense. There is nothing common about common sense. Educational educators need to be more than the voice of autobiography; they need to create the context for dialogue with the "other" so that the "other" may assume the right to be heard. But critical pedagogy is also about making links with real, concrete human subjects struggling within and against capital and against the structures of oppression that are intimately linked to capital: racism, sexism, patriarchy, and imperialism.

The principles that help to shape and guide the development of our "vital powers" in the struggle for social justice via critical/revolutionary praxis discussed at length by Allman include principles of mutual respect, humility, openness, trust, and cooperation; a commitment to learn to "read the world" critically and expend the effort necessary to bring about social transformation; vigilance with regard to one's own process of self-transformation and adherence to the principles and aims of the group; adopting an "ethics of authenticity" as a guiding principle; internalizing social justice as passion; acquiring critical, creative, and hopeful thinking; transforming the self through transforming the social relations of learning and teaching; establishing democracy as a fundamental way of life; developing a critical curiosity; and deepening one's solidarity and commitment to self and social transformation and the project of humanization. These principles are not enough by themselves. They must be accompanied by dialectical investigations of the social relations of production in which all of us toil.

MARCIA: Your own work has helped to define the tradition of critical pedagogy not only in North America but in South America as well.

PETER: The tradition of critical pedagogy in North America is not an easy history to trace. But yes, it most certainly grew out of Freire's path-breaking work in the early 1980s and its adaptation to North American contexts by Henry Giroux, Donaldo Macedo, and Ira Shor (and later by others such as Antonia Darder and Pepi Leistyna), and we can see in its varied inflections the fingerprints of John Dewey and the social reconstructionist movement in the United States that developed after the Great Depression in the 1930s; I think it is fair to say that major exponents of critical pedagogy in North America were influenced by the sociology of knowledge that was emerging from England in the early 1980s as well as the pioneering work that was produced by Raymond Williams and the cultural studies that was being undertaken at England's Birmingham School of Contemporary Cultural Studies. We would have to include the work of U.S. economists Sam Bowles and Herb Gintis, especially their book, *Schooling in Capitalist America*, but admittedly there was never much of a Marxist tradition in North American instantiations of critical pedagogy. Certainly, there were neo-Marxist interpretations and, of course, an interest in Western neo-Marxism, particularly the Frankfurt School. As in the early days of critical pedagogy, we don't in today's incarnations of critical pedagogy see much influence from Soviet Marxism and very little reference to Lenin or Trotsky. But we do see a strong Gramscian—albeit watered down—presence. Today, we see on North American shores the influence of recent international work on critical pedagogy, and I am thinking of the work of Peter Mayo and Carmel Borg in Malta as one important instance and the work of Colin Lankshear and Mike Peters from New Zealand and Australia, respectively. The work of Joe Kincheloe and Shirley Steinberg, while not Marxist, is always crucial to any development of a critical pedagogy. I have already mentioned the work of Rikowski, Cole, and Hill, as well as Allman, and for me these are the most urgent voices because of their grounding in the Marxist tradition. If we examine critical pedagogy within the graduate schools of the United States, for instance, we notice that it is highly transdisciplinary, and there are few theoretical perspectives that you can't find these days among its many exponents. Today, critical pedagogy has been cross-fertilized with just about every transdisciplinary tradition imaginable, including theoretical forays into the work of Richard Rorty, Nietzsche, Jacques Lacan, and Jacques Derrida. I have been highly critical of much of the postmodernized versions of critical pedagogy, as I am sure you have gathered from much of my recent work.

MARCIA: Brazilian educational legislation, for instance, points to the relevance of critical pedagogy but never in a political sense of the term; never as a way to better understand the complexity of our social (dis)organization. Unfortunately, *critical* means celebrating diversity and being prepared for the work market. After all, each educational law addresses critical pedagogy within a very narrow view.

PETER: While I have been very critical of much that has been going on in the academy in the name of critical pedagogy, I do not see myself as a self-appointed guardian of the term. To echo something I wrote several years ago, critical pedagogy was once considered by the guard dogs of the American dream as a term of opprobrium, but now its relationship to broader liberation struggles seems quite threadbare if not fatally terminated. While its urgency was difficult to ignore, and its hard-bitten message had the pressure of absolute fiat behind it, critical pedagogy seemingly has collapsed into limitations placed on it by its own constitutive limitations. Force-fed by a complacent relativism, it has all but displaced the struggle against capitalist exploitation with its emphasis on a multiplicity of interpersonal forms of oppression within an overall concern with identity politics. It fights capitalism's second-hand smoke without putting out the cigar. I am scarcely the first to observe that critical pedagogy has been badly undercut by practitioners who would mischaracterize or misrepresent its fundamental project. In fact, if "critical pedagogy" is examined in the context of current educational debates and reform efforts, we see the very manifestation of its forms of domestication to which Paulo Freire drew attention. I think it is not useful to try to trace this history in order to try to find the "cause" of how this pedagogy has become decanted of its revolutionary potential; it is more important, at least in this present historical conjuncture, to develop a comprehensive approach to pedagogy that can touch on the central issues around which teachers and students are currently struggling. Critical pedagogy is very much a living tradition, one that needs to be reanimated with each successive generation, which faces new and historically specific challenges.

MARCIA: How do you conceptualize your work in critical pedagogy?

PETER: For me, that is, in my own work, I employ a concept of critical pedagogy that has Hegelian-Marxist origins to it—critical pedagogy in this regard is essentially a philosophy of praxis, one that acquires its emphasis within the contextual specificity of particular class struggles. Unlike many North American critical educators who are mainly concerned with subjective or discursive manifestations of oppression (which, in themselves, surely are not unimportant), I am more concerned with the structural foundations or conditions upon which various antagonisms take root (racism, sexism, etc.): the exploitation of human labor within capitalism. Whereas between 1985 and 1994 I was primarily concerned with cultural production, since that time I have been concerned with the conditions under which humans materially reproduce themselves.

MARCIA: Can you expand on this?

PETER: To make this idea clearer, it is necessary to place the question of praxis within the larger question of consciousness in general and the development of class consciousness in particular. I have recently had the opportunity to read some interesting work on the biological roots of consciousness by Maturana and Varela, work that is making quite an impact among friends and colleagues of mine in Latin America. There is certainly something useful in their approach to human biology as grounded in autopoietic systems. According to Maturana and Varela, we enter into language through our linguistic coupling with others; we know, for instance, that those linguistic interactions play a role in the recurrent coordination of social actions. Language arose through the process of socialization, particularly cooperation, as humans continued to increase their capacity to make distinctions and engage in linguistic reflection, and the appearance of the self is essentially a distinction in a linguistic domain. Surely, it is in language that the "I" or the "self" arises as a social singularity defined by the operational interaction in the human body of the recursive linguistic conditions in which this singularity is distinguished—as Maturana and Varela so presciently note—since this accounts for the way that we are able to maintain linguistic operational coherence by means of a descriptive recursive identity as the "I." We need to admit, too, that our "languaging" is a social phenomenon; it is performed as a social coupling within the historical context of human interaction. There is no pre-given consciousness, in other words.

This is very compatible, I believe, with the way I approach the concept of human consciousness/praxis within my practice of critical pedagogy. Language, in this sense, does not reflect knowledge as much as it refracts it. That is, in Maturana and Varela's terms, language is not a tool to reveal the objectivity of an outside world as much as it is a form of behavioral coordination—a social-structural coupling—that brings forth the world as an act of knowing. Here, it is co-ontogenetic coupling that produces our identities as essentially a "continuous becoming" through a permanent linguistic trophallaxis. In this case, it becomes necessary not to presuppose an objective world with a fixed point of reference in order to adjudicate the descriptions of the world that we continually bring forth in our coexistence with others. I would amend this perspective somewhat. In doing so, I would turn to historical materialist analysis and Marx's notion of consciousness. Maturana and Varela's perspective is essentially that "knowing is doing" and that to presume a fixed objective point of view by which to judge our actions is essentially untenable since it is tantamount to assuming a view from nowhere. Here, we see an emphasis on knowing as experience, where experience is in the same sense both a poesis and praxis. Norman Fairclough makes the point that language figures in material social processes as an element of these processes dialectically related to other elements; in other words, it figures in the reflexive construction of these processes, which social actors produce as an inherent part of these processes. Discourse analysis can help us to understand how language functions in hegemonic struggles over neo-liberalism and how struggles against neo-liberalism can be partly pursued in language.

Surely there is some truth to this, but the problem is that many postmodernist educationalists stop here and thus remain mired in the trap of an ethical relativism out of which they find it hard to escape. Too often, they study the representations of the world as if they were the things that they represent. It is not the signs that produce capitalist culture; clearly signifiers are as much the products of capitalist society as they are representations that help shape it. Surely, the whole process of consumption is not the prime mover of capitalism but a result of the forces and relations of production. The fact that all theories of the world are partial and provisional—to cite a mantra of many postmodernists—does not make the world unknowable. Surely, there are approximations of the truth that are invaluable in knowing the world. In my view, critical pedagogy becomes a means not only of acknowledging language as a complex system of mediation through which we glean approximations of the world but also of developing a historical understanding of how social structures work as mechanisms of such mediation.

I agree that social structure mediates—in a multifaceted and multilayered sense—language and consciousness and that modes of production of material life condition the language we use to make sense of our everyday social life. Modes and relations of production condition all of our social, cultural, and intellectual life, which is not the same thing as arguing that all of social existence can be reduced to them. In this way, I believe we should work towards developing a general theory of social reality by analyzing the process of historical development. It is interesting to note some parallels that Maturana and Varela have with Marx, who believed that knowing was a form of doing, knowing that comes from the concrete activity of being in the world.

MARCIA: Your early work was already related to Marxism, but now it seems much more connected to it. Some of your works locate the weaknesses of postmodernism and replace them with Marxist perspectives. How would you explain your shift from postmodernism back to Marxism? What were the issues that, let me say, had pushed you back to Marxism?

PETER: In answering this question, let me say that I don't want to reject—in the main, at least—my former work, which was informed by a critical postmodernist perspective. While this work had its limitations, I always attempted to address the importance of struggling against capitalist exploitation, racism, sexism, and homophobia, as well as other issues; neither do I want to denigrate the work of other postmodernists unfairly. I have a new book that I edited with Mike Cole and Glenn Rikowski and Dave Hill that delves into most of the central limitations of postmodernist perspectives. To be fair, postmodern theory enabled me to think through the many and variegated issues of identity construction within the context of contemporary U.S. culture and lifestyle issues. But over the years, I became increasingly concerned that if we are simply little more than an "other" to somebody else's "other," staring at each "other" in an endless hall of mirrors, as a surfeit of differences produced in the "tain" of these mirrors as some unending signifying chain that descends from the sky like Jacob's Ladder in the middle of nowhere, we need to do more than affirm our right to difference as a call for dignity and respect. I began to critique postmodern rebellion as a rebellion without a rationality, without an argument, where signs are set in motion in order to shape consciousness at some "raw" (as opposed to "cooked") incarnation of unreason, where significations hustle the signifiers for the cheapest (i.e., most simple) meaning, and where social life is reduced to barroom conversations among political drunkards trapped in a sinkhole of slumbering inertia and collapsing heresies. That is not to say that I don't believe there is a place for an aesthetics of rebellion or that we cannot venture into the nonrational (or even the irrational) in order to challenge the system. But we need an overall philosophy of praxis to give our rebellion some conceptual and political ballast. We need to engage in something more fundamental, which I take to be class struggle to create the conditions in which dignity

Unique Photo # 2492
Fred Cray

emerges from the material conditions of having enough to eat, a place to sleep, and the possibility of becoming critically literate about the world in which we inhabit, a world where resources such as oil are determining the future of global relations between nations and affecting the lives of millions of innocent people victimized by imperialist wars and who are forced to migrate to other countries or who are forced to suffer because of embargoes and other forms of economic terrorism—a place where cowboy capitalism enflames an unprincipled frenzy of economic deregulation causing financial impoverishment and insecurity for the vast majority of the world's poor. In postmodernism's rejection of grand historical narratives, of central struggles that teleologically define history, of the pure historical subject, and in its argument that knowledge is constituted in diffuse power relations—that is, in discourse (which is for postmodernists the sole constitutive element in social relations)—has helped to pave the way for important discussions of the role of language in the ordering and regulation and reproduction of power. But the work of postmodernism and its perfumed vocabulary of "difference" has been in the main insufficient in helping me to understand in a more nuanced way the historical shifts within the globalization of capitalism—and I am talking here about transnational finance capitalist enterprises, those ungovernable and anarchistic capitalist movements, and the permanent structural unemployment—conditions that are cruelly manifesting themselves everywhere today and which are devastating the entire globe. There are some postmodernists who have written with great sensitivity and erudition about issues of globalization but many others who have betrayed an understanding of contemporary capitalism that is, I believe, woefully rife with misconceptions and fundamental errors. Most of them are unable or unwilling to make the connection between globalization and imperialism, which I think is a crucial flaw. For me, it is important to operate from a critique of political economy within an international framework of opposition to U.S. imperialism, an imperialism that is grounded in super-exploitation (especially of colonial and female labor) through economic, military, and political aggression in defense of the interests of the United States "Homeland" (a very Teutonic-sounding word).

For me, the postmodernists all too willingly, but by no means in all cases, detach cultural production from its basis in economic and political processes; that is, culture as a signifying system is all but sundered from its constitutive embeddedness in the materiality of social life. To put it yet another way, the relationship between cultural artifacts or commodities and their material basis is viewed by many postmodernists as little more than epiphenomenal, or only tenuously connected to the production of value. Difference is rendered opaque in that it is often unhinged from its historical embeddedness in colonial/imperialist relations. Signification doesn't take place in some structural vacuum, frozen in some textual netherworld, defanged of capitalist alienation. It is a process that occurs in historical contexts, through modes of production and circulation tied to specific social relations that produce and reproduce value formations. Anyway, I found that the work by many postmodernists devalued or downgraded and in some instances scuppered altogether the material basis of cultural production.

Of course, Marcia, I agree that culture cannot and should not be reduced to its material base, but neither can it be disembedded from it. That is the crucial issue. With this in mind, Marxism is indispensable in challenging the ideology of capitalism—i.e., the imperial hegemonic bloc of the transnational capitalist class—through both counterhegemonic struggle and the struggle for proletarian hegemony, through attempts at creating a united front against imperialist capitalism and the internationalization of slave labor—a united front that has as its goal the redistribution of power and resources to the oppressed. The key here is to understand that capitalism is no longer self-reinforcing; it needs to expand its markets constantly, invading each nook and cranny of the globe through colonization, war, competition, and military aggression. Imperialism is the carotid artery that enables capital to flow to the farthest reaches of profit maximization.

I don't want to knock everything about postmodern theory since clearly there have been important insights in this work. My overall perspective is that postmodernism often reduces class struggle to a Nietzschean "will to power" which expunges the whole notion of "necessity" out of history, out of temporal progression. Many postmodernists in the United States are engaged in "identity politics" where they center their struggle around their racial, gender, or sexual identities. While these struggles can be very important, many of the new social movements based on race and gender identities sever issues of race and gender from class struggle. I find that this conveniently draws attention away from the crucially important ways in which women and people of color provide capitalism with its super-exploited labor pools—a phenomenon that is on the upswing all over the world. Postmodernist educators tend to ignore that capitalism is, according to Ellen Meiksins Wood, a ruthless "totalizing process," which shapes every aspect of our lives and subjects all social life to the abstract requirements of the market through the commodification and fetishization of life in all of its myriad dimensions. This makes a "mockery" out of all aspirations to autonomy, freedom of choice, and democratic self-government.

MARCIA: How does your version of critical pedagogy situate Marxism?

PETER: As Valerie Scatamburlo-D'Annibale and I have argued (and if I am permitted to turn to some of our recent work), for well over two decades we have witnessed the jubilant liberal and conservative pronouncements of the demise of communism. History's presumed failure to debar existing capitalist relations has been read by many self-identified "radicals" as an advertisement for capitalism's inevitability. As a result, the chorus refrain "There Is No Alternative to Capitalism" chimed by liberals and conservatives alike has been buttressed by the symphony of post-Marxist voices recommending that we give socialism a decent burial and move on. Within this context, to speak of the promise of Marx and socialism may appear anachronistic, even naïve, especially since the postmodern intellectual vanguardist anti-vanguard has presumably demonstrated the folly of doing so. Yet we stubbornly believe that the chants of "there is no alternative" must be challenged for they offer as a fait accompli something about which progressive leftists should remain defiant—namely, the triumph of capitalism and its political bedfellow, neoliberalism, which have worked together to naturalize suffering, undermine collective struggle, and obliterate hope. I make the point here that Marxism is not built upon an edifice of all-knowing totality. It does not offer a blueprint for an alternative to capitalism. It is a form of revolutionary praxis insofar as it explores the contradictions within capitalist social relations, knowing full well that the abolition of class society is not a certainty, it is only one possible outcome of many. Critical revolutionary pedagogy, for me, adopts a perspective that knowledge is praxis; it is transforming action. In this sense, objective truth becomes a practical question. What concerns me more is the value form in which our labor is exercised. How do we produce value? Surely, it is the value form of our labor that produces capitalist ideology—in that the value form of our labor within capitalist social relations is what conditions human thought at its roots. This ideology is fostered by the imperial-sponsored circulation of market ideologies through right-wing think tanks and NGOs (nongovernment organizations). Thinking and consciousness arise from our interactions with the material world, the world in which we labor. Our social existence—embedded as it is in the material world—is what produces our consciousness. Critical agency becomes, then, from this perspective of conscious, a form of revolutionary praxis, knowing the world by bringing it forth and bringing it forth by interacting with it, by changing it. The question is, What direction should we move? And that question constitutes the present debate. Well, it isn't much of a debate in the U.S. since questions about socialism and alternatives to capitalism are the kinds of questions that are raised by those who are now called "enemies of civilization."

MARCIA: How does all of this factor into your rethinking of critical pedagogy?

PETER: The larger goal that revolutionary critical pedagogy stipulates for radical educationalists involves direct participation with the oppressed in the discovery and charting of a socialist reconstruction and alternative to capitalism. However, without a critical lexicon and interpretative framework to unpack the labor/capital relationship in all of its capillary detail, critical pedagogy is doomed to remain trapped in domesticated currents and vulgarized formations. The process whereby labor-power is transformed into human capital and concrete living labor is subsumed by abstract labor is one that eludes the interpretative capacity of rational communicative action and requires a dialectical understanding that only historical materialist critique can best provide. Historical materialism provides critical pedagogy with a theory of the material basis of social life rooted in historical social relations and assumes paramount importance in uncovering the structure of class conflict as well as unraveling the effects produced by the social division of labor. Today, labor-power is capitalized and commodified, and education plays a tragic role in these processes. According to Rikowski, education represents what he refers to as the links in the chains that bind our souls to capital. It constitutes the arena of combat between labor and capital—a clash between titans that powers contemporary history we know as the class struggle. Schools therefore act as vital supports for, and developers of, the class relation, the violent capital-labor relation that resides at the very heart of capitalist society and development.

MARCIA: Can you share your thoughts on your idea of teachers as transformative intellectuals? What is needed to be done in this regard, and how are we to do it?

PETER: Well, there is a problem with how educators have domesticated the work of Gramsci on the topic of organic intellectuals. Postmodernists overestimate the "partially autonomous" space created by civil society, and while their intentions are often good ones, they have no program for socialist struggle; in fact, many of them abhor the very idea of socialism. They have effectively remade Gramsci in terms more acceptable to the bourgeoisie. It becomes very important in this regard to examine Gramsci's use of the term "civil society" within his overall analysis of the state. According to educators such as John Holst, Gramsci viewed civil society as part of the "hegemonic" aspect of the state that essentially worked to balance the coercive aspect of the state. Civil society, while clearly a contested terrain, is a site where the ruling class exerts its hegemony over the social totality. It is not a form of complete control. From this perspective, the most radical elements of civil society must work to build working-class solidarity in a post-revolutionary society. For Gramsci, working-class organic intellectuals are to bring socialist consciousness to the working class, that is, to give the proletariat a consciousness of its historic mission. If there is spontaneous rebellion, then according to Gramsci, this should be an educated spontaneity. Gramsci's conception of the long struggle for proletarian power is one that mandates organically devised ideological and political education and preparation, including the creation of a system of class alliances for the ultimate establishment of proletarian hegemony as well as the development of workers councils. These developments are part and parcel of what Gramsci called the historical bloc, consisting of organizations and alliances as well as a permanent organization of specialists (organic intellectuals) coordinated by the party who are able to assist the working class move from a class in itself (the objective class created by relations of production) to a class for itself (a subjective understanding of its position in production and its political mission). So, essentially, revolutionary pedagogy is committed to revolutionary praxis against the power of the state.

Transformative intellectuals should set themselves against that which the Community/Labor Strategy Center here in Los Angeles links to the systematic cultivation of racist ideology, reactionary nationalism, xenophobia, male supremacy, and misogyny. Of course, racism and sexism spread independently of the material basis for imperialism.

I will elaborate further on your question, Marcia. In discussing responses to the imperial barbarism and corruption brought about by capitalist globalization, James Petras (and I will paraphrase him here as I have done in several articles) makes some very useful distinctions. For instance, he distinguishes stoics, cynics, pessimists, and critical intellectuals (categories that encompass those who serve the hegemony of empire, from the prostrated academics who bend their knees in the face of capitalism while at the same time denouncing its excesses to the coffee-sipping intellectuals of Soho) from what he refers to as irreverent intellectuals (who serve the cause of developing revolutionary socialist consciousness and a new internationalism). The stoics are repulsed by the "predatory pillage of the empire" but, because they are paralyzed by feelings of political impotence, choose to form small cadres of academics in order to debate theory in as much isolation as possible from both the imperial powers and the oppressed and degraded masses. The cynics condemn both the victims of predatory capitalism and their victimizers as equally afflicted with consumerism; they believe that the oppressed masses seek advantage only to reverse the roles of oppressor and oppressed. The cynics are obsessed with the history of failed revolutions where the exploited eventually become the exploiters. They usually work in universities and specialize in providing testimonials to the perversions of liberation movements. The pessimists are usually leftists or ex-leftists who are also obsessed with the historical defeats of revolutionary social movements, which they have come to see as inevitable and irreversible, but who use these defeats as a pretext for adopting a pragmatic accommodation with the status quo. They have a motivated amnesia about new revolutionary movements now struggling to oppose the empire (i.e., movements by militant farmers and transport workers) and use their pessimism as an alibi for inaction and disengagement. The pessimists are reduced to a liberal politics that can often be co-opted by the ideologists of empire. Critical intellectuals frequently gain notoriety among the educated classes. Professing indignation at the ravages of empire and neo-liberalism and attempting to expose their lies, critical intellectuals appeal to the elite to reform the power structures so that the poor will no longer suffer. This collaborationist approach of critical intellectuals creates a type of indignation that appeals very much to the educated classes without asking them to sacrifice very much.

In contrast to all of the above categories, the irreverent intellectual, Petras argues, respects the militants on the front lines of the anti-capitalist and anti-imperialist struggles. Petras describes them as "self-ironic anti-heroes" whose work is engaged by activists working for a basic transformation of the social order. He notes that irreverent intellectuals are "objectively partisan and partisanly objective" and work together with intellectuals and activists involved in popular struggles. The irreverent intellectuals admire people such as Jean-Paul Sartre, who rejected a Nobel Prize in the midst of the Vietnam War. Irreverent intellectuals are careful to integrate their writing and teaching with practice, and in this way Petras claims that they are able to avoid divided loyalties.

MARCIA: Can the existing schooling system, which prepares selfish capitalist pseudo-humanitarian professionals, lead us to a struggle for social justice?

PETER: For those of us fashioning a distinctive socialist philosophy of praxis within North American context, it is clear that a transition to socialism will not be an easy struggle, given the global entrenchment of these aforementioned challenges. Joel Kovel argues that the transition to socialism will require the creation of a "usufructuary of the earth." Essentially, this means restoring ecosystemic integrity across all of human participation—the family, the community, the nation, the international community. Kovel argues that use-value must no longer be subordinated to exchange value, but both must be harmonized with "intrinsic value." The means of production (and it must be an ecocentric mode of production) must be made accessible to all as assets are transferred to the direct producers (i.e., worker ownership and control). Clearly, eliminating the accumulation of surplus value as the motor of "civilization" and challenging the rule of capital by directing money towards the free enhancement of use-values go against the grain of the existing capitalist society.

MARCIA: Now, I ask you, is class struggle relevant today?

PETER: That depends on what you mean by class struggle. Critical revolutionary educators believe that the best way to transcend the brutal and barbaric limits to human liberation set by capital is through practical grassroots movements centered around class struggle. But today, the clarion cry of class struggle is spurned by the bourgeois left as politically fanciful and reads to many as an advertisement for a Hollywood movie. The liberal left is less interested in class struggle than in making capitalism more "compassionate" to the needs of the poor. What this approach obfuscates is the way in which new capitalist efforts to divide and conquer the working class and to re-compose class relations have employed xenophobic nationalism, racism, sexism, ableism, and homophobia. The key here is not for critical pedagogues to privilege class oppression over other forms of oppression but how capitalist relations of exploitation provide the backdrop or foundation from which other forms of oppression are produced and how postmodern educational theory often serves as a means of distracting attention from capital's global project of accumulation. I am arguing that capitalism is not inevitable and that the struggle for socialism is not finished—it has barely begun.

MARCIA: What are some of your concluding thoughts?

PETER: I would like to comment briefly again on the role of teachers and how it needs to change in a world rife with war and terror brought about by a number of forces that include but are no means limited to religious fanaticism, globalized capitalism, over-production, neo-liberalism, and the resource wars engaged in by the leading imperialist powers, with the United States serving as the most carnivorous Alpha Male of all these "civilized hyenas" (Lenin's term). Because there appears to be no outer perimeter to capital's destructive overreach, I see the role of teachers as that of transforming the world, not just describing or interpreting the world. It is constantly reshaping itself to meet the challenges of harmonizing relations among human beings with nature in a world convulsing in chaos. Critical educators must increasingly confront at both regional and global levels the crisis of overproduction, the continuing use of surplus value as the key to historical acceleration and social progress, ecocidal development policies and practices, and economic, cultural, and military imperialism that holds much of humanity in the combustible thrall of violence and terror. The role of the critical educator follows Marx's clarion call to transform the world and not be content with describing or interpreting the world from some frozen hinterland of presumed objectivity; his call requires a complex dialectical understanding of the ideological dimensions of teacher work and the class-based, racialized, and gendered characteristics of exploitation within the capitalist economy and its educational, administrative, and legal apparatuses. And it demands from us a living philosophy of praxis. What is the use of critical revolutionary pedagogy if it cannot help us to discover ways of feeding the hungry, providing shelter for the homeless, bringing literacy to those who can't read or write, struggling against the criminal justice system to stop it from its war on Blacks and Latinos who are imprisoned in this country in numbers that greatly exceed their percentage of the population? In fact, the prison population of the U.S. is the largest in the world. We need to create spaces and sites for the development of critical consciousness and grassroots social activism both within the schools and outside of them and in both urban and rural spaces where people are suffering and struggling to survive on a daily basis. And we need to discover ways of creating—and maintaining—a sustainable environment.

I have described in recent work critical pedagogy as the performative register for class struggle. (I am using performativity here in a sense different than Judith Butler does.) It is praxiological and is occupied with real bodies, toiling bodies, sensuous bodies, bodies bearing the weight of generations of suffering under capital and as a result of imperialist wars. Consequently, revolutionary critical pedagogy (and let me paraphrase here from recent works) sets as its goal the decolonization of subjectivity as well as the transformation of its material basis in capitalist social relations. It seeks to reclaim public life under the relentless assault of the corporatization, privatization, and businessification of the lifeworld (which includes the corporate-academic-complex) and to fight for new definitions of what public life should mean and new formations that it can take. We need to realize that civic public life (as part of the state) itself is in a state of crisis with all kinds of conflicts between workers and their bosses. We can't just exhume some notion of public from the past and apply it to the present. We need to struggle for qualitatively new and different forms of public life, while we gain some sense of direction from past struggles and accomplishments. As we lurch along the battered road towards socialist renewal, we edge closer to the social universe of which Marx so famously spoke. Our optimism may be sapped by literally centuries of defeats, yet we need to keep our spirits alive and our vision of what must be done clear-headed and measured. Of course, my success in this struggle has been modest. I am attempting to refine a philosophy of praxis on groundwork already set by people such as Paulo Freire and Raya Dunayevskaya. I am only trying to walk modestly behind their far-reaching reflections.

I advocate one more point in closing—it is this: As we begin the task of removing Marx from the museum of history and putting him back on our current reading lists, we need to affirm the central role that class struggle plays in the determination of history. We also need to remember that there are no guarantees that socialism will win the day. That will depend upon us.

References

Allman, P. (1999). *Revolutionary social transformation: Democratic hopes, political possibilities and critical education*. Westport, CT: Bergin & Garvey.

Allman, P. (2001a). *Critical education against global capitalism: Karl Marx and revolutionary critical education*. Westport, CT: Bergin & Garvey.

Allman, P. (2001b). Education on fire! In M. Cole, D. Hill, P. McLaren, & G. Rikowski (Eds.), *Red chalk: On schooling, capitalism and politics*. Brighton, UK: Institute for Education Policy Studies.

Bensaid, D. (2002). *Marx for our times: Adventures and misadventures of a critique*. Translated by G. Elliott. London: Verso.

Bowles, S., & Gintis, Herbert. (1976). *Schooling in capitalist America*. New York: Basic Books.

Cole, M., & Hill, D. (1999). *Promoting equality in secondary schools*. London: Cassell.

Cole, M., Hill, D., McLaren, P., & Rikowski, G. (2001). *Red chalk: On schooling, capitalism & politics*. London: Tufnell.

Davies, S., & Guppy, N. (1997). Globalization and educational reforms in Anglo-American democracies. *Comparative Education Review, 41*(4), 435–459.

De Lissovoy, N., & McLaren, P. (2005). Towards a contemporary philosophy of praxis. In L. Gray-Rosendale, & Steven Rosendale (Eds.), *Radical relevance: Toward a scholarship of the whole Left*. Albany: State University of New York Press.

Dunayevskaya, R. (2002). *The power of negativity: Selected writings on the dialectic in Hegel and Marx*. Boulder, CO: Lexington.

Ebert, T. (2002). *University, class, and citizenship*. Unpublished manuscript.

Freire, P. (1998). *Pedagogy of the heart*. New York: Continuum.

Gramsci, A. (1971). *Selections from the prison notebooks*. London: International Publishers.

Hill, D. (2001). State theory and the neo-liberal reconstruction of schooling and teacher education: A structuralist neo-Marxist critique of postmodernist, quasi-postmodernist, and culturalist neo-Marxist theory. *British Journal of Sociology of Education, 22*(1), 135–155.

Hill, D., & Cole, M. (2001). Social class. In D. Hill, & M. Cole (Eds.), *Schooling and equality: Fact, concept and policy*. London: Kogan Page.

Hill, D., Sanders, M., & Hankin, T. (2003). Marxism, social class and postmodernism. In D. Hill, P. McLaren, M. Cole, & G. Rikowski (Eds.), *Marxism against postmodernism in educational theory*. Lanham, MD: Lexington Books.

Lenin, V. (1951). *Imperialism: The highest stage of capitalism*. Moscow: Foreign Language Publishing House.

Luxemburg, R. (1919). *The crisis in German social democracy: The Junius pamphlet*. New York: The Socialist Publication Society.

Marx, K. (1972). *Theories of surplus value: Part three*. London: Lawrence & Wishart. (Original work published 1863).

Marx, K. (1973). *Critique of the Gotha Program*. New York: International Publishers.

Marx, K. (1976). *Results of the immediate process of production*. In *Capital* (Vol. 1). Harmondsworth, UK: Penguin. (Original work published 1866).

Marx, K. (1977). *Capital: A critique of political economy* (Vol. 3). London: Lawrence & Wishart. (Original work published 1865).

Marx, K. (1977). *Economic and philosophical manuscripts of 1844*. Moscow: Progress Publishers. (Original work published 1844).

Marx, K. (1993). *Grundrisse: Foundations of the critique of political economy*. Translated by M. Nicolaus. New York: Penguin. (Original work published 1857–1858).

Marx, K., & Engels, F. (1850, March). Address of the Central Committee to the Communist League, London.

Maturana, H. R., & Varela, Francisco. (1987). *The tree of knowledge: The biological roots of human understanding*. Boston: New Science Library.

McLaren, P. (1995). *Critical pedagogy and predatory culture: Oppositional politics in a post-modern era*. London: Routledge.

McLaren, P. (1997). *Revolutionary multiculturalism: Pedagogies of dissent for the new millennium*. Boulder, CO: Westview.

McLaren, P. (1998a). *Life in schools: An introduction to critical pedagogy in the foundations of education* (3rd ed.). New York: Longman.

McLaren, P. (1998b). Revolutionary pedagogy in post-revolutionary times: Rethinking the political economy of critical education. *Educational Theory*, 48(4), 431–462.

McLaren, P. (2000). *Che Guevara, Paulo Freire, and the pedagogy of revolution*. Lanham, MD: Rowman & Littlefield.

McLaren, P., & De Lissovoy, N. (2002). Paulo Freire. In J. W. Guthrie (Ed.), *Encyclopedia of education* (2nd ed.). New York: Macmillan.

McLaren, P., & Farahmandpur, R. (1999a). Critical pedagogy, postmodernism, and the retreat from class: Towards a contraband pedagogy. *Theoria*, 93, 83–115.

McLaren, P., & Farahmandpur, R. (1999b). Critical multiculturalism and globalization: Some implications for a politics of resistance. *Journal of Curriculum Theorizing, 15*(3), 27–46.

McLaren, P., & Farahmandpur, R. (2000). Reconsidering Marx in post-Marxist times: A requiem for postmodernism? *Educational Researcher*, 29(3), 25–33.

McLaren, P., & Farahmandpur, R. (2001a). Educational policy and the socialist imagination: Revolutionary citizenship as a pedagogy of resistance. *Educational Policy, 13*(3), 343–378.

McLaren, P., & Farahmandpur, R. (2001b). Teaching against globalization and the new imperialism: Toward a revolutionary pedagogy. *Journal of Teacher Education, 52*(2), 136–150.

McMurtry, J. (2002). *Value wars: The global market versus the life economy*. London: Pluto.

Mészáros, I. (1995). *Beyond capital*. New York: Monthly Review Press.

Mészáros, I. (1999). Marxism, the capital system, and social revolution: An interview with István Mészáros. *Science & Society*, 63(3), 338–361.

Mészáros, I. (2001). *Socialism or barbarism: From the "American century" to the crossroads*. New York: Monthly Review Press.

Neary, M. (2004). Travels in Moishe Postone's social universe: A contribution to a critique of political cosmology. *Historical materialism: Research in critical Marxist theory, vol. 12*, issue 3.

Neary, M., & Rikowski, G. (2000, April 17–20). The speed of life: The significance of Karl Marx's concept of socially necessary labour-time. Paper presented at the British Sociological Association annual conference, University of York, April 17–20.

Ollman, B. (1976). *Alienation: Marx's conception of man in capitalist society* (2nd ed.). Cambridge, UK: Cambridge University Press.

Ollman, B. (1993) *Dialectical investigations*. New York: Routledge.

Ollman, B. (2001). *How to take an exam and remake the world*. Montreal, Canada: Black Rose.

Ollman, B. (2003). Marxism, this tale of two cities. *Science and Society*, 67(1), 80–86.

Rikowski, G. (1999) Education, capital and the transhuman. In D. Hill, P. McLaren, M. Cole, & G. Rikowski (Eds.), *Postmodernism in educational theory: Education and the politics of human resistance*. London: Tufnell.

Rikowski, G. (2000a, September 9). That other great class of commodities: Repositioning Marxist educational theory. Paper presented at the British Educational Research Association Conference, Cardiff University, Session 10.21.

Rikowski, G. (2000b, September 7). Messing with the explosive commodity: School improvement, educational research and labour-power in the era of global capitalism. Paper prepared for the symposium If We Aren't Pursuing Improvement, What Are We Doing? at the British Educational Research Association Conference, Cardiff University, Wales, Session 3.4.

Rikowski, G. (2001a, May 24). The importance of being a radical educator in capitalism today. Guest lecture in the sociology of education, The Gillian Rose Room, Department of Sociology, University of Warwick, Coventry.

Rikowski, G. (2001c). *The battle in Seattle: Its significance for education*. London: Tufnell.

Rikowski, G. (2001d, June 23). After the manuscript broke off: Thoughts on Marx, social class and education. Paper presented at the British Sociological Association Education Study Group, King's College, London.

Rikowski, G. (2002). Fuel for the living fire: Labour-power! In A. Dinerstein & M. Neary (Eds.), *The labour debate: An investigation into the theory and reality of capitalist work*. Aldershot, UK: Ashgate.

Rikowski, R., & Rikowski, G. (2002). Against what we are worth. Paper to be submitted to *Gender and Education*.

Robinson, W., & Harris, J. (2000). Towards a global ruling class? Globalization and the transnational capitalist class. *Science & Society*, 64(1), 11–54.

San Juan, E., Jr. (1999). Raymond Williams and the idea of cultural revolution. *College Literature*, 26(2), 118–136.

Wood, E. M. (1994, June 13). Identity crisis. *In These Times*, 28–29.

Wood, E. M. (1995). *Democracy against capitalism: Renewing historical materialism*. Cambridge, UK: Cambridge University Press.

Wood, E. M. (2001). Contradictions: Only in capitalism. In L. Panitch, & C. Leys (Eds.), *A world of contradictions, Socialist Register 2002*. London: Merlin.

"The Path of Dissent: An Interview with Peter McLaren," was published by Marcia Moraes in the *Journal of Transformative Education, vol. 1*, no. 2 (April, 2003), pp. 117–134. Three responses to this interview by scholars from the U.S., France, and The Netherlands are also published in this issue.

multicultural education for social justice

Interview 5

critical multiculturalism and democratic schooling: a conversation with Peter McLaren and Joe Kincheloe

Shirley R. Steinberg

Shirley Steinberg and Joe Kincheloe are among my dearest friends. This article was first published just prior to my leaving Ohio for Southern California and UCLA. Joe and Shirley have taught a number of places since this interview was published, including The Graduate Center at CUNY, New York. They recently were hired by McGill University in Montreal, Quebec.

SHIRLEY STEINBERG: How has the New Right come to dominate the public conversation about education in this country?

PETER MCLAREN: Shirley, I believe that the ascendancy of the New Right in this virulent period of recycled McCarthyism is truly frightening to those who believe in democracy and believe that democracy demands more than simply opening up the floodgates of social life to the currents of free enterprise. Chester Finn may be waging a war on the very idea of "public" institutions, but in doing so he joins Ravitch, Cheney, Schlesinger, Whittle, Bennett, and others in putting their own ambition before the defense of freedom, and thereby masquerading reactionary power as democratic populism. As they rail against entrenched self-interest in patriotic hyperbole that is as self-congratulatory, self-indulgent, and self-glorifying as it is obscenely lacking in insight, they in fact are serving the interests of corporate capital and the status quo distribution of power and wealth which, let's face it, is the linchpin of conservative policy. We have seen over the last two decades brutally effective measures to domesticate the working class (which Ravitch doesn't believe exists in the United States), and curtail or prevent labor militancy. In doing so, the new conservative cabal supports the goal of American enterprise, which is to keep the populace too busy to contemplate and organize resistance to the corporate empires that enslave them by supporting a consumer ethic that creates new demands, new desires, and new forms of discontent that can only be remedied with purchasing power, with becoming sexier, thinner, more muscular, more fashionable, and more powerful in the marketplace of a consumer and service-oriented post-Fordist economy.

The repugnantly repressive moralism of the current conservative political regime, its recent counterattacks on cultural democracy and its frenetic and at times savage attacks on the underclass, and subaltern groups, as well as its militant anti-unionism and foreign interventionist policies on behalf of capitalist interest, are reflective of the steady increase in the disproportionate level of cultural power and material wealth of Americans. We are encouraged to blame the problems of America on the breakdown of family values when, in fact, the social and educational policies of conservatives actually foster such a breakdown. Witness the declining inner-city labor market, growing national unemployment rates, the drastic decline in the number of unskilled positions in traditional blue-collar industries in urban areas, the increasing number of youth competing for fewer and fewer entry-level jobs, the automation of clerical labor, the shifting of service sector employment to the suburbs and on a broader scale the deregulation and globalization of markets, trade and labor and the deregulation of local markets.

And you've got predominantly right-wing media (contrary to the perception that the media are leftist) that often, but not always, unwittingly promote the idea shared by conservatives that underclass minority youth are more prone to violence and drug use than the more "civilized" whites. These are the "wildings" that roam the streets high on angel dust, randomly hunting whites with steel pipes. These are the Rodney Kings who are presumed to be life threatening even when lying face down on the ground in an arrest-ready posture, choking on dust and their own blood and vomit. And the answer to such violence and despair in their lives is to sound the lapidary phrase: "Just say no to drugs!" Can't you hear William Bennett hollering into the smoke-filled skies of Los Angeles, megaphone clutched to his beefy manicured hand, crying: "Just say no to rioting!"?

SHIRLEY: What do Peter's ideas mean for those who are educational leaders and are committed to principles of progressive, democratic reform?

JOE KINCHELOE: Peter has much to say to educational leaders. Indeed, the ideas that Peter and I promote are concepts which many times have not been a part of the public conversation about education—a conversation dominated by the voices of Finn, Ravitch, Bloom, Hirsch, D'Souza, Bennett, and Alexander. Educational leaders need to conceive of democracy as a fragile entity, a concept which cannot survive confrontation with unequal power relations. Educational reform conceptualized in an era which has seen an unprecedented growth in these unequal power relations must be carefully examined to see how it reflects anti-democratic tendencies. For example, when the Reagan and Bush administrations have offered new strategies for education, they have been conceived almost totally outside the social and economic context. Few of the conservative reforms think in terms of the impact of accountability-driven curricula on those who fall outside the dominant culture. As long as minority youth are positioned as outsiders to the dominant culture, as long as African American and Hispanic/Latino culture is viewed as an impediment to be erased, as long as the curriculum excludes the history and culture of such peoples, educational reforms will fail the test of democracy. We will continue to view intelligence as a form of male-centered abstract rationality which has little to do with situated, contextual forms of thinking—cognitive styles which have traditionally been excluded from the definition of intelligence.

SHIRLEY: When I read or listen to Chester Finn and Diane Ravitch write or talk about educational reform, I get the feeling that they have never considered such ideas. Is that a fair assessment?

JOE: I'm not sure where they are coming from. Wherever it is, they have captured the mood of the Reagan years with the denial that socioeconomic context must be considered in educational reform.

SHIRLEY: But they are intelligent people; surely they have considered the socioeconomic context?

JOE: After studying their work, it seems to me that they are so caught up in the meta-narratives of modernism (that is, the larger cultural stories we tell about who we are as a people and the purposes our institutions serve), that they are deaf to the voices of the marginalized and the voices of those committed to economic justice. For example, Ravitch and Finn use evidence from researchers who view the improvement of standardized test scores as the raison d'être of teaching. No questions seem to have been asked here about where the knowledge on the tests comes from or whose interests it serves, what impact such tests have on the role of teachers, or the assumptions about the nature of knowledge embedded in it. Caught in the trap of objectivism, Finn and Ravitch cannot reflect on the political or epistemological presuppositions of this test-driven curriculum because they claim they don't exist. They never talk about the historical and social context which gave birth to such a curriculum. Thus, the dramatic negative effects such an education produces are swept under the neo-conservative rug.

SHIRLEY: There's a lot of discussion now among critical educators about using postmodern social theory to analyze schooling—something you and Henry Giroux pioneered at the Center for Education and Cultural Studies at Miami University about five or six years ago. It seems that those same educational critics who criticized you for being too esoteric are now writing from a postmodernist perspective. How does this perspective help you to challenge the onslaught of the New Right?

PETER: Yes, I began writing about postmodernism in 1986 in an article I did on Paulo Freire for *Educational Theory*. Postmodernism had already been on the scene for some time outside the field of pedagogy. At that time, I was worried about the cynicism that was associated with certain postmodern schools of thought, and I was trying to defend Freire's utopian thinking against such theoretical cynicism. Henry and I tried to expand on the idea picked up in cultural studies of a "resistance postmodernism" or "critical postmodernism"—something Henry has advanced brilliantly in his new book, *Border Crossings*. This follows *Postmodern Education*, which he did with Stanley Aronowitz. My work has been mainly on postmodern identity formation and the production of desire. I've tried to counter conservative perspectives on national or civic identity by arguing that identities are always multiply organized as a series of often conflicting subject positions within a structured hierarchy linked to capitalist productive relations. On this basis, I am able to challenge the New Right perspectives on patriotism and civic duty as really being monolithic and linked to the imperatives of a service economy that produces good consumers.

Think about this, Shirley. Do you want your American citizenship shaped by corporate power and the big business establishment in collusion with the Educational Excellence Network? Do you want the future of your children to be mortgaged to a corporate business rationality that seeks to create a public sphere comprised of workers with an overabundance of technical skills so it can provide cheap labor? Think of the 200 million dollars the American 2000 project will raise from the business community to create the New American Schools program. Think of the whole idea of selling school reform under the banner of choice. How can you really have choice when the government is prescribing the standards and forms of assessment? When it is regulating through national funds teaching standards and practices? This majoritarian control will lead to *less* cultural diversity, less creativity, less democracy.

Diane Ravitch, now an assistant secretary of education, Gilbert Sewall of the American Textbook Council, Lynne Cheney, chair of the National Endowment for the Humanities, and Chester Finn, a primary architect of America 2000, receive funding from conservative foundations such as the Olin Foundation and the Donner Foundation of New York. The right-wing reform initiative also has a major player, Chris Whittle, who heads a corporation that uses place-based marketing to supply television equipment free of charge in schools where his Channel One is shown in social studies, communications or art classes. Daily broadcasts of twelve minutes reach approximately 8,000 schools. Channel One produces news segments that are interspersed with commercial messages and Whittle Communications retains revenue for using them.

Whittle and his financial backers are poised to make millions on their Edison Project to start profit-making high schools, even though it is expected to cost about two and a half billion to get it off the ground. With Republican media grub Robert Ailes in his hip pocket, I have no doubt he'll make headway in creating a national private school system that is designed to create a network of 1,000 private schools. He's charging about $5,500.00 tuition with about 20% of the student population on various scholarships. Lamar Alexander, the secretary of education, was a former business advisor to Whittle and it's not a coincidence that the New American Schools project that is part of America 2000 is similar in many ways to the Edison Project. But the Edison Project appears more pernicious in my mind in its attempt to build what Russell Jacoby refers to as "McSchool Franchises" or "educational boutiques." I think Jacoby's criticisms are too kind.

It's a tragedy to see something so slick as the Whittle schools joining private enterprise and turning education into a profit-making business. Parents who can't afford to send their kids to an expensive private school will be able to send them to what Jacoby calls "McSchools" fast food versions of the comprehensive high school where rows of Whittle TV monitors can replace important human resources such as teachers. The idea of creating 1,000 for-profit schools is nightmarish. This is the ugliness of capitalism. Public schools can be thrown into the dustbin along with socialism and communism which the American psyche now treats as discarded images from a grade B horror film.

I am against corporate marketing in schools and Whittle's commercials would implicitly sanction the present role capitalism plays in democracy. It also is a question of privileging image over content and context. What gets ignored is how news stories and commercials get created and what constitutes their ideological imperative, which is to attract the largest numbers of corporate sponsors. Reality gets served up to students under the corporate banner of show business and profits. The media is already blurring the boundaries between news and advertising. Corporate ownership of the media is increasing commercial exploitation of student populations worldwide. Data systems of the world's corporations will become the curriculum of the future. We have entered Paul Virilio's perceptual field of "instantaneous ubiquity" and Baudrillard's "hyper-space of simulation" and in the words of Larry Grossberg, which refer to the title of his new book, *We Gotta Get Out of This Place*.

The whole argument that Channel One will overcome ignorance among students with respect to current events is silly and facile when you consider the way that the media articulate meaning. I'm not simply referring to the commercials that are part of the satellite broadcasts. Channel One fragments the viewer by eliminating self-reflection. While commercials construct the viewers and dependent consumers, viewers are invited to judge the validity of the advertisements. Viewers are framed monologically by providing them with the illusion that they exercise some power as interpreters of what they see and hear. Yet such a role is really illusory because self-reflection virtually collapses in television viewing. Advertisements flatter viewers into thinking they are self-constituting agents when in reality the self produced by media images is profoundly simulated. Channel One creates forms of consumer desire and models of and for citizenship in which the distinction between citizen and consumer is eliminated.

In saying this I want to make clear that I am not against the use of television, per se, in the classroom. Far from it. I think television is an inescapable and important medium. The most challenging, if not disturbing, aspect about living in a world of "virtual" realities brought about by postmodern electronic literacies is that these new information technologies or media knowledges instantaneously transform what Larry Grossberg calls our "mattering maps"—our affective investments in roles, goals, and meanings. Think of the implications for students living in a cyberspace of computers, Nintendo games, VCRs, and MTV to be suddenly wrenched back from this electronic cocoon into the nineteenth century world of linear time and mostly print technology—which is what happens in most of our classrooms. Walter Benjamin and later, Harold Innis and Marshall McLuhan, anticipated the effects of these new media technologies. The new information technologies create what Australian educators Bill Green and Chris Bigum call "cyborg couplings." The boundaries between machines and humans are constantly becoming blurred in this age of new media technologies, creating what Donna Haraway refers to as the transformation of humans into cyborgs. So whereas having television in the classroom may indeed be important in creating a postmodern curriculum for the new generation of young cyborgs that fill our classrooms, we need to be able to use such technology in ways that don't simply create what I have termed "corporate neocolonialism." Rather, as Henry Giroux and I have argued recently, helping students in the age of what Green and Bigum refer to as "technonature" or the new "digital eco-system" in which contexts are always indeterminate and contingent instead of being anchored in biological or human time, means helping them to become media literate. When people ask me why I am stressing the idea of media literacy more and more in my writings, I have to admit to them that the effect of the new media technologies in forging identities for my students far outstrips what I am able to do in the classroom unless I begin to bring popular culture into the curriculum as a central focus. This, to me, is what the postmodern curriculum is about. Providing young cyborgs with an understanding of how their identities are becoming constructed within the current proliferation of technocultures. What are the new postmodern pathologies that might emerge? Yes, I worry about this. But I also hold out some hope that students growing up in cyberspace may be able to educate us as to the possibilities of new cyber-identities, new postmodern narratives of the self that may bring about a better world. I am not overly optimistic but I think it's a challenge we must not ignore.

SHIRLEY: Joe, you've written extensively on teacher education. What are the implications of Peter's comments on postmodernism for the professional education of teachers?

JOE: Where to begin? Let's think about what Peter has said about the Edison Project and Channel One. I would argue that these educational "innovations" characterize a significant break with this country's educational past. Business involvement with education before Whittle was a bit embarrassed, taking place at a more covert level. With the Edison Project and Channel One we begin to see an unabashed merging of a public educational system with private economic interests. I get the feeling that the architects of these plans assume that any progressive opposition to their strategies would be so minimal that it would not merit serious consideration. I hope that assessment of critical progressivism is unfounded, but I do admit that I would like to see more outrage about the merging of these private and public institutions. Teachers, like most Americans, are too often incapable of analyzing the political interests of the information and the situations which confront them. A critical postmodern teacher education would prepare teachers to seek the origins of the 'knowledge' with which they have to deal and to ask questions concerning who benefits from particular portrayals of reality. Such an analytical ability would alert teachers to the power interests involved with the Edison Project and Channel One. Critical postmodern teacher education teaches students much more than just how to "do it differently." Students learn how institutions operate, how bureaucracies produce goal displacement as they confuse form with substance. In the process, prospective teachers learn about how discursive conventions in general regulate what is deemed acceptable and unacceptable, while in particular they learn how dominant power shapes the discursive boundaries of the school. The right wing has been very successful in the promotion of the Great Denial in the professional preparation of teachers. This denial involves the right wing's refusal to acknowledge the political ramifications of teacher education. In this context, Finn and his good friend, Whittle, deny that there are political dimensions to the Edison Project or Channel One. Much like the CIA, they maintain a stance of 'plausible deniability' when confronted with the political nature of their mission.

Without using the term "political," right-wing teacher educators frame their holy mission as a neo-White Man's burden, a missionary struggle between forms of civilized high culture and the poor or "off white" unwashed masses. Allan Bloom carries the flag as he portrays the culture of the masses as a disease to be cured with the magic of the traditional Western canon. Writing with latex gloves of the distasteful culture of the unwashed, Bloom turns up his nose at their music, their dancing, their television, and God forbid, their sexual impulses. Buoyed by Bloom's call to arms, right wing teacher education deploys prospective teachers on a search and destroy mission—the objective: pernicious youth culture and popular culture with their degraded use of multicultural forms.

SHIRLEY: Tell us some more about critical postmodern perspectives on teacher education.

JOE: Students in critical postmodern teacher education focus on the study of epistemology, the nature of knowledge. Not only do students learn how knowledge is produced and legitimated, but they learn that one of the most important features of a critical postmodern pedagogy involves the ability to create knowledge. Knowledge is not just created in the researcher's office or in the professor's study, but in the consciousness produced in thinking, discussion, writing, argument, or conversation. It's created when teachers and students confront a contradiction, when students encounter a dangerous memory, when teacher-presented information collides with student experience, or when student-presented information collides with teacher experience. When teachers and students speculate on the etymology and deployment of knowledge, new knowledge is created. This ability to create knowledge forms the foundation of the type of teacher education that Peter and I promote. When we find ourselves in multicultural schools, this creation of knowledge takes on even more significance. When a critical postmodern teacher who doesn't share the culture, language, race or socioeconomic backgrounds of students enters the classroom, she or he becomes not a Hirsch-like information provider but an explorer who works with students to create mutually understood texts. Based on their explorations, teachers and students create new learning materials full of mutually generated meanings and shared interpretations.

Feminist pedagogy theoretically contributes to our notion of critical postmodern knowledge production. Teachers who create knowledge must understand various ways of knowing (whether it be women's ways of perceiving or subjugated knowledges of oppressed peoples), and draw upon these perspectives when reconceptualizing the knowledge of school. These diverse ways of knowing will allow teachers to help students analyze events and interpret cultural meanings. Such ways of knowing will help teachers engage student experience in a way that allows it to be both affirmed and questioned, all the time keeping alive the possibility of self and social transformation.

It comes as no surprise that right wing critics such as Bloom, Finn, D'Souza, and Ravitch will decry such proposals on the grounds that they undermine the instruction of a core curriculum grounded on the great ideas of the Western tradition. Critical postmodern teacher education would produce students who are capable of engaging many of the ideas such critics hold dear, albeit not in the same reverential way Bloom, Finn, D'Souza, and Ravitch would. Of course, a critical postmodern curriculum would go beyond the boundaries of the West and engage ideas from Asia and Third World cultures as well.

The central point of critical postmodern teacher education, however, involves helping prospective teachers confront the epistemological shifts demanded by it. While a right-wing teacher education involves preparing prospective teachers to teach in a correct-answer-oriented curriculum with an unexamined realist epistemological base, critical postmodernism envisions a conceptually oriented curriculum with a consciously examined critical constructivist epistemological base. These critical curricular and epistemological perspectives change the purpose of teacher education programs and schools in general from vocational orientations with an emphasis on the provision of an essential body of knowledge and a set of narrow skills, to one of intellectual development and an attempt to rewrite and transform the world.

SHIRLEY: Peter, doesn't it strike you as odd that the conservative multiculturalists set themselves up as champions of diversity yet end up actually reinforcing the idea of a monolithic, singular culture?

PETER: Not at all, Shirley. Their language is very duplicitous. You need to be very careful not to take what they say at face value. That's what makes them so dangerous. The Native Americans knew this when they said early this century that white people speak with "forked tongues."

We create narrative spaces for individuals in our culture and classrooms to succeed as *a condition of whiteness*, of primarily white male values, values that stress boundaries, borders and rationality. These are certainly linked to the ideology of the old "new" conservatives like Ravitch and Schlesinger, who hide their thralldom to white culture in a measured discourse that calls for diversity and multiculturalism. That white values are held to be the apotheosis of civilization is camouflaged. In truth, it is not that the whites are the most successful players in the inter-ethnic struggle over identity and power, but the *only group allowed to play*. After all, it's the whites who primarily set the rules for the game. Educators shouldn't let Ravitch and Schlesinger trick them into thinking that whiteness is constrained by a society premised on equality because in our society, whiteness and inequality are often coterminous—they are often contiguous.

Frankly, white culture is not benign. It can be a wrathful space of delirious greed; it specializes the body and territorializes it in the service of capital. It is structured on race, class and gender inequality. The new conservatives wrest their view of culture from the turbulence of such inequality while celebrating diversity and naturalizing the preferred structures of Western values of consumer individualism.

In saying this, let me emphasize something I think is crucial. We do not simply live in white *or* Latino *or* African American cultures. There is diversity *within them* and also we must recognize, there is cross-cultural sharing that occurs across the often permeable boundaries separating them. We are, in this country, *transcultural citizens:* we occupy points of identification with many cultures. To suggest that, for instance, African Americans lose their ethnic roots if they adopt aspects of white culture or that white people lose their ethnicity by engaging Afrocentric values is to actually reinforce the marginalization of African Americans by emphasizing the binary opposition: Black vs. White. I am not trying to essentialize or romanticize differences between white and African. White culture is not *monolithic* or homogeneous or thoroughly evil. I am trying to suggest that there is a relationship among the culture of elite white men, an allegiance to capitalism, and the negation of the "other" (women, minorities, and the poor). This relationship is not acknowledged by the conservative multiculturalists.

While it's true that we no longer think of education as the same type of sorting mechanism that once served to separate out Eastern Europe and African-American and Latino immigrants from those groups more easily identified as "Western," I do think schools still serve to conscript certain forms of difference into the service of the wealthy and the privileged although today it's legitimized by different ideological methods and enhanced through privatization. One only has to read Jonathon Kozol's important new study, *Savage Inequalities*, to see how little things have really changed. Education is still the primary means for "civilizing" immigrants, for remodeling the aberrant behavior of those groups whose flesh is unacceptable but who can serve as good scapegoats for building more jails and prisons instead of schools.

For too many minorities, schools have become Cathedrals of Death, agencies for reintegration, camps for ideological internment, factories for domestication. Schools are certainly not irrelevant to the way we conduct social life in this age of post-Fordist consumer culture. Far from it. They are profoundly necessary for conservatives in a world in which cultural meaning has been transformed into one big advertising montage. If we are going to divide the world of the "haves" and the "have-nots," into the "winners" and the "losers," then we need to keep control over who will win and who will lose. And if we can do this under the banner of "choice," then so much the better. We can give certain minorities the choice of which institutions will fail them and then blame their failure on personal lifestyle of lack of good old American family virtues. Fortunately there are teachers and students out there fighting against this, along with marginal and interstitial groups. We need to build on these grass-roots struggles and for this reason the educational left must work together.

SHIRLEY: Let's go ahead and address the issue of multiculturalism.

PETER: Well, first of all, America is not only a land of immigrants. African Americans were forced to come here as slaves and the Native Americans were already here. Minorities in this country have been and continue to be historically muted; subaltern groups continue to be oppressed, policed, and demonized within patriarchal-imperialist ideological formations that exist as part of a capitalist technocracy. We are still witnessing the dissimulation of imperialism under the guise of creating a "common culture" that seeks unity and consensus in diversity. To me, we need to offer space for struggle, for conflict. The goal of a common culture is born out of a modernist legacy of trying to own knowledge, control knowledge, and is related to the Cartesian perspective of the autonomous, rational ego. It is born out of the legacy of imperialism that privileges the "high" culture of the Western Enlightenment. It's tied to the desire for objective knowledge. It's a symptom of the desire to contain and control the social by asserting a stable identity. Joe and I talk about this a great deal in our work.

The goal of a critical multiculturalism, which is how I identify my own pedagogy, is not to reverse the margins and centers of power but to displace their founding binarisms and dependent hierarchies. A critical multiculturalism foregrounds "whiteness" as an ethnic category parasitic on "blackness" so that whiteness ceases to serve as an invisible norm against which we "measure" the worth of "other" cultures. Such a move can help teachers and students question the received practical and disciplinary knowledge students bring with them to the classroom.

Joe and I talk about the importance of dislocating "whiteness" from its infusion into our political unconscious as a synonym for cultural and moral superiority. Western rationality associated with white supremacy needs to be radically decentered as the source of pristine truth. In fact, Western rationality and values are murky; they are implicated in relations of power. Dan Quayle champions family values without realizing that such values are socially constructed within particular arenas of power and privilege. His own government's creation of an underclass is able to justify its own racist and sexist social policy by turning social pathology into a question of personal choice. What gives Quayle, for instance, as a rich white male from the ruling elite, the right to pass judgment on those groups who don't share his own economic and cultural privilege? Those who do not share his values are condemned as "relativists" who have no preferred values. Quayle's position on family values is, in fact, not only morally repugnant, but intellectually dishonest. It is built upon an essentialist itinerary of white male hegemonic interests. He is unaware of the structuring influence that ideology plays in producing the discursive field in which he is situated as a spokesperson for America's morally "upright" citizens.

Diversity that somehow constitutes itself as a harmonious ensemble of benign cultural spheres is a conservative and liberal model of multiculturalism that, in my mind, deserves to be jettisoned because, when we try to make culture an undisturbed space of harmony and agreement where social relations exist within cultural forms of uninterrupted accord, we ascribe to a form of social amnesia in which we forget that all knowledge is forged in histories that are played out in the field of social antagonisms. As Joe mentioned earlier: Whose knowledge are we talking about? Whose interests does such knowledge serve? With the "diversity" that conservatives speak about comes a normative grid that *contains* cultural differences.

It is worth mentioning here that I see my work as part of much larger traditions within critical pedagogy and cultural studies that have been taking up the question of identity, difference and human agency for some time. I'm thinking of people like Phil Corrigan, Cameron McCarthy, Christine Sleeter, Jo Anne Pagano, Bill Pinar, Henry Giroux, and Paulo Freire in critical pedagogy and multiculturalism and Stanley Aronowitz, bell hooks, Homi Bhabha, Cornel West, Abdul JanMohammed, Larry Grossberg, Chandra Mohanty, and Michele Wallace in cultural studies. While none of these traditions is homogeneous, I think it's important that we acknowledge the theoretical trajectories out of which our work is forged.

Having said this, I think that the sites of our identity within postmodern cultures are various and as seekers of liberation, teachers need to recognize the heterogeneous character of their inscription into colonial and neo-colonial texts of history and cultural discourses of empire. New sites of agency are erupting all around us at the borderlines of cultural instability. I seek a pedagogy of insurrection, in the in-between spaces of cultural negation and translation. I look to the creation of hyphenated identities that struggle against monolithic models of democratic citizenship associated with Dan Quayle and the self-styled custodians of identity such as Ravitch and Schlesinger. That's why I admire and support the struggles of Latino groups and African Americans in the creation of new ethnicities that take seriously the politics of difference and cultural justice. That's why my own work is informed by feminist theory and post-colonial theory.

Henry Giroux wisely advises us to be "border-crossers." We are finished with the age of border guards and the naïve psychologism often associated with a total and autonomous self-identity. We need, as teachers, to invent ourselves in new ways, to stop looking for a natural language or a pure "ground" of being. We need to develop new theories of social criticism and transformation and not retreat from theory, as many conservatives and even some leftist teacher activists are advocating. There is a danger in yielding to the seduction of "plainspeak," because new social arrangements demand more sophisticated theories of pedagogy, culture, identity-formation, and liberation, and not the banal journalistic accounts some teacher activists think is the antidote to the new continental social theory.

Diane Ravitch and Arthur Schlesinger, Jr., as historians of the mainstream, worry a great deal about multiculturalism turning into a vitriolic factionalism—self-interest groups indulging in belligerent forms of ethnocentrism. The Committee of Scholars in Defense of History, of which they are members, serves as little more than an ideological bunker—a holding camp for subjugated knowledges—those knowledges that threaten the dominant culture's view of truth and justice. Hegemonic historians who attempt to defend the lies of the empire, Ravitch, Schlesinger, and others, fail to consider the privileging norms and articulatory effects of their own positionality as white, Anglocentric theorists.

What we need as part of multicultural curriculum is not only a social historical perspective that highlights the contributions and struggles of subaltern groups, but also one that provides us with an understanding of approaches to the study of history itself.

There's been a revolution in the social sciences that can help us to understand the ways in which historians construct the objects of their studies: how they create and often demonize their "others" through the conceptual artifacts of their own methodologies and the ideological assumptions that inform the questions they ask and fail to ask. I think we need to understand that histories of minorities are too frequently textual constructions created by the winners who, not surprisingly, are usually white and Anglo. For example, Ravitch and Schlesinger use whiteness as a cultural marker against which otherness is defined by not interrogating their own privilege as white, hegemonic historians. Whiteness does not exist outside of culture but constitutes the prevailing social texts in which social norms are made and remade. Their own Eurocentric cultural norms and logocentric rationality pass unobserved in the discourses that structure their own research. Their seeming pluralism and their lip service to diversity are belied by an allegiance to a monolithic view of citizenship steeped in a legacy of Western imperial high culture.

Shirley, I can see poor Allan Bloom still pining for the former grandeur of Greek and Roman antiquity. Late-Victorian highbrow culture cannot be resurrected in the academy, so Bloom wants to take it out on rock 'n' roll and non-Western thinkers whom he stigmatizes as the inverted and debased image of the hypercivilized metropolitan intellectual. To move away from Western knowledge and the radiantly civilized high culture of Hellenism is to descend into savagery and barbarism, into reason's Negative Other which, according to Bloom, is tantamount to Hell.

SHIRLEY: Doesn't Diane Ravitch claim that the analysis of education in light of socioeconomic class is inappropriate in the study of education?

JOE: You're right. Ravitch claims that in an egalitarian society such as the U.S., class analysis doesn't really apply. I wish all the economically disadvantaged people in our country could hear her say that. Maybe this would alert us to the mindset which has directed the educational reform movements of the last dozen years.

To personalize Peter's and my ideas about the moral failures of this neoconservative perspective, I like to tell the story of some of the kids I grew up with in the rural Appalachian Mountains of East Tennessee. For example, my friend, Larry, was a kid whose parents finished no more than six grades of schooling. His mother worked in the home and his father cut firewood during fall and winter. Larry was brilliant. Before we started school, Larry would take me into the woods behind his house and teach me the names and medicinal uses of many of the plants that grew in the hills. He was a storehouse of information. He also understood the workings of a car engine, having watched his father repair the old Ford perpetually parked out in the front yard. Sometimes when I was visiting he would take apart pieces of engine and show me how they worked. He was my teacher and I was a willing student. All of this changed when we started school. With his thick mountain accent Larry had trouble understanding the language of the school. He frequently would ask me what the teacher meant. Growing up in a home with no magazines, newspapers or books, Larry was poorly prepared for a curriculum grounded on one's familiarity with symbolic language. Moreover, because of his unfamiliarity with such linguistic conventions, he was deemed unintelligent by the evaluative instruments of school—no matter that he brought a wealth of knowledge with him, no matter that he had virtually no experience with symbolic language before coming to school. Larry's unique form of contextual understanding did not count in our school. It is the Larrys of the world who are victimized by the right wing reforms. It is real live students from poor homes and the homes of the culturally different whose futures are undermined by the right wing indifference to questions of social and economic context. The critical pedagogical tradition from which Peter and I come demands educational justice for Larry and students like him. This is why we work so hard to challenge the theoretical assumptions which undergird their perspectives—the modernist scientific tradition, unbridled free enterprise capitalism, socially decontextualized psychometrics, Eurocentrism, and patriarchy.

SHIRLEY: But Bloom, Bennett, Finn, and Ravitch attempt to frame your critique and your questions as some form of unreasonable assault on the sacred democratic success of schooling in America. How do you respond?

JOE: Part of the mythology that the right wing has created to sustain its power involves the portrayal of a golden age of American education. It was a "simpler, more natural time" when students behaved, the basics were taught, and teachers were dedicated to their noble profession. Ronald Reagan built a career on creating nostalgia for this golden age. If we would just get prayer back in the school, restore discipline like Joe Clark did in New Jersey, and teach reverence for American traditions, we could refind our lost glory. Right-wingers make little attempt to hide the fact that it was the reformers of the "permissive" 1960s that defiled our grand traditions. It was a great story and it worked beautifully. Ward and June Cleaver are under siege, the right-wing argued, by the non-traditional destroyers of the family unit—the gays, the liberals, the feminists, and the militant Blacks. To regain Wally and Beaver's utopian childhood in mythical Mayfield, we must support an Ozzie Nelson-like president and his comforting homilies about the American past.

SHIRLEY: Are you saying that the right wing created a new history?

JOE: That's exactly what I'm saying. Reagan and his educational reformers erased our "dangerous memories." Vietnam became our finest hour in defense of freedom, and the quest for social and racial justice became the clamoring of the special interests. William Bennett warned against using social studies to teach about racial issues; instead, he argues, we should be teaching the "great facts" of American history. These great facts became a code for the military and political exploits of white men—the Revolutionary War heroes, Zachary Taylor and Lewis Cass in the Mexican War, the commanders of the Army of the Potomac, Teddy Roosevelt at San Juan Hill, etc.

Such a history helps shape the consciousness of our students. It's amazing how well our memory of the "dangerous aspects" of the past has been erased. My students, for example, are virtually unacquainted with labor history or labor perspectives on history. They are shocked by stories of the "labor wars" of the late-nineteenth century. They see Vietnam through the eyes of Ronald Reagan: a noble war undercut by a drug-crazed student anti-war movement and a liberal lack of resolve.

The Iranian Hostage Crisis is a dim vestige of a distant past where an innocent America was brutalized by non-Christian savages. Let's expand on this issue for a moment to illustrate my point. It is fascinating to watch my students respond to the questions: Why were the Iranian people so angry at the U.S.? What might induce millions of Iranians to march through the streets of Tehran chanting death to the American devils? I rarely find a student who has learned in a school context that there was a historical dimension to the Hostage Crisis. They have been taught as if the crisis suddenly sprang out of history, completely out of context. Products of a media culture and schools which avoid perspectives unfavorable to the "the national interest," my students are shocked when they hear and read about the role of the CIA in overthrowing the legitimate Iranian government in 1953. The government had to go, U.S. officials agreed, when it refused to allow U.S. military installations to be constructed on the Soviet border in the North of Iran. Shocked by such revelations, my students not only begin to empathize with the anger of the Iranian people, but they begin to ask about the information they have been fed by the schools and the media. My students are fascinated by the different perspectives on the situation brought by Iranian and other foreign students. Issues such as this one begin to stimulate an awareness of the ways that their consciousness has been constructed, an appreciation of how power legitimates itself in their own lives.

SHIRLEY: Fascinating. Let's examine this concept of consciousness construction. What are we talking about here?

JOE: I use the term *critical constructivism* to help us understand the way our identity is shaped and our perception of the world is formed. A critical constructivist sees a socially constructed world and asks what the forces are that shape our construction. We need to abandon the naïve notion that our view of reality is freely made and is unaffected by power interests in the larger society. In order to understand our constructions, we must familiarize ourselves with these power interests. In a critical pedagogy, this attempt to familiarize our students with these power interests becomes a central goal. Thus, how we think becomes a political issue, not just a feature of the science of cognition. From our theoretical frames, we begin to examine cognition from a critical postmodern perspective—in the process questioning the assumptions of a cognitive science which has traditionally excluded consideration of power and social context. If critical constructivism was to be taken seriously, it would revolutionize not only elementary and secondary schools, but higher education as well. No educational institution would be unaffected, even colleges of education would be dramatically altered. A critical constructivist teacher education would transform colleges of education into serious academic institutions dedicated to an intense socio-psychological analysis of the effects of schooling. The ways that women and men construct their consciousnesses and the role that education plays in that process would become a guiding concern of teacher education—a concern which would necessitate interdisciplinary concerns and research alliances across the university.

In this context of revolutionizing the school through a critical constructivist awareness of how the "self" is produced, we are brought back to our concerns with multiculturalism. As travelers have discovered, the attempt to understand the cultural schematas of peoples from other countries often allows for a recognition of belief systems, cognitive styles, and social assumptions in oneself. When students widen their cognitive and epistemological circles by exposure to non-Western perspectives, they gain understandings which become extremely valuable in the media-saturated postmodern world. This is what critical postmodernist pedagogy refers to as learning via the power of difference. Peter and I find it phenomenal that our efforts to promote this power of difference in our advocacy of a critical multiculturalism is framed as an unwelcomed threat to American traditions and values by the right-wing. Conservatives seem to conveniently forget that the American future will be marked by greater and greater non-Anglo populations. In this twenty-first century society, the basic ability to live together and learn from one another in solidarity may be considered a survival skill. Instead of circling the Anglo wagons and attempting to save "civilization" by emphasizing our "true" language, D'Souza, Bennett, Bloom, Ravitch, and Finn might *have* to begin listening to our warnings.

SHIRLEY: What is wrong with the New Right's concept of "citizen"?

PETER: We need to consider the concept of citizen in the context of the historically developed patterns of capital accumulation and their corresponding relations of production. We also need to view citizenship in terms of how people are inscribed within civil society on the basis of gender, age, race and ethnicity, and how this occurs geopolitically in terms of locally and nationally structured identities. How are personal and public experiences co-articulated within the framework of class, gender, race and ethnic formations? Linked to capital and forms of state regulation with respect to resources? Identity formation and the construction of the self are not simply a matter of what discursive categories are available to individuals but how interests are mobilized in the securing of certain discursive forms and material benefits. The New Right perversely hides how its own perspective on citizenship is linked to how the state obliges itself to produce specific dispositions in its "youth": obedience to authority, deference to the symbols of nationhood, respect for authority and state agencies, competitiveness and a desire to compete for material possessions, and the measurement of success in terms of material wealth. The New Right's uncritical appeal to a reified notion of "citizen" is dangerous. Much of the resurgence of ethnic identities we are seeing in Eastern Europe is the result of a reaction to bureaucratically imposed homogenization and tyranny. But identity politics does not need to be cast as a politics of either separatism or the more liberal form of pluralism in which citizenship is achieved at the price of becoming married to Dan Quayle's axiologically bourgeois vision of the suburban dream.

Society is not post-conflictual. We need to recognize and appreciate difference. Our identities as citizens should not be premised on the happy idiocy of Quayle's partisan and silver-spooned vision of Mr. Rogers meets John Birch at a spelling bee where all the words are limited to two syllables.

SHIRLEY: Is it fair to say that the right wing equates good citizenship with a form of selfish, egocentric, socially unconscious, profit-seeking?

PETER: I think that's well put, Shirley. I believe that too much emphasis on the profit motive may be unhealthy for democracy and cooperative self-determination and social justice. In fact, I think racism and sexism have become an internal condition for current forms of capitalism. In my opinion, the American public—and especially teachers—need to be wary of a conservative vision of democracy that partakes of a mixture of Sunday barbeque banality, American gladiator jock sniffery, AMWAY consciousness and the ominous rhetoric of Conan the American's "new world order" jingoism. What kind of citizens do these conservative educators want produced by the schools? I think it's quite obvious that they want citizens who are committed to entrepreneurship, who will fight to keep English the official language of the country, who give lip service to democracy while really advocating a consumer culture, who will cherish and defend neocolonial imperatives of a new world order ruled by the United States. With the Cold War over, the New Right and its National Association of Scholars are attacking the so-called "politically correct" leftists in the academy. Those few professors who are openly speaking out against sedimented forms of racism, debilitating acts of patriarchy, and homophobia are being labeled as anti-Western and anti-democratic, as separatist and ethnocentric, as the return of the storm troopers, as leftist fascists. The left (which really doesn't exist in this country in the sense of an organized presence engaged to offer a socialist alternative to advanced capitalism) has been invented as a cadre of propagandists—"academic dragoons of Newthink" bent on silencing free expression and exercising censorship on behalf of a thought police resurrected from the universe of Orwell and Foucault's panopticon. Right-wing students and faculty who fear the appearance of the "New Inquisition" pine that they can no longer make jokes or unguarded statements about women, gays and lesbians, or racial minorities. Is it political opportunism or the promotion of tolerance and free speech when the New Right attacks affirmative action and minority group efforts to develop curricula and pedagogical practices that fight racism, sexism, and Eurocentric and white supremacist views of knowledge and identity? When I spoke recently at the University of Milwaukee, there were some protestors who came bound and gagged because they felt that leftist educators were taking away their right to freedom of speech. These are the same people who want to abolish "ethnic studies" programs.

When this same New Right ideology pits the search for truth against the so-called decline in academic standards brought on by lesbian, gay, and ethnic studies, not only is social amnesia involved, but an assumption that truth is immutable and seamless—that it is separate from forms of advocacy, that it ontologically resides in a metaphysical pasture for academics to graze in in order to become bloated with the truth. In other words, somehow knowledge lies outside the realm of social conflict and cultural interest. It is a knowledge that is pre-modern, and holistic—knowledge that existed before the advent of the social sciences and the logocentricity of the natural sciences. But truth is not something that can be investigated outside of its historical, geo-political or sociological situatedness or contextual specificity. Of course, the New Right needs an enemy after the collapse of communism—a Cold War substitute for the 1990s and the Willie Horton campaign of 1988. It needs a scapegoat for the shrinking U.S. economy and expanding minority populations. So they pick on the 4.9% of all U.S. college professors who call themselves leftist.

We need to retreat from metaphysical truths to ground our identities—what Wlad Godzich calls a "metasocial guarantor"—some transcendental principle such as God or what the reductionist Marxists refer to as the "laws of history." The French Revolution sanctified reason as a metasocial guarantor, and Godzich calls this reason one "that in its universality required the conquest of the world in order to free it from its pre-rational state." I like to think of this quotation in terms of how it applies to the Unites States. It seems to me that the conservative multiculturalists are still sanctifying Western rationality which they equate with being American. And non-Western people—people they associate with the Third World—are seen as non-rational, "ethnic" peoples. They prefer to see Toni Morrison, for instance, as non-Western. It seems to me that we should be wary about fixing our identities through such an appeal to a metasocial guarantor such as Western rationality because this tends to lead to a war against otherness on behalf of imperialist masculinity. It worries me. Right now the left is the scapegoat for anti-Western sentiment.

SHIRLEY: You mean Dan Quayle's "cultural elite"? Hasn't he managed to create his own Willie Horton in the leftist intellectual? The Bush-Quayle enemies list continues to grow.

PETER: Absolutely! And they conflate expressions of anti-racism, anti-sexism, and other progressive politics with intellectual barbarism.

This is not to suggest that marginalized minorities and groups who are critical of the dominant culture are always immune to dogmatism, but the "political correctness" controversy is really a misunderstanding of the political economy of knowledge—of the knowledge industry itself—and how certain knowledges become legitimated over others under the guise of objectivity and neutrality. All knowledge is *situated knowledge*, all knowledge is *partial and contingent*, and all knowledge is embedded in *contexts of production and reception*. People who are taking a progressively radical stand on issues involving the production of meaning are suddenly branded as *propagandists* and *fascists of the mind*.

The New Right talks about diversity and difference in terms of pseudoquality wrapped up in a counterfeit democracy of flags and emblems—as if diversity were simply accretive, benevolently allowing other voices to *add themselves* to the mainstream—voices that have yet to share the benefits of the American dream. In my mind, diversity is something altogether different—it is not a collection of ethnic "add-ons," like different flavored toppings on a vanilla ice cream sundae—rather, it is a form of *thinking from the margins*, seeing Native peoples, Latinos, and African Americans not as interest groups to be added on to a *pre-existing pluralism*, but rather as being at the very core of the American experience from the beginning—each offering unique dialogical perspectives to both national and local experiences. The oppressed—because they are obliged by circumstance and the imperatives of survival to know both the dominant and marginal culture—are ideally placed to launch such a politics of refusal against the oppression brought about by corporate capitalist power.

As Chandra Talpade Mohanty notes, difference cannot be formulated as simply negotiation among culturally diverse groups against a backdrop of presumed cultural homogeneity. Difference is the recognition that all knowledges are forged in histories and relations of power.

But I would ask: Is knowledge ever constructed outside the realm of the political? Whose knowledge is *most privileged?* What vantage point do we take when we proclaim what "fits in" to the so-called pre-existing pluralism and what does not? Why is it that Western values of reason, neutrality and objectivity are privileged over Afrocentric ones? Does this have anything to do with preserving what Chomsky calls "the welfare state for the rich"? Does it mean creating a common culture that is colorblind? A unity that does not recognize color? Does it really mean achieving racelessness or are the terms colorblind, racelessness, unity, and pluralism just pseudonyms for *white?*

Watching the march of nations recently on the TV coverage of the summer Olympics in Barcelona, I was struck by the insidiously banal comments of the U.S. newscaster who referred to Costa Rica, Colombia and some other countries as "discovered" by Columbus. Were there no inhabitants living in these places before Columbus arrived?

SHIRLEY: What do you feel are some of the problems facing radical teacher intellectuals committed to a critical multiculturalism?

PETER: We can't simply assume Latin American pedagogies of liberation—such as Paulo Freire's brilliant work—are transposable without taking into critical consideration their historical and cultural situatedness in Brazilian life. We need to be careful we don't betray the oppressed in our academic constructions of them as objects of our research that give our roles legitimacy. As intellectuals, we can work in solidarity with the oppressed and also extend our work into non-academic publics. But we must do so thoughtfully and conscientiously, without assuming the role of the cultural expert. Teachers as cultural workers need to make links among academic and popular and public cultures. But in doing so, they need to remain cautious about administering new forms of authoritarianism.

Our conceptual encapsulizations as academics tend to put minority cultures and oppositional cultures and subcultures in formaldehyde, turning them into frozen and lifeless artifacts fit for the cultural mausoleum. Or else we romanticize them and nominate them as candidates for the cultural vanguard or avant-garde. Furthermore, we too often mistake the cultural production of books, articles, and democratic classroom experiences as the most effective form of resistance to domination. The educational and academic spheres are only several of many oppositional public spheres.

We also need to question when the development of multicultural theory actually reinforces the distance between the margins and centers of power by our rhetoricizing moves as theorists. But I must say that critical multiculturalism is, overall, a worthy endeavor and necessary to combat corporate multiculturalism. What we, as teachers, need to understand is that the view of multiculturalism proposed by Ravitch, Cheney and others is really compatible with the corporate view which is designed to put local cultures into the service of the nation state and the global centers of power. It precipitates a conservative ideology of citizenship predicated upon possessive, consumer individualism and political consensualism.

Now that the liberal cry for disinterested knowledge, objectivity, and a neutral pluralism is being superceded by the New Right's clarion cry for the politicization of all cultural knowledge under the triumphalist banner of Western civilization, we need as educators and cultural workers, to engage in attempts to align our efforts as educators with progressive social movements. No, I'm not talking about constructing an ethically pure populism, but rather, joining in efforts to create civic, personal, public and institutional spaces of coordinated activism, spaces of critique and refusal, of possibility and provisional utopian dreaming . . . spaces of reconfigured modes of sociality and reterritorialized desire—desire uncoupled from its circuits of corporate interest—forms of desire that can be re-coupled with discourses and social relations of freedom.

"Critical Multiculturalism and Democratic Schooling: An Interview with Peter McLaren and Joe Kincheloe" was originally published by Shirley Steinberg in the *International Journal of Educational Reform*, 1(4), pp. 392–405, 1992.

Interview 6

challenges and hopes: multiculturalism as revolutionary praxis

Gustavo Fischman

Gustavo Fischman is one of the brightest young scholars in the field of education. Originally from Argentina, he lectures worldwide. Gustavo has taught me a great deal about the politics of education and he continues to do so. I had just published my book, Revolutionary Multiculturalism *and was looking forward to seeing how it would be received. The book itself was a critique of mainstream multiculturalism. I wrote it just as I was adopting a Marxist humanist analysis. If I could re-write the book, I would put greater emphasis on the relationship between race and class from a Marxist perspective. After this interview, Gustavo and I went on to co-author several articles together.*

GUSTAVO E. FISCHMAN: It is difficult to put a label on your work because you have written in so many different fields, ethnography, literacy, critical pedagogy, educational policy, curriculum, and sociology, but it appears to me that multiculturalism is a topic that crosses almost all your books and articles despite the disciplinary approach that happens to frame your project at any particular time.

PETER MCLAREN: That is true.

GUSTAVO: Among your many works, I recall four books that have multiculturalism in their title: *Multicultural Education and Critical Pedagogy* (edited with Christine Sleeter), *Critical Multiculturalism* (edited with Barry Kanpol), *Multiculturalismo Critico*, which you did for Cortez Publishers and the Paulo Freire Institute in Saõ Paulo, Brazil (and which I understand has a wide readership in Brazil), and your most recent book, *Revolutionary Multiculturalism*. There are also other books and several articles of yours that are very prominent in the field of multicultural education: *Critical Pedagogy and Predatory Culture*, and *Between Borders* (edited with Henry Giroux).

PETER: Yes, all my books deal to a greater or lesser extent with issues of race, class, gender, sexuality, the state, and power and capitalist exploitation. My readers know this and I have been fortunate to be able to publish so much since coming to the United States from Canada in 1985.

GUSTAVO: Multicultural education is a vast, complex, and in no way a homogeneous pedagogical movement. Where do you locate your works within the field?

PETER: I have learned a lot from Jim Cummings, Enrique Trueba, James Banks, Gloria Ladson-Billings, Sonny San Juan, Emily Hicks, Carl Grant, Sonia Nieto, Rudolfo Chávez Chávez, Herman Garcia, Rudy Torres, David Theo Goldberg, Warren Crichlow, Cornel West, bell hooks, Cameron McCarthy, Christine Sleeter, Antonia Darder, Joyce King, Donaldo Macedo, Joe Kincheloe, Henry Giroux, and a host of other scholars and activists. They are superb and committed scholars. What makes my work a bit different is that it is underwritten by a serious critique of global capitalism and works out of a Marxist problematic.

Some people have accused me of stressing class issues to the exclusion of race, ethnicity, and gender, for instance, because I am a working-class white guy from *el norte del norte* (Canada), but quite honestly I do believe that capitalist exploitation is the motor of the kind of systematic, institutionalized racism that has been so perniciously present in Western industrialized and post-industrialized nations. With all of our talk about racist formations, racialized discourses, binary thinking, Eurocentric tropes and conceits, and floating signifiers (which is fine, as far as sophisticated scholarly exegesis goes) we have forgotten all too perilously that racism and sexism are predicated upon the economic exploitation of the many by the few.

The academy is a vicious and hypocritical place that breeds neo-liberals masquerading as leftist multiculturalists and opportunists trying to pass themselves as selfless "solidarists" in the struggle for justice. People working across differences and building alliances are exceptions. Antonia Darder, who has initiated the call for the creation of the California Consortium for Critical Pedagogy, is one of those rare and exceptional scholars.

GUSTAVO: As a multiculturalist, how do you come to terms with your own whiteness?

PETER: My whiteness (and my maleness) is something I cannot escape no matter how hard I try. Early economic hardship cannot eradicate my whiteness because, as Mike Dyson notes, there is always a "negative culpability" on the part of whites, in the form of pleasure that some poor whites derive from not being Black. Poor whites (whites in general) still occupy a privileged space on the comparative racial taxonomy. In pursuing these questions, in living my own life as a traitor to whiteness, I cannot become lazy by failing to interrogate the epistemological, political, and ethical assumptions of my own practice. If all whites are racists at some level, then we must struggle to become anti-racist racists. We must always rethink our positionalities, platforms and affiliations, without defaulting the main game, which is to resist and transform the market system based on the maximization of corporate profits. After all, it was this system that enslaved millions of Africans in the United States and still disproportionately exploits people of color worldwide.

Of course it is not capitalism alone that achieved this. Exploitation is also made possible by systems of classification that grew out of religion, social and natural sciences frameworks that justified slavery, and other forms of oppression on the basis of the supposedly sacred and/or scientific inferiority of certain groups of people. While battling the leviathan of United States transnational capitalism and its neo-colonial clientele, and the alienation and exploitation that mark so many cultural practices of this society, the struggle ahead must include inventing life forms for ourselves where racism, sexism and homophobia have no place, where joy and love can flourish, and where we can live unfettered by the determinism of capitalist progress. This is no simple romantic anti-capitalism I am endorsing, but a challenge grounded in the tough task of historical materialist analysis and the imperative of class struggle.

GUSTAVO: What you just said reminds me that in a recent issue of *Educational Theory*, you were criticized for using a language that includes a clear call for the educational left to rethink class struggle in light of global capitalism.

The language seems quite close to traditional Marxist positions and a clear dismissal of identity politics.

PETER: I am not an old-style manifesto Marxist, as some of my critics in the *Educational Theory* issue that you mentioned have suggested, nor am I a postmodernist as other people seem to think (possibly because an article I wrote in 1986 was the first to deal with postmodernism in a U.S. educational journal so I have been told). I do learn a lot from my critics, but in this case they appeared insistent on reading much into my text that was not there. A deeper and more nuanced reading of my essay would, I hope, reveal the following. I am not against the politics of identity. After all, as Robin Kelley has so lucidly pointed out, identity politics has always been central to working-class movements. It has greatly enriched our conception of class. We should not forget that African-American social movements have been in solidarity with workers, Black male abolitionists supported women suffrage, Black radicals a century ago lent a helping hand to Irish self-determination and worked against the Chinese Exclusionary Act. Kelley also notes that in those alliances, gender and class can be conceived as "affiliations" that build unity by supporting other people's struggles.

My point was that some versions of postmodernist and post-structuralist theorizing tend to ignore the perils of global capitalism and the misery it is creating for so many people throughout the world. My argument is that we need to re-set our sights on anti-capitalist struggle before the noose around our neck is drawn too tightly. I invited readers to see how global capitalism colonizes, commodifies, and fetishizes across race, class, gender lines. Even though I explicitly stated that class should not be privileged over race, gender or sexuality and that the important issue is to understand how capitalism has reterritorialized race, class, and gender formations, some critics saw my latest works as a call for returning to the old days of Bowles and Gintis, or they claimed, rather ludicrously, that I blamed postmodern theory for the current success of global capitalism! Frankly, I still think we can learn much from the early work of Bowles and Gintis.

I think that, in general, there are postmodernist educators who will raise an objection to the "subjunctive mode" of my address—that "we should" do this or do that. They are, understandably, concerned that efforts at revolutionary praxis may contain hidden oppressions, or that the cure I propose is perhaps worse than the disease. But all that they offer in the place of revolutionary praxis is assuming an "ironic mode of address" or recognizing the indeterminacy of agency, or the multiple locations of subjectivity, and so on.

Well, I would rather build momentum against global exploitation on the basis of provisional directive than on the basis of linguistic indeterminacy, or the announcement of the impossibility of critical pedagogy to contribute to the struggle against exploitation and the process of liberation.

"Peter McLaren: A Call for a Multicultural Revolution" was published by Gustavo Fischman in *Multicultural Education*, *vol.* 6, no. 4 (Summer), 1999, 32–34. The interview was reprinted in *Multicultural Education*, Ninth Edition, McGraw-Hill. 2002. It was also reprinted in *Notes & Abstracts in American International Education*. Number 87 (*Spring*), 1999, 3–8.

Interview 7

pedagogies of dissent and transformation: a dialogue about postmodernity, social context, and the politics of literacy

Kris Gutierrez

Kris Gutierrez is one of the leading figures in cultural historical activity theory. This article is the first in a number of collaborations we have done. At the time this interview took place, I had just moved to Westwood from Cincinnati, Ohio, and was getting accustomed to my new appointment at UCLA (and learning a lot from Kris about issues of race, class, and gender in the context of Los Angeles). Kris and I realized that we had much in common in our work in multiculturalism. I had been made the international editor for the International Journal of Educational Leadership *(which has now become a mainstream journal) and this was the perfect opportunity to get our ideas across to a wide audience. My attachment to the discourse of postmodern theory is very much in evidence in this dialogue, which took place in Westwood, Los Angeles and Culver City (1993).*

KRIS GUTIERREZ: Your work on schooling, identity, and critical pedagogy is noted for its attempt to locate itself in a discussion of larger social contexts of consumer capitalism an identity formation. You are noted for discussing social and cultural issues related to power that exist outside of the classroom as much as you are nor dealing with these issues as they inscribe social relations inside the classroom. This is one of the reasons that I find your work interesting and important. The language that you use is often quite literary and is situated on trans-disciplinary theoretical terminology where post-structuralism and theories of post-colonialism, among other theoretical perspectives, play a significant role. I think, however, that this mixture of the theoretical and, if you will, poetical, has both advantages and disadvantages. While it gives you new angles and perspectives on the production of subjectivity within capitalist social formations, don't you think it tends to restrict your audience to specialists in the critical social sciences and is less likely to find its way into teacher education courses, where I would think that you would want your work to be taken up? Your view of contemporary culture is sometimes considered to be quite pessimistic—although far from nihilistic—and I wonder if your criticisms of everyday life in the United States are perhaps deliberate attempts at overstatement for the sake of shocking your readers into an awareness of the very serious social problems that face us. For instance, I read some comments by you recently in which you talked about the "structural unconscious" of the United States resembling the minds of serial killers such as Ted Bundy. You write in the book *Thirteen Questions*, "Serial killer Ted Bundy has donated his multiple texts of identity to our structural unconscious and we are living them." Is this a motivated exaggeration, a form of theoretical hyperbole for the sake of making a point about the violence that pervades everyday life?

PETER MCLAREN: Yes and no, Kris. I consider my writing to be simultaneously cynical and utopian. I think it was Adorno who once said something to the effect that in every exaggeration there exists some truth and, of course, as somebody who lives in Los Angeles, you don't need to be reminded about violence. Perhaps I focus on the more violent effects of capitalism on social formations because I really do believe that violence exists at the very heart of post-industrial capitalism as a structural precondition for it, that capitalism, in fact, is steadfastly predatory on power and that it fundamentally constitutes what could be called a "necessary contingency" within what has come to be called "the cultural logic of late capitalism." This is perhaps part of what Arthur Kroker refers to as "the contemporary human situation of living at the violent edge of primitivism and simulation, of an infinite reversibility in the order of things wherein only the excessive cancellation of difference through violence re-energizes the process."

KRIS: What about Los Angeles? In his book, *City of Quartz*, Mike Davis has described Los Angeles as existing "on the bad edge of postmodernity." Can you give us a cultural autopsy report?

PETER: Los Angeles is hemorrhaging from its social wounds. The steel fist of despotic capitalism has pulverized the soul of this city. The cowardly federal retreat from the big cities is certainly not going to help stop the bleeding of Los Angeles, a city now referred to by some as the new capital of the Third World. In fact, Los Angeles is facing at the present moment the worst economic crisis since 1938. People seem to forget that after the Watts rebellion in 1965, there were 164 major riots that spread through urban ghettoes across the United States—a period sometimes referred to as the "Second Civil War." This provoked Lyndon Johnson's administration to push its Model Cities Bill through Congress. Yet this historical fact and the recent Los Angeles rebellion have not provoked any serious action on the part of the federal government. You mentioned Mike Davis, whose work I admire very much. Davis has chronicled the crisis of Los Angeles very thoroughly and my comments simply rehearse what he has said on a number of occasions. The current crisis of Los Angeles has to be seen in the context of the combination of international finance capital and low-wage immigrant labor and what some have called the "Third Worlding" of the city (although I have problems with the way this tem is frequently used). There is little cause for optimism about the future of Los Angeles when the czar of the 1984 Olympics, Peter Ueberroth, is given the task of rebuilding Los Angeles through corporate coalition-building and voluntarism. Current government responses that center around the creation of micro enterprise zones and "infrastructure" are not a great improvement on the former Bush administration's efforts to repackage existing programs under the banner of the new while at the same time preventing small business loans and food stamps from reaching needy neighborhoods. Not to mention Dan Quayle's advice to sell the Los Angeles Airport to help rebuild the city after the uprising.

KRIS: Federal disinvestment policies have had a devastating effect on the city. But the problem is more widespread than California. Key industrial states are reducing welfare and educational entitlements. It's shameful that this could happen in a country that poured so much money into the Gulf War and the S&L bailout.

PETER: Mike Davis describes current government initiatives directed at rebuilding Los Angeles as "shoe string local efforts and corporate charity." He refers to government aid after rapid development of federal combat troops to South Central is little more than an "urban fire sale." I agree with Davis' criticism of the Republican war on big cities. During the Reagan-Bush era, big cities became what Davis describes as "the domestic equivalent of an insolvent, criminalized Third World whose only road to redemption is a combination of militarization and privatization." So now we're faced with that Davis sees as white flight to "edge cities" along the beltways and intercity corridors, the Latinization of manual labor, deficits in the jobs-to-housing ratios among Blacks, and the new segregation in cities that Davis refers to as "spatial apartheid."

KRIS: So how does this affect the average youth? I am the mother of a biracial twelve year old. Despite the fact that he has had access to and participation in academic, cultural, social, and political activities and experiences that privilege him in so many ways, his "Blackness/Latinoness," accentuated by his large frame and his ability and willingness to articulate elaborated socio-political analyses of his own life and the world around him, position him at the very margins, the borderlands, of most of his classroom communities. His strong literacy skills are not valued when they are used to write poems about the L.A. uprising or to critique or challenge the content of the classroom curriculum. For example, his honors history class was recently studying about Mecca. In an attempt to provide the students with a visual portrait of Mecca, the teacher brought in the videotape of the movie *X*. The teacher played a segment of the movie, the scene which shows Malcolm arriving in Mecca. After viewing this particular scene, the teacher asked the children to identify what was important. My son's hand shot up as he offered his response, "Well, I think that the fact that Malcolm is being followed by two white CIA agents as he goes to worship in Mecca is very interesting." He was publicly chastised for being off-topic, for not being focused. "We're studying Mecca, not Malcolm," quipped his teacher. "But can't we study history when we study geography?" asked my son. The teacher simply did not get it. His is not so much the "spatial apartheid" about which Davis writes. Instead, his is an "intellectual apartheid" that silences and marginalizes young adults in schools, particularly Black/Latino males, who take up various forms of resistance and contestation to demand the affirmation of their particular existences. But as Cornel West has asked, "How does one affirm oneself without reenacting negative black stereotypes or overreacting to white supremacist ideals?" How does this discourse of contestation not become what Foucault calls "reverse discourse?" As Henry Louis Gates, Jr., has written, this discourse "remains entrapped within the presuppositions of the discourse it means to oppose, enacts a conflict internal to that 'master discourse'"; but when the terms of argument have already been defined, it may look like the only form of contestation possible." How are these factors lived out in the everyday existence of today's urban students?

PETER: That's the key issue for me, Kris. I think we need to look beyond the transgressive desire of graffiti artists and taggers, P.T.A. groups, and anti-crime community activists to find the seedbeds of a new cultural politics. We need to begin the fight against racism and social injustice in the school. In doing so, educators need to ask themselves how students' identities are organized macrospatially and geopolitically as well as within the micropolitics of the classroom. How are students specifically positioned (in terms of race, class, gender, sexuality within the grid of late capitalist economic containment and socio-political control? How are their structures of affect (what Larry Grossberg calls "mattering maps") organized? How are students situated in both libidinal economies as well as conceptual ones? These are pressing issues, many of which have been addressed by people such as Henry Giroux, Chandra Mohanty, Larry Grossberg, bell hooks, Michele Wallace, and others. It's hard today to draw clear boundaries around the affective and cognitive modes of existence or even to identify ontological categories. This is partly due to the allegorical effects of technology, to what some writers refer to as hyper-reality or the imploded regions of cyberspace created by the new rhetoricity of our media-saturated lives. Identity has become fluid, reduced to an abstract code not simply of difference but also indifference. Today it is difficult to have an identity, let alone pursue one. We are all, in a very grave sense, always traveling incognito in hyper-reality. Students in classrooms are attempting to construct their identities through transgressive acts, through resisting those normalizing laws that render subversive, obscene and unthinkable contestatory possibilities and a pragmatics of hope.

KRIS: Fear has taken on a new meaning, it seems. It has become intensified in new ways.

PETER: Kris, I believe that we are witnessing the hyper-real formation of an entirely new species of fear. I live not far from the UCLA campus in Westwood and nearly every night I hear the wailing cries of drunken students, cries which at once evoke the empty humor of *Hee-Haw* and the more serious, reflective pain of youthful bodies responding to the slow commodification of their will under late capitalism. Their wails remind me of a desperate attempt to fill in the empty spaces of their souls with a presence-effect of pure intensity. I think that as teachers we need to ask ourselves: What does it mean to live in this fear in an arena of shifting forms of global capitalism? How does such fear direct urban policy and school policy? How is everyday life saturated by such fear and what role does this fear play in student learning? What kinds of learning need to take place in order to resist or overcome the fear of participating in the construction of terminal identities? What politics of liberation must be engaged in as part of a struggle for a better future for our schools and our youth who attend them? Brian Massumi has done a brilliant job in discussing the breaking down of the "humanistic" integrative strategy of Keynesian economics and the advent of "unapologetically ruthless strategies of displacement, fluidification, and intensification." We're talking here about the utilitarian and socially unrepentant dismantling of the welfare state and the restructuring and dissolution of identities and entire lives that follow such a dismantling. Briefly put, Kris, displacement refers to exporting industrial production to the "Third World," where the growing middle class there can provide an important market outlet for consumer durables. In the U.S. economies of the center, this means producing more information and communication services in new and mostly nonunionized domains, leaving youth to their "McJobs" (to adopt a term by Canadian novelist, Douglas Coupland in his book *Generation X*). Massumi uses the term "fluidification" to mean the increasing fluidity of capital and the workforce as well as increasing rapid product turnovers. Use-value in this case is increasingly replaced by image-value. Massumi uses the term "intensification" to refer to basically the merging of production and consumption, which is accompanied by the disappearance of leisure and a focus on self-improvement in the service of gaining a competitive edge in the marketplace. Massumi notes that the very contours of postmodern existence have become a form of surplus value as the wage relation virtually collapses into the commodity relation. Capitalism has colonized all geographical and social space and schools have not been immune. In fact, they are perhaps one of the most vulnerable social sites for this kind of colonization as we can see in the example of Channel One and the powerful forces that are being put in place by corporate logic to ensure the privatization of education. Massumi argues that capitalism is co-extensive with its own inside such that it has now become both a field of immanence and exteriority. There is no escape. There is only fear. Fear, reports Massumi, is now the objective condition of subjectivity in the era of late capitalism. In this sense, it means something more than a fear of downward mobility but rather the constitution of the self within a market culture and market morality. When non-market values disappear from everyday life—such as love and compassion—nihilism sets in. Cornel West speaks eloquently about this dilemma, especially in the context of urban settings.

I agree with Anthony Appiah when he says that Weber mistook the Enlightenment universalization of the secular for the triumph of instrumental reason. I believe, as does Appiah, that the Enlightenment has more to do with the transformation of the real into sign-value than it does with the incursion of instrumental rationality into the multiple spheres of the social. What Weber missed was the incorporation of all areas of public and private life into the money economy. There exists no autochthonous and monolithic space of pure culture or uncontaminated identity—everything has been commodified. Use-value is now supported by what Massumi calls "fulfillment-effect" or "image value." We are, all of us, subjects of capital—the point *d'appui* between wage relations and commodity relations, with commodification representing the hinge between the future and the past. According to Massumi, consummation and consumption are continually conflated under late capitalism, as we increasingly come to live in the time form of the future perfect or future anterior which can be expressed in the existential equation "will have bought = will have been." Surplus value has become, in effect, a metonym for everyday existence. Of course, all of this points to the urgency of understanding how students invest in their lives and bring meaning to everyday life. It suggests students need to understand more about the structural and more fluid contexts that produce their everyday lives and how their identities are constructed out of the vectors and circuits of capital, social relations, cultural forms, and relations of power. It means understanding more than simply how the media and dominant school curricula control the representation of the racialized "other" and influence our attitudes and desires.

I will be the first to emphasize the importance of understanding the politics of representation and the ways in which our subjectivities are constructed through the economies of signs in our media-saturated world. But as Giroux and others have emphasized, we need to go further than this. We need to understand how identities are produced through structural relations and constraints and the systems of intelligibility we have historically inherited and invented and which produce us on a daily basis. It means understanding the causes of oppression and exploitation and the material effects of economic practices and capitalist logics. Something that has struck me for quite some time has recently been articulated in a brilliant book by Rey Chow, *Writing Diaspora*. Global capitalism and its technological apparatuses of domination have ushered in what Chow refers to as "a universal speed culture." Here she is referring, after Virilio, to the mediatization of information. Such mediatization and human life, while incompatible, are now interchangeable. Electronic communication makes this possible. She notes that human labor is "finally exchangeable in digitalized form, without going through the stage of the concrete commodity whose mysteriousness Marx so memorably describes" (180). We now live in a world of what Chow calls "electronic immigrants" who work in countries such as India and the Soviet Union where well-trained but jobless technical professionals sell their labor-power for low wages to U.S. computer companies. They work through the phone lines (where there are no import duties) as cheap data processors. This digitalized form of labor has implications for how we should be developing critical forms of literacy in school. Moving now to the question of schooling, you have been developing a politics of literacy that I think is extremely important in helping educators to understand how knowledge is constructed within a variety of social contexts. Can you talk about the role social contact plays in your own work with immigrant Latino children?

KRIS: As you know, Peter, the focus of my work involves communities and schools here in Los Angeles and concerns itself primarily with how contexts of learning in schools influence the nature of the teaching and learning of literacy for linguistically and culturally diverse student populations. This means doing intensive ethnographic fieldwork in both the schools and the communities. In the course of doing this ethnographic work, we[1] have examined how certain contexts provide or deny access to particular forms of learning and literacy learning in particular. I believe this kind of work helps make visible the ways in which literacy instruction continues to function as a way of socializing historically marginalized students into particular forms of knowing and being that make access to critical forms and practices of literacy in either their first or second language difficult. What becomes evident in this work is how this socialization process cannot be understood apart from the socio-historical context in which it occurs and implicates how teachers' beliefs influence who gets to learn and how.

PETER: It seems to me, Kris, that teachers have a mandate to understand their own process of identity formation as well as those of their students. And in order to do this they need to at least have a rudimentary understanding of how their subjectivities are produced. They need to break free from the time-encrusted conceptions of identity, which, throughout the history of liberal humanism, have given credibility to the idea of the transparent ego, the autonomous will or the metaphysical illusion of self-identity. They need to escape from the hallucinatory idea of the boundaried, self-sufficient agent of history and see how seemingly anonymous political and economic structures colonize their life-worlds, instrumentalize forms of human agency, and sediment forms of desire. And then they need to engage such practices of colonization with some normative and regulative idea of justice and human freedom. Which is not to suggest teachers develop some metaphysical or transcendental platform of ethico-political judgment.

KRIS: That's true. However, this country has found itself completely unprepared and, in some cases, unwilling to address the educational and social needs of its multicultural student population. As a result of the shortage of multicultural, multilingual teachers, teachers are given emergency credentials to teach. These teachers have little opportunity to develop an understanding of what it means to teach in a multilingual and multicultural society. Moreover, teacher preparation programs continue to focus on the teaching and learning of monocultural and acontextual "models" of instruction such as the seven-step lesson plan. Who needs to be critical and reflective if the continued use of decontextualized "teacher proofed" methods, materials, and curricula is the normative practice in schools?

PETER: How do your studies help teachers in this task?

KRIS: I would argue that these long-term, classroom-based studies help us understand how teachers themselves, through their own experiences as students and through their preservice and inservice experience, have been socialized to particular understandings of "knowing" and "doing." Further constrained by deplorable working conditions and inadequate preparation, these teachers have little opportunity for reflective, critical practice. Understanding how these cycles of socialization influence classroom culture helps explain how the structures—that is, the social and discursive practices of many classrooms—reflect the relations of power and systems of knowledge distribution and the larger society. Critical theorists such as yourself, Michael Apple and Henry Giroux provide the needed meta-analysis of the function of schools in corporate capitalistic societies and the effects of its pedagogies on multicultural student populations. However, to truly transform the nature of teaching and learning requires work at multiple levels and requires the development of situated understandings of what counts as teaching and learning in classrooms and the larger social context.

PETER: I agree with you. Your attentiveness to multiple levels of analysis is what I admire so much about your work. Of course, social life would be impossible without some form of discursive and non-discursive domestication. All forms of nomination—of naming—are in some ways violent in that the world is reduced to objects of knowledge. I'm not opposed to naming social life but I am opposed to certain values that are embodied in the formation of the social at the level of micro-politics as well as macro-politics, whose persistent and motivated un-naming further reproduces existing relations of power and privilege.

KRIS: I know that some critical theorists are critical of microanalytic educational research and I certainly agree with much of the criticism, of the failure to locate the dynamics of classrooms and school life in larger socio-political contexts. I also believe that much of educational research does not discuss the ways in which hegemonic classroom practices are both the co-construction of particular sets of individuals and the reinstantiation of larger socio-historical processes and practices; however, I think that some critics of classroom-based, action-oriented research have not spent enough time in schools and thus, do not understand that unless we can also unpackage the construction of these hegemonic practices at the microlevel, we will not be able to assist teachers in their attempts to transform the contexts for learning and their roles in that process.

PETER: Yes, Kris. I agree. But we need to be wary of researchers who supply us with specific contextual data in ways that enable such data to become unwittingly recoded and reconverted so that teaching practices professing to be liberatory actually become complicit in the dominant ideology of colonialism.

KRIS: That's always an important issue. As Gramsci reminded us, intellectuals are experts in legitimation and in defining what counts as knowledge. I'm reminded of linguistic anthropologist Charles Goodwin's analysis of the first Rodney King case. In his essay, he demonstrated how the prosecution recodified the data frame by frame, created new schemas and provided an institutionalized scientific language to redefine Rodney King as the violent, crazed aggressor and the police's behavior as the appropriate and measured response to imminent danger. The data were recodified and, thus, redefined the obvious brutality. A good lesson here. The fact that a researcher is engaged in an anti-imperialist ethnographic study is no guarantee that a transformative politics and pedagogy will always emerge; it does not prevent at some level the recuperation of some of the very colonialist discourses one is contesting. That's what makes our work so difficult. I'm sure you noticed the reaction to Willis' *Learning to Labor* by feminist researchers and to your early ethnographic work. I believe some of the engagements you had in your formative years as an ethnographic researcher with your critics have helped deepen and extend your own methods of analysis.

PETER: I try to be ruthlessly self-critical about my own work. When you are engaged in a collective struggle, the stakes are always higher.

KRIS: The task for transforming instruction is an urgent one and, as you know, action-oriented, ethnographic research is one way of advancing this struggle. I believe that many teachers recognize the need for radical change. But teachers also need assistance in reimagining instructional contexts in which a problem-posing curriculum, an organic curriculum, emerges from the socio-cultural and linguistic experiences of the participants, contests in which the teaching and learning of literacy leads to critical, reflective practice.

PETER: Kris, elaborate if you would on the kind of ethnographic work that you feel is central to the emancipatory agenda of criticalists in the field.

KRIS: I'm interested in ethnographic research that is informed by transdisciplinary work—cross-cultural, socio-cultural, socio-political, and socio-historical perspectives concerning the relationships among language, development, culture and power. The work of Jean Lave, Barbara Rogoff, Elinor Ochs, and Marjorie Goodwin comes to mind. It is these kinds of studies that I believe are extremely useful in helping us understand the socio-historical and socio-cultural nature of development and in producing contextualized or situated understandings of the effects of current schooling practices on particular groups of students. But such work has to also have a social and political agenda to be transformative.

PETER: When you talk about effects on "particular groups of students," I take it that you mean the contextual specificity of schooling practices in relation to the construction of gendered, classed, and racialized subjects.

KRIS: Precisely. Classroom-based research that identifies what counts as knowledge in classrooms and that describes how that knowledge is constructed, as well as whose knowledge gets constructed, is essential to transforming schools from the bottom-up and for understanding the social construction of classroom culture, of how gendered, classed and racialized subjects are constructed. The hegemonic practices that structure the teacher-centered pedagogy of so many of the classrooms of bicultural students, for example, must be unpackaged at the micro level; that is, in the moment-to-moment interactions of teacher and students as they participate in everyday classroom routines. I have found that this kind of research provides teachers with both the theoretical and analytical tools, as well as a language, for transforming their own pedagogies. This process of becoming a critical teacher/researcher, however, requires a redefinition of the hierarchical social relationships between researcher and classroom teacher; it requires movement away from the traditional objectification of those studies to action-oriented research in which both teacher/researcher and researcher are brought together to define the research agenda, as well as their own positions in those processes. In short, these research agendas have social and political consequences.

PETER: What concerns me about the hegemonic articulations of dominant schooling practices is the way in which teachers participate in institutionalized structures, practices, and discourses that set up forms of racial differentiation and differential exclusion. It is the "whiteness" of the dominant ideology that metonymizes the standard curricula and constructs the legitimating norms for our pedagogies. I'm talking here about what David Theo Goldberg refers to as "the constitution of alterity." Goldberg is referring to the hold of racialized discourses and racist exclusions over subject formation and expression. I don't think that, as educators, we have carefully thought through this issue in our day-to-day teaching practices, especially the way in which racist discourses become conjoined with the discourses of class, gender, nation, and capitalism. As Goldberg notes, all racisms have to do with exclusions on the basis of belonging to particular racial groups, even though there is not a single transhistorical meaning of the work "race." I think we need to do more ethnographic work on how racial groups are constituted discursively and how race is inscribed by the interests of different groups and institutions and how racial preferences are assigned. Some of my recent visits to Brazil have been very illuminating in terms of understanding the discursive constitution of racialized subjects. For instance, racialized descriptions of individuals based on morphology and skin color are much more nuanced there. Some of the descriptive categories include the mulatto escuro (dark skin) and the mulatto claro (light skin), which refer to persons of mixed racial groups (Caucasian and Afro-Brazilian). The sarara has light skin with blonde or red kinky hair and varied facial features, while the moreno has dark curly hair but light skin that is not white. The cabo verde has thin lips and a narrow straight nose, whereas the preto retinto has black skin and a broad nose and kinky hair. The cabra and cabrocha are lighter than the preto but darker than the cabo verde. Whites are also subclassified according to skin color, hair, and facial attributes. Here in the U.S. our system of classification is primarily in terms of binary oppositions—black versus white—whereas in Brazil there is a complex system of differences based more on distinctions. But these distinctions are still made on the basis of privileging whiteness. One of my students recently pointed out how offensive the term "mulatto" actually is, since it derives from the term "mule." Whiteness is still a marker of special distinction and one has to see this historically and link it to the capitalist elites who have the power to suture racist ideological discourses to material relations of political, social and economic advantage. How will global capitalism continue to reinforce such distinctions? That, to me, is an important issue. We need more qualitative work in this area.

KRIS: But these distinctions are also made here in the U.S. For example, Chicano sociologists Eddie Telles and Ed Murguia have identified how phenotype influences which Chicanos have access to particular academic and economic opportunities. Still, I agree that we need more qualitative work that allows us to see how privileging on the basis of whiteness, language and class is instantiated in the classroom. I also believe that qualitative work that is informed by a very different epistemology allows us to see the effects of uni-directional socialization processes of schools. For example, the socializing nature of institutional contexts is made evident in the institutional nature of the classroom discourse and interaction among participants and in the instantiation of teacher beliefs in the contexts for learning. For example, we have observed how the uniform turn-taking pattern of speech in the many classrooms we have studied exhibits overwhelming adherence to institutionally appropriate procedures—procedures that are both historically and socially situated. In particular, a differential and restricted system of knowledge distribution and access to meaningful conversation and participation characterize the normative teaching and learning practices of many classrooms of linguistically and culturally diverse children. In these contexts, we found that the rules and rights of participation were set by the teacher; that is, the teacher determined who was allowed to speak, how often, for what purpose. Thus, the social hierarchy and the asymmetrical social relationships among participants and their roles in the learning process privileged teacher's knowledge in the knowledge exchange system. Consequently, the linguistic and socio-cultural experiences of these Latino children rarely became incorporated into the classroom narratives, as they were routinely denied access to meaningful and legitimate participation; that is, access to practice as a means of learning. Moreover, access to the means and forms of learning for Latino children is restricted at several levels of instruction. For example, these students are provided limited opportunities to develop comprehensive literacy skills (i.e., reading, writing, talking, critical thinking, as well as the socio-cultural knowledge needed for successful participation in this discourse community) in both their native and second language—they have few opportunities to become biliterate. Further, the classroom discourse which serves as the medium of instruction is itself restrictive and thus limits opportunities for students to engage in and produce the very discourse they are expected to learn. Even when they are encouraged to produce written and oral text, they are not encouraged to use literacy in ways that allow them to narrate their own experiences, much less to critique the socio-political and economic realities of their everyday lives. In this way, both the language of instruction and the form of discourse reconstruct and preserve the traditional forms of language use, interaction and the traditional knowledge exchange system constitutive of teacher-centered instruction—instruction that is centered around a decontextualized and uncritical curriculum. Thus, the relationship between discourse, power and forms of knowledge is made evident in everyday practices of literacy instruction. (See Gutierrez & Larson, 1994, for more discussion.)

Current language practices in schools, despite attempts to incorporate bilingual instruction, provide the most effective means of denying access to both knowledge and practice. Richard Ruiz's research on language policies and practices, for example, points out that particular language policies are, in fact, responses to the presence of particular language communities rather than a need or desire to improve or expand language practices. Current language policies aimed at quickly moving children from native language usage to English are no different.

Such language programs are historically rooted in the policies and practices of a monocultural and monolingual society in which assimilation is highly valued and necessary. Multiculturalism and multilingualism are seen as threats to the social, political and cultural stability of this country. In these times of economic crisis, as support for the wave of anti-immigrant legislation increases, it becomes even more critical to understand how these sentiments manifest themselves in school policies and practices, in classroom instruction.

In our literacy studies, we find that the linguistic, economic, educational and socio-cultural needs of immigrant Latino children, particularly the Mexican immigrant, are still defined by the same Eurocentric lens used to define earlier immigrant experiences. However, these children are not monocultural or monolingual; they and their families transmigrate from Los Angeles to Mexico, for example, at least several times each year. The sociocultural, political and linguistic realities of their everyday lives require them to draw on their bicultural experiences and their various languages and discourses. If we continue to define these students' experience as being similar to the immigrant experience of European-American and even of other linguistically and culturally different immigrants, we simply will not be able to understand the educational and larger social needs of this immigrant student population. In defining them as traditional immigrants, we fail to understand how transmigration better explains their existence; to understand how these students are not monocultural but bicultural children in a multicultural society. From this perspective, the linguistic and cultural characteristics of this student population are not the same as those of children who have previously immigrated to this country. Thus, a more appropriate response to the linguistic needs of these students would be to create language policies that move beyond monolingualism and bilingualism to policies that promote biliteracy; that is, language practices that focus on the acquisition of a more comprehensive set of literacy skills, including writing, in both the native and second language.

Such policies and practices acknowledge the complex linguistic and social needs of a multicultural society. Further, this recognition is an important first step in redefining bicultural children as a tremendously valuable national resource. This redefinition, however, will necessarily challenge the folk knowledge that currently informs so much of school practice and will also challenge current attitudes that underlie the growing anti-immigrant sentiment in our country.

PETER: One of the crucial issues for criticalists working in the field of literacy is to rethink the conditions of possibility for the subaltern to speak, to escape the labyrinth of subjugation, to make critical counterstatements against the logic of domination that informs the dominant white supremacist ideology of patriarchal capitalism and to transform the ideological precepts that make up the "imponderability" of everyday life where social relations of power and privilege are naturalized throughout the curriculum. As Brackette Williams has pointed out, if you use the term "American" without a hyphen you are taken to be white and if you do hyphenate the term, then you are not only categorized as non-white but also as "ethnic." Non-white groups are often defined in our schools as "problems," a status which Vine Deloria argues "relegates minority existence into an adjectival status within the homogeneity of American life." The conservative multiculturalists writing under the sign of whiteness are trying to protect the unitary cohesiveness of cultural life, making culture isomorphic with the logic of assimilation and homogenization and a unified racio-national configuration. Even the difference-in-unity of the liberals and left liberals attempts a cultural balancing act in which harmony and consensus are sought while minorities continue to be excluded and oppressed. Interestingly, David Theo Goldberg suggests that capitalism's new demands for flexible accumulation loosen the socio-cultural and spatial boundaries that help to promote racialized antagonisms. There is a greater opportunity for transgressing "the established racialized limits of spatial confines and political imagination." At the same time, Goldberg notes that diversity in the public domain is challenged and delimited by the privatization of "univocality, exclusion, and exclusivity." In other words, diversity itself has become commodified in the interests of corporate capitalism. Multiculturalism is one of the hottest commodities presently circulating in the global marketplace. I want to know more about the direction of your work in relation to multiculturalism.

KRIS: In our work, we attempt to redirect the discourse on multiculturalism from an exclusively socio-political discussion to one that is also informed by theories and research that help us better understand the relationship between language, culture, development and power. To make the shift to include socio-cultural frames, however, requires an understanding of how socio-economic and socio-political forces gave rise to the emergence of multiculturalism. Although multiculturalism is most often identified with educational reform movements, the roots of multiculturalism are grounded in economic and socio-political processes. From a world systems perspective, for example, multiculturalism is the ideological reflection of two medium-term processes that have unfolded in the core area of the world system (e.g., Europe and the U.S. and the other rich countries of the advanced capitalist societies). The first process is a structural response produced by the workings of global capital in the post-World War II era. These world processes are eroding and recreating national boundaries and are diffusing the notion and practice of nation stateness. Thus, global production and simultaneous widespread global migration are challenging the notion of monoculturalism—a concept inextricably linked to the concept of nation building. From this perspective, multiculturalism has emerged as a consequence of global capitalism and its accompanying great migration has thrown monoculturalism into a crisis; multiculturalism in part, then, has emerged as an unintended consequence of these worldwide socio-economic processes.

PETER: But we need to be reminded of the specificity of these processes, especially in light of the growing nationalisms in places like the former Soviet Union and Yugoslavia.

KRIS: Of course. It's also important to understand that the need for multiculturalism has also been created by socio-political forces. For example, multiculturalism is also the socio-political challenge of the subordinated peoples both in the peripheral areas of the global world system and in the racialized areas of the core countries, the people participating in national liberation struggles in the Third World and those struggling for human and civil rights in the First World.

Multiculturalism is a new paradigm of race relations; a new concept of the proper relations between ethnic groups and races and is a reflection of the post-World War II challenge by people who have been marginalized and colonized. The ethnic and discriminated races have challenged the assumption of the inherent superiority of European cultures and have demanded the elevation of their cultures to equal those of Europe or white America. This particular sociological analysis attributes the emergence of multiculturalist movements to the inability of the monocultural systems to control the processes of globalizing capital and to enforce the sustained subordination of a racialized strata of its working people. However, until an overarching concept of nationhood is created—a concept that accommodates the globalizing tendencies of post-industrial capitalism and the inherent instability it creates—multiculturalism itself cannot serve to resolve the crisis, as you point out in the examples of the former Soviet Union and Yugoslavia.

Thus, despite its limited impact, multiculturalism has already begun to challenge monoculture beliefs and practices and has begun to destabilize Eurocultural strongholds. Yet, we need to recognize that we are in a period of transition for which the social order has yet to be established. We need to understand that monoculturalism requires a hierarchy of cultures and particular power relations. Multiculturalism requires a transformation of these hierarchies and the accompanying social relationships among diverse populations.

In an educational context, however, few who are doing work in multicultural education address the necessity of transforming traditional hierarchical relationships and redefining the purposes of education. Some forms of multicultural education have emerged as a means for celebrating difference. But these are additive models that do not challenge existing paradigms and frames of reference. Educators, then, have come to terms in limited ways with addressing some issues of ethnicity but still have difficulty understanding how to deal with culturally and linguistically diverse communities. The discourse around the education of bicultural children still defines the educational and social needs of these Black, Latin, Native American and Asian children as problems that need to be addressed. Cornel West underscores this point: ". . . we confine discussions about race in America to the 'problems' black people pose for whites rather than consider what this way of viewing black people reveals about us as a nation." That's why you and others are using the term "critical multiculturalism" to distinguish the critical multiculturalist agenda from those of conservatives and liberals.

Thus, to fully understand the difficulty in reforming practices that promote inequity, we must recognize that such practices, as David Theo Goldberg suggests, are deeply and historically rooted in beliefs about racial hierarchies and capacities; beliefs that are an inherent part of monocultural/monolingual societies. So part of the resistance to the implementation of radical pedagogies that call for transformative practice, such as language programs that promote biliteracy, for example, is a resistance to multiculturalism and multilingualism and other changes that disrupt the maintenance of racialized ways of life.

PETER: I'm wondering if we can discuss some of the possibilities that are emerging from criticalist work such as yours.

KRIS: While I recognize that only limited change can occur without major reform on a wider scale, critical educators, in collaboration with classroom teachers, must begin the process of rethinking teaching and learning in a multicultural society. I'm very hopeful about the possibility of transforming classrooms into very different kinds of communities in which dialogic rather than monologic forms of instruction are evident, heteroglossic communities in which the social relationships and discourses are dramatically transformed. In our studies of the social contexts of literacy, so many of the classrooms we studied reinstantiated traditional social relationships of teacher as information giver and student as receiver of knowledge and, thus, created very restricted forms of learning and limited opportunity for the linguistic, social and cultural experiences of the children to become organically constitutive of classroom life. However, we did identify some classrooms in which very different contexts for literacy learning existed. In these classrooms, the co-construction of discourse, activity and knowledge were the normative practices for both teacher and student. Instruction was not driven by what Stanley Aronowitz calls methodologically oriented practice; instead, in these more interactive contexts for learning, or what we call "responsive/collaborative" classrooms, the nature of participation for both students and teachers has transformed and created new, as well as more, opportunity spaces for students to function as apprentices and as experts in the literacy learning process. In these communities of practice, the socialization process was bi-directional and students with varying levels of experience and expertise were full participants in legitimate and meaningful praxis. They were not relegated to skill-drill-and-kill work; instead, meaningful discourse and practice were both the means and the ends to critical literacy. (See Gutierrez, 1994, for a comparison of the effects of various contexts for learning on bicultural children.)

In these more democratic classrooms, there were zones of possibility for both teachers and students to dialogue, to pose critical questions, to co-construct both process and product. They were critical ethnographers in both their classrooms and surrounding communities. In this way, the curriculum of the classroom relied on "funds of knowledge" that existed in children's families, social networks and communities. (See Moll, 1990, for more discussion of the notion of "funds of knowledge" in Chicano communities.) Literacy learning, then, necessarily addressed the lived experiences of children. While it's true that these classrooms had not resolved issues of power relations, racism and sexism, these were themes that informed many of the classroom narratives. In this way, I believe that responsive/collaborative classrooms set up the conditions for problem-posing pedagogy and increase the potential for radical pedagogy, for different representations of and stances toward knowledge and different ways of "doing and being student and teacher." It's an encouraging beginning. (See Marc Pruyn, 1994, for a discussion of the social construction of critical pedagogy in elementary school classrooms.)

As we develop new pedagogies for teaching the new student population, there is much to be learned from the struggles in ethnic, women, and cultural studies. For example, cultural studies programs have brought together transdisciplinary perspectives and methods of inquiry to more comprehensively examine the social, economic, political, cultural and historical dimensions that shape the lives of America's ethnic and racial groups. Thus, cultural studies reflect the intersection of issues of race, ethnicity, class, gender, culture and power.

One of the central aims of ethnic studies, for example, has been to make visible the essential philosophies, cultures, and histories of ethnic peoples and, thus, to produce a complete scholarship that necessarily challenges prevailing Eurocentric thought and methods. From this perspective, then, ethnic studies is not the inclusion or integration of new themes or experiences into the existing curriculum; that would simply require studying new subjects through the same Eurocentric lens, rather than a process by which students, teachers, and researchers develop new forms of agency. Instead, ethnic studies seeks to locate itself in a much broader socio-cultural terrain in which groups of color and women of color are integral to the understanding of everyday life in a U.S. context.

Because ethnic studies was not conceptualized as an addition or an appendage of existing curricula, the development of ethnic studies provided the occasion not only to create a new epistemology but necessarily became an occasion to substantively transform both pedagogy and curricula, to develop a very different stance towards the production of knowledge. Curricular transformation, then, was not an inadvertent by-product of ethnic studies. Rather, the epistemological roots of ethnic studies were reflected in the interdisciplinary and cross-disciplinary nature of its methodology, in the content of the curriculum and its pedagogy. In this way, ethnic studies was constitutive of a coherent content, methodology and pedagogy which allowed the development of curricula that focused on an examination of the interactions among particular groups of people and others and on the explication of these experiences within and across the total population. Transforming the general curricula for a multicultural student population requires the same processes. I would argue, however, for a pedagogy that does not promote an essentialist agenda.

I spend a great deal of time working with teachers and working in the teacher education programs. There's so much to be done. This transformation is not about using the right materials, reform-oriented pedagogies or celebrating ethnic life in the form of food, fun and fiestas, or simply "retraining" teachers so that they become tolerant or sympathetic to difference. It's about developing a very different space for teachers, students and parents in the educational process.

PETER: I think one of the biggest problems in establishing a criticalist movement in pedagogy on a wider scale than presently exists has been the pervasiveness of the way experience is understood and employed by bourgeois educators. There has been a strong tendency to essentialize experience, to view experience as self-evident. Some groups argue that there is an essential Chicano or Chicana experience, or Anglo experience, or African-American experience or gay experience. Personal history is spoken about as if it somehow affords transparent access to the real, as though it were removed from the effects of larger structures of mediation. This is to hold to the mistaken belief that experiences constitute some ordinary or foundational event. Identity is therefore conceived as an original authorship, as possessing the means to foreclose contingency and stabilize or impose a unity on the process of signification. It's my contention that in such cases the employment of experience as a referent for a transformative pedagogy needs to be rethought because too often it leads to the reproduction of those strategies of containment, regulation, and normalization that one is trying to contest. I've been in classes where students demand to speak from their own experiences and where the voice of experience becomes for them a license to render as the ultimate authority whatever they happen to "feel" about an event. Classes based on the privileging of personal experience and a fear of theory tend to degenerate into a forum for telling personal anecdotes or stories. Now, I believe stories are extremely important since they narrativize our cultural world in important ways. And life experiences are absolutely crucial to identity formation and historical agency. But, as I have argued elsewhere (along with Henry Giroux, Joan Scott, and others), experience is fundamentally discursive. That is, we cannot separate experience from language and the conflict among and contradictions within systems of signification. Experience permits us to establish a system of similarities and differences. But we can never "have" an experience and then simply attach a word or concept to that experience. Because experience is always a form of languaging—it is always an event. A material event in the sense that language always reflects and dialectically re-initiates social relations, structural relationships to otherness, and the world of objects and events. But it is always an after-effect, too, since it is always housed within particular conceptual frameworks and can never exist in a pure state unsullied by ideology or interest. Experience, in other words, never occurs outside of its specific forms of intelligibility or signification. It always occurs in relationship to the normativizing power of social life and the exclusionary logics of dominant subject positions. All experiences occur with more or less established regimes of signification or meanings. We need a theoretical language if we want to be able to interrogate the manner in which we enable our experiences to be understood and acted upon. Joan Scott notes that since experience is discursive, it "is at once always already an interpretation and is in need of interpretation." She adds something very insightful when she says: "Experience is a subject's history. Language is the site of history's enactment." We cannot separate experience from language. After all, experience is produced by systems of intelligibility that help to recognize it as experience. When we acquire a new language of analysis, we reinvent experience retroactively, for instance, when my social and cognitive consequences of schooling, to understand classroom culture is constructed, how certain contexts for learning deny or increase access to particular forms of literacy, and to understand the importance of developing agency and new frames of reference for both students and teachers. These teachers are not intimidated by research and theory; instead, they co-construct the discourse of theory and practice. In this way, we are attempting to conduct research that has multiple agendas—that is, research that has academic, social and political consequences.

Notes

1. I will use "we" to talk about this research because research assistants have always been an important part of the ongoing study. Assistants such as Joanne Larson, Marc Pruyn, William Saunders, Terese Karnafel, Cindy Tuttle, Tracy Rone, and Claudia Ramirez should be acknowledged for their contributions.

References

Aronowitz, S. (1993). Paulo Freire's radical democratic humanism. In P. McLaren, & P. Leonard (Eds.), *Paulo Freire: A critical encounter*. London: Routledge

Chow, R. (1993). *Writing diaspora*. Bloomington and Indianapolis: Indiana University Press.

Coupland, D. (1991). *Generation X: Tales for an accelerated culture*. New York: St. Martin's Press.

Davis, M. (1993). Who Killed LA ? A political autopsy. *New Left Review, 197*, 3–28.

Davis, M. (1993a). *City of quartz*. New York: Verso.

Deloria, V., Jr. (1987). Identity and culture. In R. Takaki (Ed.), *From different shores: Perspectives on race and ethnicity in America*. New York: Oxford University Press.

Delpit, L. (1988). The silenced dialogue: Power and pedagogy in educating other people's children. *Harvard Educational Review*, 58(3), 280–298.

Gates, H.L., Jr. (1989). Transforming of the American mind. Paper presented at the annual meeting of the Modern Language Association, San Francisco.

Giroux, H. (1992). *Border crossings*. New York and London: Routledge.

Goldberg, D. T. (1993). *Racist culture: Philosophy and the politics of meaning*. London and Cambridge: Blackwell.

Goodwin, C. (1993). The discursive constitution of Rodney King. Paper presented at the annual meeting of the American Anthropological Association, Washington, D.C.

Goodwin, M. H. (1990). *He-said-she-said: Talk as social organization among black children*. Bloomington, Indiana: Indiana University Press.

Gutierrez, K. (1994). How talk, context, and script shape contexts for learning: A cross case comparison of journal sharing. *Linguistics and Education*, *5*, 335–365.

Gutierrez, K. & Larson, J. (1994). Language borders: Recitation as hegemonic discourse. *International Journal of Educational Reform*, *3*(1), 22–36.

Kroker, A. (1992). *The possessed individual: Technology and the French postmodern.* Montreal: New World Perspectives.

Lave, J. & Wenger, E. (1991). *Situated learning: Legitimate peripheral participation.* Cambridge: Cambridge University Press.

Lefebvre, H. (1991). *Everyday life in the modern world.* New Brunswick and London: Transaction Publishers.

Massumi, B. (1993). Everywhere you want to be: Introduction to fear. In Brian Massumi (Ed.), *The politics of everyday*. Minneapolis: University of Minnesota Press.

McLaren, P. (1992). What is the political role of education? In Joe Kincheloe & Shirley Steinberg (Eds.), *Thirteen questions: Reframing education's conversation.* New York: Peter Lang.

Moll, L. (1990). Introduction. In L.C. Moll (Ed.), *Vygotsky and education: Instructional implications and application of sociohistorical psychology.* Cambridge: Cambridge University Press.

Ochs, E. (1988). *Culture and language development.* Cambridge: Cambridge University Press.

Pruyn, M. (1994). Becoming subjects through critical practice: How students in one elementary classroom critically read and wrote their world. *International Journal of Educational Reform*, *13*(1), 37–50.

Rogoff, B. (1990). *Apprenticeship in thinking: Cognitive development in social context.* New York: Oxford University Press.

Ruiz, R. (1992). Language and public policy in the United States. In W.A. Van Horne (Ed.), *Ethnicity and public policy revisited: Selected essays.* Milwaukee: Institute on Race and Ethnicity.

Scott, J. (1992). Experience. In Judith Butler & Joan Scott (Eds.), *Feminists theorize the political.* New York and London: Routledge.

Telles, E. & Marguia, E. (1990). Phenotypic discrimination and income differences among Mexican-Americans. *Social Science Quarterly*, *71*(4), 682–696.

West, C. (1993). *Race matters.* Boston, MA: Beacon Press.

Williams, B. (1993). The impact of the precepts of nationalism on the concept of culture: Making grasshoppers of naked apes. *Cultural Critique*, *24*, 143–191.

"Dialogue with Kris Gutierrez: Pedagogies of Dissent and Transformation: A Dialogue about Postmodernity, Social Context, and the Politics of Literacy" was published by Kris Gutierrez and Peter McLaren in 1994 in the *International Journal of Educational Reform*, *3*(3), 327–337.

popular culture and urban schooling

Interview 8

a radical educator's views on media

Mashhood Rizvi

Mashhood Rizvi is the co-founder and editor-in-chief of Pakistan's first progressive magazine on education and development, EDucate! *Several years ago, I was one of the critical educators contacted by Mashhood to contribute to his magazine and some of the interviews we did subsequently ended up in cyberspace, such as this one. Recently I met Mashhood in Karachi, Pakistan, where I was invited to give several talks on critical pedagogy. Mashhood and his wonderful family were magnificent hosts, and I was able to learn a great deal about pedagogical issues as well as the politics of post-colonialism and neo-colonialism from Mashhood, his colleagues, and his family.*

MASHHOOD RIZVI: Can you share some of your general perspectives on the media?

PETER MCLAREN: I think it is important to understand that we cannot treat the media as some kind of autonomous entity. Media sectors interpenetrate in various ways, but overall the media are overwhelmingly structured by the state and function, by and large, to service the interests of capital. I would begin by arguing that the current commercialization of broadcasting actually substantially undercuts public systems of communication. Public systems of communication are really at the mercy of the market. Today, it appears as if the hypertrophy of financial capital has become the functional grid in which media economies are secured. We need to understand that media serve the interests of national capital and its hydra-headed entanglements with transnational economic relations. So that the media need to win the support of the transnational money markets. I would argue that it is impossible for the media to foster democratic social relations when they do not challenge the principle of private ownership and profit. If the media and the capitalist state work hand-in-glove, how is it possible for the media to really be an instrument for helping the poor and powerless in the United States? We live in precarious and ominous times, Mashhood.

The destinies of the media—and the ideological interests that they serve—are interlocked with the vagaries of the "free" market. When you begin to comprehend the enormous power and global reach of the U.S. media, the challenge becomes overwhelming. The media cartel of AOL Time Warner, Disney, General Electric, News Corporation, Viacom, Vivendi, Sony, Bertelsmann, AT&T, and Liberty Media do their best to ensure that the news media continue in their role as the servants of the dominant ideological instruments. Jack Welch, CEO of General Electric (NBC's corporate parent) is an arch conservative; Michael Jordan, the head of CBS (Westinghouse) is a staunch conservative set against government regulation; Michael Eisner of Disney is a Democrat, but a political centrist; and Rupert Murdoch, who heads News Corporation (and owns Fox Television) is a right-winger. In fact, right-wing conservatives dominate the three major opinion-shaping forms in the U.S.: TV, talk radio, and syndicated columns (Coen, 2002). That, and the fact that the majority of public broadcasting outlets in the U.S. rely on large corporate-backed think tanks to offer "expert" opinions to their audiences, are just a few of the reasons why the United States population has been so willing to give up its long-cherished democratic freedoms for promises of security from bin Laden and his chthonic warriors.

The media serve to mystify the process of human value production. Social relations linked to capitalist production are glossed over and never explained in terms of the consequences that they have for the powerless and the poor. According to Mark Crispin Miller, the cartel's favorite audience is that stratum of the population most desirable to advertisers. Thus, we are faced with the media's complete abandonment of working people and the poor. Traditionally, the role of the press has been to protect us against those who would abuse the powers of government. However, the current media cartel is unwilling to take on the powers that be. Why should they? Their value systems are too similar and the powers that be share their own interest in the accumulation of surplus value. As Miller notes, media journalists now appear to work against the public interest—and for their parent companies, their advertisers and the political administration that holds sway in Washington. Miller argues, and I agree, that we have to take bold steps in order to liberate the media from oligopoly, so as to make the government our own.

MASHHOOD: Don't regulations exist to help prevent the formation of cartels?

PETER: Yes, but historically they have been ignored. And now they are being overturned altogether. A few weeks ago, the District of Columbia Court of Appeals overturned one of the country's last-remaining regulatory protections against media monopoly. The court overturned the rule that had prevented one company from owning both television stations and cable franchises in a single market. The court also ordered that the FCC either justify or rewrite the rule that bars a company from owning television stations which reach more than 35 percent of U.S. households, stating that left as is, the rule is arbitrary and illegal. If you look at the broadcast TV markets in the United States, one-seventh are monopolies, one-quarter are duopolies, one-half are tight oligopolies, and the rest are moderately concentrated. In addition, while the number of TV stations has increased from 952 to 1,678 between 1975 and 2000, the number of station owners in the same period of time has actually declined from 543 to 360. Let me give you an example of what a media monopoly can do. One of the primary ideological vehicles of the new media mafia is Fox News. Fox News Channel and 26 television stations are owned outright by Rupert Murdoch's News Corporation. Fox News is rapidly gaining a wide and committed audience on the basis of its appeal to right-wing white male viewers. Its political catechism is spiked with testosterone and rage and gives ballast to the logic of transnational capitalism and U.S. militarism. James Wolcott aptly describes this gang as the "Viagra posse."

> The corporate media have driven out any hope for even left-liberal news coverage or commentary in the United States. Labeled as "leftist" pundits, the likes of Sam Donaldson, Cokie Roberts, George Stephanopoulos, Bill Press, Michael Kinsley, Beckel, Margaret Carlson, Al Hunt, Mark Shields, David Broder, Juan Williams, and Susan Estrich are paraded before the American public as an attempt to balance right-wingers such as Limbaugh, Buckley, Novak, McLaughlin, Buchanan, Robertson, Liddy, and North. The

> truth is that the so-called "leftists" are, at their most extreme, "centrists" and more often than not tilt politically to the right. With virtually no leftist representation in the media, the U.S. public is being ideologically massaged by opinions and positions that serve the interests of the ruling class. The myth of the liberal media talked about so much by right-wing pundits is simply a lie (*Extra!* July/August, 1998).

Take as one example, popular Fox Television commentator Bill O'Reilly. His mind is rarely burdened by a dialectical thought, O'Reilly frequently berates with autocratic homilies those few guests he invites on his show who dare offer an explanation for the events of September 11. He enjoys sparing his audiences insight and lifting from them the burden of comprehension, preferring instead a spectacle of self-congratulatory belligerence and Stygian anger. The majesty of O'Reilly's self-regard is propped up by a stubborn conviction that unsupported opinions presented in a mean-spirited fashion are preferable to complex analysis. Proud of his simple patriotic (i.e., warmongering) advice to kill the enemy because the enemy is evil, he admonishes anyone offering critical analysis as giving evil credibility and as comforting our enemies.

But the worst offenders in the media are not always the drooling reactionary pundits such as O'Reilly. They are also organizations like National Public Radio. On January 10, FAIR (Fairness & Accuracy In Reporting) put out an Action Alert asking people to write to National Public Radio about the politics of its Middle East reporting. NPR had been referring to the situation in Israel and Palestine around the New Year as a period of "relative calm" or "comparative quiet." NPR went on to clarify this description by noting that "only one Israeli has been killed in those three weeks." What NPR failed to acknowledge was that during this "quiet" period, an average of one Palestinian per day was being killed by Israeli. (See http://www.fair.org/activism/npr-israel-quiet.html.) Despite protests organized by FAIR, this distortion continues to be repeated. But think about it, Mashhood, the Left in the United States does not have a lot of money behind it. Do you know how much it costs to enter the national media market, let alone the international market?

MASHHOOD: How is the struggle for media reform linked to the larger struggle for democracy?

PETER: There is no question in my mind that the struggle for media reform is an essential part of the struggle for democracy. McChesney and Nichols

(2002, 16–17) have argued (if I may be permitted to paraphrase them here) that media reform proposals need to apply existing anti-monopoly laws to the media; restrict ownership of radio stations to one or two per owner; fight the monopolization of TV-station ownership, break the lock of newspaper chains on entire regions, create reasonable media ownership regulations, establish a full range of low-power, noncommercial radio and television stations across the United States; invest in public broadcasting so as to eliminate commercial pressures and to serve low-income communities; allow tax credits to any non-profit medium; lower mailing costs for nonprofit and significantly non-commercial publications; eliminate political candidate advertising as a condition of a broadcast license; require that stations that run paid political broadcasts by politicians run free adds of similar length from all the other candidates on the ballots immediately afterward; reduce or eliminate TV advertising directed at children under 12; and decommercialize local TV news with regulations that require stations to grant journalists an hour daily of commercial-free news times; and set budget guidelines for those newscasts based on a percentage of the station's revenues. In his magisterial work, *Rich Media, Poor Democracy*, Robert McChesney writes that media reform cannot be successful if isolated from other struggles for democracy. He writes that media reform will not, and cannot, be won in isolation from broader democratic reform. He argues that the only way to gain some control over media and communication from the giant firms that overrun the field will be to mobilize some kind of a popular movement. He also notes that while media reform is a cornerstone for any type of democratic movement, it is not enough. This must be accompanied by electoral reform, workers' rights, civil rights, environmental protection, health care, tax reform, and education. In other words, McChesney links media reform to the larger struggle for democracy. In this sense his advice is similar to that of Chomsky and Ed Herman, both of whom I greatly admire, along with McChesney.

MASHHOOD: What about information technologies?

PETER: Well, I believe that information technologies—when they are embedded heart and soul in the capitalist marketplace—can actually increase alienation in the sense of commodifying information. A marketplace—even one that has been digitalized—is still a marketplace. The digitalized information systems so necessary to capital help to speed up its circulation and production. The speeding up of circulation and production does little, however, to demystify the world and in fact creates mystification at a higher register. On the other hand, alternative media that challenge marketplace values are very important in the struggle for democracy. Magazines like yours (*EDucate!*), *Z Magazine*, *Covert Action Quarterly*, *High Times*—as well as many Internet magazines—all of these publications are crucial in providing information and analysis crucial to challenging dominant ideological and political interests. Can the new media technologies create through forms of cyberactivism a new global "cognitariat" capable of challenging capital's law of value and the digital networks of the international financial system? Let's just say that I am hopeful but not optimistic.

MASHHOOD: What can radical educators do?

PETER: Wherever and whenever possible, radical educators have been implementing critical media literacy classes in high school and university classrooms. Examining the politics surrounding media policy and practices from a historical materialist perspective (i.e., looking at the media in the context of the creation of a transnational capitalist class), critical media literacy educators also employ a critical semiotics to analyze the media as a form of popular culture—a popular culture that carries a lot of unexamined ideological freight; it investigates the form and content of commercial broadcasting; and it examines representations of race, class, gender, and sexual relations as a form of ideological production. I have students at UCLA who work in working-class communities, helping young people create their own media representations of themselves and their communities through alternative media. Of course, examining the media critically and creating alternative views—especially with respect to the Bush administration's war on terrorism—at this particular historical juncture in the United States risks charges of anti-patriotism. Yet, from a critical perspective one could argue that patriotism that is not at the same time conjugated with introspection, sustained critical self-reflexivity, and the possibility of transcending the reified knowledge and social relations of the corporate capitalist state, is a patriotism that does an injustice to the meaning of the word. One of the best features of a democracy lies in its provisions for the ability to be self-critical, to challenge, or affirm, as the case may be, what has been presented by the dominant capitalist media as commonsense. That feature has been effectively eroded by increasing corporate control of the media. Democracy cannot exist in a society whose media are owned and run by the transnational capitalist elite. From where I stand, a socialist alternative is the only possibility for democracy to be secured.

References

Coen, Rachel. (2002). *New York Times* buries stories of airstrikes on civilians. *Extra!*, (February), 3.]

Cummins, Bruce. (2002). Reflections on 'containment.' *The Nation, vol. 274*, no. 8, 19–23.

Field Guide to TV's Lukewarm Liberals. (1998). *Extra!, vol. 11*, no. 4 (July/August).

Hart, Peter, & Ackerman, Seth. (2001). Patriotism & censorship. *Extra!, vol. 14*, no. 6 (December), 6–9.

Hart, Peter. (2001). No spin zone? *Extra!, vol. 14*, no. 6 (December), 8.

Massing, Michael. (2002). Black hawk downer. *The Nation, vol. 274*, no. 7 (February 25), 5–6, 23.

McChesney, Robert W. E (1999). *Rich media, Poor democracy: Communications politics in dubious times*. New York: The New Press.

McChesney, Robert W.E., & Nichols, John. (2002). The making of a movement: Getting serious about media reform. *The Nation, vol. 274*, no. 1 (January 7/14), 11–17.

Miller, Mark Crispin. (2002). What's Wrong with This Picture? *The Nation, vol. 274*, no. 1 (January 7/14), pp. 18–22.

Wolcott, James. (2001). Terror on the dotted line. *Vanity Fair*, January, 50–55.

"A Radical Educator's Views on the Media: An Interview with Peter McLaren" was published by Mashhood Rizvi in *ZNet* on March 10, 2002. This interview was also published 2002 in *EDucate! A Quarterly on Education and Development, vol. 1*, issue no. 4, 66–69.

Interview 9

educating for social justice and liberation

Mashhood Rizvi

Mashhood Rizvi first contacted me about five years ago. As director of programs, operations and research of the Sindh Education Foundation (a semi-autonomous organization established in Pakistan in 1992). Mashhood wrote to me in his capacity as editor-in-chief of a portfolio of publications that included an innovative magazine called EDucate! *The line-up of contributors he wanted me to join was impressive and included Noam Chomsky, Henry Giroux, and Robert McChesney. I wrote regularly for* EDucate! *magazine over the next several years. Mashhood was kind enough to invite me to present the keynote lecture in Karachi at a Conference called Re-envisioning Quality in Education in June, of 2005. The following interview took place over the Internet.*

MASHHOOD RIZVI: What do you feel about the current state of educational criticism across the world? We hear terms such as democratic schooling and progressive schooling? Are they for real? What would these look like?

PETER MCLAREN: Well in order to answer your question adequately, I will have to specify the context in which such "democratic" and "progressive" education takes place. The educational left is finding itself without a viable critical agenda for challenging in the classrooms and schools across the world the effects and consequences of the new capitalism. For years now we have been helplessly witnessing the progressive and unchecked merging of pedagogy to the productive processes within advanced capitalism. Capitalism has been naturalized as commonsense reality—even as a part of nature itself—while the term "democratic education" has, in my mind, come to mean adjusting students to the logic of the capitalist marketplace. Critical educators recognize the dangers of capital and the exponentiality of capital's expansion into all spheres of the life-world, but they have, for the most part, failed to challenge its power and pervasiveness.

Today capital is in command of the world order as never before, as new commodity circuits and the increased speed of capital circulation work to extend and globally secure capital's reign of terror. The site where the concrete determinations of industrialization, corporations, markets, greed, patriarchy, technology, all come together—the center where exploitation and domination are fundamentally articulated—is occupied by capital. The insinuation of the coherence and logic of capital into everyday life—and the elevation of the market to sacerdotal status, as the paragon of all social relationships—is something that underwrites the progressive educational tradition. What we are facing is educational neo-liberalism.

MASHHOOD: What does this term mean in the context of the critical educational tradition?

PETER: As my British colleagues, Dave Hill and Mike Cole, have noted, neo-liberalism advocates a number of pro-capitalist positions: that the state privatize ownership of the means of production, including private sector involvement in welfare, social, educational and other state services (such as the prison industry); sell labor-power for the purposes of creating a "flexible" and poorly regulated labor market; advance a corporate managerialist model for state services; allow the needs of the economy to dictate the principal aims of school education; suppress the teaching of oppositional and critical thought that would challenge the rule of capital; support a curriculum and pedagogy that produces compliant, pro-capitalist workers; and make sure that schooling and education ensure the ideological and economic reproduction that benefits the ruling class.

Of course, the business agenda for schools can be seen in growing public-private partnerships, the burgeoning business sponsorships for schools, business "mentoring" and corporatization of the curriculum, and calls for national standards, regular national tests, voucher systems, accountability schemes, financial incentives for high performance schools, and "quality control" of teaching. Schools are encouraged to provide better "value for money" and must seek to learn from the entrepreneurial world of business or risk going into receivership. In short, neo-liberal educational policy operates from the premise that education is primarily a sub-sector of the economy.

MASHHOOD: Can you be more specific in terms of what distinguishes progressive educators from more conservative ones?

PETER: The challenge for progressive educators is vigorous and varied and difficult to itemize. Unhesitatingly embraced by most liberals is, of course, a concern to bring about social justice. This is certainly to be applauded. However, too often such a struggle is antiseptically cleaved from the project of transforming capitalist social relations.

Mainly I would say that liberal or progressive education has attempted with varying degrees of success to create "communities of learners" in classrooms, to bridge the gap between student culture and the culture of the school, to engage in cross-cultural understandings, to integrate multicultural content and teaching across the curriculum, to develop techniques for reducing racial prejudice and conflict resolution strategies, to challenge Eurocentric teaching and learning as well as the "ideological formations" of European immigration history by which many white teachers judge African-American, Latino/a, and Asian students, to challenge the meritocratic foundation of public policy that purportedly is politically neutral and racially color-blind, to create teacher-generated narratives as a way of analyzing teaching from a "transformative" perspective, to improve academic achievement in culturally diverse schools, to affirm and utilize multiple perspectives and ways of teaching and learning, to de-reify the curriculum and to expose "metanarratives of exclusion."

MASHHOOD: These sound like worthwhile goals, do they not?

PETER: I am not saying these initiatives are wrong. Far from it. They are, undeniably, very important. I am arguing that they do not go far enough and in the end support the existing status quo social order. And for all the sincere attempts to create a social justice agenda by attacking asymmetries of power and privilege and dominant power arrangements in society, progressive teachers—many who claim that they are practicing a vintage form of Freirean pedagogy—have, unwittingly, taken critical pedagogy out of the business of class struggle and focused instead on reform efforts within the boundaries of capitalist society.

MASHHOOD: Your own work has been identified with the tradition of critical pedagogy. What is critical pedagogy?

PETER: Well, there is no unitary conception of critical pedagogy. There are as many critical pedagogies as there are critical educators, although there are certainly major points of intersection and commonality. There are the writings about critical pedagogy that occur in the academy, which are many and varied. And there is the dimension of critical pedagogy that is most important—that which emerges organically from the daily interactions between teachers and students. Some educators prefer the term "postcolonial pedagogy" or "feminist pedagogy," for instance. Some reject critical pedagogy for focusing mostly on class struggle, and embrace "critical race theory" or "critical multiculturalism" because they feel it focuses more on race. Some would say that critical pedagogy and multicultural education have melded together so much these days that they are virtually indistinguishable. Some might want to use the term, "postmodern pedagogy."

As I recall, the term critical pedagogy evolved from the term radical pedagogy, and I came to associate both terms with the work of my dear friend, Henry Giroux, whose efforts brought me from Canada to the United States in 1985. I have attempted in recent years (with varying degrees of success) to introduce the term "revolutionary pedagogy" or "revolutionary critical pedagogy" (after Paula Allman) as a means of redressing recent attempts to domesticate its practice in teacher education programs throughout and in school classrooms. I would be remiss if I did not include the works of Foucault, Bourdieu, Deleuze, Guattari, Antonio Negri, and many other European thinkers who have been lumped under the label of "postmodernist" and/or "post-Marxist theorists." Also, feminist theory, post-colonial theory, and literary theory have made important contributions to critical pedagogy.

We can also connect critical pedagogy to the Latin American tradition of popular education, to Latin American pastoral traditions of liberation theology and to European currents of political theology. We need to recognize that political struggles of African Americans, Latinos, and other minority groups have greatly enhanced the development of critical pedagogy, as have liberation struggles of oppressed groups worldwide. We need to make a distinction here between academic critical pedagogy, and the critical pedagogy engaged by oppressed groups working under oppressive conditions in the urban settings and in rural areas throughout the world.

MASHHOOD: Is critical pedagogy the same as radical education or does there exist a significant difference?

PETER: Radical education is a wide-net term that refers to everything from liberal progressive approaches to curriculum design, policy analysis, educational leadership and classroom pedagogical approaches to more radical approaches. You will find many approaches to critical education that are anti-corporate, anti-privatization, but you won't find many people positioning their work as anti-capitalist or anti-imperialist. It is incoherent to conceptualize critical pedagogy, as do many of its current exponents, without an enmeshment with the political and anti-capitalist struggle.

MASHHOOD: Can you share your thoughts on your idea of teachers as transformative intellectuals? How and what is needed to be done in this regard?

PETER: This is an important question. I admire Giroux's important call for teachers to develop themselves into transformative intellectuals. To the question of what is to be done, I follow Gramsci in his concept of developing organic intellectuals. But it is glaringly evident to me that most educationalists offer a perniciously narrow reading of Gramsci that situates the body of his work within the narrow precinct of reform-oriented, counter-hegemonic practice, largely in its forced separation of civil society from the state. It should be remembered that Gramsci's conception of the long struggle for proletarian power is one that mandates organically devised ideological and political education and preparation, including the creation of a system of class alliances for the ultimate establishment of proletarian hegemony as well as the development of workers councils.

Now, I am not saying that the struggle to build organic intellectuals today is identical to the struggle that Gramsci articulated in his day. I see the challenge of transformative (organic) intellectuals today as developing strategic international alliances with anti-capitalist and working-class movements worldwide, as well as with national liberation struggles against imperialism (and I don't mean here homogeneous nationalisms but rather those that uphold the principles of what Aijaz Ahmad calls multilingual, multidenominational, multiracial political solidarities). Transformative intellectuals should be opposed to policies imposed by the International Monetary

Fund and the World Bank on "undeveloped" countries because such measures are the actual cause of economic underdevelopment.

Transformative intellectuals should set themselves against imperialism. In discussing responses to the imperial barbarism and corruption brought about by capitalist globalization, critical intellectuals frequently gain notoriety among the educated classes. Professing indignation at the ravages of empire and neo-liberalism and attempting to expose their lies, critical intellectuals appeal to the elite to reform the power structures so that the poor will no longer suffer.

MASHHOOD: Can the existing form of schooling system lead us to a struggle for social justice?

PETER: In so far as our goal is to create a society where real equality exists on an everyday basis, it is impossible to achieve this within existing capitalist social relations. To challenge the causes of racism, class oppression, and sexism and their association with the exploitation of living labor, demands that critical teachers and cultural workers re-examine capitalist schooling in the contextual specificity of global capitalist relations. Here the development of a critical consciousness should enable students to theorize and critically reflect upon their social experiences, and also to translate critical knowledge into political activism.

A revolutionary critical pedagogy actively involves students in the construction of working-class social movements. Because we acknowledge that building cross-ethnic/racial alliances among the working class has not been an easy task to undertake in recent years, critical educators encourage the practice of community activism and grassroots organization among students, teachers, and workers. They are committed to the idea that the task of overcoming existing social antagonisms can only be accomplished through class struggle, the road map out of the messy gridlock of historical amnesia.

MASHHOOD: Another challenge that I have been faced with is the immediate dismissal from the teachers that these concepts look good and work well only on paper or these only work in theory, but in real life situations there is no classroom application for such intellectual jargon. What would you say to that?

PETER: Well, that is a fair question. In most public schools, and in most private schools for that matter, there are no provisions for classroom applications of these concepts. There are some courageous alternative schools that are trying to employ revolutionary critical pedagogical imperatives into the curriculum, to be sure. But the public schools could not function within capitalism if revolutionary critical educators were to challenge the very foundations upon which they rest. Of course, revolutionary critical pedagogy is a dialectical approach that works with both the concepts of reform and transformation.

Reform efforts are important so that resources are distributed equally among schools in every neighborhood, so that curricula include the voices of ethnic minorities, so that there is equality of access and outcome in education. But we also look towards the transformation of capitalist social relations, at least keep that goal in sight and working in whatever capacity we can towards its realization. While such a transformation is unlikely in our lifetime, or even in our children's lifetime, it is important to keep the dream of another world—a better world. And, we need to believe that a better world is possible.

MASHHOOD: Can you expand on this?

PETER: The problem is that while schools should serve as the moral witness for the social world in which they are housed, they are today little more than functional sites for partnerships between business and higher education. The corporate world basically controls the range and scope of the programs and, of course, military research is being conducted on campuses. As Ramin Farahmandpur and I have argued, universities are now becoming corporations. They embrace the corporate model. We talk in our classrooms about the values of openness, fairness, social justice, compassion, respect for otherness, critical reasoning, political activism, but look at how the university treats its employees, the service workers, and the graduate students who are exploited as assistants to the professors. Many of the campus workers in the cafeterias and in the warehouses and in the offices are paid wages on which they can barely subsist, and they have few, if any, health benefits and little job security. Graduate students assistants often teach most of the classes but are paid very small wages, while the professors earn robust salaries. We need to make the university mirror the social justice that many professors talk about in their classrooms.

Recently in a talk I gave at a university in the Midwest, I talked about trying to establish more links between the university and social movements for justice that operate outside of the university; there was a lot of opposition from the professors in the audience. When I called for socialist principles and practices to resist corporate principles and practices, I was called "totalitarian" by one well-known professor. When I talked about the problems with capitalism, and the relationship between the university and the corporate state, many professors became very offended. They did not like me using the word "state" because, to them, it sounded too "oppressive." They told me that they preferred to think of universities as places of hope. I replied that "hope does not retreat from the world, but radiates outwards into the world" and gives us the strength for a principled opposition to the imperialist practices that surround us, there were some very angry statements from the professors.

Under these circumstances, I see the role of teachers as that of transforming the world, not just describing or interpreting the world, and this means understanding the ideological dimension of teacher work and the class-based nature of exploitation within the capitalist economy and its educational and legal apparatuses. For me, the most immediate challenge is to discover ways of feeding the hungry, and providing shelter to the homeless, bringing literacy to those who can't read or write. We need to educate political workers to create sites for critical consciousness both within the schools and outside of them in urban and rural spaces where people are suffering and struggling to survive, and we need to discover ways of creating a sustainable environment. My work in critical pedagogy is really the performative register for class struggle. It sets as its goal the decolonization of subjectivity as well as its material basis in capitalist social relations. It sets as its goal the reclamation of public life under the relentless assault of the corporatization, privatization and bussinessification of the life-world (which includes the corporate-academic complex).

MASHHOOD: What message would you want to convey to the *EDucate!* readers?

PETER: The challenge is to create an authentic socialist movement that is egalitarian and participatory—not merely a different form of class rule. This means struggling against the forces of imperial-induced privatization, not just in education, but in all of social life. In this imperially dominated world, I can say that I live in the "belly of the beast." To support collective struggles for social change, to support a de-hegemonization of civil society by the economic superpowers, and to support a positive role for the national state to play—all of this requires steadfastness and focus. The struggle for co-operation, sustainable development, and social justice—which includes efforts to transform gender, political, race, ecological, and international relations—is a struggle that we should not leave solely to social movements outside the sphere of education.

Educators need to be at the heart of this struggle. This is a very difficult proposition to make here in the United States. In my travels around the country, professors in schools of education are inclined to support the status quo because of the benefits that it has provided for them. Yet currently, the top one-half of one percent of the population of the United States hold about one-third of all wealth in the United States. We have 31 million poor people, which is approximately the entire population of Canada. We have 3 million people who live on the streets. And I live in the richest country in the world. This is the belly of the beast, a beast that in the process of maintaining its great wealth for a few and misery for the vast majority, is destroying the globe.

As I have argued with Noah de Lissovoy, Greg Martin, Nathalia Jaramillo and Ramin Farahmandpur, struggling against imperialist exploitation means dismantling a Eurocentric system of cultural valuations that rationalizes globalization as "development" and "progress," and portrays those who suffer its violence—especially the masses of the South—as the beneficiaries of the favors of the magnanimous and "advanced." We know this to be a lie. From the belly of this lie, the effects of imperialism worldwide are recycled and re-presented as proof of the need for intervention by transnational corporate elites. Dismantling imperialism means destroying this unholy marriage of capitalist accumulation and neo-colonial violence, and creating the possibility of anti-colonial reconfigurations of politico-cultural space at the same time as systems of socialist production are initiated. This is only a vision at this particular historical moment, but it is one that we must continue to defend.

In this regard, no impatient ultimatums can be delivered to the masses from the sidelines. Critique is essential, but it must arise from the popular "common sense." In the terminology of Paulo Freire, the productive ground for the operation of liberatory praxis will be found in the "generative themes" that are truly lived in the "limit-situations" of the people.

"Educating for Social Justice and Liberation: An Interview with Peter McLaren" was published by Mashhood Rizvi in *ZNet* on August 19, 2002.

Interview 10

popular culture and pedagogy

Dianne Smith

Dianne was a graduate student when I taught at Miami University of Ohio. She was not my advisee but I do remember some very interesting discussions we had in those days. After Dianne graduated and became a recognized scholar, researcher, editor and teacher, she was kind enough to invite me to do this interview with her. Dianne provided the topic, and I appreciated this interview not in the least because it was a chance for me to reflect on the concept of popular culture, a topic that I had addressed years earlier but had not engaged again until this interview.

DIANNE SMITH: Peter, why do you think academics are distrustful of popular culture?

PETER MCLAREN: In general, Dianne, I believe that academics are distrustful of the fact that popular culture constitutes a legitimate focus for scholarly work. This is likely because popular culture deals with the all-too-familiar and messy world of the mundane, of quotidian life, of the daily grind, much of what is deemed overly commercialized, often crass and vulgar, and considered to be of little merit aesthetically or intellectually. Popular culture is often considered by academics to be disembarrassed of values that are culturally redemptive or have symbolic ameliorative effects. But these are pretty obvious reasons: the tendency of academics to distinguish between high culture and the culture of the masses, the cultural elitism of the academy, and so on. Often we are presented with the example of the critical theorist as cultural snob, and so on. Culture here is seen in Manichean terms as the hammer that shapes barbarism into civilization. Such a notion of culture puts limits on our understanding of cultural agency and the range of modalities and articulations of popular agency that can challenge regnant social and cultural determinations that are part and parcel of current manifestations of global capitalism. Part of the reason for what you label "distrust" lies in the fact that scholars have not mined the important debates surrounding culture outside of the traditional languages of cultural criticism, nor have they apprised themselves of the new theoretical vocabularies available for studying the complex articulations of culture and the effects of cultural practices in contemporary spaces and places of capitalist production. If one sees, as I do, culture as inextricably connected to the production of particular political effects—albeit in different ways, depending on the particular sites of cultural production and the particular technologies of power and cultural practices involved—then culture becomes a terrain of contestation, not only at the level of everyday engagement with "ordinary" events (those extraordinary ordinary events), but in the way that we theorize culture, problematize culture; in other words, Dianne, what becomes important for me is to challenge the current philosophy of culture (current systems of intelligibility) that both constrains and enables our theorization of culture as a site of the production of identity and difference, power/knowledge, relations of production, and so on. Of course, as cultural workers, there will always be limits placed on our claims to authority. As a cultural and political worker, I see my role as creating spaces of possibilities within cultural sites, including the university, recognizing the limitations of my own positionality, my own affiliations, my own discursive and institutional practices, and so on. I have to recognize the contractions of my own work, my own formation, and not presume to have the answers beforehand. And I would hope that in the process, my students will be able to recognize the strengths and limitations of their own understandings, their own role in the shared political future of their community, and humanity in general.

DIANNE: How can we begin to capture the multiple voices of popular audiences into our works and our understanding of doing popular culture?

PETER: Well, what I think is important that "doing popular culture" be linked to a larger project of emancipation from exploitation and oppression.

I am using the term "oppression" here in the distinctly Freirean sense. The central question in my own work has been to focus on exploitation as the central condition of global capitalism. The world is constantly remaking itself, and within that process we have an opportunity to intervene and effect transformations at both the level of theory and practice—in a more Freirean sense, at the level of praxis. Doing popular culture, as you put the term, has, over the last few decades been committed to understanding culture as—in the main, I would say—a politics of identity and difference. And of course I have perhaps been too ungenerous with the way cultural theorists have relied on neo-Weberian approaches to social life, but I feel they misrecognize and elide the centrality of class relations. But that is the subject of another discussion, perhaps. I have also been critical of identity politics that bracket out relations of class (class as problematized and articulated within Marx's labor theory of value). The question that many people raise is "how do you intervene"? How are conditions created for the subaltern to speak? Who creates those conditions? How are those conditions created? Can we work with the "other" without negating the "other"? Does speaking as a "we" necessarily reinscribe relations of patriarchal, capitalist, heterosexist domination? Can we employ the term "we," as Larry Grossberg suggests, in a non-referential or non-singular way? Can it be used multifunctionally? How are alliances formed? In what contexts? There are a host of questions that come to the fore here. Regardless of the way we choose to approach them theoretically, politically, on so on, we can never bracket out configurations and effects of power, whether we are referring here to semantic, semiotic, spacial, temporal, material, or affective (libidinal) processes or relations. But power, for me, is most importantly linked to the production of value through the dialectical contradiction between labor and capital. It is certainly possible to see this process as cultural and material.

DIANNE: How does hegemony affect what we think and practice relevant to the insertion of multiple voices into curriculum?

PETER: As Hoffman and others have pointed out, the first group to apply the term hegemony were Russian Social Democrats, and then Lenin. Lenin looked at hegemony from the perspective of proletarian leadership by means of the vanguard party. He used it in the context of the dictatorship of the proletariat as well as in the context of bourgeois class rule. Both Lenin and Gramsci associated hegemony with the moral and intellectual leadership of the dominant class (Gramsci borrowed the concept of hegemony from Lenin's

Two Tactics). Although hegemony is achieved in the process of class struggle, hegemony does not refer to the complete absorption of subordinate classes into ruling class ideology and cultural domination—it does not refer to the total subordination of the working classes to the dominant capitalist class. It is not a mechanical principle. The relationship between coercion and consent can be read dialectically. But I am more interested in the structural determinants of hegemony, that is, with how systems of production are organized. I am more interested in this relationship than, say, in the role of class leadership and political and ideological processes that contribute to how hegemony is "won" or secured. The material world and the world of ideas are linked, they mutually constitute each other, but I think educators interested in popular culture in the main fail to link ideas sufficiently to capitalist relations of production. The issue for me is not that the oppressed—the working classes—are ideologically indoctrinated and therefore do not exercise their rights to vote, etc. It is the fact that the political and economic orders are formally separated under capitalism and therefore socialism is precluded as a relevant choice—this is a point made by Perry Anderson and others. Bourgeois democracy presents to the oppressed their unequal location in civil society as if they were equal to the bourgeoisie. Žižek has pointed out recently how Lenin makes the important point that within bourgeois democracy, formal freedom is really a form of unfreedom because to opt for democracy entails giving up social security. Actual freedom, according to Žižek's understanding of Lenin, means moving beyond choosing between certain options within a pregiven set of coordinates, but choosing to change the very set of coordinates within which the pregiven choices are generated. Freedom within class struggle—does it constrain or enable the fundamental revolutionary choice for socialism? Certainly within a bourgeois democracy such as ours, socialism is not a valid choice.

In order to explain what I mean by creating a counter-hegemonic struggle, let me expand on Marx's dialectical approach to exploitation because this is really the centerpiece of my position.

The antagonistic relation between labor and capital, or the relation between production and circulation and exchange, constitutes the essence of capitalism. The labor of workers is utilized within the capital-labor relation. Workers may be said to constitute the dialectical opposite of capital and within a capitalist society enter into a value creation process. The basis of the rift or split within capitalist labor is the relation internal to labor: labor as a value producer and labor as a labor-power developer. One of the oppositions always benefits from this antagonistic internal relationship. Capital (the positive relation) structurally benefits from its relation to labor (the negative relation). To free itself from its subordinate position, labor must abolish this internal relation through the negation of the negation.

To understand class society in this way offers a more profound analytical lens than operationalizing notions of class that reduce it to skill, occupational status, social inequality, or stratification. This is because what is at stake in understanding class as a dynamic and dialectical social relation is undressing the forces that generate social inequality. This can only be accomplished by analyzing the value form of labor within the entire social universe of capital, including the way that capital has commodified our very subjectivities. This mandates that we grasp the complex dialectics of the generation of the capital-labor relation that produces all value. The labor-capital contradiction constitutes the key dialectical contradiction that produces the historically specific form of capitalist wealth or the value form of capitalist wealth. It is important to remember that the worker does not sell to the capitalist the living active labor which she performs during the hours of her work but rather sells her labor-power or her capacity to work for a certain number of hours per week. In exchanging her labor-power for wages, the worker receives in return not wages but what Marx called wage goods. That is, the worker gets what is determined in amount by what is required for her maintenance and her reproduction as a worker. Thus, she gets no general or abstract form of power over commodities in exchanging her labor-power for a wage. She only gets power over those particular commodities which are needed for her maintenance and for the reproduction of other workers. It is the capitalist who has the power to consume the labor-power which he has bought.

Labor-power purchases for the worker only exchanges with values. Labor, as distinct from labor-power, is the exercise of labor-power and it is labor that produces value. The worker is paid for the availability of her labor-power even before commodities have been produced. A certain proportion of the values produced by the worker by means of her labor are over and above the value that she has received as equivalent to the availability of her labor-power. When the capitalist consumes what he has paid for, he therefore receives a higher value than that which is represented in the wages paid out to the worker. The capitalist receives a surplus value created by the worker's labor. The wages the worker receives are therefore not the equivalent of her labor, or her value-producing activity.

What appears to be an equal exchange—the social transaction of wages for work done as equivalents—is actually a relation of exploitation. It is a relation between persons reduced to a relation between things. The labor/wage relationship as one of equal exchange is only equal from the perspective of its relationship to the market. But what appears to be the exchange of equivalents is actually an exploitative extraction of surplus value by the capitalist. What we are dealing with here, in other words, is the fetishized appearance of a relation of equality. The value produced by labor is "fetishistically" represented equivalently by wages. The dialectical contradiction or internal relation inheres in the fact that the capitalist mode of production of wealth premised on an exchange of equivalents is in essence a relation of exploitation through the extraction of surplus value on the part of the capitalist.

There is no way to approach the analysis of class within the social universe of capital without addressing the central relation of class struggle that permeates all of social life within capitalist societies. Schools, for instance, serve as production sites for human capital. But not only schools. Popular culture is certainly a site where value is produced through human capital. The central struggle for me is against capitalist social relations and capital's value-form of labor, wherever they are produced. Capitalist society needs the expenditure of our labor-power. We can resist this manipulation, this forced exploitation. We need to terminate the value-form of labor, of capitalism, of capital. My own particular task has been to find ways of resisting capital's social form in school sites. But that is but one site of possible resistance. Other sites—such as sites of popular culture—also provide us with the possibility of counter-hegemonic struggle. A socialist curriculum, a curriculum that I advocate, would address how the production of knowledge is located within the labor/capitalist divide. Of course, this also mandates the challenge of analyzing how the labor/capitalist divide works at the level of race and gender. In other words, class relations are always racialized and gendered. Analyzing this from the perspective of how racism and patriarchy are produced in the larger context of capitalist society is one of the important challenges of a socialist education.

"Popular Culture and Pedagogy: An Interview with Peter McLaren" was published by Dianne Smith in *Journal of Curriculum Theorizing, vol. 18*, no. 2 (Summer, 2002), 59–63.

Interview 11

capitalism, critical pedagogy, and urban science education

Angela Calabrese Barton

This interview came as a total surprise because it was for a science teaching journal, and I am not very familiar with the topic of science teaching. Angela has more expertise in this area than anyone I know and is recognized as one of the top scholars in this area in the country. I could not resist having a discussion of Marx and revolutionary pedagogy appear in a mainstream science teaching journal. I learned a great deal from my discussions over the email with Angela. I hope that the readers of the journal learned a little about Marx, socialism, and critical pedagogy.

Introduction: The questions which frame urban science education

We have prepared this discussion of capitalism, critical pedagogy, and urban science education in conversation format in order to keep problematic the contextualities of privilege, power and knowledge in urban settings. The conversation begins with a discussion of key issues in education (more generally) and then leads into a critique of the relationships between capitalism, science, and education. This more general beginning is important because it sets the stage for making a case that in science we are not looking in the right places to bring about meaningful reform based upon social justice. Only when we see the problems in science education as problems at a societal level, which always mediates the other problems, can we aspire to any hope. Indeed, McLaren makes three key claims here: (1) That the relationship between capitalism and urban education has led to schooling practices which favor economic control by elite classes; (2) That the relationship between capitalism and science has led to a science whose purposes and goals are about profitability rather than the betterment of the global condition; (3) That the marriages between capitalism and education and capitalism and science have created a foundation for science education that emphasizes corporate values at the expense of social justice and human dignity. We conclude this conversation by describing the implications that critical pedagogy has for how these three main issues might be productively confronted in urban settings.

ANGIE CALABRESE BARTON: Urban science education raises several challenges for science educators because of the vast inequalities in terms of resources, social privileges, and capital control which play out in inner-city settings, in general, and inner-city schools, in particular. You have been writing about education and inequality for over twenty years. In particular, a major theme of your work over the past two decades (in particular in your book, *Life in Schools*) has been to understand teaching in cultural, political, and ethical terms with the goal of building strong links between the classroom and our efforts to build a more just world through critical pedagogical practices and analyses. From your critical theory perspective, what would you say are the key issues with which the science education community must come to terms in urban settings?

PETER MCLAREN: For me, the key questions about urban science education raised by a critical approach include: How is the social practice of science organized? Or of education organized? How are social classes constituted through these practices? How are social practices constituted *prior to* these practices, since capital works to limit and control intellectual and scientific activity? What kind of scientific knowledge or school-based knowledge has the greatest exchange value in society? How is labor-power—the selling of one's ability to work—implicated in the reproduction of scientific knowledge? What type of science has ownership of the most prestigious research capital? What happens to scientists who have become alienated by the corporate community? Or by the student or science teacher who has become alienated by the school community? What about those who have more political and economic capital? Are they able to interpret the knowledge produced by these scientists or educators but also interrupt such knowledge when it does not serve—or works against—the interests of the ruling elite?[1] Since the discourse of science does not contain within itself the conditions of its own intelligibility, it needs to be analyzed critically from the perspective of the social, cultural, and historical determinations that produces it.

The relationship between capitalism and education

ANGIE: The problems of science education are just a small subsection of the problems endemic to education and capitalism. It seems to me, then, underlying your key issues, or rather your key questions, is the claim that school science reform has aligned itself to the imperatives of the capitalist marketplace rather than the goals of a democratic socialist struggle. In other words, science education has become more about presenting students the science they need to fit into society rather than about educating students about how they might produce, use, and critique science to work with and transform society—going to school does not enhance one's chances, because even if everybody was learning something, schooling is still leading to stratification and the shaking out of those lower in the strata.

PETER: Yes. Perhaps the best way for me to expand upon these points you raise is to share with you and your readers some serious concerns I have that shape my present perspective on education in general, science in general, and then urban science education in particular. The first point that I want to make is about the relationship between education (generally) and capitalism. Our society's unfettered capitalism has become a dangerous prejudice in the U.S. and worldwide and has impacted our social, political, scientific and education structures. Everywhere you look today, learning is being marginalized by its stress on capitalist accumulation. Scientific research, education, and capitalism serve each other so intimately that it is hard to think of one without the others. No where is this more dangerous than in economically and politically oppressed communities. While capitalism, having emerged from the shadow of Marx's incubus with the fall of the former Soviet Union, continues to make good on its promises of providing considerable consumer advantages available to large numbers of people in advanced industrial nations, it also functions systematically as a form of global pillage. The neo-liberal economic politics of the developed capitalist states (marked by the elimination of the public sector, the imposition of open-door free trade policies, and a draconian curtailing of state subsidies, compensations and social protections) have created staggering disparities in wealth among populations in advanced democracies. They have also intensified and expedited the flow of surplus values from poor countries into the U.S., leaving unprecedented levels of poverty, starvation, disease, and homelessness in those very countries that the U.S. ostensibly attempts to assist (McLaren & Farahmandpur, 2001a and 2001b).

ANGIE: Yet some argue that education will become more efficient and productive in a fiercely competitive marketplace and that this is just what urban school systems need. Indeed, this relationship between capitalism and education seems to be the central thesis in the recent Bush administration's approach to school reform.

PETER: And, this link is reinforced by coinciding profitability and the educational system, transforming it into a billion-dollar marketplace ripe for corporate investment and profit. An education which is subordinate to transnational capital can only be detrimental to any attempts to bring about social justice through education (McMurtry, 1998). Let us step back for a moment to sketch out how this relationship between education and capitalism has developed because how this relationship developed (and continues to develop) is just as important as its outcomes.

In many respects, the deregulation of markets and the marriage between knowledge production and profit-making have taken on the form of a transcultural prejudice, underwritten by capitalism's law of value, and what appears to be the unstoppable march of capital accumulation. Never in the history of human wealth-creation have fortunes been amassed so quickly by so many. The U.S. now has 300 billionaires and approximately 5 million millionaires. Silicon Valley alone adds about 64 new millionaires every day, according to recent reports. Nine million Americans have household incomes above $100,000 a year, up from just 2 million in 1982, many of the new millionaires profiting from the science/technology industries (i.e., Bill Gates or Hendrik Verfaille (CEO of Monsanto)). It has been said that if Great Britain was the first country to produce a mass middle class, the U.S. is the first country to produce a massively large upper class.[2] But let's not forget that the majority in the U.S. are not rich or middle class—but are working class. The working class, in the broadest sense, are those who have to sell their labor-powers to survive; those people who can't just live on assets. In a more pointed sense, the working class comprises those workers that produce surplus-value for capital. There are three issues important to how our society makes a distinction between the working and professional class besides the kind of labor which occupy people. First, there is the issue of control over work (its content, pace, conditions and so on) the working class lacking in this area of social life. Second, there are the cultural aspects of class—dress codes, speech, mannerisms and so on—more significant in countries like England perhaps, than here in the U.S., but relevant nonetheless. Political power, of course, is the third issue and is particularly significant when analyzing the ruling class—as C. Wright Mills pointed out many years ago. As Michael Zweig (2000) and other commentators have noted, the political power of the economic elite is at least as great as it was in the 1920s, perhaps even more so since today there are fewer challenges from other class interests. Contrary to the popular claims of the postmodernists, class struggle has not disappeared. It is simply being reconstituted. In fact, while class struggle from below may have temporarily disappeared from the discourses of many scholars, class struggle has strengthened from above. Since the early 1980s, under the leadership of Reaganomics and Thatcherism the ruling class has waged all-out class warfare from above against the working class. These continued struggles around class must remain central analytic themes in our work in urban centers.

ANGIE: Democracy and capitalism in many ways seem opposed. And yet in the popular imagination they appear indissoluably linked.

PETER: To argue that capitalism is fundamentally democratic is like saying Harry Potter is a Trotskyite or Leninist, on the basis of his wearing round-rimmed glasses.

ANGIE: Or a Lennon-ist!

PETER: Right. Lenin—the Russian, not the Beatle—was correct when he wrote that bourgeois democracy, which was invaluable for educating the proletariat, was also narrow, hypocritical, spurious and false, and always remained a democracy of the rich and a swindle of the poor (Lenin, 1943). The structural inability of capital to provide for the majority of the world's population and its creation of historically structured systems of inequalities between men and woman, social classes, and developed and undeveloped countries, marks the imperialist character of its current efforts to dominate the globe. What you are seeing today is the result of economic policies that date back nearly a decade. Capitalism's revanchist ascension to public education in recent years, under the guise of a neo-liberal restructuring of the educational system through education-business partnerships, privatization, school choice, accountability schemes, and standardized tests, and the like, can be traced back to the early 1990s.

ANGIE: At least to 1994.

PETER: Exactly. My central claim is that you can't divorce educational policy today from the transmogrification of the world economy into a global financial system overrun by speculators and modern-day robber-barons who act not in the interests of social justice, but for the cause of unchecked private interest and profit at any cost. Take the World Trade Organization for example. In 1994, the World Trade Organization replaced the General Agreement of Tariffs and Trade (GATT). This program established the framework and political architecture necessary for the U.S. to acquire free access to the global market. Consequently, the WTO, the World Bank and the International Monetary Fund created a barrier between the poorest and most vulnerable of the world's population and big Western capital, mostly U.S. capital. Those in power in the U.S. hold onto the best jobs and export the most menial, low-wage, polluting industries.

In such a climate of outlaw capitalism and corporate orthodoxy, is it any wonder that education has been reduced to a sub-sector of the economy—a zone of free capital investment? Indeed, the corporate agenda for public and higher education fundamentally contradicts education in principle. Any value system that maximises the private monetary interests of major stockholders without opposition or resistance is both anti-educational and complicitous with superclass interests. Educators must keep the veneration of capital and the sacerdotal status of corporate rule out of education. We must provide students with opportunities to develop "robust reflexivity" (Harding, 1998). We must also engage in critical agency that moves beyond competitively selling knowledge as priced commodities for profit and private returns. Take, for example, the more than 1,000 corporate scientists in Monsanto headquarters building genetically engineered food systems more about turning a profit than about real food safety. I am not suggesting that genetically altered food is unsafe—indeed, I do not think we actually know the longer term impacts of adding new genes and proteins to plants, to our bodies, or the larger global ecosystem. What I am suggesting is that we find ways to critically examine the relationship between corporate power and the knowledge we label for our students as "objective" and "true."

The rude contradiction in all of this is that, where for-profit enterprises have been introduced in education, there is little evidence that students actually perform better or that high school graduates are getting better jobs (Zweig, 2000). What do you think of the fact that the leading private education company, Edison Schools, Inc., is consistently losing money? When private firms successfully compete with the government it is usually because they take only the most potentially profitable segments of the market. In addition, private schools often screen out students who often need more attention (i.e., cost more money). In the final analysis, private schools are a "niche item" that allows some students to do better (Zweig, 2000). Thus, once we realize that capitalism's link to democracy is really a chimera, we can begin to examine how educational policy and practice—and this includes urban science education—are largely controlled by superclass political dominance through an invisible class empire and control of the shadow political industry and the information industry (Perrucci & Wysong, 1999).

The relationship between capitalism and science

ANGIE: Are you saying that science and education serve primarily the superclass? In other words, the oppressors, to use Paulo Freire's term?

PETER: Yes, and your question brings me to my second major point: the relationship between capitalism and science has led to "corporate science." More and more these days, capitalism and science are moving into a shared orbit, as the earlier Monsanto example shows. If we conceptually undress the role science plays in the larger society, we can see how it stabilizes dominant social relations. If we make problematic the commonplace notion that science equals progress, we can begin to develop a different view of how science works. When I talk about science serving the interests of the dominant class, I am not only talking about paradigmatic historical exemplifications of scientists participating with, say, fanatical regimes of power, such as the Nazi scientists who helped to advance the "final solution" or members of the medical profession who have proved indispensable to military juntas for their work in perfecting "interrogation techniques" to be used during "information gathering sessions" with dissidents and political prisoners. I am also talking about the ways in which corporate life and profitability shape and influence the directions and products of science.

ANGIE: This all sounds very abstract.

PETER: But the consequences are not. As underscored by Canadian philosopher, John McMurtry (1998), the fact that corporate-directed science and medicine devote little or no research funds to resurgent malaria, dengue fever or river blindness (whose many millions of victims lack market demand to pay for cures), while it invests billions of dollars into researching and marketing dubious and often lethal drugs to treat non-diseases of consumers in rich markets, reveals a principle of selection of problems that is highly suspect. How else do you make sense of the millions dying in Africa from treatable diseases, such as tuberculosis, malaria, and sleeping sickness or the fact that the country that spends the most on AIDS research—the U.S.—is ignoring the plight of Africans who account for 70 percent of new AIDS cases worldwide. The reason that U.S. scientists are searching for a vaccine for a subtype of AIDS present in the North Hemisphere is that drug companies don't find it profitable to sell drugs to dirt-poor Africa.

As David Trend (2001) has recently noted, university research has been transformed into a privately sponsored affair driven mainly by industries in bioscience and information technology. Projects that can produce new drugs, genetically engineered cotton, and faster microprocessing chips are reaping huge profits. In the pharmaceutical industry, large research projects are no longer dedicated to saving lives of millions of people in the developing world but to creating lifestyle drugs for impotence, obesity, baldness, and wrinkles. Trend mentions that new resistant strains of malaria, tuberculosis, and respiratory infections killed 6.1 million people last year. Yet of the 1,223 new medications introduced last year, only 1 percent were developed for those specific illnesses. Viagra sales totaled more than one billion dollars its first year alone. But total global expenditures for malaria treatment stand at 84 million.

ANGIE: And you could also have mentioned the biotech revolution—such as the recent case in South Africa, where the drug companies backed down on suing the country for attempting to import cheap drugs to deal with their AIDS epidemic.

PETER: Absolutely. Think about the vast amounts of capital poured into genetic engineering research, the genetic manipulation of corn and soybeans, not to mention the "modification" of animal reproduction or the human genome project. The point I am trying to make is that advances in science and technology are firmly lashed to the mast of capital's value form. Indeed, scientific value has been engineered, not for the improvement of the quality of life for all but for profit. Can you imagine sometime in the near future, the CEO of a biogenetic corporation calling his or her corporate quislings into the office and announcing: "We need to recall several life forms which may be flawed." This scenario is unlikely, especially when products are so intimately connected to the next quarter earnings. Perhaps I appear squalidly pessimistic, here, but the stakes are too high. Let me be clear, Angie. I don't want to collapse innovations in technology with social and political institutions. As Callinicos (1999) points out, technology can be improved without changing its nature, but the same cannot be said about capitalism. To improve capitalism would require a fundamental change of its nature since it has as a constituent feature an inherent tendency towards crises. The major problem today is the widely held belief that there is no alternative to capitalism.

Corporate Urban Science Education

ANGIE: So, it seems then, that the corporate approach to urban science education might not be so different from the corporate approach to science. Let me be more specific. The challenges in urban science education are layered, and these layers are deeply connected to each other and to issues of power and control. I am concerned that science education has not incorporated the needs or concerns of children in poverty and children from ethnic, racial, and linguistic minority backgrounds. These "gaps" can be seen in high-stakes tests, mandated curricula, and daily school practices. I am also concerned that science—as a culture and practice—has developed along elitist lines resulting in a knowledge base and a cultural practice reflective of those already in power and uses the unobtainable ideals of truth and objectivity to hide its singular focus. Finally, I am concerned that schooling itself and the workaday practices of low-level worksheets, discipline through humiliation, and teacher-student bargaining (to name only a few) in urban centers strips children of their cultural identities, their right to learn, and their dignity as human beings. In short, I see schooling practices and the practice and content of science as potentially oppressive and schools and science as contributors to the colonization of people's minds (whether that be students, teachers or anyone else). Are you arguing that the neo-conservative agenda of implementing standards, assessing students' technical knowledge and understandings, and engaging in cross-national comparisons of student achievement ignores the ways in which the practice of schooling and the organization and intent of school science are structured to support capitalist goals which benefit the few at the expense of the many? Isn't this what the "weeder" introductory college science courses are supposed to accomplish anyway?

PETER: Yes, and this brings me to my third major point: that the marriages between capitalism and education, and capitalism and science have created a foundation for science education that emphasises profitability and control at the expense of social justice and human dignity. As long as society uncritically accepts the relationship between capitalism, science and education, then science educators will continue to be bound to discourses and social practices responsible for needless human suffering. Instead, science education needs to be directed to assisting an educated population with managing a large-scale investment program for a sustainable future for humanity. The wealth of our nation (and of the nations of the world) should be measured by the elimination of class exploitation, racism, sexism, homophobia, and other forms of oppression, by the health of a people, their creative capacities, their standard of living and their well-being. I feel strongly that a corporate approach to science in our classrooms has failed to raise questions dealing with what knowledge counts most, for whom, and for what purposes. I also feel that it has distanced science from confronting the objectifying and mediating functions of capitalist production and exchange relations, deflected attention away from how the advanced imperialist order of contemporary capitalism actually works in the production of knowledge, swept away contradictory class interests, and cultivated an engineered misunderstanding of how the geography of capital accumulation helps perpetuate bourgeois power and suppress workers' rights and aspirations.

ANGIE: So I can link your point about distancing science from class interests to, on the one hand, how we "teach" about developing countries in science class—the rare moments when developing countries are talked about in the typical science textbooks tend to be in relation to disease and pollution (i.e., the typical biology textbook picture of the poor African woman with a goiter). The sad parallel is that on the other hand I can link this very example to how little mention (or no mention) is given in these same texts to how these poorer countries often serve as the first clinical test beds for new drugs. Let us not forget what is also happening in our poor centers in the U.S.—Hispanic and African-American children were immunized with the EZ measles vaccine in Los Angeles, and their parents were not informed that the vaccine was not licensed in the United States (Trafford, 1996). How would you say these ideas translate pedagogically?

PETER: The issue for me is to create pedagogical sites where educators and students collectively can "speak truth to power." One of my goals is to develop learning contexts—both in schools and in community settings—where the local habitation of such a struggle for socialism can take root. For me, the educational system is an important possibility in this regard. It is here that critical pedagogy can be employed in the teaching of science. At present there is a haunting absence of critical approaches to the teaching of urban science, an enigmatic silence with respect to attempts at conscripting teaching science into the service of social justice.

ANGIE: Can you expand a bit on what you mean by critical pedagogy and why this approach may help to foster social justice and "science for all" in urban settings?

PETER: I believe that a critical pedagogy of urban science approached from a Marxist perspective[3] evaluates educational policy and practice using the following criteria as a yardstick: Does it mobilize the working class to engage in activities that address those contemporary dynamics of advanced capitalism—especially its fundamental and irresolvable contradictions—that place education in a subordinated partnership with imperialist capital? Does it promote unity of political purpose within a diversity of experiences (race, gender, class, sexuality)? Does it promote gender equality and the destabilization of patriarchal structures of oppression? Does it promote racial/ethnic equality and dismantle the hegemony of white privilege? Does it improve the overall lives of the working class? Does it provide leadership in challenging the injustices that are constitutive of capitalist accumulation? Does it provide opportunities for an analysis of the contradictions between the forces and the relations of production?

ANGIE: So how do you see critical—or rather revolutionary pedagogy intersecting with the production of scientific knowledge in classrooms? And, how might we think about this intersection in our work with urban youth? In other words, you have outlined a stance towards science and a stance towards education, both of which emerge from a critique of the democracy-capitalism couplet. My concern now is so what does it mean to bring these ideas together in our efforts to build a more socially just science education in urban settings especially in the daily practice of classroom life?

PETER: Although it is hard to speak about the practicalities of classroom life because students and teachers are situated differently from day to day and from place to place, I will share some general thoughts on the kinds of classroom practices in urban settings which may underpin these more abstract ideas. It seems important that the practice of teaching has to be constructed differently. Urban teachers are confronted, on the one hand, with "being accountable" to district and state standards with the expectation that they are there merely to transmit the epistemologies and cultural practices foundational to these standards. On the other hand, urban teachers interact daily with diverse groups of students who may, as cultural groups, be semiotically and physically excluded from the very assumptions which drive those standards at the same time that they are confronted with limited resources, time, or decision making authority to do anything serious or systematic about what or whom they need to be accountable to or serve. To think about teaching differently means that we must think about what it might look like in classrooms to reject this structured and regimented practice and begin to question not only "what or how it is" that teachers are "supposed to teach," but how it is that the very structure of schooling works to silence any kind of critical conversation about what or how teachers are supposed to teach. In other words teaching becomes about not only critically assessing the science and how it may intersect with the lives of students who are most often on the fringes of science but also critically assessing why it is that conversations about power and authority at both local and global levels are generally not allowed in science class.

Take, for example, the case of Beta, a grade-eight teacher in a major urban center. As part of a unit intended to teach her students about temperature gradients and the function of insulators, she had her students design "the ideal cooler" big enough to fit a six-pack of soda. She had prepared a set of experiments to test out different materials for their ability to insulate. She also prepared different activities to help the students think about size, scale, measurement and design. Although her students would have to work in groups because she did not have access to a wide swath of resources, she believed that this experience might at least get them thinking about science outside the text. Her implementation of the unit was not as she anticipated. Her students verbally and physically indicated their disinterest in the project. Yet, Beta took their resistance and turned it into a class-long discussion about "what the class should do with the topic of insulators" given that she was bound by certain district learning standards and limited resources. She learned that her students preferred to design insulated lunch bags that held their lunches rather than a six-pack cooler, and they preferred to make individual bags because they wanted to keep them and use them. She also learned that the aesthetic quality of the materials was also important as the students intended to actually use these bags for their lunches. Through the story of one student's experiences with the family's icebox in the Dominican Republic (DR), she also learned that they had ideas more complicated, real-world, simulated experiments to test out the viability of the lunch bag design along with other experiments to test out other insulating and cooling devices. Students' concern about inequalities, both local and global, also emerged: differences in the availability of insulating and cooling devises in different places, such as refrigeration in the U.S. versus the poorer communities of the DR, or the differences in air conditioning systems between the affluent and poor school districts in the city entered the conversation. Finally, the students voiced their belief it was more important for the school to spend money on better and more materials than the kinds of things the school typically purchased (paper for too many worksheets, overhead projectors, and metal detectors).

This seems like a simple story, but indeed it raises questions about what it means to think about teaching and science differently. By allowing her students to see "inside" the expectations that schools place on teachers—by turning the classroom talk about why build lunch bags over coolers into talk about the science standards for the quarter—Beta's students turned science class into political space where the learning of science was coupled with learning about (and critiquing) the schooling process and the purposes and goals of doing science and its connections to social control, economic trade-offs, and human welfare. Beta and her students not only created new spaces to design and build lunch bags—something that was important to them in their day-to-day lives, but also critiqued the purposes behind why making lunch bags was a necessary and important project for them to engage in as students. It made public the profound differences between learning a regulated list of science standards for the purposes of fitting into a particular mold of scientific literacy and engaging in a practice of science for the purposes of youth development.

This story also helps us to begin to reflect upon what it means to interrogate how science education is framed through profitability and control at the expense of social justice and human dignity. The youth re-centered the goals of science class as about agency and learning to use and produce science in situationally meaningful ways rather than as about good studenting and capitulating to the contemporary dynamics of advanced capitalism that place education in a subordinated partnership with imperialist capital (i.e., where learning to be an obedient student is more important than learning to be critical of how power, knowledge, and culture interact to facilitate particular definitions of science and schooling). Here the difference is more powerful yet more subtle: the youth enacted a critique of "do we do science in ways and times set out by others in order to keep systems moving smoothly or do we do science in ways that turns those systems on their heads—in ways that uncover just how much the process of learning science is embedded with issues of hegemonic control as can be the very construction of science itself." Yet even more could have happened and may still happen in Beta's class—the youth could see their actions as students building lunch bags and as students critiquing their school and science as part of a larger global effort to better understand how structures like school and science help to perpetuate global inequalities and social injustices.

This example also shows the ways in which transforming what it means to teach positions students and science with and among each other differently. It makes asking questions about why some ideas are taught at the expense of others or how it is that some scientific practices elevate certain cultural beliefs and practices over others a part of the discursive practices of the science classroom. Indeed, it creates the kinds of spaces that allow students and teachers to interrupt the practice of learning and doing science in order to uncover the unacknowledged aspects of culture that historically underwrite and shape the social practices out of which science education is produced through experiences like end-of-year exams, textbooks, or state and local curriculum objectives. Think about it. This story could have turned out many ways. Beta could have made her students make the coolers. She could have listened to her students and allowed them to make the lunch bags without exploring the deeper intentions in such a decision. Rather she chose to politicize the students' choices as a vehicle for helping her students (and herself) uncover the assumptions which guide the practice of schooling in urban centers.

ANGIE: Your point that position matters in the science we teach and how we choose to teach it centralizes both the importance of how we think about the purposes and goals of science education as well as the roles that students and teachers play in that process.

PETER: Yes, and indeed, one of the keys for me is vantage point (Althusser, 1975) and how this ideal in light of revolutionary pedagogy shapes classroom practices. For Foucault (1972, 1973), local knowledges must be reactivated against the scientific hierarchy of knowledges. Harding (1991, 1998) has made some important advances in this regard in her development and refinement of "standpoint epistemologies." For Harding, standpoint epistemology sets the relationship between knowledge and politics at the center of its account. It explains the effects that different kinds of political arrangements have on the production of knowledge and knowledge systems. Empiricism tries to "purify" science. Yet, Harding has shown that these empirical methods never reach greater objectivity for they exclude thought from the lives of the marginalized. For Harding, who draws upon post-colonial, feminist and post-Kuhnian social studies of science and technology as well as Latour's notion of technoscience with its tension between local and global science practices—all attempts to produce knowledge of any kind are socially situated and some of these objective social locations are better than others as starting points of research. Harding points out that, for instance, when physics is permitted to set the standards for what counts as nature and what counts as science, knowledge becomes truncated and is often misapplied, limiting our ability to produce knowledge in ways that can assist aggrieved populations.

So the question arises: What are the knowledge opportunities for the marginalized and disenfranchised, especially for those youth who live and go to school in poor urban settings? To use Harding's terminology, these groups occupy the "borderlands" as "outsiders within." The dominant conceptual frameworks, criteriologies, systems of intelligibility and classification don't reflect their input or their interests. When decisions are made as to what kind of scientific studies should be undertaken, these groups rarely have a voice. Similarly, when decisions are made as to what kinds of science should be taught in school, these groups, again rarely have a voice. Indeed, the example of Beta involving her students in her decision-making process was not the norm, and if Beta continued this practice throughout the school year, she may even have found herself in trouble with her administration. The dominant epistemologies and truth claims exercised by the bourgeois science establishment dehistoricize knowledge conflicts within science and fetishize them as permanent and unavoidable features of the scientific enterprise instead of seeing them as conflicts produced by class struggle, by patriarchal oppression, by heteronormative and homophobic perspectives. But doing science, both in the scientific workplace and at schools, from the perspective of the oppressed—whose lives bear a disproportionate share of the costs of these activities—can bring a wealth of important knowledge to the table. In Beta's case, it wasn't making the lunch bags that was so important—rather it was that the youth questioned the process of how decisions to make a cooler or a lunch bag get made, why they get made, and the implications this has for what students learn and do in school. This questioning pulled into the public discourse their lives, the intentions of the school system (i.e. the standards), the issues faced by urban schools (the lack of resources, the distance between the prescribed curriculum and the students lives) and the overwhelming focus, at least in her district, on passing the test, and the larger connections between science, schooling and the perpetuation of inequalities (why the difference between availability of cooling and insulation systems in affluent versus poor communities?).

In urban science education circles—both in schools and in universities—we must begin to ask hard questions about what and how we teach and research: How is science integrated with and across diverse communities such that scientific advantage accrues to some but not to others? How do we interrupt this process? What are the unacknowledged aspects of culture that historically underwrite and shape the social practices out of which science is produced? What sort of science education is produced through experiences like end of year exams, text books, or state and local curriculum objectives? How are women, racial/ethnic minorities, and the working class functionally excluded from the dominant practices of doing science? Of course, for me the struggle is not only about a more just and equitable distribution of resources but transforming existing contradictory capital-labor relations in such a way that the system itself does not generate such contradictions.

ANGIE: Yet, some have described standpoint epistemology as relativist and indeed, some have argued that this only further oppresses youth in marginalized settings because it denies them opportunities to "learn the canon" or to "have access to the culture of power." After all, with the push towards greater accountability, how much will it matter to students if they learn to see the intersections between science and culture yet fail to learn the western canon of science?

PETER: "Learning the canon" and "learning-critiquing-re-visioning how culture and science intersect" are not mutually exclusive. Indeed, finding ways to access the canon is a central part of critique and revision. It is that the focus is different. Harding points out that this kind of diametric thinking confounds power with cultural differences. Differences are historical and material. They also stem from a confusion that empiricism is politics-free; that the canon is apolitical, ahistorical, and acultural. Standpoint epistemology is more sophisticated than this in that it constitutes a powerful socio-historical analysis of how dominant discourses of science work to serve the interests of the powerful by masking their claims in a neutral "view from nowhere" position. What I like about the way Harding uses standpoint epistemology is that she doesn't assume that because a standpoint is articulated from the position of the oppressed, that it is necessarily the best position. Freire (1971) used the term "basism" to describe this. In other words, consciousness is not determined by social location but it is greatly influenced by it. Just because somebody is oppressed does not mean their statements or opinions are exempt from critical scrutiny. But the political underplot of Freire's work (1978, 1993) opens up the process of becoming literate to the idea that the oppressed are in a unique position to reclaim authority for their experiences in the struggle to end exploitation on the basis of race, class, and gender. My position is not to reduce science education solely to politics. Rather I want to assert that position *does* matter both in terms of the science we teach and in the ways we choose to engage students in a critical understanding of that science. Adam Katz articulates the relationship between science and politics that I am trying to underscore here:

> If the service science provides to politics is in explaining its conditions of possibility, eliminating as many false paths as possible, and demystifying obscurantist ideological generalities, this is, first of all, in the interest of a science that itself depends upon a politics that defends its conditions of possibility by opening spaces previously closed to scrutiny; furthermore, this displays before science the limits and terms of its own tasks, and it sets science in motion by opening itself for critique. Politics, likewise, is interested in a science that protects the foundational political categories upon which politics and science both depend—categories, in the case of Marxism in particular, whose demystification stands at the origins of the science itself and whose various appearances, semblances, and mystifications set the terms for science or revolutionary theory. (2000, pp. 24–35)

My struggle to promote socially just education, especially for children and youth in poor urban settings, stems from a critical analysis of my own experiences as an elementary school teacher. Indeed, I know the very ideas I present here are difficult to live in the big machine of schooling. Yet, if we do not try, we will have given over our lives as educators to a future filled with inequality, oppression and unlived lives. I believe deeply that we must commit in urban science education circles to work with and for youth to make the science they learn and the science they do a part of the practice of working towards social justice in our urban centers here in the U.S. and especially in developing countries. No other goal will bring us closer to science for all.

Notes

1. I need to add this qualification. I don't agree with some of the Frankfurt School theorists who reduce the physical sciences to instrumental rationality. In other words, I don't believe that the sciences are only forms of domination, bourgeois impulses seeking to master the laws of nature and the physical environment. The epistemological critics of science—Lakatos, Bachelard, Popper, Canguilhem—postulate a relative autonomy of theoretical science through the idea that sciences serve as a type of heuristic (Callinicos, 1999). What interests me is how scientific knowledge is integrated into private corporate power.
2. These figures are taken from *The Economist*. "The Country-Club Vote." May 20, 2000, page 42.
3. In looking at critical pedagogy, it is important to demarcate its staging ground and political trajectory (McLaren & Baltodano, 2000). It is primarily a dialectical approach to understanding the contradictions within social life grounded in a commitment for encouraging each group—defined in racial, ethnic, gender, or other ways—to claim a notion of the good. My particular approach to critical pedagogy is Marxist, and I have often chosen to refer to it as 'revolutionary' pedagogy. The critical pedagogy that I am seeking bears a kinship to the Marxist humanism developed by Raya Dunayevskaya and more recently, by Peter Hudis. It emphasizes the way in which Marx's work was deeply immersed in the dialectics of the revolution. It is grounded in Marx's notion that capital is a form of congealed abstract labor and that the transcendence of alienation proceeds through a "second negativity" (Hudis, 1997; Marx, 1975). The first negation would be the negation of private property—that is, to get rid not only of the capitalists but capital itself. The negation of the negation—i.e., the negation of the negation of private property and the political overthrow of the bourgeoisie—must occur if capital is truly to be abolished (Dunayevskaya, 1989). This notion of self-movement through absolute negativity is what Marx meant as the basis of permanent revolution (Hudis, 1997).

References

Althusser, A. (1975). *Lenin and philosophy and other essays*. New York: Monthly Review Press.

Callinicos, A. (1999). *Social theory: A historical introduction*. New York: New York University Press.

Dunayevskaya, R. (1989). *Philosophy and revolution, from Hegel to Marx to Mao*. New York: Columbia University Press.

Foucault, M. (1972). *The archaeology of knowledge and the discourse on language*. Translated by A. M. Sheridan Smith. Pantheon Books: New York

Foucault, M. (1973). *The order of things: An archaeology of the human sciences*. New York: Vintage.

Freire, P. (1978). *Pedagogy in process: The letters to Guinea-Bissau*. Seabury: New York.

Freire, P. (1993). *Pedagogy of the oppressed*. Continuum: New York.

Harding, S. (1991). *Whose science? Whose knowledge?* Ithaca: Cornell University Press.

Harding, S. (1998). *Is science multicultural? Postcolonialisms, feminisms, and epistemologies*. Bloomington and Indianapolis: Indiana University Press.

Hudis, P. (1997). Conceptualizing an emancipatory alternative: Istvan Mészáros's beyond capital. *Socialism and Democracy, 11*(1), 37–54.

Hudis, P. (2000a). The dialectical structure of Marx's concept of 'revolution in permanence.' *Capital & Class, 70*, 127–142.

Hudis, P. (2000b). Can capital be controlled? *The Hobgoblin, 2*, 7–9.

Katz, A. (2000). *Postmodernism and the politics of culture*. Boulder, Colorado: Westview Press.

Lenin, V.I. (1943). *What is to be done?* New York: International Publishers.

Marx, K. (1975). *Early writing*. Harmondsworth: Penguin.

McLaren, P., & Baltodano, M. (2000). The ruture of teacher education and the politics of resistance. *Teaching Education, 11*(1), 31–44.

McLaren, P, & Farahmandpur, R. (2001a). Teaching against globalization and the new imperialism: Towards a revolutionary pedagogy. *Journal of Teacher Education, vol. 52*, No. 2, 136–150.

McLaren, P, & Farahmandpur, R. (2001b). Class, cultism, and multiculturalism: A notebook on forging a revolutionary politics. *Multicultural Education*, Spring, 5–11.

McMurtry, J. (1998). *Unequal freedoms: The global market as an ethical system*. West Hartford, CT: Kumarian Press.

Perrucci, R., & Wysong, E. (1999). *The new class society*. Boulder, CO: Rowman and Littlefield.

Trafford, A. (1996). Bitter medicine. *Washington Post*, July 2, Z–6.

Trend, D. (2001). *Welcome to cyberschool*. Boulder, Colorado: Rowman and Littlefield.

Zavarzadeh, M., & Morton, D. (1994). *Theory as resistance: Politics and culture after (post)structuralism*. New York: The Guilford Press.

Zweig, M. (2000). *The working-class majority: America's best-kept secret*. Ithaca: Cornell University Press.

"Capitalism, Critical Pedagogy, and Urban Science Education: An Interview with Peter McLaren" was published by Angela Calabrese Barton in the *Journal of Research in Science Teaching, vol. 38*, no. 8, 847–859.

Interview 12

pedagogy for revolution against education for capital: a dialogue on education in capitalism today

Glenn Rikowski

Glenn Rikowski is one of the most important Marxist educational theorists in the world. In the early 1990s, Glenn, Mike Cole, and Dave Hill of the United Kingdom all took me to task privately and in their own writings for my postmodernist approach to social transformation. They did this even though, at the time, I was friends with both Mike and Dave (Glenn I met much later, in Brighton, in 2004 and we have since become fast friends). Fortunately for me, I listened to them. It led me to a rediscovery of the centrality of Marx's writings for anyone seriously interested in social change through education, and I began the long and arduous task of engaging once again with Marx's work (having tried to read Marx in the 1960s and later as a graduate student). This time I was better prepared. Glenn, Mike, and Dave have been writing as Marxists for years, but there are few well-known Marxist scholars in education in the United States. So for many students of education in this country, Marxist theory is something that is completely new to them. Given the political atmosphere in this country at the moment, it is not an easy task to encourage educators and educators-in-the-making to read Marx. But it is an important task, nonetheless. This is one of my most in-depth discussions of education from a Marxist perspective.

Introduction

PETER MCLAREN: Well, Glenn, it's great to have the opportunity for this dialogue with you. We've corresponded by email now for nearly four years, and this situation is set up well for me to bring together a number of points. I would like to ask you about your work and politics, your "project" maybe—if you're not offended by the Blairite connotation!

GLENN RIKOWSKI: It's wonderful to share this platform with you, Peter, and we both owe it to *Cultural Logic* for giving us this slot. I have read your work closely over the last few years, and I have used it to try to radicalize further my outlook on education and its place in social transformation. And most certainly this is a magical opportunity to pose some questions to you with these ends in view. For me, this kind of thing is really about pushing our own views further and in new directions, to go beyond where we have gone in our published work, and also seeking to move the other person on that basis too. It's also about giving explanations and accounts of aspects of our own work, to show why we are doing what we are doing and in the style that we are doing it. On all these fronts it's about taking risks for an open future.

PETER: Yes, Glenn, I'm with you on your account on what we are doing here. Certainly, one thing we have both done in various ways is to have taken risks, risks that some have criticized us for—and we'll get on to those later. Also, Glenn, despite the range of topics you address in your work, the various empirical studies you have done, there are some strange silences too. I hope to kind of "flush you out" on some of those gaps. I'm intrigued as to why you don't write about certain issues. I first became aware of your work through that monster article you did for *British Journal of Sociology of Education*, "Left Alone" (Rikowski, 1996). Your honesty in that article was exemplary. You seemed to be facing the crisis within Marxist educational theory head-on, trying to grasp the depth of the crisis resulting from the deficiencies of what you called the "old" Marxist educational theory that was based on Sam Bowles and Herb Gintis *Schooling in Capitalist America* (1976) and Paul Willis (1977) *Learning to Labour*. You also launched an attack on me in that article, on the more "postmodern" moments within my work!

Postmodernism

GLENN: Indeed I did, Peter, as you've reminded me from time to time! Perhaps it would be useful if you could take me through where you stand now on postmodernism. I mean, without rehearing your objections to postmodernism, which would take several articles to do the job, can you give me some of your recent thinking on the subject —something, say, that you have not yet written about?

PETER: Let me begin to answer this by trying to give you a sense of where I situate my own analysis, first.

GLENN: Fine. It's a good way in.

PETER: I pretty much follow some of your ideas on where to begin my critique. I take the position that capital grounds all social mediation as a form of value, and that the substance of labor itself must be interrogated because doing so brings us closer to understanding the nature of capital's social universe out of which our subjectivities are created. Because the logic of capitalist work has invaded all forms of human sociability, society can be considered to be a totality of different types of labor. What is important here is to examine the particular forms that labor takes within capitalism. In other words, we need to examine value as a social relation, not as some kind of accounting device to measure rates of exploitation or domination. Consequently, labor should not be taken simply as a "given" category, but interrogated as an *object of critique*, and examined as an abstract social structure. Marx's value theory of labor does not attempt to reduce labor to an economic category alone but is illustrative of how labor as value form constitutes our very social universe, one that has been underwritten by the logic of capital. As you have underscored in your own work, Glenn, value is not some hollow formality, neutral precinct, or barren hinterland emptied of power and politics but the "*very matter and anti-matter of Marx's social universe*," as Mike Neary and yourself have indicated (in Neary & Rikowski, 2000). The production of value is not the same as the production of wealth. The production of value is historically specific and emerges whenever labor assumes its dual character. This is most clearly explicated in Marx's discussion of the contradictory nature of the commodity form and the expansive capacity of the commodity known as labor-power. In this sense, labor-power becomes the supreme commodity, the source of all value. For Marx, the commodity is highly unstable and non-identical. Its concrete particularity (use-value) is subsumed by its existence as value-in-motion or by what we have come to know as "capital" (value is always in motion because of the increase in capital's productivity that is required to maintain expansion). Raya Dunayevskaya (1978) notes that "*the commodity in embryo contains all the contradictions of capitalism precisely because of the contradictory nature of* *labor.*" What kind of labor creates value? Abstract universal labor linked to a certain organization of society, under capitalism. The dual aspect of labor within the commodity (use-value and exchange value) enables one single commodity—money—to act as the value measure of the commodity. Money becomes, as Dunayevskaya notes, the representative of labor in its abstract form. Thus, the commodity must not be considered a thing, but a social relationship. Dunayevskaya identified the "soul" of capitalist production as the extraction from living labor of all the unpaid hours of labor that amounts to surplus value or profit. I think that too much stress is being placed on the market and not enough on the process of production itself. There needs to be more analysis of the fetishism of the commodity form.

GLENN: I agree. You see this in "left" educational theorizing especially. A garage full of emphasis on education markets and quasi-markets, but not much recognition of education as production or the products of education.

PETER: Yes, Glenn, the issue here is not simply that workers are exploited for their surplus value but that all forms of human sociability are constituted by the logic of capitalist work. Labor, therefore, cannot be seen as the negation of capital or the antithesis of capital but capital's human face. Capitalist relations of production become hegemonic precisely when the process of the production of abstraction conquers the concrete processes of production, resulting in the expansion of the logic of capitalist work. We need to move beyond the fetishized form of labor (as organizational forms of labor such as labor movements or new forms of work organization) and concentrate instead upon new forms of human sociability. The key question that drives much of my work can be captured in the following question: How is labor constituted as a social relation within capitalism?

GLENN: So the key here is that teachers need a better grasp of the inner dynamics of capitalism? Is that it, Peter?

PETER: Yes, that's it precisely, Glenn. Living labor creates the value form of wealth that is historically specific to capitalism. What drives the capitalist machine, in other words, is the drive to augment value. We need to explore the inner dynamics of capitalism, how it raises social productivity to a level of mind-numbing enormity yet that does nothing to limit scarcity. Paula Allman talks about how capitalisms relations of distribution are simply the results of the relations of production, placing a limit on consumption by limiting the "effective" demand of the vast majority of the world's population. She reveals, in turn, how material use-values are only available in the commodity form, and how use-value is internally related and thus inseparable from the exchange-value of the commodity, which is determined by labor-time. She writes that the wealth that is constituted by capitalist societies is not just a vast array of use-values (it appears as this), but value itself. Wealth in capitalist society takes a perverted form. I agree with her that capitalism is perhaps best understood as a *global quest to produce value*. We need to focus our attention on capitalism's totalizing and universalizing tendencies. Its forms of global social domination are, of course, historically specific. Allman uses some of the insights of Moishe Postone (1996) to argue some very important points. One is that while capitalist exploitation through the production of value is abstract, it is also quasi-objective and concrete. Allman notes, correctly in my view, that people *experience* abstract labor in concrete or objective formations that are constituted subjectively in human actions and in human feelings, compulsions and emotions. Value produced by abstract labor can be considered objective *and* personal. How else can you account for the "hold" that abstract labor has on each and every one of us?

GLENN: I concur on that point. Alot hangs on it; the capitalization of humanity flows from that point.

PETER: Furthermore, Allman reveals how the value form "*moves between and binds all the social relations and habituated practices of capitalism into an interlocking network that constitutes what is often referred to as the social structure of capitalist society*." All critical education endeavors need to address the antagonistic terrain of capital that is inherent in the labor-capital relation itself and to lay bare the contradictions that lay at the heart of the social relations of production. The value form of labor which gives shape to these internal relations or contradictions not only affects the objective conditions within which people labor, but also the domain of subjectivity or human agency itself. This mediative role is far from innocent.

GLENN: This is the deep horror of capitalist reality. The difficult thing is to acknowledge that horror in a process of overcoming it —collectively, and on a world scale.

PETER: Yes, at the level of individual psychology the fact that our personalities are penetrated by capital is not that appealing! Of course, many Marxist educators advocate a fairer distribution of wealth, arguing that the current inequitable distribution that characterizes contemporary capitalist societies results from property relations, in particular, the private ownership of the means of production. For Paula Allman, and others, including yourself, Glenn, this doesnt go nearly far enough. The real culprit (as both you and Paula Allman have maintained) is the internal or dialectical relation that exists between capital and labor within the capitalist production process itself—a social relation in which capitalism is intransigently rooted. This social relation—essential or fundamental to the production of abstract labor—deals with how already existing value is preserved and new value (surplus value) is created. It is this internal dialectical relationship that is mainly responsible for the inequitable and unjust distribution of use-values, and the accumulation of capital that ensures that the rich get richer and the poor get poorer. It is this relation between capital and labor that sets in perilous motion the conditions that make possible the rule of capital by designating production for the market, fostering market relations and competitiveness, and producing the historically specific laws and tendencies of capital.

GLENN: But what about private property? "Traditional" Marxists make a big deal of that, Peter.

PETER: True, private property is a concern, I don't want to downplay this. But private property, commodities, and markets all pre-date the specific labor-capital relations of production and serve as pre-conditions for it. And once capital develops they are transformed into the results of that relation. This is why you, Paula Allman, Mike Neary and others emphasize as fundamental the abolition of the labor-capital relationship as the means for laying the groundwork for liberation from scarcity.

GLENN: The abolition of capital, as a social relation and social force, is crucial, as you say, Peter. To get rid of private property and the capitalist without abolition of capitalist social relations clearly leaves a vacuum into which the state can enter, making for a pernicious *state* capitalism. Okay, Peter, now that you have situated your own work firmly within the Marxist tradition, how does your position enable you to criticize postmodernism? We still haven't got to my original question on where you stand on postmodernism today!

PETER: For me it is important to be able to help students understand various postmodern theories as contributing to a re-functioning of capital. Rather than rehearse —even briefly —my critique of postmodernism, I'll start somewhere specific.

GLENN: You are never brief, Peter!

PETER: Okay, instead of itemizing my general criticisms of postmodern theory, it might be more productive to share my recent reading of the work of David McNally, because I think he has done a tremendous job of deepening the critique of postmodern theory from a Marxist perspective.

GLENN: Shoot!

PETER: McNally has recently published a wonderful critique of Saussure, Derrida, and the post-structuralists—as well as a celebration of Volisinov/Bahktin, and especially Benjamin—in a book called *Bodies of Meaning* (McNally, 2001). His basic argument, since I can't recall all the details without reference to my notes, is that economic concepts figure centrally in their approaches to linguistic science. I recall that he argued the following points. Postmodern theorists model language on their specific understanding of the capitalist marketplace. McNally makes a good case that, in the process of such modeling, formal linguistics turns language into the dead labor of fetishistic commodities. It does this by decapitating signifiers and their meaning-making process from their fundamental connection to living labor. For example, Saussure and Derrida equate the general phenomenon of linguistic value with the role of "money" as a general equivalent of exchange. McNally calls Derrida the philosopher of fictitious capital. Derrida criticizes Saussure for positing an invariant or transcendental signified, or what McNally calls a "gold standard" against which signs can be measured or interpreted. Derrida, as you will recall, argues that there is only *differance*, that unknowable form prior to language, that condition of undecidability and the very condition of possibility of that undecidability that permits the endless play of reference that Derrida famously discusses in his large corpus of work (Derrida seems enraptured by difference and enraged by sameness, norms, standards). When Derrida makes the claim that *differance* is the most general structure of the economy he denies the praxis and labor that ground economic relations. That's because money lacks a referent, according to Derrida. It has no material foundation; money circulates without any referents. You can, for instance, have bad cheques, fraudulent credit cards—and these function as money. Credit and speculation become a form of "fictitious" capital.

GLENN: Sounds a lot like Baudrillard. Smells like postmodern virtual spirit.

PETER: Exactly. Actually, McNally goes on to discuss Baudrillard, and how in his system sign values are independent of external referents, they refer, in other words, only to *themselves*. Baudrillard's is an economy of internal relations, following its own code. Baudrillard lives in a techno-crazed universe of techno-mediatic power where labor is always already dead, where political economy is dead, where everything is virtual, the economy is virtual, and where use-values have disappeared. Use-values do not transcend the codes that encapsulate them and give them life.

GLENN: Right, the sign economy. We don't have exchange-value or use-value in the Marxist sense anymore, we have an information economy that trades in images, and status, and all of that. It's a good story if you can get people to believe it. A lot of Internet magazines seem convinced: *Fast Company, Business 2.0* and the like.

PETER: There is something compelling about it, I admit, as long as we realize it's science fiction. Scientologists beware! You have competition for Battlefield Earth! Baudrillard maintains that we consume fictitious identities by purchasing the sign value of, say, an Armani suit, or a pair of Guess jeans. We dress ourselves up in abstractions—literally. Contrast this with what Marx had to say, that in capitalist societies, concrete labor is reduced to a quantum of total social labor, as something translated into the socially necessary labor-time—a process that is part of the circuit of production and exchange. The key point here, according to McNally, is that, for Marx, abstract labor is not a mental abstraction but the *real social form of labor* in capitalist society. This is an important point. It's an absolutely crucial point. When labor-power itself becomes a commodity (a special kind of commodity) in the very act of laboring itself, then this abstracting process becomes generalized. But what we are talking about here is surely more than a linguistic phenomenon and McNally is very critical of Derrida's linguistification of life. If this were just a linguistic phenomenon then we would have to go along with Wittgenstein, and maybe in the process have to concede that Marxist theory was the result of a linguistic error! *Contra* Baudrillard and Derrida, signifiers do not replace use-value in a virtual economy of signs. True, capitalism entails an abstracting process, but it is one in which concrete labor is translated into abstract labor—into a labor that resembles interchangeable bits. But this is not just a concept, or a signifier, it is a real social form within the process of production; it is, as McNally notes, a systematic process of abstraction wherein capital compels the translation of concrete labor into abstract labor. Labor-power becomes value only when it assumes a value-relation, an objective life as a commodity, an abstraction from the body-work of the laborer, and hence from the use-values produced by the efforts of laboring subjects. This is alienated labor, the subsumption of concrete labor by abstract labor. McNally writes that no matter how abstracted things become, the exchange between money and a commodity always entails exchanges of labor. Capital is not self-birthing; it is never an independent source of value. For instance, interest-bearing capital does not escape a connection with human labor but is merely the purest fetish of them all. In their rage against Marx's obsession with decidability, post-structuralists deny the origin of value in labor, in the life-giving, toiling, body in labor.

GLENN: Which is why we need materialist critique.

PETER: Precisely. McNally describes historical materialist critique as a struggle against idealism, against the subordination of the world of bodies, nature, objects, and labor to subjectivity, and a struggle against objects being subsumed by concepts. It is a direct challenge against the autonomy of thought, that is, against objective, concrete, sensuous life being subsumed by the self-movement of thought.

GLENN: So, then fetishes are not a figment of the imagination?

PETER: No, they are tangibly real. Marx believes that they are necessary forms of appearance of alienated life. McNally brilliantly notes that in Derrida's economy of fictitious capital, our birth into language is—how did he say it?—right, our birth into language is detached from our origin in the bodies of others. This is very important for us to grasp. He likens Derrida's approach to language to the way that money-capital is treated as self-generating, without an origin in labor.

GLENN: And how do we abolish these fetishes?

PETER: By undressing them, and undoing them, and through revolutionary praxis, abolishing capitalist social relations.

GLENN: But developing revolutionary praxis surely means uncovering redemptive possibilities within the commodity form, too? I mean, you can't escape the commodity form entirely, you can't work fully outside the seductive thrall of capital, altogether?

PETER: That's an excellent point, Glenn. Let's follow some of McNally's observations further. He notes that Walter Benjamin realized the redemptive possibilities within the de-mythified and barren landscape of capitalism. In his work on the *flâneur,* for instance, Benjamin conveyed that everyone in capitalist society is a prostitute who sells his or her talents and body parts. We live in the charred world of capital, a dead zone inhabited by corpses and decaying commodities. Such a realization can help break through the naturalization of history and enter the terrain of historical action. According to McNally, Benjamin ruptures the myth of the self-made man. We are all dead objects awaiting the meanings we have yet to write, as McNally puts it. McNally sees Benjamin as establishing a political project in which the oppressed class must reclaim the libidinal energies it has cathected onto commodities and re-channel them into a revolutionary praxis, a praxis of historical struggle towards emancipation, towards liberation. It was Benjamin, after all, who said, "*money stands ruinously at the center of every vital interest.*" Revolutionary action involves the dialectics of remembering and forgetting, of challenging the repressed bourgeois desires linked to the rise of capitalism, and embodied in the collective dreams of a pathological culture, a society gone mad—something we don't have time to explore here. But it is something I have touched upon in my earlier work, especially in my *Critical Pedagogy and Predatory Culture* (1995). In other words, we need to have a theory that helps us to resist the social practices of exploitation linked to the social relations of production, but, dialectically, our resisting also helps us to have theory. In fact, this resisting is in many ways the basis of our theory.

GLENN: What about modes of resistance that you and I are more familiar with in our everyday praxis: the strike, protest rallies, and the like?

PETER: Yeah, Benjamin writes very little about these. But in his *One-Way Street*, Benjamin does stress the centrality of physical action. According to McNally, Benjamin views the body as the site of a transformative type of knowing, one that arises through physical action. Revolutionary practice, for Benjamin, means cultivating a "bodily presence of mind." We need to locate new energies—in hip-hop, in art, in protest demonstrations (like the Zapatistas)—without being re-initiated into the giddy whirl of bourgeois subjectivity, its jaccuzzi reformism, and its lap-dog liberalism. That can only happen when you have a collective political project to give direction and coherence to your struggle. For me, that direction comes from a commitment to defeat the capitalists, but also capital. Admittedly, we are consigned by history to live in the disjunction between the defeat of capital and the recognition that such a defeat is not likely to happen soon. Glenn, you have quizzed me about how I now see postmodernism, but I am puzzled by your *own* attitude towards it. I know you have critiqued postmodern theory with Mike Cole and Dave Hill in your 1997 article (Cole, Hill & Rikowski, 1997), but what exactly is your own position on it?

GLENN: Well, you're correct that I haven't written as much on the critique of postmodernism as yourself, or as much as Dave Hill and Mike Cole. This does need some explaining, perhaps. It's not just a case of slothfulness! In the late 1980s and early 1990s I read a shed full of material in education journals written from various postmodernist and poststructuralist perspectives. At the time I thought I could see where it was all leading: to various doors labeled "Nihilism," "Relativism" or "Solipsism." With hindsight, I think that gut judgement was validated by what actually occurred. Also it seemed that educational postmodernism was on the road to totally eclipsing Marxist educational theory by absorbing any form of potential radicalism and spitting it out as a fashion statement. But I formulated a particular reaction—a strategy if you like—to the situation. I decided I would stop reading all the secondary, derivative stuff and go straight to the heart of the postmodernist beast by reading the postmodern Godfathers: Foucault, Deleuze, Baudrillard, Lyotard, Derrida and the rest. That was a very short phase, for I realized that Nietzsche had heavily influenced all these theorists. Thus: I needed to dive deeper to get to the real roots of postmodernism. So from 1992 to around 1996 I read most of the works of Nietzsche. Some I read twice. I pretty much continued to ignore the postmodernist stuff written after 1992—though for the Cole, Hill and Rikowski article (1997) I had to backtrack and read a bit in order to make my contribution to that article useful. Then in 1996 Geoff Waite published his monumental and masterly critical study of Nietzsche (Waite, 1996). Waite got right to the core of Nietzsche's *intentions*, what the philosopher with a hammer was really up to. According to Waite, Nietzsche's project was to attempt to bring about an eternal rift within humanity between an elite (that would venerate Nietzsche as one of its own) and the mass. The mass would have the role of sustaining the elite in conditions where their creativity could remain vital and flourish—which was why Nietzsche was obsessed with the state of culture and society in his own day. For Waite then, the Eternal Return of the Same is the Eternal Return of the elite/mass duality. The doctrine is an attempt to engineer a future where the corpse of Nietzsche would be continually rejuvenated as the elite lived an idealized Nietzschean existence and his corpus (the body of his work) venerated in the process.

That's not all. Waite explains that Nietzsche obviously needed the help of intellectuals, politicians, media people and educators to bring this about. He had to *seduce* us. Nietzsche had to write in an esoteric way that recruited us to the project of realizing his abominable Eternity. Furthermore, Waite indicates the forms and processes of Nietzschean textual, conceptual and discursive seduction; the many tactics he used, and the fishhooks and tests he put in our way. On this account, Nietzsche's corps has two main officer blocs overlaying a postmodernist infantry. First, there is what Waite calls the Nietzsche Industry—those apologists and so-called "interpreters" of Nietzsche who avoid or sanitize Nietzsche's real game. Second, there are the postmodern Godfathers—Derrida, Lyotard and the rest. These are the upper tiers of Nietzsche's corps. The interpreters of postmodernism are the footsoldiers, the infantry, of Nietzsche's corps. They are legion, and they cast a huge cloak of obfuscation, denial, mind-fucking mediocrity and inverted pomposity on the question of the implication of themselves within the realization of Nietzsche's Project of Eternal Return. For me, postmodernism does not just collude with Nietzsche's project for humanity and his resurrection through his followers; it is a vital force within that project. So, through the work of Geoff Waite, I wish to simultaneously uncover the roots of postmodernism and Nietzsche's dangerous project for humanity's future. I'm more interested in exposing this—because I think it's more important—than just criticizing postmodernism *per se*.

PETER: You said there were two aspects to your outlook on postmodernism: what's the other one, Glenn?

GLENN: Yes, there is a second aspect of my take on postmodernism. I do believe postmodern thinking has inadvertently hit on something with its foregrounding of a de-centered, fragmented and multi-faceted "self." Basically, the postmodernists and poststructuralists are interesting on this. But the key task is the *explanation* of this fragmentation. Now, for me, the role theorists of the 1960s and early 1970s and the work of Erving Goffman and R.D. Laing had explanations of the "divided self" that surpass any stuff on "discourse" produced by most postmodernists and poststructuralists. This work is largely forgotten nowadays. For me though, the task is to explore the "divided self" through Marxism as an exercise in developing Marxist science. Thus, the analysis of "the human" as a contradictory phenomenon, where these contradictions are generated by value relations as they flow through labor-power, is the starting point. Labor-power is inseparable from personhood, though labor recruiters and personnel managers necessarily reify it as a collection of attributes in the recruitment process. This impossibility of separation is a problem for capital, as the single commodity that can generate more value than that constituted at the moments of its own social production—labor-power—is an aspect of the person of the laborer that is controlled by a potentially hostile will. Holding "that the will has no existence" sidesteps the issue, as acts of willing (whether there is a "will" or not) have the same effect. The "will" itself, moreover, can also be explored as a set of contradictory forces. Of course, I can see the inevitable objection; that whilst I have criticized forms of Marxist educational theory that embrace determinism, I have opened the door to a reconfigured determinist embrace. But I hold I've done the opposite; the clash of contradictory drives or forces within the "human" engenders *indeterminacy*, openness. One could, of course, introduce a new determinism on the basis of some presupposition regarding the relative *strength* of particular social drives and forces as they come into contradiction within the "human." Not only would this be undesirable, but also for Marxist science it would avoid the problem of explaining changes in the power and strength of these contradictory drives and forces. Furthermore, the core dynamic antagonism is denied on such determinism: the contradiction between our "selves" as labor and ourselves as *capital*, human-capital. I am capital. We are human-capital, the human-as-capital, but this is constituted by and through ourselves as labor; we haunt ourselves in a creative loop within the constitution of our personhoods. We are inherently contradictory life forms, but these very contradictions drive us on to try to solve them within our everyday lives (including within "ourselves"). On an individual basis this is impossible. Marxist psychotherapy is pointless. We require a *politics of human resistance*. This is a politics aimed at resisting the reduction of our personhoods to labor-power (human-capital), thus resisting the capitalization of humanity. This politics also has a truly negative side: the slaying of the contradictions that screw-up, bamboozle and depress us. However, only collectively can these contradictions constituting personhood (and society: there is no individual/society duality) be abolished. Their termination rests on the annihilation of the social relations that generate them (capitalist social relations), the social force that conditions their development within social phenomena, including the "human" (capital) and the dissolution of the substance of capital's social universe (value). A collective, political project of human resistance is necessary, and this goes hand in hand with *communist politics*, a positive politics of social and human re-constitution. This is the collective process of re-designing society, revolutionary socialist transformation as Paula Allman (1999) has it. We need to simultaneously engage in this as we struggle for abolition of the social domination of capital. As I see it, Marxist science and politics and a politics of human resistance to capital are forms and aspects of each other. Communist society already exists on this view; it is a suppressed and repressed form of life within capitalism.

PETER: And where does this leave postmodernism, Glenn?

GLENN: Well, Peter, postmodern thinking just becomes a liability, a block, on even raising these sorts of issues and questions, let alone getting any kinds of answers. Postmodernists don't like answers, it seems to me; as you said earlier they celebrate "undecidability," and hence they fight shy of explanation. But this disarms us. These are big hang-ups that we can't afford. We need to move on. The development of Marxist science (a negative critique of capitalist society) and a politics of human resistance are just more important, and also more interesting, than criticism of postmodernism. Though, on the basis of forestalling a Nietzschean future, we have to expose postmodernism as the blight on humanity that it is, whilst also using it if we actually do find something worthwhile residing within it.

PETER: Well, your answer raises a lot of issues, questions and problems, Glenn, and I want to take some of these up later. You packed a lot of punches into a few rounds there! But where do you stand on those who have tried to leave postmodernism through Nietzsche? I have people like Nigel Blake and his colleagues in view here (Blake *et al.*, 2000). You sent me an unpublished paper of yours, *Nothing Becomes Them: Education and the Nihilist Embrace* (2001a) where you lavish fulsome praise on Nigel Blake and his pals for moving from postmodernism to nihilism through Nietzsche. This seems weird when Mike Cole, Dave Hill and yourself castigated Nigel Blake in an earlier article (Cole, Hill & Rikowski, 1997) for supporting postmodernism that, on the analysis there, was on track to run into nihilism which the three of you thought was the last stop before hell! Secondly, on what you said previously, moving from postmodernism to Nietzschean nihilism looks to have thrown Blake and company smack into the arms of something far worse than postmodernism: Nietzsche's Project of Eternal Return! Where's the redeeming features of the track taken by Blake and friends? I must admit, I can't readily see them!

Nihilism and Nietzsche

GLENN: Straight for the weakest link, Peter, nice one! I know what I've said seems strange, but I'll try an explanation. When I moved *back* from reading derivative postmodern writings to reading the postmodern Godfathers and then to reading Nietzsche, this was, in my view, a kind of progression. Nigel Blake, Paul Smeyers, Richard Smith and Paul Standish have made a similar movement in their book *Education in an Age of Nihilism* (2000), though I get the impression that they didn't actually engage with the first base (the derivative stuff) as much as it did. So, by the same token, they have moved in a productive direction. It should be noted, however, that they have not moved wholly away from the postmodern Godfathers, so their *Nihilism* book is transitional. Secondly, through the concept of nihilism, they have forged a deep and wide-ranging critique of many aspects of contemporary education and training in England. They indicate how the abyss of nothingness (the de-valued values) at the core of education policy, where discussion about the purposes and goals of education is substituted by instrumentalism and managerialism, is the centrifugal (but negative) force conditioning developments in contemporary education and training. The "crisis of value" in education is a precondition for the generation of such phenomena as the school effectiveness/improvement movements, targets, funding systems umbilically tied to outputs, the drive to produce human capital and much else in this gloomy educational landscape. Thirdly, they contrast this state of affairs with Nietzsche's affirmative attitude towards life. The quest to overcome nihilism in education parallels Nietzsche's attempt to transcend nihilism through a process of self-overcoming. Blake and colleagues seek to show how education can be made more vital, intense, interesting and worthwhile when the overcoming of nihilism radicalizes educational processes, forms and content. They aim to bring moral *commitment* back to the educational enterprise. Thus, for Blake and co-writers, education after Nietzsche is implicated in the quest to overcome nihilism by creating the conditions where new values can emerge, values that do not de-value themselves as we attempt to realize them (as did the old, tired values underpinning modernism). Fourthly, Blake and company note that they wish to *use* Nietzsche, not just interpret him, not just be part of the Nietzsche Industry. I too argue that Nietzsche needs to be used, used to subvert his own goals! I now don't go along with Geoff Waite (1996) that we should just not mess with Nietzsche at all; that gives Nietzsche too much respect. Waite seems almost paranoid, or at least fearful, about what Nietzsche's texts can do to us. After I read his book I could understand why he held this. But on reflection I think I was wrong, and that Blake and colleagues attitude towards Nietzsche is healthier.

PETER: Explain why and how this is so, Glenn.

GLENN: Well, now, for me, it seems that Blake and associates have produced a serious and important critique of certain trends and developments within contemporary education and training that Marxist and socialist educational analysts have also highlighted. Indeed, their critique is deeper and more interesting than in some Marxist and socialist accounts. They attack the very *roots* of education policy and change—not just the effects of these. Unlike a standard postmodern "deconstruction" of education policies, Blake and his collaborators have a dreadful, but strangely productive, vantage point—nihilism—from which to illustrate the dread at the heart of contemporary education. In doing this, they make critique of today's education significant and interesting whilst offering an apparent way forward through Nietzsche. For me, this is preferable to infinite deconstruction and "questioning of concepts" from no position whatsoever (as positions are denied). Blake and colleagues face up to the fact that postmodernism entails nihilism; they are honest. Once they face this they creatively turn this insight into conceptual dynamite for the critique of education and society.

PETER: I see, but there's a downside? I mean, I've seen some of your unpublished stuff on Nietzsche.

GLENN: Yes, there is. Their avoidance of Nietzschean interpretation also insulates them from the growing anti-Nietzsche work. Most of all, they seem oblivious to Geoff Waite's critical analysis. The implications of their analysis is that "the strong should be protected from the weak" in education and society as a whole. The weak masses are sacrificed to the potential for creativity and innovation of the strong, the elite whose heroic members are capable of forging new values. This becomes the ultimate *new value* of the education system. They say:

> The strong—those who can affirm life—need to be protected from the life-sapping nihilism of the weak, and this is not to be realized through the nostalgic restating of values, through the monitoring and rubber-stamping of standards, for these are only guises of the Last Man. It must reach its completion by passing through the Last Man, but going beyond him to the one who wants to perish, to have done with that negativity within himself: relentless destruction of the reactive forces, of the degenerating and parasitic, passing into the service of a superfluity of life (Blake et al., 2000, 63)

For Marxist science and Marxist educational theory, the hope is precisely in those "reactive forces" incorporated within the masses collectively expressing themselves as concrete forms of definite danger to the social domination of capital. In running counter to this possibility, Blake and his collaborators open themselves up to the full force of Geoff Waite's critique. Furthermore, their analysis of nihilism does not go deep enough; they fail to raise the question of the *form* that nihilism takes in contemporary capitalist society, to explore the relation between *value*, values, nothingness and meaninglessness (they tend to see nihilism in terms of meaninglessness). This work has yet to be undertaken. Thus, I am suggesting that their critique can be radicalized further through engagement with Marx, and that taking this route can neutralize Nietzsche's program for humanity as we come to grasp that there is no "self-overcoming" without dissolution of the capitalist universe. Self-overcoming is synonymous with overcoming capital, as the "self" is a form of capital, human-capital.

PETER: This last point of yours, Glenn, fits in with something that you have raised in your work, and which you hint at in this dialogue previously: the relation between labor power and human capital. What is that relation? Also, you have stated on a number of occasions, that education policy in England rests on human capital development. Perhaps you could illustrate how these pieces fit together?

Human Capital and Labor-Power

GLENN: Well, I'll try. The first bit's controversial. First, although I am interested in Marx's *method* of working and in his method of presentation, I am not one of those who believe that there is a "Marxist method" that can simply be "applied." I'm certainly not one of those who believe in some "dialectical" Marxist method (deriving from a Hegelian reading of Marx) that we can take ready-made off-the-peg either. Certainly, I learnt a tremendous amount from reading the works of Derek Sayer (1979–1987), but I tend to start from asking a simple question: what is the *form* that this social phenomenon assumes within the social universe of capital? Now, labor-power is in the first instance a transhistorical concept. There must be labor-power of some sort of another; a capacity to labor that is transformed into actual labor within a process of laboring—the labor process—for any human society to exist. However, labor-power takes on different forms as between social formations. Marx talks about labor-power in ancient societies based on slave labor, and the feudal form of labor-power. Marx was most interested in the *historical social form* that labor-power assumed in capitalist society. In capitalism, I have argued, following Marx, labor-power is a commodity. Furthermore, it takes the form of *human capital*. Human capital production and enhancement are at the heart of New Labor's education policy (Rikowski, 2001c).

But it is not strictly accurate to say that human capital and labor-power are *identical*, though as convenient shorthand they can be viewed as such. The form of labor-power varies between social formations, whereas human capital is a phenomenon tied to capitalist society, but when we refer to "labor-power within capitalist society" then *de facto* this fixes the form of labor-power as human capital. In my "Education, Capital and the Transhuman" article I demonstrate their virtual identity in capitalism in detail, with reference to Marx's work (Rikowski, 1999).

Secondly, labor-power also has the potential to be expressed in non-capitalist, anti-capitalist modes, and in the transition from capitalism to socialism it will be. This point indicates the fact that labor-power can *exceed* its contemporary social existence as human capital. Finally, the possibility for internal struggle, within the person of the laborer, *against* the capitalization (i.e., the subsumption) of her/his personal powers and capacities under the domination of capital for value-creation, is a potential barrier to the capitalization of labor-powers. For me, *this is the class struggle within the "human" itself; a struggle over the constitution of the "ourselves" as capital through the practical definition of labor-power.* Today the class struggle is everywhere, as capital is everywhere. Human capital is labor-power expressed as capitalist social form. As labor-power is intimately linked to personhood then "we are capital" to the extent of its incorporation within our personhoods and its expression in our lives. Thus, a really useful *psychology of capital* would be an account of our "selves" as capital. This would be a parasitic psychology, for capital is a blind social force (created by us) that has no ego of its own (as noted by Moishe Postone, 1996), but is given life through us, as we become (are taken over, transformed into) it.

What I call "liberal left" critics object to this account on two main fronts. First, they argue that labor-power is not a commodity as people "are not sold on the market or produced for sale on the market," and if they were that would be a society based on slave labor, and not essentially capitalist society based on formally "free" labor. Humans, therefore, cannot be "capital." Secondly, some have put it to me, in private conversations that I am quite perverse in taking the concept of "human capital" seriously at all. After all, they would say, is this not just a hopeless bourgeois concept? Does it not just reduce education to the production of skills and competencies? And is this not what we are *against?*

PETER: So what are your replies to these critics, Glenn?

GLENN: Let's explore the first point: labor-power is not a commodity. Well, labor-power is in the first instance, within the labor market, the capacity to labor, not labor itself. It is this capacity that the laborer sells to representatives of capital as a commodity, *not her or his total personhood*, nor "labor" as such. We have many skills, abilities and knowledges, but from the standpoint of the capitalist labor process, only those that are significant for value-creating labor have direct social worth, validity or relevance. Representatives of capital buy labor-power, but not the whole person. However, it is most unfortunate for capital's managers that this unique value-creating power is incorporated within a potentially volatile and living body—the laborer. There is no getting round this. The task of getting the laborer to yield up her or his special power, labor-power, for value-creation, to channel the laborer's talents and capabilities into the process of generating value, is the material foundation of business studies, human resource management and other branches of management studies. Furthermore, the sale is made only for a specific duration and the laborer can take her/himself off to another employer, subject to contractual procedures. In all of this, the fact that labor-power is incorporated within the personhood of the laborer is a source of much vexation and frustration for representatives of capital. On the other hand, the flexibility that this implies, where the constitution of labor-power changes with demands made upon the laborer within the capitalist labor process, is an aspect of labor-power that capitalists appreciate. Management "science" is littered with eulogies to flexibility and adaptability. Indeed, a study I made of the UK Institute of Personnel Managements and also the Industrial Society's journal going back to the First World War showed that flexibility and adaptability in school-leavers were attributes that employers were looking for in youth recruits right back to that time. They also expected schools and colleges to play their part in producing such forms of youth labor. Thus they were looking for labor-power, or human capital, of a certain kind.

PETER: And the second point, Glenn, what's your reply there?

GLENN: Yes, on the second point: this is that "human capital" is a bourgeois concept therefore we should have nothing to do with it. For me, this constitutes an abandonment of serious critical analysis of society. Marx remember, in his *Capital*, was not giving a better "socialist" form of political economy, but a *critique* of political economy. Marx held that political economy was the most highly developed and condensed form of the expression of the social relations of society within bourgeois thought. It was society viewed from the "standpoint of capital," as capital. The critique of political economy was simultaneously a critique of the social relations, and especially the form of *labor* (the value-form), within that society. I maintain that the concept of "human capital" expresses something quite horrific; the *human as capital!* The critique of this concept is, therefore, of the utmost urgency. It is precisely because "human capital" is a bourgeois concept, and one that expresses such deep horror, that critical analysts of capitalist society should place it center stage. Running away from it, like superficial liberal left critics, gives capital and its human representatives an easier time and avoids the potential explosiveness that its critique can generate for unsettling capitalist thought and social relations. We should take the concept very seriously indeed. In fact, I would argue that human capital theorists do not take their own master concept seriously. This is because they cannot, for to do so would explode the full horror of the phenomenon the concept expresses. There is real horror lurking within this concept of human capital; Marxists have a special duty to expose it, as no other critical analysts of society seem to have the stomach for it. The politics of human resistance is simultaneously a *politics of horror*, as it includes fighting against the horrific forms of life that we are becoming. For although "we are capital" the process is historical; it develops in intensity over time. Fortunately, the more it occurs the greater its obviousness, and the more paranoid supporters of the system (those who gain millions, billions, of dollars on the foundation of suppressing this insight) will become.

PETER: The thing with reading this stuff, Glenn, is that I find myself seeing your explanations of my questions and then I also find that there are further ideas that you use to give the explanations that are also interesting, and that I would like to follow up on these! It would be great to read more about what you say on capital as a "social force," what your views are on the nature of the "human" in capitalist society and what you have to say on the "social universe of capital." But for now, could you expand on what elsewhere you have called the "social production of labor-power" in capitalist society—in your conference paper for the British Educational Research Association, "That Other Great Class of Commodities" paper (Rikowski, 2000a). Because this seems to me to be the point where your Marxism connects directly with education, and in quite specific ways, Glenn.

The Social Production of Labor-Power in Capitalism

GLENN: Yes, Peter, what I have called the social production of labor-power in capitalism is crucial for the existence and maintenance of capitalist society today, and education and training have important roles to play in these processes of social production. For Marx, labor-power is defined as the aggregate of those mental and physical capabilities within a human being which they exercise when they produce a use-value of any kind (Marx, 1867). Now, the significant issue, for me, is what is included in "mental capabilities." The standard response is to view these as skills, competencies or the ability to draw upon different knowledges in labor-power performance. But I argue (in Rikowski, 2001b, for example) that "attitudes," personal values and outlooks and personality traits are also included within "labor-power." I argue this on a number of counts. First, empirically, recruiters of labor search for work attitudes and personality traits above all other categories of recruitment criteria (and many recruitment studies show this). Second, the first point indicates a key feature of labor-power. This is that a laborer can have three PhDs, a bunch of IT qualifications and a Nobel Prize in physics, but from the perspective of capital the key questions is whether s/he is motivated and committed to expending all these wonderful capacities and capabilities within the labor process. For representatives of capital this is the essential point—and why I include attitudes to work and work-related personality traits within the orbit of labor-power. Third, at the global level, it is essential that labor-power is expended sufficiently to create surplus-value; thus not only must the "wills" of individual workers be subsumed under their own labor-power in the service of capital (value-production), but the working class *in toto* must be. It is therefore an aspect of social domination, and that indicates reconfiguration of the collective social life of the laborers on the foundation of capital. Fourth, and most important, including attitudes, values and personality traits within labor-power both *radicalizes* Marx and *radicalizes* the concept of labor-power.

PETER: But again, it could be argued that you have produced another form of determinism—with no escape. Aspects of our very personalities "become capital" as they are incorporated within labor-power. So, what happens to agency? Where is the space for self-activity? And where does education come into this? You still have to explain that.

The Problem of Agency

GLENN: The incorporation of aspects of "personality" (attitudes, values and personality traits) changes nothing. Remember earlier that I said it is clashes of contradictory forces and drives within the "human" that make determinism impossible. These oppositional forces within personhood ensure *openness* within the social universe of capital; a universe that moves and expands on the foundation of the clashing of drives and forces within its totality. This openness does not exist within postmodernist *aporias*, or in some social spaces "in the margins," or in the borders of this social universe. There are no such social spaces, in my view. There is nowhere to hide. The social universe of capital *is all that there is*. Rather, the openness results from the clash of social forces and drives. This partly contradicts what I said earlier, for although none of these forces and drives are inherently stronger or superior there is one that has the capacity to destroy the whole basis of the social universe of capital. This is the collective social force of the working class acting on a global scale to destroy capitalist social relations, to annihilate *capital* itself, and this is the *communist impulse* at its most vital, when there is a massive movement of social force and energy. The capitalist social universe, whose substance is value, *implodes* when this social force to move human history on from pre-history generates sufficient pressure. In the routine running and expansion of the social universe of capital, this force is *suppressed*—it only has virtual existence. But it is our hope for the future.

PETER: Yeah, but, pressing you still: what is agency in the social universe of capital?

GLENN: Well, first I'll get the mess out of the way. The conventional agency/structure problem, so-called, is insoluble. Basically, it's a recasting of the freedom/determinism problem within social life, capitalist social life in fact. Thinking "agency" has the effect of dissolving "structure" and *vice versa*. An experiment: just try to think both at the same time! Purported solutions such as Anthony Giddens's "structuration theory" evade the impossibility of simultaneous existence of agency and structure. I explain all this in more detail in my article "The Which Blair Project" (Rikowski, 2000b), so I won't enter into it here. Agency, for me, can be understood like any other social (and it is social, not an individual) phenomenon within the social universe of capital: by inquiring into its social *form*. I haven't followed this through in detail, so I'm literally "thinking on the keyboard" here, but I would probably argue that agency in capitalist society exists to the extent that individuals partake in a social project of human emancipation through imploding the social universe of capital. This implosion *opens up* human futures to possibilities where agency can have real (not just virtual, or repressed, or suppressed) social existence. This applies to many other "moral" or "social value" phenomena too, such as social justice. In the struggle against capitalist social existence, the abstract and virtual begin to take on real social form, but its substantive reality is repressed and suppressed. Thus, "agency" and "social justice," for example, in capitalist society, are only ever virtual. In this sense, agency in capitalism can only be the *struggle* for agency, the struggle to make it substantively *real*—as opposed to the abstract reality (as real abstraction) it attains in capitalist society. The same for social justice: in capitalist society, social justice is *the struggle for social justice* (as I explain this in greater depth in an experimental paper I wrote a year ago: Rikowski, 2000c). Capital, as Moishe Postone tells us (Postone, 1996), is "without ego." There is therefore, not just an absence of any standpoint on which to base *values*, but no *substance* that can make values possible. The postmodernists and nihilists are expressing something at this point. In capital's social universe, "values" have no substance, but value *is* the substance. Morality, is the *struggle for* morality, the struggle to make it real, and this can only be a possibility (still only a possibility) in the movements of society post-capitalism. Moral critiques of capitalism are in themselves insufficient, as Marx held (though they are understandable, and may energize people and make them angry against the system, and this anger may lead to significant forms of collective struggle). However, the *struggle to attain morality*, the struggle to make values possible, continually crashes against the fabric of society. It is this that makes struggles for gender equality, "race" equality and so on so explosive. In capitalist society, these forms of equality (like all other forms of equality) are impossible. But the struggle for their attainment exposes their possibility, a possibility that arises only within a post-capitalist scenario.

On this analysis, collective quests for gender and "race" equality are a threat to the constitution of capitalist society; they call forth forms of equality that can have no social validity, no existence, within the universe of capital—as *all forms of equality are denied except for one*. This is equality on the basis of *exchange-value*. On the basis of exchange-value we are all equal. There are a number of aspects to this. First, our *labors* may be equal in terms of the value they create. However, as our labor-powers have different values, then 10 weeks of my labor may be equal to a single day of the labor of some highly paid soccer player. Equality here, then, operates on the basis of massive substantive *inequality*. Secondly, the value of our labor-powers may be equal; so one hour's labor of two people with equal labor-powers (in terms of labor-power quality) creates the same value. In a paper of last year, I go on to show that although these are the only forms of equality socially validated within the social universe of capital, practically they are unattainable as other social drives break these forms of equalization (Rikowski, 2000c). For example, the drive to enhance labor-power quality as between different capitals, national capitals and between individuals pursuing relative "self-investment" in their own labor-powers would constantly *disrupt* any systematic attempt to create equality of labor-powers through education and training. Although forms of equality on the basis of exchange-value are *theoretically* possible, the first (equality of labor) is abominable as it is compatible with massive inequalities of income and wealth, whilst the second (equality of labor-powers) is practically hopeless. The outcome of all this is that struggles against inequalities in capitalist society are struggles for forms of equality that cannot exist within capitalism. Yet they nevertheless constitute struggles against the constitution of capitalist society, and also *for* equality than *can* attain social existence on the basis of the dissolution of the social universe of capital.

PETER: So now we get round to the "social production of labor-power" in capitalism? We seem to keep churning out new issues. In your published work, as far as I can see, you have not really expanded tremendously on this, though you have hinted that it is at the foundation of what you want to say about education and training in capitalist society, Glenn. How would you sum up what you call the "social production of labor-power," Glenn? What are the main characteristics and features?

Return to the Social Production of Labor Power

GLENN: Sure! This is a big topic. First I want to summarize why labor-power, and then education and training, are so crucial in capitalist society. Labor-power is transformed into labor in the labor process, and in this movement value, and then at a certain point surplus value, is generated. There are two aspects to labor: it is a process of producing use-values and also value (a valorization process). There are not two separate processes going on here; they are both expressions of the one and same set of acts within the labor process. If the product is useless, then value is not realized at the point of sale. Labor-power consists of those attributes of the person that are used in creating a use-value (the use-value aspect of labor-power), but labor power also has a quantitative, *value*-aspect too. Through the activity of the worker (labor) in the labor process, some of our personal powers (labor-power) also become expressed as value-generation. Thus: labor-power is the unique, living commodity that is the foundation of value, the substance of the social universe of capital. We create the social universe of capital.

Now, I have argued (e.g. Rikowski, 2000a) that education and training play a key role in the *social production* of labor power. Definite productive forms of this can be located empirically. Empirical studies I have undertaken, on apprentice recruitment for example, illustrate this. However, processes of labor-power production are extremely fragmented on an institutional and organizational basis (between forms of education and training, work-based learning). Thus, we see relatively "weak" forms of labor-power production. But this misses the key historical point, which is that over the last fifty years processes of the social production of labor power have become socially defined and delineated more clearly and definitely. This is because the social drive to reduce all education and training to *labor-power production* has gained ground historically. This reflects the deepening capitalization of the whole of social life. Thus, education and training increasingly operate as systems and processes of labor-power production, and it is labor-power that generates value. Value is the substance of the social universe of capital. In this chain of transformation and production we can see that education and training, therefore, have a key role to play in the *maintenance and expansion of the social universe of capital*. The social power of teachers, trainers and all those involved in socially producing labor-power rests on this fact.

Representatives of capital in business, state bureaucracies and government are fundamentally aware of the significance of education and training in terms of labor-power production, though they call it "human capital," but we know what that means! Indeed, read any UK Department of Education and Employment report of the last twenty or more years and they illustrate the intense concern regarding the quality of UK labor-power. It is, of course, all wrapped up in such euphemisms or proxy concepts as "employability," "human capital," "work-ready graduates," school kids who are able to "meet industry's needs" and the like. Teachers and trainers have huge strategic importance in capitalist society: they are like "angels of the fuel dump," or "guardians of the flame," in that they have intimate day-to-day responsibility for generating the fuel (labor-power) that generates what Marx called the "living fire" (labor) (Marx, 1858, p. 361). Their roles start to explain the intense efforts of representatives of capital in state bureaucracies, government, business and the media in attempting to control the labor of teachers and trainers. Teacher's and trainer's labor is channeled into labor-power production, and increased pressures arising from competition to enhance the quality of labor-power within nation states (as one response to globalization), spurs on efforts to do this. The implications are massive: control of curricula, of teacher training, of education unions, training organizations and much more. There are many means of such control, and empirical and historical investigations are important here. Letting the law of money loose (though education markets) is just one strategy. Attempts to control the processes involved is another, but increasingly both are used in tandem (though these strategies can come into conflict).

So, there are strong forces at work to ensure that teachers and trainers labor is reconfigured on the basis of labor-power production. But also, teachers and trainers are in a structural position to *subvert* and *unsettle* processes of labor power production within their orbits. Even more, they can work to enshrine *alternative* educational principles and practices that bring into question the constitution of society and hint at ways in which expenditure of labor-power does not take a value form. This is a nightmare for representatives of capital. It is an additional factor making for the control of teachers and trainer's labor. And this highlights, for me, the central importance of radical or critical pedagogy today, and why your work, Peter, has such momentous implications and consequences for the anti-capitalist struggles ahead.

PETER: And for me, it highlights the significance of education for today's anti-capitalist movement. As you have put it, radical pedagogy and the anti-capitalist struggle are intimately related: that was also one of the messages I aimed to establish in my Che/Freire book (McLaren, 2000).

GLENN: Your Che/Freire book really consolidated the relation between anti-capitalism and radical pedagogy for me. You see, Peter, when I was younger, I used to think that it would be better being in some industrial situation where the "real action" was going on, rather than in education. However, labor power is capital's weakest link, as it is incorporated within personhood. Labor-power is the commodity that generates value. And education and training are processes of labor-power production. Give all this, then to be in education today is to be right at the center of the action! There is no better place to be. From other things I have said, it follows that education and training, insofar as they are involved in the production of labor-power, that, in capitalism, takes the form of human capital, then they are also involved in the capitalization of humanity. Thus: a politics of human resistance is necessary *first of all* within education and training. These are the places that it goes on in the most forced, systematic and overt way. Radical pedagogy, therefore, is an aspect of this politics, an aspect of *resisting processes within education and training that are constituted as processes of reducing humans to labor-power (human capital)*. On this account, radical pedagogy is the hot seat in anti-capitalist struggles. The question of pedagogy is critical today, and this is where our work productively collides.

You have written extensively on Pedagogy for Revolution (though also increasingly, and more directly on the critique of capitalist schooling in recent years). I have concentrated more on the negative analysis of Education for Capital, and said little about pedagogy, though I now realize its absolute importance more clearly after reading your wonderful *Che Guevara, Paulo Friere, and the Pedagogy of Revolution* (McLaren, 2000). Both are necessary moments within an exploration of what Paula Allman (1999) has called socially transformative praxis. My negative critique of Education for Capital exposes the centrality of the question of pedagogy, I believe. From the other direction, your work on the centrality of pedagogy for the anti-capitalist struggles calls for an exploration of the constitution of society and a negative critique of education as labor-power production. This also provides an argument about the necessity of radical, transformative pedagogy as a key strategy for use in terminating the capitalization of humanity and envisioning an open future. It grounds the project of radical pedagogy; shows its necessity in capitalism today. We can contrast Education for Capital (as an aspect of the capitalization of humanity) with Pedagogy for Revolution (that transforms social relations and individuals, and seeks to curtail the horror of capital within the "human"). I was wondering if that was how you saw it, Peter. Although we have come at things from different angles, we have arrived at the same spot. Capital is like a labyrinth.

PETER: That's a good way of putting it. I think you have spelled out the connections between our work from the development within your own ideas and experience. I might see it slightly differently in some respects. I think I have a stronger notion of Marxism as a *philosophy of praxis* than you have in your own work, is that fair and accurate?

GLENN: I think it is in the sense that is I would not place so much store by the notion of philosophy, though *praxis* is hugely significant for me. You may say the two go together. My Marxism was learnt largely through debates within the Conference of Socialist Economists, their journal *Capital & Class*, participating in the (now defunct) Revolutionary Communist Party and going to Socialist Workers Party meetings in the mid-to-late-1990s, but most of all through reading Marx. Theorists such as Derek Sayer, John Holloway, Simon Clarke and Kevin Harris were very important for me, and more recently Moishe Postone and the works of Michael Neary (Neary, 1997; Neary and Taylor, 1998). But what do you think, Peter? How do you see Marxism as, for lack of a better word, a philosophy? And how does it link up with your work on pedagogy for revolution?

Marx, Marxism and Method

PETER: Yes, Glenn, as I see it Marxism is a philosophy of praxis. This is so in the sense that it is able to bring knowledge face-to-face with the conditions of possibility for its own embodiment in history, into contact with its own laboring bodies, into contact with its forgotten life-activity, its own chronotype or space-time co-ordinates (i.e., its constitutive outside). Knowledge, even critical knowledge, doesn't reproduce itself, for to assert this much is to deny its inherence in history, its insinuation in the social universe of production and labor. But I guess that's okay with some post-structuralists who tend to reduce history to a text anyway, as if it miraculously writes itself. Postmodern theory is built upon the idea of self-creation or the fashioning of the self. Self-creation assumes people have authorized the imperatives of their own existence, the conditions in which they form or create themselves. But Marxism teaches us that people make history within, against, and through systems of mediation already saturated by a nexus of social relations, by a force-field of conflicting values and accents, by prior conventions and practical activities that constrain the possible, that set limits to the possible. Raya Dunayevskaya (1978) describes Marxism, as I recall, as a "theoretical expression of the instinctive strivings of the proletariat for liberation." That pretty much captures the essence for me. Paula Allman (1999) notes that Marx's efforts were directed at exposing "the inherent and fundamental contradictions of capitalism." I agree with her that these contradictions are as real today as they were in Marx's time. She enjoins readers to dismiss the criticisms of Marxism as essentialist and teleological and to rely not on the perspectives of Marxists but on the writings of Marx himself. After all, Marx's works constitute a critique of relations historically specific to capitalism. We need to try to understand not only the theoretical concepts that Marx offers us, but also the manner in which Marx thinks.

GLENN: It sounds as if there is a role for philosophers in the revolution then.

PETER: I think the concrete, objective crisis that we live in today makes philosophy a matter of extreme urgency for all revolutionaries, as Dunayevskaya puts it. You may not be interested in philosophy, but I am sure philosophy is interested in you. Well, the specific ideologies of capitalism that frame and legitimize certain philosophical approaches and affirm some over others are interested in your compliance, perhaps that is a better way to put it. My own interest here is in developing a philosophy of praxis for educators. The key point for me is when Marx broke from the concept of theory when he wrote about the "working day" in *Capital*. Here we see Marx moving from the history of theory to the history of the class struggle. The workers struggles at the time shifted the emphasis of Marx's work. Dunayevskaya (1978) notes that

> From start to finish, Marx is concerned with the revolutionary actions of the proletariat. The concept of theory now is something unified with action. The ideal and the material became unified in his work as never before and this is captured in his struggle for a new social order in which "the free development of each is the condition for the free development of all."

GLENN: Certainly, the role that something called "philosophy" plays in my own work has not been clarified—which is ironic really, as philosophy was my major subject for my first degree and I taught philosophy in the early 1990s. On Dunayevskaya, I am a Marxist-Humanist of sorts; the problem I have with it is the notion of the "human" and humanism, but I won't go into that here. Just to say that Marxist-Humanism is the struggle to attain an open future for humanity: that's how I see it.

PETER: You see, Glenn, I think that this is one of the silences in your work—the role of philosophy. Let's recast the issue, so we come at it at an angle that more clearly does crash into your work. You have given me an idea of some of the general forces flowing through what you call the "social universe of capital," and I can see your points about how our work meets up, and so on. What puzzles me though is how you see all this meeting up with what some might call the "level of appearances," or "everyday life." I mean, you make your living as an education researcher (though you research training processes too, if we want to make that distinction). But what are the connections between your work as an education researcher and your Marxist educational theory, or your "labor power theory," as you might prefer to call it? Can connections be made? What is the role of "education research" in relation to what you have said so far in this dialogue?

GLENN: From my perspective, those questions have colossal significance today, Peter! The connection between the phenomena structuring life within capital's social universe and "everyday life" in capitalism has been a key issue in Marxist theory since Marx's death. The usual starting place is to make the distinction between essence and appearance and then try to show that what we observe empirically, on the surface of society, can be explained with reference to the deeper phenomena (value, abstract labor and so on). For me, this suggests that, ontologically, there are two realms of existence: the real and the abstract, or essence and appearance. This allows some to argue that we can understand things like competition, price and money without recourse to any "deeper reality" (value, abstract labor, surplus value, and so on). It is a short step from there to exploring "everyday life" in terms of markets, price and competition without recourse to value, abstract labor and others' ideas central to Marx's analysis of capitalism.

A concrete example of this is the work on education markets and the marketization of education. In the UK there is a massive literature on education markets, quasi-markets and related empirical studies of the marketization of schools and colleges. These studies, however, are extremely superficial in that they incorporate no sustained analysis of what the "products" of education are. Thus, we have "education markets and missing products," as I explained in a paper to the Conference of Socialist Economists in 1995 (Rikowski, 1995). However, I would not wish to say that production, value and labor-power and so on constitute some kind of "deeper *reality*." I read Marx as saying that the phenomena pinpointed as key by the educational marketization writers are *phenomenal forms* of essential relations. There is no "analytic dualism" involved here, or a Critical Realism that is founded on such a dualism, as in the writings of Robert Willmott in England (e.g., Willmott, 1999). The phenomenal forms are an *expression* of value, not some radically different ontological "level" or order. I would want to argue that this is so even for the phenomena of "everyday life" too. So when I say "I am money," or "I am capital," or "I am value," I am heralding the ways in which money, capital and value literally are "me" and flow through my life as aspects of observable things that I do and say. But the former (capital, value, and money) does not constitute some analytically distinct level apart from "everyday life." "Real life" *is* abstract. Although we can use the power of abstraction to abstract *from* reality, to indicate generalities, a really radical approach to abstraction demonstrates and indicates how concrete, "real life" is also *abstract*. We are indeed "ruled by abstractions," but these abstractions are not separate from lived experience; we live the abstractions through the concrete (and *vice versa*). It's as with labor. The same labor has two *aspects:* first, the concrete, qualitative, use-value aspect; and secondly the quantitative, abstract value-aspect. There are not two different acts of labor going on. Now, I want to argue that the whole of social, "everyday life" is like that. There are concrete and abstract aspects to social phenomena in capitalist society. One of the tasks of Marxist science is to explore these aspects as "living contradictions." Of course, getting funding for this type of "Marxist research" will not be easy. Furthermore, if it is to have any real value then the lessons learnt from this research must be fed into the wider anti-capitalist movement, and ways for disseminating it have to be addressed.

PETER: But have you done this, Glenn? I mean have you actually examined particular social phenomena in capitalism in this way? And if you have, how have you done this?

Aspects of Labor-Power

GLENN: Yes: labor-power. I have attempted to uncover various aspects of labor-power: the use-value, exchange-value, value aspects in particular, but also the collective and subjective aspects (Rikowski, 2000a). And this work shows that it is not a case of "applying" concepts to reality; aspects of capitalist social life are expressed in such a way that these ideas are produced in thought at the moment of grasping the aspects and essential relations. In capitalism, social reality writes itself through us, as *ourselves*, as we live its forms and aspects. There is no determinism involved here; as there is no duality. The phenomena are not separate in capital's social universe (its totality) in the way that determinism in the classical sense presupposes. Causality also has no purchase either on this outlook; the phenomena are aspects and forms of each other within the totality. There is no separation of phenomena as in bourgeois social science. What is required is a communist scientific language adequate to the expression of movements, transformations and metamorphoses of phenomena within a social universe whose substance is value. Thus, we talk of totality, social universe, infinity, relativity, process, transformation, movement, metamorphosis, morphing, aspect, contradiction, generation, form, intensity, density, force, implosion, explosion, dissolution and other concepts, that explain social transformations and relations. The processes of labor-power formation or surplus-value generation, when examined through these ideas, rather than notions of cause/effect, determination, base/superstructure and the ideas of what Moishe Postone (1996) "traditional Marxism," are *radicalized*. Unlike "postmodern thinking," this process truly unsettles through exposing the bareness of capitalist social relations as we live them. The gap between lives lived and lives theorized about closes.

PETER: A couple of points. First, this must make the social production of labor-power a tricky process! If labor-power incorporates various "aspects," as you call them, presumably these are in contradiction. Secondly, what's the role of empirical research? Do Marxists do that? Is there any point to it? After all, will not analysis of our own lives be sufficient? Why research anyone else when we can research ourselves with the same degree of validity?

GLENN: Yes, the social production of labor-power is made difficult by the fact that labor-power incorporates aspects: use-value, exchange-value, value, collective and subjective aspects—that do express a whole bunch of contradictions. Schools are in the business of producing a living commodity that incorporates contradictions! You can see the enormity of what they are up against! This conditions contradictions in education policy; state functionaries have to try to make sense of the absurd. Result: education policies that reflect the contradictions or skip around from one prong of the fork to the other. Of course, sometimes they are suppressed too. This is fascinating stuff, as you can see these contradictions playing themselves out within peoples' lives, within government policies and thinking—everywhere! Empirical studies can give these insights power and relevance. Secondly, the social production of labor-power, *as a process*, crashes against social *re*-production and maintenance of laborers and their families through the wage form. I show this contradiction in relation to the phenomenon of the student-worker, nominally full-time students who work to survive (Rikowski, 2000d). Education policies are riddled with contradictions flowing from these considerations also. Mainstream academics attempt to make sense of, to rationalize these concepts, these processes, at war! Empirical and historical studies are crucial for uncovering the forces that we are up against.

And this gets on to your second point, Peter, the point of doing empirical research. First, it's true that "researching ourselves" can get us a lot further than previously envisaged. Autobiography attains importance; we can locate the contradictions within our own personhoods as they are transformed and flow throughout our own lives. However, the *intensity* of some of the contradictions within personhood as capital and between persons and groups varies.

Sometimes these living contradictions can be illustrated and demonstrated more easily by exploring the lives of others, rather than merely examining your own "self" as contradictory social entity. But most importantly, from what I have said previously, the concrete is also the abstract, so an empirical exploration of some aspect of education is never just empirical and concrete. There is a place, therefore, for Marxist research in education and in other areas of social life. The obvious problem is getting resources and time to do this work. In the UK, the school and college effectiveness and improvement are being driven increasingly strongly from the centre through the Department for Education & Employment (DfEE). The Economic and Social Research Council (ESRC), the premier funding body for serious social science research, is under increasing pressure to narrow the limits for "acceptable" education research. A National Educational Research Forum is being established which is dominated by the school/college effectiveness/improvement industry. Of course, you can try to get something through this system—but it's getting extremely difficult. There are more big programmes (such as the Teaching and Learning Research Programme) and the establishment of megabucks research centers through the DfEE that make any critical research program difficult to get off the ground in any substantial manner. There are ways round this; hidden agendas and so on, but it's tough. I'm reading Russell Jacoby's book, *The Last Intellectuals* (Jacoby, 2000)— the new edition—and he's great at showing the processes through which even mildly critical research, let alone any Marxist research, gets squeezed out, and how left academics get marginalized, victimized and worse.

PETER: You said that empirical studies can give us insight and also relevance into the ways that contradictions within personhood and within processes of the social production of labor-power itself —within which education and training are implicated heavily—through empirical studies. On the "relevance" aspect, what did you have in mind exactly?

GLENN: *Political* relevance, principally. In my pamphlet, *The Battle in Seattle: Its Significance for Education* (Rikowski, 2001c), I show how the WTO agenda for education is related to New Labor's education policy. However, for me, the really important part is the second half of the book where I explore the significance of education for anti-capitalism post-Seattle. At that point, the links between labor-power, radical pedagogy and the need for organisations that can seriously take on the kind of politics of human resistance to processes of our capitalization—in particular, the key role that education plays in these processes, these links can all be made. They can be made for political strategy. That is the full force of the "relevance" I am thinking of. In England, sadly, I have received criticism from some who hold that we should not mix up writing about Marx with writing about something like the WTO education agenda and New Labor education policy—and these criticisms from the Left too! These criticisms come from elements within what I call the liberal left, and they induce us to separate theory from empirical study, radical pedagogic practice and education politics (and politics in general). I have been called a "radical poser" (and worse) on the basis that I dare bring Marx up front into education analysis and politics. It will "put people off," I am told, and I "will make a fool of myself!" Obviously I care about "putting people off." My answer is that in education theory, analysis and politics we really ought to be trying to *radicalize* Marx, to make him more relevant and *exciting*. That is a project for writing, analysis, critique and practical politics to demonstrate. As to "making a fool of myself," let history decide! Marx didn't seem to worry about that very much; he took tremendous risks with his own personae and public image—on the basis that he believed that it would be for the good of the movement. Surely, the goal is to bring Marxist analysis, theory and politics together within the sphere of education together—I argued this years ago (Rikowski, 1996). Marx is neither an embarrassment nor an idol. He is there to be used, as still the greatest critic of capitalist society today. Anyway, I tried to bring this all together in *The Battle in Seattle* booklet; to give a materialist analysis of today's new anti-capitalist movement that would indicate how social movements are engaged in *one fight, one struggle*—for only on this basis can they win out.

PETER: Establishing the unity of diverse struggles is important, surely. Seattle brought that to the fore with tremendous practical force. The key point is that we collectively crash through the walls of capitalist society.

GLENN: Yes, Peter, but in what direction is it possible to move in order to transcend the entrapment of capital? In other words, in what direction should we labor?

PETER: There are specific modes of production, some of which are historically bound up with capitalism. Not all modes of production are capitalist. A core feature of the capitalist mode of production is that the labor that is operative within it contains a duality, as use-value and exchange value. Living labor therefore incorporates concrete and abstract labor. Abstract labor, for capital, is the foundation of value. Bruno Gulli (1999) mentions the fact that labor is an ontological power, a creative power, which is why capital wants (must have) it for its social existence! Living labor is turned into productive labor because of its special relationship with objectified labor. Peter Hudis (2000a-b) poses the crucial question: What kind of labor should a human being do? It seems to me that strategizing against capital means working with those in the technologically underdeveloped world, and part of the challenge stipulates that we go beyond empirical treatments of categories developed by Marx and engage them dialectically. Capital, as Marx has pointed out, is a social relation of labor; it constitutes objectified, abstract, undifferentiated—and hence alienated—labor. Capital cannot be controlled or abolished through external means without dispensing with value production and creating new forms of non-alienated labor. Creating these new forms of non-alienated labor is the hope and promise of the future. This is something that you have talked about in your own work, Glenn.

Let's consider for a moment the harsh reality of permanent mass unemployment, contingent workforces, and the long history of strikes and revolts of the unemployed. It is relatively clear from examining this history that the trajectory of capitalism in no way subsumes class struggle or the subjectivity of the workers. We can relate this to the work of Raya Dunayevskaya and Peter Hudis and bring Hegel into the conversation here. What for Hegel is Absolute knowledge (the realm of realized transcendence), Marx referred to as the new society. While Hegel's self-referential, all-embracing, totalizing Absolute is greatly admired by Marx, it is, nevertheless, greatly modified by him. For Marx, Absolute knowledge (or the self-movement of pure thought) did not absorb objective reality or objects of thought but provided a ground from which alienation could be transcended. By reinserting the human subject into the dialectic, and by defining the subject as corporal being (rather than pure thought or abstract self-consciousness), Marx appropriates Hegel's self-movement of subjectivity as an act of transcendence and transforms it into a critical humanism. The value form of labor (abstract labor) that has been transmogrified into the autonomous moment of dead labor, eating up everything that it is not, can be challenged by freely associated labor and concrete, human sensuousness. The answer is in envisioning a non-capitalist future that can be achieved, as Hudis notes, after Dunayevskaya, by means of subjective self-movement through absolute negativity so that a new relation between theory and practice can connect us to the idea of freedom. Hudis (2000b) argues that the abolition of private property does not necessarily lead to the abolition of capital. We need, therefore, to examine the direct relation between the worker and production. Here, our sole emphasis should not be on the abolition of private property, which is the product of alienated labor; it must be on the abolition of alienated labor itself. Marx gave us some clues as to how transcend alienation, ideas that he developed from Hegel's concept of second or absolute negativity, or "the negation of the negation." Marx engaged in a materialist re-reading of Hegel. In his work, the abolition of private property constitutes the first negation. The second is the negation of the negation of private property. This refers to a self-reflected negativity, and what Hudis refers to as the basis for a positive humanism.

Bruno Gulli makes a similar point when he notes that the "both/and" bourgeois logic used to resolve contradictions is not an alternative to capital. The possibility of change does not reside in a "both/and" logic but rather can be located in a "neither/ nor" logic. He writes that

> In reality, the *both/and* modality enjoyed by the few is the condition for the *neither/nor* modality of a growing majority. *Chiapas* is an example of this. The possibility of a change does not reside in the acceptance of the *both/and* mentality but in the creation, out of a double negation, of a new radicality, one in which the having become of becoming is resurrected again to return to the immediacy of its subject. . . . The logic which breaks that of capital is a logic of *neither/nor,* a logic of double negation, or, again, a logic of double resistance and absolute affirmation. Through this logic, labor returns to itself, not posited by capital as valorizing labor, but posited by itself as *neither productive nor unproductive* labor: as living labor or form-giving fire (Gulli, 1999, note 28; paragraph 35).

GLENN: Absolute negativity in this sense is a creative force.

PETER: Yes. Of course, Marx rejects Hegel's idealization and dehumanization of self-movement through double negation because this leaves untouched alienation in the world of labor-capital relations. Marx sees this absolute negativity as objective movement and the creative force of history. Absolute negativity in this instance becomes a constitutive feature of a self-critical social revolution that, in turn, forms the basis of permanent revolution. Hudis raises a number of difficult questions with respect to developing a project that goes beyond controlling the labor process. It is a project that is directed at abolishing capital itself through the creation of freely associated labor: The creation of a social universe not parallel to the social universe of capital (whose substance is value) is the challenge here. The form that this society will take is that which has been suppressed within the social universe of capital: socialism, a society based not on value but on the fulfillment of human need.

GLENN: This brings us together, facing a common enemy in order to struggle for the realization of those human needs. At this point, the question of social movements asserts itself: different struggles it appears, but do they form just *one* struggle from the perspective of anti-capitalism? For me, the social movements have a common enemy: capital—and the ideologies (especially neo-liberalism) that sustain it. But what is your perspective on social movements, Peter? You indicated by email some while back that you where rethinking the significance of social movements. What are the problems with social movements?

Social Movements and Critical Pedagogy

PETER: I find the creation of multi-class formations exceedingly problematic for a number of reasons, several of which I would like to mention, without excessive adumbration. Others have gone into this in capillary detail but for the purposes of this discussion I want simply to mention that, for the most part, such movements serve mainly the petit-bourgeoisie and their interests. Secondly, these groups rarely contest the rule of capital. The laws of motion of capital and social relations of production to some seem the central objects of their attack, and, frankly, too often they are not even regarded as the central issues around which their struggle coalesces. Their efforts are too often reform based, calling for access to capitalist forms of democracy, for redistribution of resources. Thirdly, in their attempt to stitch together a broad coalition of groups, they often seem rudderless. Should we be for "social justice" that works simply to re-institute capitalist social relations of production? Of course, these are issues that we need to debate in schools of education. The whole issue of rights-based justice is predicated on the capitalist right to property. Can we shift the focus to the abolition of private property? I don't see these discussions occurring with any consistency within the tradition of critical pedagogy in the United States.

GLENN: How so?

PETER: What seemingly gives them ballast—emotional, conceptual, political—is their all-encompassing rallying cry for "counter-hegemonic struggle at all costs" without, as it were, ever specifying what they mean. There is a lack of contextual specificity in tying their interests together. In other words, is all counter-hegemonic struggle a good thing? It reminds me of the clarion call of the multiculturalists for diversity, for social justice. Is the struggle for diversity always transparent, always self-evident? I think not. Today the great benefactors of diversity are the multinational corporations. Especially when you consider that we have arrived at a point in our history where democracy and social inequality proceed apace, in tandem. In today's global plantation, diversity—ethnic, gender, sexual—functions in the interests of capital accumulation. The questions we need to raise are: Diversity for what purpose? In whose interests? By what means? Who benefits? Just look at the Republican Party and the calls for diversity during its national convention. Diversity for "compassionate" conservatism? Diversity for boosting big business? For taking money from the poor and putting it in the pockets of the rich? Is this what we mean by "diversity"? Is this what we mean by counter-hegemony? What are we countering, precisely?

I should think that the strategic centrality of counter-hegemony very much depends on what you are attempting to counter. I would much prefer to see the various new social movements linked by a singular commitment towards a protracted, all-embracing assault on capital, not just capitalism. Wouldn't it be more productive for the center of gravity in such a project to be the struggle for mass, collective, working-class struggle, for proletarian hegemony so that we can create conditions that capture Marx's concept of "from each according to their ability, to each according to their need"? As Marx and Engels noted, our concern cannot merely be the modification of private property, but its abolition, not the amelioration of class antagonisms, but the abolition of classes, not the improvement of society but the establishment of a new one. This is no easy task but it requires working-class internationalism at a time of a powerful diversity within the international division of labor.

GLENN: I would see things slightly differently. Whilst I agree with you that the struggle against capital is *the* struggle, the critical engagement, I don't think this is a majority position within the post-Seattle anti-globalization movement. However, I do think its appeal is growing within that movement, as the various fragments come to realize the impossibility of finding real solutions within the framework of capitalist society. For me, the issue is to bring the anti-globalization movement towards its constitution as an anti-*capitalist* movement. The arguments for that transition have to be continually made. But Peter, backtracking a tad, you said that critical pedagogy has the potential to become a challenge to private property rights, and a challenge to the domination of capital itself. It can also articulate social injustices as they relate to education and the wider society. Yet, for you, it is clear that the so-called Critical Pedagogy School has to date signally failed in realizing its potential. The issue of critical pedagogy is where our contributions meet up—as I indicated earlier. My work on labor-power shows that critical or radical pedagogies have the potential to disrupt the smooth flow of the social production of labor-power by raising issues of social justice and inequalities in capitalist society. Further, radical pedagogy is an essential moment within revolutionary social transformation; it is at the heart of truly revolutionary transformative praxis, as Paula Allman (1999) convincingly argues. So what, Peter, in your view, has gone so wrong with the Critical Pedagogy School? I am afraid if we don't center our question on pedagogy now then we might not have time enough to do it justice. Specifically, where is the problem with critical pedagogy in the United States?

PETER: I like to say there exist critical pedagogies, in the plural, because the few of us who write about it, and practice it, have definite ideas about what makes a pedagogy critical, or vulgar and domesticating, or reproductive, or what I have been calling of late, revolutionary. I won't give a nuanced rendition of these debates, but offer you my simple but straightforward impression of what's wrong.

GLENN: Okay, just the outline of the tragedy then.

PETER: Critical pedagogy has, in the main, been defrauded of its legitimacy, defunded of its revolutionary potential, at least the critical pedagogy that I am thinking about. In my discussions last year with my dear comrades in Finland, Israel, Brazil, Mexico, Australia, and Taiwan, I noticed that there was a great enthusiasm surrounding the possibilities of critical pedagogy, and a misperception that it was finding its way into the classrooms of the United States. In the United States, it is has been sadly vulgarized and emasculated to what I call "the democracy of empty forms"—seating arrangements in circles and semi-circles, teachers serving as "facilitators" and promoting informal discussions of students' experiences, and the like. On the one hand, when critical pedagogy is taught in university settings it is dismissed as being elitist. There are constant attacks on the language of critical pedagogy as it is used in the academy, for instance. On the other side of the debate is populist elitism. This is a heavily charged feeling among some activists that the closer in proximity that you are to the oppressed (that is, if you are a teacher in South Central or Watts or East Los Angeles) then the closer you are to the "truth" of the teaching enterprise. It also puts you nearer to interpreting the experience of students. Hence, professors who teach critical pedagogy are accused of being ivory tower intellectuals who offer theoretical approaches that make little sense in actual classroom situations.

GLENN: The "ivory tower" no longer exists, if it ever did. Studies of higher education show that it too is increasingly under the truncheon of capitalist social relations. I have David Harvey's excellent article in *Capital & Class* in mind here (Harvey, 2000), but also I also have in view important work in this journal by Teresa Ebert, Deb Kelsh and others.

PETER: Absolutely, Glenn, but on the specific issue of classroom teachers, I do believe that this proximity gives teachers a unique vantage point for interpreting their experiences, but I don't think it guarantees the truth of their own experience or that of their students. There are a lot of teachers and students who work in the barrio who don't betray—or strive for—what might be called "critical consciousness." We can apply the same criticism to professors of education, of course. But I do think that the teachers and students from aggrieved communities have the potential to build a powerful revolutionary movement. The pressing question for me—whether we work in inner-city areas in classrooms or whether we work in the precincts of the academy—is whether or not our approach to making sense of experience is a dialectical one. That is, that it locates students, schools, curricula, policies and pedagogical and social practices within the larger social totality or social universe of capitalist social relations. My focus here is not on analyzing schooling from the perspective of social relations of exchange or consumption as much as it is analyzing the schooling process and the formation of students within it from the perspective of the social relations of production. Behind the exchange of things—knowledge, information, and commodities—there is always a relationship to production. Students are not only consumers, they are also casualties of a perverse production process. They therefore become casualties of history. When I talk about interrogating our experiences as learner-practitioners or teacher-learners, I am trying to find ways of forging a collective revolutionary praxis and creating contexts where students can shape history through their own actions in, through and against the world. Language and experience are not pristine, unmediated, fully transparent, or sealed off from society but rather are refracted by dominant values as well as stabilizing and conventional discourses. Experiences need to be both affirmed and critically interrogated, but the point behind our affirmation of and challenge to the "common sense" character of our experiences is the commitment to transform our experiences. We need to make a connection between our collective revolutionary aspirations and personal experiences of oppression. But our attempts at the transformation of social relations of exploitation must pay attention to the appropriate forms that our cultural action should take as a mode of revolutionary praxis. Paulo Freire underscored the notion that cultural action in order to be transformative must also be a preparation for cultural revolution. And such a revolution is most fully developed when we are engaged in the struggle to bring about the dictatorship of the proletariat. The point I want to make here is that we can't be passively bound by our experiences—even populist ones (perhaps especially populist ones when you consider the fact that it is a form of populism that is currently informing the politics of George W. Bush). This is because critical knowledge means an encounter with dialectical analysis in order to smash the oppressor within. Paula Allman reads Freire brilliantly—and "bodily"—when she notes that *"dialogue enables us to experience the alternative or certain aspects of it for a period of time and in a specific context."* The structure of society resides in the structure of experience. We carry this in our musculature, in our gestures, our emotions, in our dreams and desires. Our subjectivities are commodified (a process that Lukács described as "reification").

GLENN: This was a central theme of your *Schooling as a Ritual Performance* (McLaren, 1999), was it not?

PETER: Yes, I was trying to find a way of exploring the link between labor and the language of symbolic gesture, between knowledge and the commodification of desire. Unfortunately I was not schooled in the work of Marx as much as I should have been when I wrote that book. But let's get back to the idea of commodification. The whole process of commodification should be more central in discussions and practices of pedagogy. These commodities, these reifications, are not illusions but objective social processes. Commodification regulates our social lives. We can't just "think" away the commodification of our subjectivities, our "structures of feeling" as Raymond Williams put it. We need to find our freedom in our actions, in new sets of actions that explode the prison-house forged out of the grammar of capitalism. Our truth will be found in our actions, in our praxis. Marx wrote, *"man must prove the truth, i.e., the reality and power, the this-worldliness of his thinking in practice."* That is, the truth of our ideas exists only in practice. Lukács quotes Lenin thus: "*the concrete analysis of the concrete situation is not an opposite of 'pure' theory, but—on the contrary—it is the culmination of genuine theory, its consummation—the point where it breaks into practice.*" Lukács follows this with the remark: "*Without any exaggeration it may be said that Marx's final, definitive thesis on Feuerbach—'The philosophers have only interpreted the world in different ways; the point, however, is to change it'—found its most perfect embodiment in Lenin and his work.*" In other words, Lenin's revolutionary struggle is illustrative of what is meant by a philosophy of praxis. All critical educators need to become philosophers of praxis. So that to summarize and give you the gist of my argument, and I fear that I have been meandering terribly here, Glenn—I believe that critical pedagogy needs to focus on interrogating and transforming the constituent results of the complex and concrete social totality. We need to explore the "fertile dungheap" of capitalism's contradictions, through which all of us live and labor. We need to get back to this messy work of historical materialist critique in order to build momentum in our revolutionary praxis. This is so especially given the often grave misperceptions about Paulo Freire's pedagogy that have proliferated over the last several decades, following in the wake of what has been a steady domestication and embourgeoisment of his work.

GLENN: This is a key element in your Che/Freire book, Peter (McLaren, 2000). You exhibit the tragedy beautifully but with an obvious sadness of heart.

PETER: Yes, Glenn, what I aimed to show in that book was why a dialectical critique of capitalism needs to underlay the development of critical consciousness. This point is essential, and, in part, it can be achieved through the act of decoding everyday life, and, in the process, liberate students to deal critically with their own reality in order to transform it. Students need to understand that they do not freely choose their lives, that their identities, their dreams, their actions in and on the world, as well as their objects of consumption are adaptive responses to the way that the capitalist system manipulates the realm of necessity. Commodification regulates social lives. Something Paula Allman points out is exceedingly important: that Freirean educators are unwaveringly directive. Paulo confirmed this in numerous discussions with me. Teachers have something to say, something to offer in creating the context for students to name their world, and through dialogue come to creatively reshape their historical reality. Freire did not approve of attempts to turn teachers into passive facilitators. To ask students to "read the world" critically in order to transform it in a way that will foster humanization is, after all, prescriptive. To demand that the world needs transforming and that education should play a critical role in this effort is, again, prescriptive. Educators should use their authority that comes from their own critical reading of the world as well as their understanding of Freire's philosophy of education in their work with students. As Paula Allman asks: Isn't the most facilitative, non-prescriptive and non-directive form of progressive teaching doubly prescriptive in the sense that it is a prescription for non-prescription as well as for political domestication and adapting successfully to the social universe of capital and the law of value? Freirean educators direct and prescribe, but do so in a spirit of co-operation and mutuality, with an eye to collective action and with a Marxist grasp of the fact that the truth of thinking exists only in practice.

GLENN: I detect a deep disappointment in what you say, Peter, and this flows from your account of really existing critical pedagogy as, more or less, a renunciation of its *criticality* so that it has become more of a liberal pedagogy. That is, it is severed from the social drive of the working class to transform society. Is that correct?

PETER: Critical pedagogy must be tied irrevocably and implacably to our faith in the ability of the working class to shape society in the interest of freedom and justice. How do we enjoin our students to create conditions for escaping from the capitalist compression that necessarily splits value-preserving labor (that reproduces use-value) from value-creating labor (exchange-value that gives shape to capital)? It seems to me that we need to focus with students on how they can become active social agents in shaping the sphere of revolutionary political praxis. How can we get them interested in anti-capitalist political praxis: including mass strikes, establishing workers councils, overthrowing the state, and establishing a revolutionary party? These are questions that are currently challenging my thinking and my praxis. How can we make the anti-capitalist project (the struggle for working-class hegemony) a salient, coherent, and viable project, one with a force that will make history explode? How can we generate new horizons of experience, language, and struggle? These are issues that brush against the grain of most efforts at establishing critical pedagogy projects in classrooms.

GLENN: Although you emphasize the collective moment here, Peter, yet, at the same time, I get the impression that, for you, truly radical pedagogy is also a very *personal* thing. I have in mind your work on Che Guevara's pedagogy in your *Che Guevara, Paulo Freire and the Pedagogy of Revolution* (McLaren,

2000)—and also the stuff on Freire too. The co-operative moment, the mutuality that you speak of is manifested through the lives of individuals. So, although Che did not write huge tomes on pedagogy, his life was lived as pedagogic form for others. We just have to know how to "read" it, and that is where radical educators come in. Is that how you see it, Peter? Of course, at that point, personal histories, biographies become the "texts" of the collective learning that aims to transform social existence. How does the personal life link in with life as critical educator? Perhaps you could say a bit on this in relation to your own trajectory.

Personal History, Intellectual Life, and Education

PETER: My intellectual life had lowly origins; my body kept getting in my way of my mind. No, I'm not talking about a preoccupation with sex, but with the "event," with the fusion of idea and action, argument and activity. Pivotal ideas meant that you crouched on them and used them as a springboard for action. Sometimes they were too slippery or too narrow to get a good footing. But reading Malcolm X, and Frantz Fanon lit a fire under me and I leap-frogged into the streets. Those two figures built a launching pad for urban action that was as large as an aircraft carrier. And Che Guevara, well, his was a platform the size of a continent. At the end of the 60s, my activities became more bookish, starting with attempts to engage the existentialism of Sartre, really. Merleau-Ponty was a strong influence for years, as was Pierre Teilhard de Chardin, especially in my early engagement with Catholicism and Catholic mysticism, and, for a brief period, the theosophical tradition.

GLENN: Are you serious?

Peter: Yes, all that bourgeois muck, as they say. And I felt no sense of shame in luxuriating in the metaphysics of Krishnamurti and indulging in the self-scrutiny of Thomas Merton with an unappeasable frenzy, but in the case of Merton, I was starting to sniff a little Catholic triumphalism in the air and so I backed off.

GLENN: We were all young once, I suppose.

PETER: Don't tell me, Glenn, that you have never thumbed through a deck of Tarot cards! Or I suppose you used them as bookmarks in your readings of *Capital!*

GLENN: Well, there was the ouija board thing, and that put me off the Tarot. Okay, what was next?

PETER: Then the pastoral tradition of liberation theology swept through my life like a Kansas tornado. That is what spirited me away in the 1960s and 70s. Then I was introduced to Althusser and Balibar. There was not much of a link for me at that time with the tradition of Hegelian Marxism, although I was alerted to Lenin's shift to a Marxian dialectics, and encouraged by friends to indulge his ideas with some serious reading. From Althusser it was a brief engagement with Lacan, at first through the influence of Anthony Wilden's work. I worked my way back to the dialectic through the Budapest School, Lukács, Heller, and, of course, Korsch. There was little discipline attached to my reading here, but I recall a rather dutiful engagement with the Frankfurt School, Fromm and Marcuse mostly, and only later Adorno, Horkheimer and Benjamin. Of course, Gadamer, Habermas, Ricoeur, they all made an impact. By that time I was working in education and had to engage Dewey, which was quite a worthwhile endeavor. But not as worthwhile as discovering Freire. Of course, Foucault came next, followed by Eco; next up, the post-structuralists and the intellectual high fashion at the time—what a competitive enterprise it was! —and still is—and then, well, I've pretty much rehearsed that part of my intellectual history elsewhere. I think most people will find this boring, so let me conclude by saying that my journey back to Marx, and hence my journey forward politically, carefully sidestepped rational-choice theory and analytical Marxism—to which I was temperamentally averse but begrudgingly respectful—as I made an effort to re-engage the Hegelian Marxist tradition. I read Karil Kosik, and Lenin, and Luxemburg, and, of course, the great Marxist-humanist, Raya Dunayevskaya. Of course, I am leaving out the Birmingham School here, and my subsequent engagement with the cultural turn brought about by a specific reading of Gramsci; a turn which I now find highly problematic, and believe it to be a significant vulgarization of Gramscis radical politics. Suffice it to say that I am still very much a student of Marx and the Marxian tradition. Just when you think the old bearded devil is down for the count, he rises up stronger than ever. Marx was uncannily prophetic—and eerily prescient—about the internationalization of capital. But there is more to Marx than his ability to anticipate crisis. I am currently very much impressed with the work of Terri Ebert, E. San Juan, James Petras, Masud Zavarzadeh, Ellen Meiksins Wood, Terry Eagleton, Alex Callinicos, well, I will stop there because if I try to list everyone, I'll inevitably leave some important names out.

GLENN: Yes, Peter, but how much of what you have read has informed, or continues to inform, your activism?

PETER: Glenn, the issue isn't what you've read. I've often been asked what influences have been vital to my intellectual formation, as if they all appear in the pages of a book. It really is a question of *what you actually do with the knowledge that you have:* what concrete events you helped shape, but also what concrete events helped to shape the contours of your subjectivity, of your action both in and on the world, within the social order and against it. I remember in the 1960s when I was arrested for the first time. After being thrown against a black-and-white, I was taken to the police station, and into a cell, alone, and beaten with a flashlight by a sadistic cop. It was that sense of feeling the arm of the state (literally and concretely) on my skull that helped to shape the direction of my life. And wearing the scars of the encounter months later was a reminder, as was—and is—the memory, still. I had similar experiences in school—the strap, of course, on the palm of my hand—but my most powerful memory of corporal punishment is the slashing metal ruler brought down in hacking motions on the top of my hand, below my knuckles, by a sadistic industrial arts teacher.

GLENN: Given the current context of global capitalism, how would you describe your current contribution to educational debates and struggles in the U.S.? I'm thinking of a quotation from your *Preface* to Paula Allman's new book:

> The vagaries and vicissitudes of capitalist domination and the conceptual apparatuses that yield our means of rationalized it are unceremoniously exposed. It is revealed as a world-system, an abundant and all-permeating social universe that, in its endless and frenetic drive to expand, co-operates in implacable and irreparable denials of social justice and shameless practices of exploitation. Such is the pervasive reach of capital that no aspects of the human condition are left untouched. Indeed, our very subjectivities are stuck in the muck of capital. And the momentum capitalism has achieved makes it unlikely that it can be derailed without tremendous effort and sacrifice. It constitutes a resplendent hemorrhaging of the labor-capital relation, where commodities vomited up from the vortex of accumulation are hungrily consumed by tormented creatures, creatures who are deliriously addicted not only to new commercial acquisitions, but to the adrenaline rush of accumulation itself. Here the individual essence, in Gramsci's

sense, is equivalent to the totality of social relations within global capitalist society (McLaren, in Allman, 2001).

PETER: If you'll permit me to express myself—with decidedly less dramatic flair—let me share the fact that, unlike many postmodernists, I don't believe that humanity has entered a qualitatively new epoch. I don't subscribe to the picture that we are breaking away from the (Fordist/industrial) era of modernization and entering the new world of globalization where the economy is operating at a transnational level and where the nation state is no longer the political formation seeking to regulate the economy. I don't maintain—as do many left-liberal educationalists—that the major actors can be found in the realm of civil society in the form of new social movements and NGOs who work to expand, extend, defend, and strengthen civil society, as well as to render it more inclusive. In other words, I don't assume that civil society is relatively autonomous from the state, capital and the market, even when you consider the ongoing informal and non-formal efforts of the new social movements and their accompanying NGOs, to advance the cause and the practice of citizenship. It is misguided to view the arena of civil society as a space where public policies of social justice can be pursued in a spirit of co-operation and civic participation, and where a critical education approach can be enacted within a reform-oriented politics of inclusion, influence, and democratic accountability. Those of us who have attempted an activist politics in the domain of civil society know it isn't inherently benign. It's not a warm or co-operative space of dialogue and identity-formation. John Holst correctly notes that civil society is not antiseptically removed from the social relations of production. In fact, it is perfectly compatible with the emphasis that the free marketeers place on self-sufficiency, enterprise zones, "capacity building" and grassroots empowerment initiatives. But what is worse is that it simply transfers the costs of structural reform onto civil society. Radical pluralists, for instance, in arguing for personal and community responsibility, in schemes like the self-management of public housing and public schools and the privatization of welfare, derail the guaranteeing of basic social services by the state. My recent work has been an attempt to challenge the reformists from a classical Marxist position. Thus, I have of late being trying to re-ignite politically and conceptually some old debates that need to be exorcised from the musty North American vaults of the educational imagination. I suppose that if I am making any kind of contribution to the field, and I dare say it is a modest contribution at that, then it's in the area of challenging this radical pluralist/

radical democracy school (you can also read this as the postmodernist school of educational criticism) in terms of its considerable and ongoing impact on critical theory and critical pedagogy. I would like to re-route educational theory away from its secure precincts in civil society and back to Marx. Well, actually, it really hasn't made much of an engagement with Marx to begin with there are scattered about the field some good Marxist educators, but for the most part the field is pretty much empty of Marx. But I would say that my work—especially recent work with Ramin Farahmandpur—is attempting to spark an interest among educators in Marx and the Marxist tradition. There are others, like Richard Brosio, and John Holst, and a handful of others in the United States, who are writing against the liberal grain. I suppose, then, what I am attempting to do is to renovate educational theory in terms of Marx's labor theory of value and to make some Hegelian Marxist incursions into the educational literature.

GLENN: Your Che/Freire book has made a significant impact, Peter. I know that it has been reaching young readers in their early twenties and readers in their teens. They are relating to your work, I think, on a number of levels, and are initially drawn to your work by the way you present yourself. You mentioned to me recently that you read a book review that attacks you personally for the Che tattoo you display in the author's photo but also for the prefaces to the book written by distinguished scholars.

PETER: Thats right. In failing to deal substantively with the ideas, concepts, and arguments in the book, Ken Zeichner, a teacher educator, focussed instead on my physical appearance, as well as on the series editor's preface and a preface by an internationally respected Latin American scholar—two prefaces that, I might add, were published word-for-word, and title-for-title, exactly as they were sent to the publisher (mercifully, he omitted any commentary about the Foreword written by Nita Freire, Paulo Freire's widow). Prefaces or introductions by a series editor are standard fare in academic publishing and in this case the editor, Joe Kincheloe, complimented my writing style. My unorthodox style has received quite a bit of critical commentary over the years because it is considered by some educators to be overly literary and too esoteric to be of much practical use for teachers or pre-service students seeking to improve the educational system. I guess Zeichner feels that I should have asked the publishers to halt the presses so that Joe could have time to write a less-flattering preface, maybe asking readers to put the book down and read something by somebody who professes to have more humility, somebody perhaps like Zeichner. Zeichner also found it self-indulgent of me to be in a book graced by a second preface, written in the form of a poem by Chilean Marxist, Luis Vitale. Vitale entitled his poem "A Salute to Peter McLaren" (a poem, by the way that mentions me only once). *Webster's Unabridged New Universal Dictionary* defines "salute" as "to greet or welcome in a friendly manner." So, in Zeichner's mind, to be "greeted" by a respected Latin American Marxist in a poem that mentions the author only once, and to be complimented on one's writing by the series editor somehow illustrates a character flaw in the author. Zeichner finds the ultimate index of my lack of humility in the fact that a tattoo of Che Guevara is visible on my arm in the author's photo.

GLENN: So what should you have been wearing in your author's photo?

PETER: Whatever Zeichner wears, I guess. Maybe a tweed or corduroy sports jacket and a turtleneck? A patch-pocket blue blazer with an embroidered gold wire crest from a private university? Coffee-stained Dockers and button-down cotton Levis shirts? A sharkskin suit? I have never seen him so I have no idea what he wears and, frankly, don't care, but I'd put money on the fact that he doesn't wear leather pants or sport a tongue stud. You can tell he doesn't live in Hollywood. Here I pretty much blend into the crowd. The point is that if you take Zeicher's logic about glowing prefaces a bit further then even blurbs about one's book should equally earn censure for self-indulgence. That would apply to every author whose book is festooned with the usual endorsements.

GLENN: Or a tattoo.

PETER: My advice to authors: cover those arms and keep the blurbs tame.

GLENN: In addition to commenting on your appearance, Zeichner infers that you rarely leave your university campus in Westwood so you couldn't know the real world of teachers and teaching.

PETER: I am not impressed by Zeichner's knowledge of Los Angeles. It might be interesting to put him in my shoes for a week, and see how he holds up. Then again, maybe that isn't such a good idea; he might not feel comfortable wearing Doc Martens.

GLENN: The point of the Che/Freire book then?

PETER: The point of the Che/Freire book was to launch an all-out critique of capitalism from an historical materialist perspective and to encourage educators to consider socialist alternatives. The global restructuring and retrenchment of capitalism should be the starting point for any serious analysis of and engagement with teacher education. My work since the Che/Freire book has gone even further in postulating what this might mean in terms of revolutionary class struggle.

GLENN: For some, this might sound a bit "fundamentalist." I mean, I have heard it said by some educators in the United States, that in your work, in particular, critical pedagogy at its best is too preoccupied with issues of social class. Your Marxism in your current work swamps concerns with "race," gender—with the social movements in general. Is there any truth to this?

Too Much Class?

PETER: I am glad you raised this question, Glenn. What do we mean by social class? That's part of the issue. You, Dave Hill, and Mike Cole all have objected strenuously—and courageously—to the way that the official classification of social class in Britain is based upon status and associated consumption patterns and lifestyles. If you say somebody is upper class and then designate somebody else as lower class, the assumption is that there is a middle class and the upshot of this classification system is the naturalization of the notion of progress within capitalism. All you do is to lend credence to the myth that it is possible for everyone to move up the ranks on the basis of hard work, fortitude, and perseverance. This justifies the social division of labor and class differentiation and mystifies the agonistic relation among the classes. When we talk about "white collar" and "blue collar" workers, we hide the existence of the working class and the fact that this class has common class interests. We hinder the development of a common class-consciousness among fractions within the working class. I prefer the term "ruling class" or "capitalist class" on the one hand, and "working class" on the other.

GLENN: Okay—so not much room for the predominant neo-Weberian view of class there. I'm totally with you on this. Last summer I went to a conference at Kings College, London on education and social class, and all the presentations presupposed a neo-Weberian stance that reduces "class" to status, income and consumption groups (with the usual cultural overlay—which is important in England). Anything approaching a Marxist class analysis of education was lacking, sadly. I think there are serious problems in Marxist class analysis. Marx never left us a developed class theory. *Capital* volume three ends with, well, basically a neo-Weberian "box people" approach that today's sociologists of education feel very at home with. But Peter, I do feel you have sidestepped the issue of an apparent prioritization of social class in your work—above gender, "race" and so on. I'll press you on this one!

PETER: Well, it is important that we continue this discussion. But let me shift here to your comment about privileging class oppression over other forms of oppression. I hold that in general class struggle modifies the particularities of other struggles, that there is a strategic centrality to class struggle in that capitalism is the most powerful and far-reaching process of commodification imaginable. I hold, too, that the working class does pose a credible threat to the viability of the capitalist system. The charge that I privilege class exploitation over other forms of oppression is usually leveled at me by bourgeois left-liberals (some with pretensions to neo-Marxism). These people claim that advocating for anti-capitalist struggle is mere rhetoric. They also maintain that a stress on class detracts from anti-racist efforts in education, or efforts to de-claw patriarchy. This is an insult to feminists and to activists of color who have historically played an important role in the struggle against capitalist exploitation. I see an indissoluble link among "race," class, and gender forms of oppression.

GLENN: I totally agree on this, Peter. I indicated earlier in our dialogue that it is difficult to make the links, but we shouldn't duck the responsibility for making them.

PETER: Yes, Glenn. My point is that capitalism will find ways to survive the challenge of multiculturalism and feminism by co-opting these struggles. Many of the new social movements are seeking resource re-distribution, not the overthrow of capitalist social relations. That's my point, plain and simple. I support projects that undress the conspiracy between capitalism and racism, and capitalism and sexism, and capitalism and heteronormativity. But there is a strategic centrality to my work that I won't deny, or apologize for, that seeks to unite new social movements with the old social movements, so that anti-capitalist struggle becomes a unifying priority.

GLENN: This is interesting, on how the social movements relate to the anti-capitalist struggles of the future. It touches on the old, but still significant debate about reform *versus* revolution and the "problem of centrism." This debate is playing itself out in the emerging anti-capitalist/globalization movement post-Seattle. Furthermore, there are problems of leadership and strategy, and these problems are being discussed within the anti-capitalist/globalization movement throughout the world. How do you see things, Peter? Can social movements congeal into a force for anti-capitalism?

PETER: I find the creation of multi-class formations exceedingly problematic for a number of reasons, several of which I would like to mention, without excessive adumbration. Others have gone into this in capillary detail but for the purposes of this discussion I want simply to mention that, for the most part, such movements serve mainly the petit-bourgeoisie and their interests; secondly, these groups rarely contest the rule of capital. The laws of motion of capital and social relations of production do not seem the central objects of their attack, and, frankly, too often they are not even regarded as the central issues around which their struggle coalesces. Their efforts are too frequently reform based, calling for access to capitalist forms of democracy, for a redistribution of resources. Thirdly, in their attempt to stitch together a broad coalition of groups, they often seem rudderless. Should we be for a form of "social justice" that works simply to re-institute capitalist social relations of production? Of course, these are issues that we need to debate in schools of education and elsewhere. The whole issue of rights-based justice is predicated upon capitalist rights to property and entitlement to the extraction of surplus value in measures unimaginable. Can we shift the focus of such a struggle to the abolition of private property and the abolition of the private ownership of the means of production? To new social relations, political cultures, and forms of free, creative, and collective association not trapped within the social universe of capital? I don't see these discussions occurring with any consistency within the tradition of critical pedagogy in the United States.

GLENN: But this, for me, is not just an issue for the United States. In your own work, Peter, you have continually stressed the international dimension when thinking through how critical pedagogy, social movements and anti-capitalist struggles relate.

PETER: Yes, this is important, absolutely essential. What you see, for instance, in Eastern Europe and the Soviet Union is not a disappearance of the hidebound and monolithic structures of power, or the disappearance of the previous socio-economic orders—i.e., centrally planned socialism—of the old regime, so much as its transmogrification: the capitalist consolidation of power over markets and property—i.e., via spontaneous privatizations or voucher privatizations, and the like; power over the means of the extraction of surplus value; the power to merge civil society more fully into capital; the power to increase dependence on Western economic systems; the power to legitimize what amounts to a swapping of elites in the name of democracy. A capitalist revolution without capitalists, a bourgeois revolution without the bourgeoisie, as some commentators note. Attempts at integration to the capitalist world economy have increased misery and poverty—through a vertical international division of labor—on a world-historical scale, and this also relates to Latin American economies in general. In fact, in light of the restoration of the comprador elites, many of the present-day Eastern European countries, by means of their prolonged austerity and increasing unemployment, the exacerbation of the rifts between the ruling class and labor, and the deepening of class divides, are beginning to resemble the peripheral capitalist countries of Latin America. Here the dreams fuelled by the consumer promise of a better life in capitalism fall and shatter on the pavement of hard truths: that the so-called "transition to democracy" will see the authoritarian regimes of Eastern Europe come in through the back door. A class system riven with such disparities—even when overhauled by neo-liberalism—cannot afford a real participatory form of political representation, but must rely more and more upon brute state repression or authoritarian populism. Witness also recent events in Spain with respect to government policies on immigrants.

GLENN: These facts point to some of the tasks ahead for the anti-capitalist movement. People like to point to Seattle, Washington, Prague, Nice and so on—but in some countries the anti-capitalist movement and working-class action are at lower levels. Basically, though, are you optimistic about the future?

The Future

PETER: Occupying the horizon of the future—the immediate future, at least—is the continuation of life as warfare, of war against the poor, against women, against people of color, against gays and lesbians and transgendered peoples. I lament the continuing contempt that the ruling class betrays towards those who do not mirror its values. I mourn daily for the revolution that has not yet come to pass. How can one not recoil from the refuse of history that litters the charred path to emancipation, to freedom? So much agony, so much bloodshed and misery. I may not be able to summon optimism, but I still hold on to hope, as fragile as my grasp might be. I am careful to reject a facile optimism, so prevalent in the current craze of bourgeois self-fashioning, yet I refuse to be burdened by a politics of despair. Nor do I seek to aestheticize despair and turn it into a coffee klatch therapy session for academics, or to make it an art-form—or forum—to succor more bourgeois self-indulgence for the metropolitan art scene crowd. Now is the time to become intoxicated with the struggle for freedom, to get drunk on the possibility that comes from the horizon of the concrete. Look at the general strikes that have occurred in countries all over the world. Look at Seattle, Washington, and beyond. Look at the revolutionary movements that continue to forge a new politics of the possible. But before we in the North become drunk by such anticipation we need to become awakened to the tasks ahead. The tasks that Freire, Gramsci, Lenin, and Luxemburg have put before us. If we accept the terms of capital, then one has already conceded defeat at its hands. That's where critical education comes in, and that is where I believe I have been granted a special gift. The gift of being able to work with teachers and students from all walks of life, and being given the privilege to fight alongside of them for working-class power.

GLENN: What about the struggle, the pragmatics of it. Take the Zapatistas. You have written about their struggle and admire it. But does it go far enough?

PETER: You mean, are the "cuernos de chivo" just postmodern props today? Is the ammunition ready to be chambered, if necessary? The question is this: Is it the correct time? That depends, of course, upon where you happen to be standing when you are asking that question. Take the recent split between the Revolutionary Party of the Insurgent People (ERIP) and the Popular Revolutionary Army (EPR) in Oaxaca and Guerrero.

GLENN: You have written about the Zapatista?

PETER: Yes. I am also encouraged in hearing about the Armed Ecologist Group who are defending communal forests from timber exploitation, and the National Indigenous Guerrilla Triple Alliance (TAGIN), a joint command of three armed groups in the Sierra del Sur, Morelos, and Mexico state: the Indigenous Campesino Revolutionary Party (ERIC), the Nationalist Army of Insurgent Indigenous Mexico (ENMII) and Armed Campesino Command of Indigenous Liberation (COACUAUHTLI). There is an interesting and informative article on all of these groups by Bill Weinberg in a recent issue of *Native Americas*. A major concern Weinberg identifies is the whole issue of the drug war as counterinsurgency. Here the Pentagon has played a role in advancing what it has called "Guerra de Baja Intensidad" or low-intensity warfare that consists of limited and protracted politico-military struggle designed to put economic, psychological and diplomatic pressure on insurgent groups. The Pentagon has imparted this doctrine to the Mexican National Army. Weinberg notes, for instance, that 1,500 Mexican military officers received training from 1996 to 1997. The training is supposedly for counter-drug interdiction operations, but it is obvious that it is for counterinsurgency against the guerrillas. There are clear signs of tension between and within some guerrilla factions. For instance, the ERPI basically split from the ERP on the grounds that the ERP was becoming too militantly orthodox, too messianic. The EPR and Comandante Jose Arturo refuse to dialogue with the Mexican government and criticize the Zapatistas' "armed reformism." The ERPI wants to operate in a bottom-up fashion, with the direction coming directly from the people. They want to be the Army of the People, not the Army of the Party. The guerrilla command should obey the will of the people, and not the other way around. The question of organization is crucial, and always will be. Weinberg cites an exchange by Arturo and Subcomandante Marcos. Arturo criticized Marcos by arguing that "poetry cannot be the continuation of politics by other means" followed by Marcos's reply: *"You fight to take power. We fight for democracy, freedom and justice. It's not the same thing. Even if you are successful and win power, we will go on fighting for democracy, freedom and justice."* This really reflects a lot of the debates around issues of organization, of how revolutionary movements can become authoritarian and despotic once they take power. On the other side of the issue is the difficult task of achieving real, structural change by operating in the civil sphere. This brings us to the debates around the relationship of civil society to the state.

GLENN: Where do you stand on this issue, Peter?

PETER: It has a lot to do with the issue of how hegemony is forged. Radical pluralists, neo-Marxists and post-Marxists rely a great deal on the democratizing potential of civil society. They wish to portray civil society as largely free from the tentacles of the state. Like Marx, I view civil society as an arm of the state. Hegemony is forged there, too, as well as at the site of production. Individuals consent to the dominant ideology because of the position the dominant group in the world of production attains. The class that constitutes the ruling material force in society forges the dominant ideology. Gramsci, as far as I know, didn't use the concept of counter-hegemony because it speaks overwhelmingly to a reformist politics. I think that operating in the civil sphere alone is problematic. I believe that as a result of each and every solution that is put forward by liberal democratic pluralists, or NGOs, or liberal or left-liberal multiculturalists, to the suffering of labor, labor will continue to suffer, precisely because these solutions don't directly challenge the rule of capital.

GLENN: You can, of course, trace this back to Hegel.

PETER: Yes, for Hegel the state becomes the site where alienation experienced in civil society is overcome. But Marx criticized Hegel's notion of civil society and the state as an imaginary idealist relation. For Marx, the state was another form of alienation, a central site of ruling-class oppression. The state becomes a means for civil society to create the natural cosmopolitan citizen. John Holst has some provocative things to say about this. According to Holst, rejecting as outmoded and romantic Lenin's dream of taking over the state, and skipping around Marx's project of overthrowing capital, radical pluralists merely champion the cause of the new progressive social movements and organizations dealing with feminism, anti-racism, sexuality, and environmental issues whilst leaving capitalism intact. Nevertheless, they view this as a necessary defense of the life-world and a courageous deepening of democracy through their engagements with civil society. On the other hand, notes Holst, revolutionary socialists seek alliances between the old (community-labor organizations/trade unions) and new social movements. They reject, for the most part, the new social movements as the center of progressive change on the basis that they cleave away from the basic tenets of classical Marxism, especially when read directly against the work of Marx and Gramsci.

GLENN: And what's your view on it, Peter?

PETER: I believe that forging a counter-hegemonic bloc with new social movements could be problematic and should be encouraged only when the primacy of working-class struggle against capital remains the overwhelming objective. Of course, let me say without further qualification that I believe today's dialectics of liberation, of self and social transformation, must include all forces of revolution: proletarian, women, gays and lesbians, people of color. Of course, Marx famously put it that "labor in the white skin cannot be free so long as labor in the black skin is branded." But I believe fervently that such forces should always be united against capital. I think it is possible to address the heterogeneities and differences in society based on, for example, race, gender, age, ability, locality, religion, culture, and the like, and still concentrate on class struggle. This brings us—does it not—to the inevitable discussion of Antonio Gramsci, and don't all educational roads always seem to lead to Gramsci?

GLENN: Well, for me they never did! Gramsci has played virtually no part in my intellectual development. Peter, we come from very different intellectual traditions, and that has to be acknowledged. I think that gives our conversations a certain edge. In the States, it seems that critical/radical pedagogy came principally through Gramsci and Freire, with Dewey sometimes in attendance. In Britain, the critical/radical pedagogy phenomenon has always been very much weaker as compared with the United States. Direct reading of Marx, labor process theory, Marxist critiques of education policy and Marxist historical writings on education (I have the work of the legendary Brian Simon in mind here) have been the main referents.

Furthermore, I don't really go along with the notion that we have to work only with the "maximum program" (abolition of capitalism). I've seen too much of what happens with that in England. The key issue is how you build for anti-capitalism, and I'm not convinced that "taking the message neat" necessarily works best. I witnessed the early history of the Revolutionary Communist Party (as the Revolutionary Communist Tendency in its early years) as indicating the weakness of the "all or nothing" approach. Maybe I'm being unfair. But please go on, Peter, on Gramsci.

PETER: We shall take those points down-line, Glenn, for sure!

GLENN: Okay!

PETER: We, all those involved in anti-capitalist practice, need to discuss these vital issues. But yes, back to Gramsci, and I believe this is something we both agree on. It is important to expose those left liberals and radical reformists who have emasculated and vulgarized the political center of gravity that informs Gramsci's revolutionary theories, thereby distorting his legacy as a committed communist.

GLENN: Yes, absolutely with you there, Peter. In both our countries the liberal left approach to critique of education policy is dominant.

PETER: Right, Glenn. The crucial point is this: John Holst's reading of Gramsci is similar to the position held by British scholars such as Paula Allman and John Wallis (1995). Allman and Wallis contend that Gramsci did not have in mind loose coalitions of social movements when he spoke of creating an historical bloc in civil society. The war of position and the creation of proletarian hegemony mean that the majority of the working-class population needs to be mobilized by class alliances. And this mobilization is directly undertaken to challenge the state. It is crucial to locate Gramsci within the historical context of his attempt to forge proletarian hegemony. He was interested in bringing forth a revolutionary class. We need only examine his emphasis on the pedagogical dimensions of the revolutionary party. Holst re-situates Gramsci—including his ideas of the state, the political party, organic intellectuals, spontaneity, hegemony, and alliances—within Marx's problematic. Gramsci saw civil society as a fundamental aspect of the state. I realize there are major debates on this issue, but even if we should concede that Gramsci saw private, civil society as distinct from the state, or political society, we have to agree that he saw both as the domain of ruling class economic power and political interest. The ruling class exerts its authority over the social order in the arena of civil society. So while I agree that you can't foist socialism on workers, I have not abandoned the notion of the vanguard. The issue for me is what such a vanguard should like. Ideally, the entire people should comprise the vanguard.

GLENN: Right, I think we are nearer on the account you are giving now, Peter.

PETER: For me, Glenn, the key issue is the central role that can be played by education. Socialism must first be "embodied" or "enfleshed" by workers in a type of struggle-in-motion, a collective internal dialogue, one directed towards emancipation from capital. After all, as Gramsci notes, historical acts can only be performed collectively. And this is to occur through the creation of a cultural-social unity in which toilers who reflect *"a multiplicity of dispersed wills"* are welded together on the basis of a heterogeneous, single aim: that of *"an equal and common conception of the world, both general and particular."* This is the future that inspires and powers my work and life.

GLENN: Well, from Europe, the notion of vanguard party building has perhaps a different resonance. In Britain, we have witnessed the fortunes of many far-left groups that have in one way or another subscribed to the notion of a "vanguard party" deriving from Leninist principles of organization. Examples are the Workers Revolutionary Party, the Revolutionary Communist Group, the Revolutionary Communist Party, Workers Power, and the Socialist Workers Party—and many smaller groups. On the whole, the results have not been impressive. We have seen examples of brilliant critique and analysis (the early writings of the Revolutionary Communist Tendency—their *Revolutionary Communist Papers*, for example, which I still use now). There have been some fantastic campaigns and solidarity building (around many strikes), and so on. But no real big anti-capitalist party or group has emerged that has posed a really substantial threat to the British state and capital. The Leninist model has not been that successful in enabling these parties and groups to hold on to members either. The Socialist Workers Party has clearly been most successful, and I have great respect for them. When Ruth Rikowski and Howard Bloch were victimized by the managers of Newham Library Service in the mid-1990s (both were librarians at the time), the SWPs campaigning was impressive. At the college I worked at up to 1994 (Epping Forest College), it was the SWP members who were really great at organizing the fightback against management—over new contracts, staff appraisal and other issues. Maybe, Peter, I have not made the distinction you might wish to make between a vanguard *party* and vanguard anti-capitalists, where the latter are not necessarily members of a particular party.

A concrete example may help develop this last point. Last weekend (4th February) Ruth Rikowski and I attended the Globalize Resistance Conference in London. What impressed us was the way that the SWP were becoming a part of the anti-capitalist movement, rather than trying to dominate or get it "oriented" in classical Leninist mode. In terms of the future, that Conference demonstrated that there is indeed "something in the air": it brought the Greens, the SWP, Workers Power, the Revolutionary Communist Group, the environmental movement, Jubilee 2000, Drop the Debt and other organizations together to work for what Kevin Danaher calls the "Peoples' Globalization." There was a wonderful finale with a speech by a striking London Underground worker being cheered to the rafters! I admit that there are problems and debates around the organization of the movement against capitalist globalization. Ruth Rikowski summarizes the event in *Link-up* (Rikowski, R. 2001—a journal for Third World information workers) and argues that the movement has come a long way in a short time. But obviously, it needs to attend further to organizational and democratic forms, and left political parties are in a process of discovering their role *vis-à-vis* this rapidly developing movement. The SWP in particular are really trying hard to do this. People talked about a "new politics" in relation to postmodernism, and in relation to Blair's New Labor. The former was a kind of anti-politics, the latter a continuation of Thatcherite neo-liberalism with a homespun gloss. But the rising anti-capitalist movement is a genuinely new politics; it places the future of capitalism itself on the chopping block of history. The anti-capitalist movement that has developed throughout many countries in the last five years also—given a massive boost post-Seattle— points towards an open future. This is a future no longer dominated by capital. It is a future worth fighting for. More than that: we are *driven* to fight for this future by capitalist development itself. We must not fail; the survival of our planet depends on the success of the anti-capitalist movement and the abolition of capital.

PETER: There are clearly issues requiring further discussion, Glenn, especially in relation to the notion of vanguardism. I've enjoyed this e-dialogue and look forward to further discussions with you.

GLENN: It's been great, and I feel that I've clarified and deepened some of my own ideas. I have also deepened my understanding and appreciation of your work, Peter. In addition, I've also got a clearer grasp of where our work interlocks most strongly for the project of human liberation. I look forward to developing our dialogue some more in other contexts with this project in view.

References

Allman, P. (1999). *Revolutionary social transformation: Democratic hopes, radical possibilities and critical education*. Westport, CT: Bergin & Garvey.

Allman, P. (2001). *Critical education against global capital: Karl Marx and revolutionary critical education*. Westport, CT: Bergin & Garvey.

Allman, P., & Wallis, J. (1995). Gramsci's challenge to the politics of the Left in our times. *International Journal of Lifelong Education*, *14*(2), 120–143.

Blake, N., Smeyers, P., Smith, R., & Standish, P. (2000). *Education in an age of nihilism*. London: Routledge/Falmer.

Bowles, S., & Gintis, H. (1976). *Schooling in capitalist America: educational reform and the contradictions of economic life*. London: Routledge & Kegan Paul.

Cole, M., Hill, D., & Rikowski, G. (1997). Between postmodernism and nowhere: The predicament of the postmodernist. *British Journal of Educational Studies*, *45*(2), 187–200.

Dunayevskaya, R. (1978). *Marx's Capital and today's global crisis*. Detroit, MI: News & Letters.

Gulli, B. (1999). The labor of fire: On time and labor in the *Grundrisse*. *Cultural Logic: An Electronic Journal of Marxist Theory & Practice, vol.* 2(2) (Spring). Retrieved from http://eserver.org/clogic/2–2/gulli.htm.

Harvey, D. (2000). Alienation, class and enclosure in UK universities. *Capital & Class*, no. 71 (Summer), 103–132.

Holst, J. (2001). *Social movements, civil society, and radical adult education*. Westport, CT: Bergin & Garvey.

Hudis, P. (2000a). The dialectical structure of Marx's concept of revolution in permanence. *Capital & Class*, No. 70 (Spring), 127–142.

Hudis, P. (200b). Can capital be controlled? Retrieved from *News & Letters Online* from http://www.newsandletters.org/4.00_essay.htm.

Jacoby, R. (2000). *The last intellectuals: American culture in the age of academe*, 2nd Edition. New York: Basic Books.

Marx, K. [(1973). *Grundrisse: Foundations of the critique of political economy*.Translated by M. Nicolaus. Harmondsworth: Penguin. (Original work published 1858.)

Marx, K. (1977). *Capital: A critique of political economy*–(Vol. 1). London: Lawrence & Wishart. (Original work published 1867.)

McLaren, P. (1995.) *Critical pedagogy and predatory culture: Oppositional politics in a postmodern era*. New York & London: Routledge.

McLaren, P. (1997). *Revolutionary multiculturalism: Pedagogies of dissent for the new millennium*. Boulder, CO: Westview Press.

McLaren, P. (1999). *Schooling as a ritual performance: Towards a political economy of educational symbols and gestures*, 3rd Edition. Lanham, MD: Rowman & Littlefield.

McLaren, P. (2000). *Che Guevara, Paulo Freire, and the pedagogy of revolution*. Lanham, MD: Rowman & Littlefield.

McNally, D. (2001). *Bodies of meaning: Studies on language, labor, and liberation*. Albany, New York: State University of New York Press.

Neary, M. (1997). *Youth, training and the training state: The real history of youth training in the twentieth century*. Basingstoke: Macmillan.

Neary, M., & Rikowski, G. (2000). *The speed of life: The significance of Karl Marx's concept of socially necessary labour-time*. A paper presented at the British Sociological Association Conference 2000, Making Time—Marking Time, University of York, April.

Neary, M., & Taylor, G. (1998). *Money and the human condition*. London: Macmillan.

Postone, M. (1996). *Time, labor and social domination: A reinterpretation of Marx's critical theory*. Cambridge: Cambridge University Press.

Rikowski, G. (1995). *Education markets and missing products*. a paper presented at the Annual Conference of Socialist Economists, University of Northumbria, Newcastle, July 7–9.

Rikowski, G. (1996). Left alone: end time for Marxist educational theory? *British Journal of Sociology of Education*, *17*(4), 415–451.

Rikowski, G. (1999). Education, capital and the transhuman. In D. Hill, P. McLaren, M. Cole, & G. Rikowski (Eds.), *Postmodernism in Educational theory: Education and the politics of human resistance*. London: Tufnell Press.

Rikowski, G. (2000a). *That other great class of commodities: Repositioning Marxist educational theory*. A paper presented at the British Educational Research Association Conference 2000, University of Cardiff, Wales, September 9.

Rikowski, G. (2000b). The Which Blair project: Giddens, the third way and education. *Forum for Promoting Comprehensive Education*, *42*(1), 4–7.

Rikowski, G. (2000c). *Education and social justice within the social universe of capital.* A paper presented at the British Educational Research Association Day Conference Approaching Social Justice in Education: Theoretical Frameworks for Practical Purposes, Faculty of Education, Nottingham Trent University, Clifton Hall, April 10.

Rikowski, G. (2000d). The rise of the student-worker. In M. Gokulsing, & C. DaCosta (Eds.), *A compact for higher education*. Aldershot: Ashgate.

Rikowski, G. (2001a). *Nothing becomes them: Education and the nihilist embrace*. Unpublished paper, Faculty of Education, University of Central England, Birmingham, January 14.

Rikowski, G. (2001b). Education for industry: A complex technicism. *Journal of Education and Work, 13*(1), 27–47.

Rikowski, G. (2001c). *The battle in Seattle: Its significance for education*. London: Tufnell Press.

Rikowski, R. (2001). Globalise Resistance Conference, (Spring), pp. 6–8. *Link-up: The newsletter of Link —a network for North-South library development*.

Sayer, D. (1979). *Marx's method: Ideology, science and critique in Capital*. Hassocks: The Harvester Press.

Sayer, D. (1987). *The violence of abstraction: The analytical foundations of historical materialism*. Oxford: Basil Blackwell Ltd.

Waite, G. (1996). *Nietzsche's Corps/e: Aesthetics, politics, prophecy, or, the spectacular technoculture of everyday life*. Durham & London: Duke University Press.

Willis, P. (1977). *Learning to labor: how working class kids get working class jobs*. Farnborough: Saxon House.

Willmott, R. (1999) Structure, agency and the sociology of education: rescuing analytical dualism. *British Journal of Sociology of Education, 20*(1), 5–21.

"Pedagogy for Revolution Against Education for Capital: A Dialogue" was published by Glenn Rikowski in 2001 in *Cultural Logic, vol.* 4, no. 1, (October) , 1–44.

philosophy, marxism and revolution

Interview 13

pedagogy against capital today

Glenn Rikowski

Glenn and I decided to publish in a British Marxist journal and we chose to submit this to my favorite, Hobgoblin. *It is affiliated in the United States with a very important Marxist organization, News & Letters, which has had a major impact on my work.*

" . . . all of us are enemies of the people until we prove otherwise." (Walter Rodney, The Groundings, *as cited in Tunde Adeleke, "Guerrilla Intellectualism,"* Journal of Thought, *Spring 2000, p 42.)*

GLENN RIKOWSKI: Peter, I've followed your work closely since the mid-1980s, and it seems to me that in the last few years you have moved away from what could be called "left postmodernism," or "postmodernism of resistance" and decisively towards Marx and Marxism, and indeed towards Marxist-humanism. Now, let's be frank; educational theory and research are something of a backwater in Marxist circles. You are one of the few Marxists working in the fields of radical pedagogy and educational theory today. For readers not familiar with the current state of Marxist educational theory and critical pedagogy, perhaps you could start by summarizing these fields, and situating your own work and praxis within them.

PETER MCLAREN: Since the mid-1990s Marxist educational theory has undergone a renaissance. Its previous high point was in the mid-late-1970s, with the work of Samuel Bowles and Herbert Gintis, *Schooling in Capitalist America* (1976), and Paul Willis *Learning to Labor: How Working Class Kids Get Working Class Jobs* (1977). Critical and radical pedagogy—flowing from the work of Paulo Freire—had degenerated into *un*critical liberal education detached from revolutionary social transformation by the end of the 1980s (with a few honorable exceptions). In the early 1990s, postmodern educational theory became the fashionable home for dissident "Left" educators and researchers. By the mid-1990s, Marxist writings on education and training appeared on a scale not known for many years. More importantly, however, these writings were moving in a number of directions and were increasingly no longer tied to the "old" Marxist educational theory flowing from Bowles and Gintis and Willis. Finally, radical pedagogy had reasserted itself by the mid-1990s through showing the links between Paulo Freire and Antonio Gramsci and Karl Marx. Thus, radical education was made truly *radical* once more. In the last six years, there has been an impressive output on Marxist educational theory and radical pedagogy. The beginning of the new writing on Marxist educational theory can be traced to Richard Brosio's, *A Radical Democratic Critique of Capitalist Education* (Peter Lang, 1994) and Kevin Harris, *Teachers: Constructing the Future* (The Falmer Press, 1994). Paula Allman's two books, *Revolutionary Social Transformation: Democratic Hopes, Radical Possibilities and Critical Education* (1999) and *Critical Education Against Global Capital: Karl Marx and Revolutionary Critical Education* (2001) (both Bergin & Garvey) have established her as one of the world's leading Marxist educational theorists and radical educators. Your work, along with that of Mike Cole and Dave Hill has argued for the centrality of social class within left writing on education and education politics, while providing trenchant critiques of postmodernism in educational theory. Meanwhile, the writings of Grant Banfield, Ramin Farahmandpur and Helen Raduntz herald a second wave of Marxist educational theorists. In his article "Schooling and the Spirit of Enterprise: Producing the Power to Labour" (in *Education and Social Justice*, 2(3), 2000), Banfield shows how Marxist educational theory can explain and illuminate the phenomenon of "enterprise education." Farahmandpur has written a number of articles on Marxist educational theory, the critique of postmodernism in educational theory and critical pedagogy. Finally, Helen Raduntz has produced a number of conference papers on teachers' labor, with special reference to un/productive labor. My own work is multidisciplinary, and I work at the cusp of a number of disciplines: sociology, pedagogy, critical social theory with an emphasis on Marxist theory, and ethnography. In recent years I have become disillusioned with postmodern theory, and have concentrated on revolutionary social theory, as my work has moved securely within a historical materialist approach to schooling and society. I have also become keenly interested in the Marxist-humanist tradition, especially the works of Hegel, Marx, and Dunayevskaya.

GLENN: Your latest book *Che Guevara, Paulo Freire, and the Pedagogy of Revolution* (McLaren, 2000) is the most decisively Marxist of all your books. Could you give an account of, or explanation why your own Marxism has deepened within your writings in recent years?

PETER: I became increasingly irritated by left poseurs in the academy, especially those who flirted with post-structuralism and hypertext theory and who indulged in what I call "fashionable apostasy." Many students were led down the path of disconnecting theory from revolutionary praxis and I saw them become engineered into severing whatever remaining ties they had to workers and their everyday struggles. The elitism bothered me. At the same time, I was reading more Marx and Hegel, and trying to work out my own sense of what revolutionary pedagogy was all about. I was spending more time in Latin America, most especially Brazil and Mexico, and had the good fortune of meeting professors who worked in the academy yet remained very active in community politics, as well as national and international movements. Freire became an import example for the engaged, the truly committed intellectual, and my work has tried to prevent the domestication of his work in the United States. I've also sought to demonstrate the relevance of his work to U.S. urban education.

GLENN: From my reading of the situation, urban education in the United States is in turmoil and has been for years.

PETER: Yes—and there are many reasons for this, and there has been much discussion on this issue. However, in their discussions of structural racism in the United States, particularly as it affects education, not many people have delved into the history of the founding of the American comprehensive high school, in particular, the connection between the founding of the comprehensive American high school and the Cold War. Dean MacCannell has written provocatively on this subject and some of his insights are apposite here—especially in understanding the historical roots of racist schooling in the United States. MacCannell links the politics of the Cold War and United States nuclear strategy—specifically post-Hiroshima strategic foreign policy—to what he calls the "nuclear unconscious" that was instrumental in structuring urban education in the 1950s and 1960s. He sees educational policy as connected in an unconscious way to the doctrine of deterrence and the concept of limited survivability. Directly after World War II, the dominant thinking amongst U.S. military strategists was that cities of over a million people were the only targets of sufficient economic value to warrant the use of atomic weapons. The U.S. believed that the Soviets would strike first, and many cities would be wiped out. Yet it was also believed that a sufficient number of people outside the cities would survive an attack and rebuild U.S. society—and as we shall see, this would be white people. Rural white folks and those living in smaller cities outside the large metropolitan areas were those that were slated for saving the reigning values of free enterprise after a Soviet first strike. The cities would therefore be "cured" of their officially designated social problems (crimes, disease, and high mortality rate). The idea was that the city would absorb the attack so that damage minimally spilled over into surrounding "survival areas" made up of predominantly white populations. To try to defend the cities by "hardening" them would only intensify the attack, and it might spill over to white communities. Along with the accelerating nuclear arms build-up in the1960s came massive withdrawal of upper to middle-class white folks, including many of the intelligentsia, into small towns beyond the suburban fringe. In the 1970s and 1980s rural areas continued to grow at a more rapid rate than urban areas. As MacCannell points out, rather than moving towards a form of Euro-socialism, where minimal standards of living (housing, health care, income) would be created for impoverished ethnic communities, or opting for a renewed commitment to educational and legal justice, the U.S. began to warehouse its marginalized citizens in large cities. Interestingly, about this time, fiscal policies of public spending to increase investment and employment were replaced with monetary policies that regulated interest rates, moderated investment and accelerated layoffs. Harvard University president, James Bryant Conant, who had been a member of the secret National Defence Research Committee, and had helped to target Hiroshima and Nagasaki—in particular, workers and their homes—became an influential educational reformer in the 1950s and early-1960s. In fact, he helped to create the public school system that we have today in the U.S. Conant's national-level involvement in planning the inner-city school curriculum advocated vocational education for Puerto Ricans and African Americans, and recommended school counselor-student relationships on the model of the relationship of a probation officer to a parolee that extended four years after completion of high school. He also recommended public works projects to provide ghetto-based employment for Black male youth. The idea, of course, was to keep them contained in the cities, which were expendable under the "first strike" scenario. He questioned the relevance of having African Americans in the Civilian Conservation Corps working on forest projects that would keep them out of the city. In fact, he was opposed to any program that would move Black youth out of the city, even temporarily. Conant also argued that the private enterprise that was moving outside the city should not be responsible for the welfare of inner-city inhabitants whom he referred to a "inflammable material." He was against busing, even voluntary busing, and argued that ghetto schools must require students to "rise and recite" when spoken to and suggested boys wear ties and jackets to school. As MacCannell argues, we see the nuclear unconscious at work in Conant's vision of public schooling and public life. He placed the future hope in society's projected survivors (overwhelmingly white) who would live in small cities of populations of 10,000 to 60,000. When you examine the current decay and neglect of urban schools in the United States, some of this can be traced right back to Conant's reform measures for the comprehensive high school.

GLENN: Well, Peter, given this grim picture, how does philosophy figure in such a conflictual pedagogical arena?

PETER: Is philosophy really an Archimedean lever that can be used to bring about human liberation? It's a question that has been posed to me often by those who remain skeptical of philosophy and see it primarily as an academic enterprise. Raya Dunayevskaya would, I believe, answer in the affirmative.

GLENN: In what sense? Please elaborate, Peter.

PETER: In the sense that philosophy can bring us closer to grasping the specificity of the concrete within the totality of the universal—for instance, the laws of motion of capital as they operate out of view of our common sense understanding. Furthermore, philosophy plays a key role in enabling our understanding of history as a process in which human beings make their own society, although in conditions most often not of their own choosing.

And further, the practice of double negation can help us understand the movement of both thought and action by means of praxis, or what Dunayevskaya called the "philosophy of history." The philosophy of history proceeds from social reality and not from abstract concepts (the latter is the bourgeois mode of thought). Here it is necessary that critical educators seek to help students go through "the labor of the negative" in order to see human development from the perspective of the wider social totality. By examining Marx's specific appropriation of the Hegelian dialectic, Dunayevskaya shows us how we can comprehend more clearly how the positive is always contained in the negative. It makes clear how every new society is the negation of the preceding one, conditioned by the forces of production, which gives us an opportunity for a new beginning. While it is true that ideas are conditioned and correspond to the economic structure of society, this in no way makes history unconditional. In his *Theses on Feuerbach*, Marx wrote that circumstances are changed by human beings, and not by abstract categories, and that the educator herself must be educated. Economic structures constitute the drive-wheel of history, but that doesn't mean that everything can be reduced to the sum of economic conditions. That a future society comes into being as a negation of the existing one (whose habits and ideas continue to populate it) finds its strongest expression in class struggle. The idea of freedom wobbles precariously on shaking foundations, on the scaffold of empty bourgeois dreams. Haven't we entered that monopoly stage of capitalism that Lenin called imperialism—in which nearly the whole world has been drawn into the capitalist system? Marx noted that, in the words of philosopher Georg Lukács, that "the commodity-form penetrates every corner of the social world." Aren't we very close to this monstrous eventuality at the current historical moment? Isnt the neo-liberalism that has emerged with the collapse of state demand-management and the Keynesian welfare state a particular species of imperialism, one in which the inner contradictions have become exacerbated beyond imagination? Witness the continuing "epidemics of overproduction," and the explosion in the industrial reserve army of the dispossessed that stake themselves out on the streets of our urban metropolitan centers. Aren't we experiencing a re-feudalisation of capitalism, as it refuels itself with the more barbarous characteristics of its past? While in the developed Western economies at least, wages have not been pushed down to subsistence levels as Marx predicted, he was spot-on in his predictions that oligopolistic corporations will swallow the globe and industry would become dominated by new technologies.

GLENN: Yes, but even with all of this, Peter, in the minds of the vast proportion of the population, both in the U.K. and in the U.S., it is assumed that there is no alternative to capitalism. This makes things easier for politicians to promote the extension of capital into all spheres of social life. Witness, for example, current moves to privatize education, to bring schooling into the orbit of capital. New Labour's recent Green Paper on education, *Schools: Building on Success*, seeks to extend and legitimatize the take-over of schools by corporate and venture capital.

PETER: It can also be seen at the level of pedagogy itself. One indication of this is how the work of Paulo Freire has become reconciled to capitalism. In the United States context at least he is often reduced to a liberal humanist interested in dialogical communication among students and teachers in a way that alarmingly disconnects literary from capitalist exploitation and class struggle: in short, in a way that side-steps praxis. What I think is different in the U.S. from the U.K. is that few among the United States educational left talk about workers anymore, or class struggle. There is an implosive reduction of the labor capital opposition to a single, uniform, denial of structured class conflict. When this antagonism is posited, labor and capital often cancel each other out. Part of it is the reproduction of the ideology of "classlessness" in the United States: that every decent human being is at least middle class. And part of it is the Marxaphobia produced within the commercial cultural industries, particularly the mass media. There are no popular narratives about the struggle for class formation among worker movements that students can share. The current political culture certainly does not help to foster such narratives. School texts rarely devote more than a few pages to workers' struggles. This can be traced to a residue of the McCarthy era as well as the Cold War. As Joel Kovel points out in his Foreword to *Marxism and Freedom* by Dunayevskaya, during the McCarthy era even university courses that were blatantly anti-Marxist were banned simply for exposing Marx's name to a generation of growing minds. A case in point. Recently I was having a conversation with one of the locals at a coffee shop I frequent in West Hollywood. Over his lifetime he had become a millionaire two or three times, but this time, for the first time in his life, he had lost everything—which was 2.1 million dollars—in the recent stock market plunge. His wife is on heavy medication and their regular gambling trips to Vegas have been cancelled. (A friend of his had lost everything in the recent plunge as well. But he had a buffer—an ageing relative who had put him in his will owns twenty thousand shares of Phillip

Morris). He told me that he can't afford to eat out in his usual restaurants on Sunset Strip, and that he is forced now to eat at places like Soup Plantation (which, by the way is where I often eat). He was desperate and depressed, and was railing at the government. Eventually I leaned over the table and said to him: "it's enough to make you a Marxist." He nodded and added: "Or a thief, a drug addict, or a murderer." For him, a Marxist was a perfect fit in the category of criminal. Let me give you another example. At a recent protest march and rally at the University of California, Los Angeles, against the ban on affirmative action initiated by the Board of Regents and their academic parvenus, I noticed that all the speakers decrying the repeal of affirmative action emphasized race but didn't mention social class. Most speakers structured their position from an anti-racist and anti-sexist perspective but failed to connect these to the social relations of production under capitalism. There was, in other words, no attempt to connect affirmative action to intrinsic features of capitalism. Relations of class were displaced to questions of identity politics. A better analysis would have been to identify the crucial link between the ban on affirmative action and the current intensification of capitalist exploitation and attacks on the working class—especially as we have seen reflected in measures recently taken by George W. Bush and his administration. Why the connection among race, gender, and wider systemic capitalist exploitation was glaringly missing would be an exploration in itself. The speakers failed to situate the elimination of affirmative action within a wider political optic of current attacks on unions, workers, and labor in general. There was a danger of race becoming an absolute category, foreclosing alliances with working-class groups. I am not saying that we need to disqualify the class character of this student movement because its impulse was not to obtain state power. But the radical students are still working within a liberal framework, hence tacitly accepting the rules set by capital. Radical students need to embrace a multiracial proletariat struggle.

GLENN: What kind of pedagogy is needed for that to occur?

PETER: Well, we require a pedagogy that meets the conditions of the current times. We need to understand that diversity and difference are allowed to proliferate and flourish provided that they remain within the prevailing forms of capitalist social arrangements, and this includes hierarchical property arrangements. Once anti-racism and anti-sexism begins to contest the hierarchical imperatives of advanced capitalism, *then* such struggles are resisted by all the power the state can muster. My own work has been to support anti-racist and anti-sexist pedagogies, but to recast them within a larger project of class struggle, particularly the struggle against the globalization of capital. I have emphasized the need to educators to revisit the works and lives of Paulo Freire and Che Guevara. Furthermore, I believe that critical pedagogy (or what I have come to term "revolutionary pedagogy") could greatly benefit from exploring the work of Raya Dunayevskaya, and other Marxist-humanists such as Peter Hudis and Kevin Anderson. Dunayevskaya was critical of both United States capitalist democracy and the state capitalism of the Soviet Union—and for good reasons. Both were concerned with the extraction of surplus labor from workers, although in different ways. The current conditions in both countries are growing more similar, as both countries are experiencing variations of tycoon, or gangster capitalism. Because at the present historical juncture, the contradictions of capitalism are pushed to such unbearable extremes, Dunayevskaya felt it was important that history and consciousness be examined from the perspective of the development of labor. Her work on double negation captures the continuous process of becoming. Her philosophy of absolute negativity as a self-moving, self-active, and self-transcending method has a lot to offer critical educators in the schools.

GLENN: What about the common objections from students that Marxism is based on an archaic economic reductionism, or that it's hopelessly teleological, and what about the controversies surrounding the "base-superstructure" relation?

PETER: In addition to requiring my students to engage the works of Hegel, Marx, Lenin, Lukács, Luxemburg, and others, I have my students read Peter Hudis on dialectics, and, of course, a large sampling of the works of Dunayevskaya. The key points that I try to emphasize with students is that the struggle to understand the primary causal role in capitalist society—is it the forces of production or the forces of ideas, culture, politics, law, etc.?—is to grasp their *dialectical interaction*. If the forces of production were the key determinants, then class struggle would be useless because it, too, would be determined, or overdetermined, by the forces of production. Marx was certainly aware of the influence the superstructure had on the forces of production. But unlike Hegel, Marx did not see the consciousness of Mind as ultimate reality. Whereas Hegel viewed the material world as a manifestation of mind, Marx viewed the material world as the ultimate ground of being, and mind was a manifestation of the material world: mind, in other words, is *reflected in and refracted through* the forces of production. Hence, Marx was concerned about what was real, and what was mere appearance, a mere phantom of the mind, or an ideological mystification. In other words, capitalist society was, for Marx, "an imagined association" of freely associated human beings. The challenge, of course, is to make free association a reality within a society of collective producers. Thus, the forces of production for Marx play a fundamental role in the movement and purposefulness of history.

GLENN: Purposefulness? Therein lies teleology?

PETER: The purposefulness of history for Marx was to liberate human capacities through the development of the productive forces. Marx had a distinctly materialist conception of history. But that did not mean history has to move unstoppably in the direction of progress. While there are underlying laws governing the past and present, it is still possible—perhaps even more probable, depending on the circumstances—that humanity will retreat towards barbarism. Or, conversely, it is possible to move forward; to advance to a time when the "mystical veil" draped over our life-processes within capitalism is lifted by a community of freely associated producers. At that moment, when the value of a product becomes its use-value used to satisfy the needs and desires of the people, when production can be planned for the development of humankind's creative capacities, when the forces of production can develop to the fullest in a co-operative way and in concert with the all-around development of individuals, *then* society becomes *humanized*—in opposition to its current track of capitalization. The overthrow of class society is a path that history has opened, but nothing will happen if that path remains untraveled. History is purposeful—but not in a transcendental sense or in the sense of Hegel's universal mind—and it can achieve its purpose when workers *recognize their central role in making history*, and struggle to overthrow the forces and relations that exploit them. Marx gave himself over to the forces of history by preparing the way for workers to be able to realize such recognition. The significance of pedagogy comes into play here, particularly the pedagogy of Paulo Freire. Drawing on Marxist insights, Freire wanted workers to make this recognition: that they are central actors in history *for themselves*. He did this—most famously in his book, *Pedagogy of the Oppressed*—by creating a pedagogy in which individuals can become critically literate, in which they learn to "read the word and the world." This entails educators committing class suicide in order to be baptized into the popular character of the culture of the students.

GLENN: In your most recent writing you have moved towards exploring education, pedagogy as an educational theory through Marxist-humanism and the works of Raya Dunayevskaya in particular. Why this turn to Marxist-humanism, Peter? What were the motivations? What special contribution can a Marxist-humanist educational and pedagogic outlook yield for radical and critical educators? What aspects of Dunayevskaya's work are the most central to the pedagogy of liberation you are envisioning?

PETER: Well, Glenn, most radical educators in the United States operate out of a concern with a more democratic form of economic distribution. They are concerned with the antagonism between capital and labor in general, and with labor relations in particular. While this is fine as far as it goes, rarely is the rule of *capital* itself challenged. This is true of many union organizations, including teacher unions. What is important about Dunayevskaya's work—and your work, too, Glenn, I might note—is her stress on challenging the very rule of capital. Dunayevskaya undertook this challenge most formidably through her work on the value form of labor. Incorporating and extending the ideas of Marx and Lenin, Dunayevskaya notes that the value form of labor—which is the specific character of labor under capitalism—pervades and encompasses all of social life under capitalism. She emphasizes in her *Philosophy and Revolution* that the relation of subject to object within capitalist social formations is fundamentally perverse since it alone contains the reduction of the many and varied concrete labors into one abstract, undifferentiated mass. All critical education endeavors need to address the antagonistic terrain of capital that is inherent in the labor-capital relation itself, and to lay bare the contradictions that lay at the heart of the social relations of production. The value form of labor which gives shape to these internal relations or contradictions not only affects the objective conditions within which people labor but also the domain of subjectivity or human agency itself. This meditative role is far from innocent in so far as our very *personalities* are penetrated by capital. Following insights put forward by Dunayevskaya, I would argue that one of the central concerns of critical educationalists is to help their students understand how capital grounds all social mediation. Because capital grounds "the social" as a form of value, it follows that the substance of labor itself must be interrogated because doing so brings us closer to understanding the nature of capital's social universe out of which our subjectivities are created. In other words, we need to understand value as a social relation, not as some kind of accounting device to measure rates of exploitation or domination. Living labor creates the value form of wealth that is historically specific to capitalism. Dunayevskaya notes that the reason that capital is inherently driven to crisis is because in the process of production, labor creates value greater than that incorporated within itself. What drives the capitalist machine, in other words, is the drive to augment value. In a value-producing society, the worker is always a "producer of overproduction" because the means of consumption cannot be bigger than the needs of capital for labor-power. I agree with educators such as Paula Allman, Mike Cole, and Dave Hill who argue that capitalism is perhaps best understood as a *global quest to produce value*.

GLENN: How do these ideas play out in our classroom discussions?

PETER: Students in the classroom need to be able to ask the questions: what has society made of me that I no longer want to be? How can I become other than what I am? How is the direction of my desiring engineered in ways that escape my daily comprehension? Every student has a right to ask questions such as these, and critical educators have a responsibility to help them answer those questions. But in order to answer these questions, educators need to understand how identities have been forged within the crucible of capital, within the social universe of capital.

GLENN: So, they need to understand how we, as human subjects, have been capitalized—the "human" as capital; thus the struggle for humanism is necessarily a struggle against capital, and against a specific form of social being as capitalized life form. That places the struggle to be "human," the decapitalization of our existence, at the center of contemporary and capitalist struggles. In turn, that situates Marxist-humanism at the core of any project to implode capital's social universe, as a vital resource for de-capitalizing our individual and collective social existences and the value-form of labor on which all this rests. Is that how you see it, Peter?

PETER: Exactly! The Marxist-humanist educator recognizes that because the logic of capitalist work has invaded *all* forms of human sociability, society can be considered to be a totality of different types of labor. What is important here is to examine the particular forms that labor takes within capitalism. Consequently, labor should not be taken simply as a "given" category, but interrogated as an *object of critique*, and examined as an abstract social structure. Educators like yourself and Paula Allman have argued that the real problem is the internal or dialectical relation that exists between capital and labor with the capitalist production process itself—a social relation in which capitalism is intransigently rooted. This social relation—essential or fundamental to the production of abstract labor—deals with how already existing value is preserved and new value (surplus value) is created. It is this internal dialectical relationship that is mainly responsible for the inequitable and unjust distribution of use-values, and the accumulation of capital that ensures that the rich get richer and the poor get poorer. It is this relation between capital and labor that sets in perilous motion the conditions that make possible the rule of capital by designating production for the market, fostering market elations and competitiveness, and producing the historically specific laws and tendencies of capital.

GLENN: We need to remember here that the production of value is not the same as the production of wealth.

PETER: Correct. The production of value comes into being whenever labor assumes its dual character as both use-value and exchange-value. Peter Hudis notes, following Marx, that this dual character is not simply the distinction between use-value and exchange-value but within value itself, in the distinction between value and exchange-value. In order to see value, we have to abstract from exchange-value. Value always *reveals itself* in a relation of exchange. This enables us to emphasize the particular social character of labor that produces commodities. What we need to focus on is how education has become commodified, and how, in the process, it has commodified the very subjectivities of those who live within its precincts. We need to understand how education has become reduced to a sub-sector of the economy but also how human beings have been turned into educational commodities. You've written a great deal on this topic, Glenn.

GLENN: Yes, certainly here in the U.K. there has been a massive amount of work from what I call "liberal left"—educators, researchers and theorists—on education markets and quasi-markets. However, this work hardly ever addresses the question of the "products" of schooling, education as a form of production. So, we have "education markets and missing products"—the title of a paper I presented at the Conference of Socialist Economists in 1995. The social production of labor-power and the role that education and training (and other practices of labor-power development) are central, for me, in exploring education as production. Today, the social production of labor-power through education and training are central to the reproduction of the capitalist form of class society. But today, class, in a Marxist sense, is a topic that is more difficult to raise in educational circles than 15 or 20 years ago. Is it like this in the U.S. today too? I mean do you feel that it is more difficult to discuss class today with your students than it was, say, 20 years ago, Peter?

PETER: Yes, no question. There is a real complexity in discussions of class these days, it seems both on the part of Marxists and post-Marxists. Some radical sociologists, such as Stanley Aronowitz, argue that classes are historical and their effects are interlinked with their historicity, and that class composition changes at every level of the social structure. He feels that social groups can assume class formations, depending upon such factors as relationships of power, degree of mobilization, and whether a group's demands can be integrated into the prevailing power bloc. According to this view, classes are more than groups arrayed on the basis of productive labor or ownership of capital—i.e., productive capital—but that class formations are connected to all domains of power. Pierre Bourdieu has argued that class struggles constitute contestation over the value of signs as well as economic conditions. He argued that class struggle involves many different forms of capital.

GLENN: Different forms?

PETER: Yes, what Perrucci and Wysong would describe as *consumption capital* (having to do with wages or salary), *investment capital* (having to do with a surplus of consumption capital that you can invest and on which you can earn interest), *skills capital* (having to do with specialized knowledge that people accumulate through their work experience, training, or education), and *social capital* (having to do with the network of social ties that people have to family, friends, and acquaintances, as well as the collectively owned economic and cultural capital of a group). *Cultural capital* is a factor, too, and this has to do with values, attitudes, dress, mannerisms, personal style, etc. Teachers often respond more favorably to students who exhibit cultural capital that is most similar to theirs. And while I would like to stress ownership and control over the means of production and the central axis of class, the key concern is to make sure that class movements do not become transformed into their opposites. Class struggle must entail the struggle over new economic arrangements. This is essential.

GLENN: New arrangements that move beyond simply dividing up the capitalist pie?

PETER: Absolutely. Peter Hudis poses the crucial question: What kind of labor should a human being do? It seems to me that strategizing against capital means working with those in the technologically underdeveloped world and part of the challenge stipulates that we go beyond empirical treatments of categories developed by Marx and engaging them dialectically. Capital, as Marx has pointed out, is a social relation of labor, it constitutes objectified, abstract, undifferentiated—and hence alienated—labor. Capital cannot be controlled or abolished through external means without dispensing with value production and creating new forms of non-alienated labor. Creating these new forms of non-alienated labor is the hope and promise of the future. Let's consider for a moment the harsh reality of permanent mass employment, contingent workforces, and the long history of strikes and revolts of the unemployed. It is relatively clear from examining this history that the trajectory of capitalism in no way subsumes class struggle or the subjectivity of the workers. What separates Marxist educators from liberals is that Marxists are not content with advocating for better wages and working conditions, although that is certainly an important goal. Of course, Marxist educators advocate for a fairer distribution of wealth, arguing that the current inequitable distribution that characterizes contemporary capitalist societies results from property relations, in particular, the private ownership of the means of production. However, to suggest that Marxism merely seeks elimination of economic exploitation is to underestimate it. It pushes a great deal further than the call for a fairer redistribution of wealth. As Dunayevskaya teaches us, Marxism is profoundly humanistic in that it works not only for a more equitable redistribution of economic resources but also *for the liberation of humanity from the rule of capital.*

GLENN: Perhaps Dunayevskaya's greatest contribution is her reanimation of the Hegelian dialectic and her breakthrough work on the negation of the negation.

PETER: Dunayevskaya rethought Marx's relations to Hegelian dialectics in a profound way, in particular, Hegel's concept of the self-movement of the idea from which Marx argued the need to transcend objective reality rather than thought. Dunayevskaya notes how Marx was able to put a living, breathing, and thinking subject of history at the center of the Hegelian dialectic. She also pointed out that what for Hegel is Absolute knowledge (the realm of realized transcendence) Marx referred to as the new society. While Hegel's self-referential, all embracing, totalizing Absolute is greatly admired by Marx, it is, nevertheless, greatly modified by him. For Marx, Absolute knowledge (or the self-movement of pure thought) did not absorb objective reality or objects of thought but provided a ground from which objective reality could be transcended. By reinserting the human subject into the dialectic, and by defining the subject as corporal being (rather than pure thought or abstract self-consciousness), Marx appropriates Hegels self-movement of subjectivity as an act of transcendence and transforms it into a critical humanism. As Peter Hudis has revealed, in her rethinking of Marx's relationship to the Hegelian dialectic Dunayevskaya parts company with Derrida, Adorno, Marcuse, Habermas, Deleuze, Mészáros, and others. She has given absolute negativity a new urgency, linking it not only to the negation of today's economic and political realities but also to developing new human relations. The second negation constitutes drawing out the positive within the negative and expressing the desire of the oppressed for freedom. Second negativity is intrinsic to the human subject as an agent; it is what gives direction and coherence to revolutionary action as praxis.

GLENN: This shall be a form of praxis that takes us outside the social universe of capital?

PETER: Yes. Abstract, alienated labor can be challenged by freely associated labor and concrete, human sensuousness. The answer is in envisioning a non-capitalist future that can be achieved, as Hudis notes, after Dunayevskaya, by means of subjective self-movement through absolute negativity so that new relation between theory and practice can connect us to the realization of freedom.

GLENN: A freedom, surely, that is incompatible with private property.

PETER: Yes, but we need to remember something Hudis emphasized, which is that the abolition of private property does not necessarily lead to the abolition of capital. We need therefore, to examine the direct relation between the worker and production. Here, our sole emphasis should not be on the abolition of private property, which is the product of alienated labor; it must be on the abolition of alienated labor itself. Marx gave us some clues as to how to transcend alienation, ideas that he developed from Hegel's concept of second or absolute negativity, or "the negation of the negation." Marx engaged in a materialist re-reading of Hegel. In his work, the abolition of private property constitutes the first negation. The second is the negation of the negation of private property. This refers to a self-reflected negativity and what Hudis refers to as the basis for a positive humanism.

GLENN: Absolute negativity in this sense is a creative force.

PETER: Yes. Of course, Marx rejects Hegel's idealization and dehumanization of self-movement through double negation because this leaves untouched alienation in the world of labor-capital relations. Marx sees this absolute negativity as objective movement and the creative force of history. Absolute negativity in this instance becomes a constitutive feature of a self-critical social revolution that, in turn, forms the basis of permanent revolution. Hudis raises a number of difficult questions with respect to developing a project that moves beyond controlling the labor process. It is a project that is directed at abolishing capital itself through the creation of freely associated labor: The creation of a social universe not parallel to the social universe of capital (whose substance is value) is the challenge here. The form that this society will take is that which has been *suppressed* within the social universe of capital: socialism, a society based not on value but on the fulfillment of human need. For Dunayevskaya, absolute negativity entails not just economic struggle but the liberation of humanity from class society. This is necessarily a political and a revolutionary struggle and not only an economic one. This particular insight is what, for me, signals the fecundating power of Dunayevskaya's Marxist-humanism—the recognition that Marx isn't talking about class relations only but *human* relations. Critical pedagogy is too preoccupied with making changes within civil society or the bourgeois "public sphere," where students are reduced to test scores and their behavior is codified in relation to civic norms. Marx urged us to push beyond this crude type of materialism that fails to comprehend humanity's sensuous nature and regards humans only as statistics or "averaged out" modes of behavior. We need to move towards a *new social humanity*. This takes us well beyond civil society. We need to work towards the goal of becoming associated producers, working under conditions that will advance human nature, where the measure of wealth is not labor-time but solidarity, creativity, and the full development of human capacities. This can only occur outside the social universe of capital.

References

Allman, P. (1999). *Revolutionary social transformation: Democratic hopes, radical possibilities and critical education*. Westport, CT: Bergin & Garvey.

Allman, P. (2001). *Critical education against global capital: Karl Marx and revolutionary critical education*. Westport, CT: Bergin & Garvey.

Allman, P., & Wallace, J. (1995). Gramsci's challenge to the politics of the Left in our times. *International journal of lifelong education*, 14(2), 120–143.

Cole, M., Hill, D., & Rikowski, G. (1997). Between postmodernism and nowhere: The predicament of the postmodernist. *British journal of educational studies*, 45(2), 187–200.

Dunayevskaya, R. (1978). *Marx's Capital and today's global crisis*. Detroit, MI: News & Letters.

Hudis, P. (2000a). The dialectical structure of Marx's concept of revolution in permanence. *Capital & class*, no. 70 (Spring), 127–142.

Hudis, P. (2000b). Can capital be controlled? News & Letters. Retrieved from http://www.newsandletters.org/Issues/2000/April/4.00_essay.htm.

Lukács, G. (1997). *Lenin: A study in the unity of his thought*. London and New York: Verso.

Lukács, G. (2000). *A defence of history and class consciousness: Tailism and the dialectic*. London and New York: Verso.

MacCannell, D. (1984). Baltimore in the morning . . . after. On the forms of post-nuclear leadership. *Diacritics*, (Summer), 33–46.

Neary, M., & Rikowski, G. (2000). *The speed of life: The significance of Karl Marx's concept of socially necessary labour-time*. A paper presented at the British Sociological Association Conference 2000, University of York, April 17–20.

Perrucci, R., & Wysong, E. (1990). *The new class society*. Boulder, CO: Rowman and Littlefield.

"Pedagogy Against Capital Today" was published by Glenn Rikowski in *Hobgoblin: The Journal of Marxist Humanism* (England), No. 4, Winter 2001–2002, 31–38. (A shortened version was previously published in *News & Letters, volume* 46, no. 4, May 2001, 10–11.)

Interview 14

traveling the path of most resistance: Peter McLaren's pedagogy of dissent (parts 1 and 2)

Kenneth McClelland

Ken McClelland is a doctoral candidate who works with my friend John Novak, one of the most prominent Deweyean educators in Canada. John was responsible for getting my first position as a professor at Brock University in 1984 (my official title was senior lecturer) but was not responsible for me being fired the very next year because of my sharing of my radical political perspectives in my classes. After this interview, which touched on the basis of human nature, Ken and John wanted to set up a debate between me and Peter Singer. But that could not be worked out, much to my disappointment.

Part 1

KENNETH MCCLELLAND: Hi Peter! We are happy that you have been able to take some time to talk with us here at *Professing Education* and address some of the problems surrounding the miseducation of the democratic public.

PETER MCLAREN: Thanks, Ken, for offering me an opportunity to put a few of my ideas on the table for your readers to consider.

KEN: In the wake of the kind of confusion and horror generated by the recent attacks on the United States, its leaders have responded with confidence—their answer, among other things, involving the forceful display of "democracy" abroad in what we might assume will be an expanding web. It seems to me that this brash confidence belies the real confusion that can be the only result of such terror tactics. To your thinking, do confident answers in this case represent the easy way?

PETER: Well, long before the Bush gang took power (illegally, in my view) in January 2001, the present architects of U.S. foreign policy at the Project for the New American Century (PNAC), recognized the need to maintain the dominant position of U.S. capitalism by advancing such American values through a policy of "peace through strength." It has turned out to be more like war through war. Permanent war.

Americans like to plump for the Bush gang's tough stance against terrorism while forgetting that transnationals who are flooding the market with cheap and subsidized food are forcing millions of farmers into bankruptcy, including thousands per week in the U.S. Forgotten are the millions of urban homeless and unemployed and those who cannot afford medical insurance. Forgotten is the environmental degradation in the Homeland, and the toxic waste we are dumping not just on Native American lands but also exporting to developing countries as the solution. Forgotten is California's energy crisis that was stage-managed by Kenny Boy Lay, the darling of Bush W., who still runs free even after the collapse of his company, Enron. Well, the corporate media helps us forget. And FOX-News virtually *commands* us to forget. As I have tried to document with Valerie Scatamburlo-DAnnibale, Ramin Farahmandpur, Greg Martin, Noah De Lissovoy, and Nathalia Jaramillo in a torrent of articles over the past year, ultra-right-wing mouthpieces have been busily trying to craft George W. Bush as a fraternity brother version of Ronald Reagan, while labeling critics as un-American and unpatriotic. Recently, pro-war columnists and radio and television gasbags have begun a testosterone-driven campaign to have anti-war dissidents arrested by invoking the Sedition Act of 1918. It has become dangerous to think, to ask too many questions, or to look beyond the surface of whatever commentary is served up to us by politicians, the military, and the infantilizing screeds of talk-radio pundits.

As far as linking Bush military strategy to neo-liberal economics, my focus, Ken, has been on monopoly capital theory which traces the developments in finance capital, the concentration and centralization of capital as part of a new phase of neo-liberal globalization, stagnation tendencies in the capitalist center, and imperialist exploitation in the countries located on the periphery (developing capitalist economies).

Well, we know that all the talk by the U.S. ruling elite about exporting democracy really boils down to exporting neo-liberal free market ideology, policy, and practice. In my view, neo-liberal economics is incompatible with democracy, and later on I'll try to give you a rather technical answer directly from Marx—*Capital, Volume 1* to be precise—that speaks to why I feel this to be the case. Occupied by the military forces of the U.S. and British coalition, Iraq is slowly being turned into a vassal state—a protectorate, if you will—of its conquering imperialist powers. The Security Council of the UN granted these occupying forces full powers to control the economy and the future politics of Iraq, which it is doing by virtue of a campaign designed to terrorize the population into submission. We've already read about the thousands of civilians who have been and continue to be killed. We have seen what happened to Iraq's cultural heritage in the mass lootings, and now its national wealth, i.e., oil will be sold in order to pay U.S. corporations, who, without bidding, have been granted huge reconstruction contracts. If, in Iraq, citizens decided by free election to keep their oil socialized, then the U.S. would never permit that election to stand. The U.S. occupying powers are saying that the Iraqis must take "baby-steps" toward democracy before they will be permitted to govern themselves in full (the U.S. has such a colonial view of the Iraqis it is sickening, and it reminds me of the patronizingly pathetic way the Anglo-Europeans viewed the Indians or African slaves: as underdeveloped children). The U.S. is prohibiting elections until the conditions are ripe for a government to be elected that will favor the institution of free-market capitalism. They need to propagandize first and get their ideological machinery institutionally in place. And they need to build a loyal capitalist class, with the help of their imported Iraqi exiles (Iraqi workers are already complaining that their wages were higher when Saddam's state tightly controlled the economy). And, of course, they need to purge the socialists and communists. Then, when the occupying powers are assured that the government will remove any impediments to letting the U.S. and other developed democracies exploit their cheap labor and natural resources, then and only then will they be given a green light to hold elections. And God forbid if the Iraqis wish to elect an Islamic fundamentalist government. (Of course, the U.S. helped to cultivate the most reactionary Islamic fundamentalists possible when it worked with bin Laden and Pakistan's secret service to help expel the Soviets from Afghanistan.) And what will happen when Iraqi citizens start to press for the right to organize independent unions and to collective negotiation? History has shown that the U.S. will militarily pummel or covertly destabilize any country that refuses the great dream of free-market capitalism, because, frankly, the U.S. needs the markets (it is trying its best to topple Venezuela and it has failed for decades to finish off Cuba). Anything considered remotely socialist is linked to the evil of the gulag. The key point here is that whether they opposed the war or not, all countries that are at the mercy of the international institutions that are devoted to neo-liberal capitalist globalization (G-8, World Bank, IMF, European Union, or "free-trade" agreements like the FTAA on the American continent) are forced to implement policies of "structural adjustment" and counter-reforms that are totally directed against rights that have been gained through courageous and relentless struggle by workers over decades.

Even the United Nations (although it had a minor revolt by the Security Council over the war in Iraq) is perceived by many in the U.S. as a feral socialist body that attempts to impede the will of the United States, even though historically it has genuflected to the interests of U.S. imperial policy-making on nearly every occasion.

One thing to keep in mind is that the U.S. has always acted militarily to pursue its imperial interests and maintain its economic hegemony. As the philosopher Hobsbawm (2003) has pointed out, the imperial reach of the U.S. differs from that of Britain a century ago in that the U.S. does not practice colonialism but relies on dependent and satellite states, resorting to armed intervention when the natives get restless and start refusing to buckle down. Whereas the British Empire was based on a singularly British purpose, the U.S. is based on a universalist conviction that the rest of the world should follow its example of free market capitalist democracy.

But the Bush Doctrine has relegated the notion of "just war" to the realm of absurdity. There is, as Ellen Meiksins Wood argues, no more real aim to war, since its results can never be achievable. The means—attack by the most powerful military ever known—are no longer proportionate to the ends: eliminating evildoers. The economy, just like evildoers, is boundless. It's not just that the means are disproportionate to the ends—attacking countries like Afghanistan whose GNP amounts to less than a B-52 bomber—but when you have an open-ended declaration of perpetual war, what achievable goals can you hope to postulate in order to justify it? And Meiksins Wood argues how this notion of perpetual war, this war without end, *answers the needs of this new imperialism, by the universality of capitalist imperatives*. Anyway, suffice it to say that the Bush gang has emerged as an indispensable guarantor of "super-profits" for the drive to world economic domination. Think about this, Ken, in the context of education for a moment. We now have the concept of "life-long learning" that is designed to replace the principle of a basic public school education before entry into the workforce. This reduces workers to human resources designed to serve the new flexibility of the corporate sector and the internal needs of individual companies. In other words, the concept of life-long learning means that workers could be compelled to work at any job, at any age, and under any conditions that the employer sees fit. This is paving the way for NGOs to take over the business of education, as it has already done in places such as Haiti. Education must be de-linked from the IMF, the World Bank, and the international financial institutions since the multinationals see a potential market in education of U.S.$2.2 trillion dollars a year. Given the crisis in world capitalism, corporations cannot afford to lose this potential market. Thus, one of the battles we are fighting is the privatization and dismantling of education in any form: private teaching; subcontracting or externalization of public school and university work to private companies, associations, or non-governmental organizations (NGOs); transnational "free-trade" agreements; decentralization and the fragmentation of public services; the establishment of voucher systems and the substitution of "competencies" for "qualifications." (These points were made at the recent International Conference Against War and in Defense of Public Education was held in Paris, on June 14–15, 2003.)

For a while it seemed that capitalist imperialism could do the work of what formerly was accomplished by military means by imperial states and colonial settlers. This is no longer the case. The new imperialism needs a doctrine of war, but the former doctrine of the "just war" is no longer sufficient. It needs a new doctrine of war—a doctrine of endless war, of war without boundaries. It needs a new model of imperialism, so watch how the U.S. rebuilds Iraq—with particular attention to how it restructures public services, education, labor codes, etc.

You are familiar, I am sure, with the frequently invoked quotation made famous by Prussian military officer, Karl Marie von Clausewitz (1780–1831): "war is the continuation of politics by other means" (cited in Mészáros, 1993, 18). However, István Mészáros notes that this definition no longer is tenable in our time. This is because such a definition "assumed the *rationality* of the actions which connect the two domains of politics and war as the continuation of one another" (2003, p. 18). For this definition to hold, war had to be winnable—winnability in war was its absolute condition, for even a defeat in war would not destroy the very rationality of war between competing nation states. This absolute condition for Von Clausewitz's definition no longer exists, maintains Mészáros, if we consider that today, the objective of a winnable or feasible war is tied to the objective requirements of imperialism, which is "*world domination* by capital's most powerful state, in tune with its own political design of ruthless authoritarian 'globalization' (dressed up as 'free exchange' in a U.S. ruled global market)" (2003, p. 18). This situation is clearly unwinnable and could not be considered a rational objective by any stretch of the imagination. War as the mechanism of global government is untenable because the "weapons already available for waging the war or wars of the twenty-first century are capable of exterminating not only the adversary but the whole of humanity, for the first time ever in history" (2003, p. 19). Mészáros warns that Bush's National Security Strategy "makes Hitlers irrationality look like the model of rationality" (2003, 19).

Once Iraq, for instance, is made sufficiently vulnerable to the rules of the imperial marketplace, the U.S. no longer needs to rule by military occupation. But Iraq must always be threatened by military force if it no longer complies. The smashing of Iraq was also a lesson for other countries that defy free-market imperatives. The cruel irony here is that U.S. military and economic imperialism is most certain to promote more terrorism than it is able to prevent. The U.S. is after total war as a form of unilateral world domination. Now if we want to talk about the world system today, then I would follow again the arguments made by Enrique Dussel and argue that we can locate the dependency of less developed countries at the level of competition and the distribution of surplus value. Were it not for space limitations, I would focus here on Marx's notion of the fall of the rate of profit as a result of the growth of monopoly capitalism or as simultaneous with the growth of the mass of profit, which will take us into the whole arena of overcapacity or overproduction—a situation that I hold in large measure responsible for driving the recent imperialist hegemony of the United States. That might be a good discussion for another interview.

KEN: How might those who are attempting to profess education in the wake of such traumatic events start coming to terms with the questions not being asked then, and what might a few of those questions be?

PETER: It is important for any educator to spend time with real people, in real life struggles, to understand how they engage with society from the bottom up.

It is important to be part of struggles outside of the seminar room. My own activity as a revolutionary socialist is premised on the notion that democracy as a set of discourses or principles or political philosophy is simultaneously re-functioned at the level of everyday social relations as an instrument of exploitation. And where I have become the most outspoken is in my critique of liberal reformism. It seems obvious to me that most of the educational left speaks from a discourse of reformism. However, in my own work, I refrain from dogmatically posing an either-or option of reformism or revolution but rather take a both-and dialectical position. Dialectics is about mediation, not juxtaposition, most surely, and I approach the reform versus revolution question dialectically. Of course we have no choice but to act within capitalist social relations, but my position is that while we are living and struggling within the belly of the beast we need to develop a vision of working towards a society outside of capitalism's value form of labor. I don't offer a blueprint, but a glimpse of some possibilities.

My work on developing a post-capitalist society is mostly in the subjective "what if" mode and not the imperative "it must look like this" mode. However, in my critique of capitalism I am less tentative. In fact, it has been described as downright ruthless. We need to be clear that we don't have on the agenda in the United States a revolutionary perspective, especially in education. We have militant movements in the U.S., true, but most of these operate within the larger optic of reformism. Approaching reformism from the perspective of the classical distinction posited between reformism and revolution by Luxemburg and Lenin (in the era of the Second and Third Internationals), Alex Callinicos has written some insightful commentaries on the dangers of reformism (reformism used here as the gradual improvement of capitalism rather than the revolutionary transformation of society) that I believe need to be rehearsed. Now I know I make a lot of people in the field of education nervous—especially in a post-9/11 environment—when I talk about the revolutionary transformation of the state. I am not talking about armed revolution here but rather the ability of workers to take control of society through means other than its violent overthrow. I am reminded of the revolution that occurred in Paris in late February, 1848, triggering revolutionary activity throughout most of Europe. During this time Marx had returned to Paris from Brussels to help organize the communist movement and he was adamant in discouraging armed resistance as reckless adventurism. He urged winning a democratic, political revolution with a view towards pushing ahead to achieve socialism. When I talk about revolutionary transformation, I am talking about education, the development of revolutionary social consciousness as a direct challenge to reformist consciousness, a critique of political economy rather than tinkering with capitalist redistribution, resistance that at times would surely constitute civil disobedience and protracted class battles, but I am not talking about armed revolution, so let's be clear on that. And I have always taken a strong stand against terrorism, whether that is state terrorism or individual acts of terrorism.

Well, back to the concept of reformism. Even militant anti-capitalist movements can be reformist if they attempt to redress neo-liberalism by strengthening the state, but at the same time do little to challenge the basis of the inter-imperialist rivalry we are seeing throughout the globe (in contrast to the insights of Hardt and Negri, I might add, in their world bestseller, *Empire*). To defeat reformism, we need patience, obviously, and we need to move in a number of directions. As Callinicos notes, we need to create a united front, which means winning the working-class base of the electorate over to the struggle for a socialist alternative to capitalism. We need to build our struggle around demands and through organizational forms that can be shared by diverse political forces. This means increasing efforts at radicalizing the labor movement, which works overwhelmingly within a reformist logic. Struggles along this line have never been easy in the United States. Since the Battle of Seattle, there have, however, been promising signs. The anti-war movement, especially the ANSWER (Act Now to Stop War and End Racism) coalition, was able to bring together divergent groups that took a strong stand against the war, and against U.S. imperialism, although it did take a lot of media criticism for its association with the Workers World Party. Strategically, it makes little sense to work toward the construction of a mass revolutionary party here—the objective conditions just don't exist. I favor the notion put forward by Callinicos, which is that of regroupment, which means revolutionary Marxists working on a non-sectarian basis in which there exist multiple interpretations about what revolutionary socialism might mean but which takes seriously the concept of building an anti-capitalist movement within the context of the notion of a permanent revolution. In other words, any effective anti-capitalist struggle needs to be international in scope. Now, within education, my role is singularly more modest. My goal is simply to educate teachers and teacher educators about Marx's ideas and the Marxist tradition, and dispel the lies and distortions that have crusted over Marx's legacy since the United States emerged victorious from the Cold War. This was never an easy task and has become more difficult now in the

United States since 9/11. I am also committed to the notion that teachers need to become part of the united front in their personal lives. When you see the country—and nearly all countries of the world, in fact—ruled by a small cadre of the capitalist class, serving the neo-liberal agenda which has led to the virtual impoverishment of working people and the destruction of the planet's ecosystems, and the superexploitation of women throughout the globe, how is it possible to remain, as an educator, detached from larger social movements struggling against this?

KEN: It is assumed that certain pre-conditions are necessary for intelligent criticism of existing social conditions. Those who profess education can play an integral part in deciphering and establishing some of these pre-conditions. Can you speak to what some of these pre-conditions for intelligent criticism might be, and what challenges do today's professors of education face when so many of society's associations seem bent on taking arms against such efforts?

PETER: Preconditions for generating a critical pedagogy that can address the world situation today—and thereby avoid its current domesticated incarnations in college classrooms—mean a lot of things, obviously. I can catalogue a few of them. Especially after 9/11, it means a societal commitment to freedom of speech, a willingness to challenge the current Bush regime's definition of patriotism (where an analysis of the root causes of terrorism is tantamount to aiding and abetting the enemy), a willingness to permit open investigations of the U.S. government which means its connection to its intelligence agencies, what these agencies were willing to share with the United Nations, an open examination of U.S. attempts to destabilize foreign governments, its links to transnational corporations, and a commitment to critical self-reflexivity and dialogue in public conversations. Greater efforts must be made to enforce the separation of church and state in principle as well as more pressingly as a means of countering the Likudites in the Bush administration as well as Bush's own rabid brand of Christian fundamentalist beliefs (Bush is trying to turn the U.S. into a covert theocracy). It also means struggling for a media that does not serve corporate interests. How can you have a democracy when you have the ideological state apparatuses in the hands of the corporations, which are connected to the military industrial complex, etc.? Which develop monopolies and which in turn shamelessly take up the agenda of the Bush regime (FOX TV and Clear Channel are just two examples). I could talk about any one of these, and more, but I want to concentrate on another pre-condition for a critical pedagogy: Understanding the fundamental basis of Marx's critique of capitalism.

Since I am well aware that Marxism is fairly marginalized in the academy—and especially the revolutionary critical pedagogy that has come to inform my work as a Marxist humanist—I will take the time to situate my first answer with a bit of a theoretical overview. Since critical pedagogy's current phase of theoretical gestation does not deal adequately with the issue of class as a social relation, I feel it necessary to dispatch the reader for a couple of paragraphs into the very technical and, for those who are not accustomed to it, the sometimes esoteric and off-putting language of Marxist theory, but I don't see any way to avoid that. I hope that your readers will bear with me for a few paragraphs. Answering this question will serve to form the basis of the position that I have been taking in my work since coming to California and grounding my work in Marxist humanism. It might seem at first blush that I am trying to avoid the specifics of your question but this background information is crucial for subsequent answers. In other words, I believe this concept of value linked to the exploitation of labor-power—something British educationalist, Glenn Rikowski has written about in powerfully nuanced ways—is a crucial precondition for having an extended discussion about educational transformation. Without it we are stuck in what I have called the logic of "reformism," which I will discuss later on in the interview.

About a decade ago I decided to revisit Marx to get a better grasp of how capitalism works at its roots. Much of this was due to frequent visits to Latin America and spending time with Marxist activists there, and from conversations with British educationalists such as Paula Allman, Glenn Rikowski, Mike Cole, and Dave Hill as well as U.S. educationalists such as John Holst, Wayne Ross and Rich Gibson. Rikowski encouraged me to re-visit Marx's *Capital, Volume 1*, and especially the labor theory of value and to explore the distinction between labor and labor-power. So I dusted off my volumes of Marx, and Marx and Engels, and began a new journey into Marxist theory. Well, let me get started. Casting aside for the moment current debates about the whole question of the "knowledge economy" and "fictitious capital" and related issues of "cyber-capitalism" (after all, our space is limited) I have come to the conclusion, along with many Marxists, that capital as a form of exploitation takes place fundamentally at the level of production, not at the level of circulation or exchange or in the sphere of consumption (which is not to say that these other spheres are unimportant in our analyses). It is to be aware of Marxist fundamentals—what Marxists and liberation theologians and others have been saying for decades—that the worker does not sell his or her labor to the capitalist, but rather he sells his labor-power or his labor capacity (that is, his skills, level of education, competencies, etc). The worker sells this labor-power as a commodity at a price or money equivalent of the value of his or her labor-power, and the value or price paid by the capitalist is determined by the quantity of labor required to produce and maintain the worker's existence (whatever it takes to educate the worker in the required skills and whatever is necessary to raise children who can replace the worker on the labor market, etc.). The worker in return gets no real wealth or power over commodities in general, but only power over the commodities that are needed to maintain him and perpetuate the class of laborers of which the worker belongs. The key point here—and really, this a very fundamental idea known as the labor theory of value—is that human labor-power expends more time than is necessary for its maintenance, and this labor-power creates no value for the worker but does create surplus value for the capitalist, for, in other words, private interest. Profit, or surplus value, is the result of living labor-power, or the exploitation of the living labor of workers. The value of labor-power is measured by the amount of labor required to reproduce itself as labor-power. The value of this special commodity known as labor-power is concretized in a certain amount of consumer goods that enable workers to sustain themselves and reproduce their offspring. When the value of consumer goods diminishes, the value of labor-power also diminishes, and this remains the case even though the physical quantity of goods consumed by the worker remains the same. Likewise, if the productivity of the worker increases, the value of labor-power may decrease. Living labor produces all value, including the surplus value that valorizes capital, or that turns capital into a profit for the capitalist. The wages received by workers are only part of the value that they actually produce. The capitalists appropriate as their surplus value or profit the other part of the value produced by the workers. Living labor is subsumed by capital. That is, the labor-power of the worker is the source of all value in capitalist society.

Capital, therefore, is not a self-sufficient totality, but exists only by incorporating living labor outside of itself. In fact, a good argument has been made by the philosopher Enrique Dussel that all forms of surplus value (profit, interest, rent, etc) are derived from the surplus value of workers. The value of a commodity, because it is realized in circulation, gives the illusion that it arises from the process of circulation, and not production. In effect, labor-power produces nothing (its use-value is that it produces exchange value), but when it is exercised through the act of laboring, it produces value. Put another way, labor-power is a commodity, but of a special kind. Its use-value is the act of laboring itself and the creation of value. It is this commodity that is purchased by the employer. The secret of capitalism is in the use that is made of this commodity by the capitalist after its purchase. Here is the key. Before anything is actually produced by the worker, the worker is already paid for his or her wealth-creating capacity or the availability of his capacity to labor, so that the proportion of the values which the worker produces by the actual act of laboring is more than the values he or she receives as equivalent to the availability of his or her labor-power. But this unpaid labor takes the semblance of an equal exchange. In other words, surplus value is uncompensated labor. In effect, it is what the wage worker gives to the capitalist without receiving any value in return. Surplus value, then, is the difference between the value created by work and the amount the worker needs in order to subsist.

The point I want to stress is that once you understand capital as a social relation—the subsumption of concrete labor by abstract labor, the negation of concrete/particular labor time by abstract/general labor time—well, then you need to consider irrefutably that this social relation is one of exploitation and it presupposes or characterizes all social relations within capitalism. This is the ironclad logic of capital. I mean if it really is a matter of improving the level of consumption in materialistic terms of all workers, then there is no reason to get rid of capitalism. A worker's standard of living could continue to improve without marking any lessening of the degree of exploitation! In reality, workers cannot prevent the value of their own labor-power from diminishing or the theft of their surplus value from increasing exponentially. In other words, capitalism is given ballast, or is bolstered by a corrupt morality, or by a set of ideologies that perpetuates the false notion that the relation between capitalists and workers is one of free and equal exchange, that what in fact the workers receive in terms of wages is equal to their contribution to production. Similarly, it is a lie to assume that capitalists receive as surplus value or profit, a contribution equal to their role in production given the factories and machines that they own and control. All of capitalist society is a theft of the surplus value of workers. Society becomes an independent alienated entity from humankind precisely through the process of commodity fetishism. Workers hallucinate their labor as a property of the products themselves and the value form of labor that is produced. And of course, the corporate media help to perpetuate this mass hallucination.

The point I wish to underscore, Ken, is that the standard of living of workers can rise without this representing any diminution of their degree of exploitation, just as an improvement in the economy can actually result in greater numbers of people fired from their jobs. The point Marx is making is that capitalism is a system of slavery. Workers are not allowed to reproduce themselves unless they agree to labor for free for a certain number of hours during the day in order to provide surplus value for the capitalist. The workers need the permission of the capitalists to feed themselves and their families. This permission will be denied unless the workers agree to these terms, to work a certain length of time for the exclusive benefit of the capitalist. Now I have deliberately not addressed the issue of bourgeois property relations as they emerged on the basis of the development of commodity production as the shape by which the laws peculiar to commodity production assert themselves. But I don't want to get more technical here than I have already. Well, many educators today are writing about global capitalism, and that's a good thing. But not enough of them are looking at Marx's central premises surrounding the commodification of human labor and its value form.

Part 2

KENNETH MCCLELLAND: Democracy as a form of government and democracy as an ideal for the guiding of one's conduct in life represent two different aspects of what democracy might be about and for. Can you speak briefly to what this means for professors of education, to the notion that teaching for intelligent and effective citizenship might involve criticism not only of the external political sphere but also of one's own personal sphere of conduct?

PETER MCLAREN: Let's look at the epistemological and axiological basis of democracy, just for a moment. I very much oppose judging a society primarily on the basis of maximizing minimal well being for the poor and the powerless. Relative improvement in conditions for the subaltern, for society's poor and powerless, for the castaways, for *los olvidados*, does not cut the mustard for me. Nor did it for Marx, from whose work I draw my inspiration. Your question gives me an opportunity to explain why, in the main, I shy away from the concept of education as social justice when the concept of social justice generally is reduced to the redistribution of material wealth. I think to understand my position I need to address this issue.

My own work has moved away from a liberal, Rawlsian or Habermasian conception of social justice premised on the idea of a democratic society preoccupied by the logic of reformism, to, as I mentioned earlier, the idea of a socialist society actively engaged in revolutionary transformation. Let me give you the conceptual basis of the reason that my work has taken this shift. When the production of inequalities begins to affect the weakest, only then does capitalist society consider an injustice to have occurred. Daniel Bensaid (2002), following Marx, points out the irreconcilability of theories of justice—such as those by Rawls and Habermas—and Marx's critique of political economy. Liberal theories of justice attempt to harmonize individual interests in the private sphere. But Bensaid points out, correctly in my view, that you can't allocate the collective productivity of social labor individually; the concept of cooperation and mutual agreement between individuals is a formalist fiction. You can't reduce social relations of exploitation to intersubjective relations. In the Rawlsian conception of the social contract, its conclusions are built into its premises. Bensaid elaborates on his Marxian critique of Rawls by arguing that within political theories of justice, the concept of inequality is tied to the notion of creating a fair equality of opportunity and that these conditions of equal opportunity are to serve the greatest benefit to the least advantaged in society. It is possible for inequality to exist as long as such inequalities make a functional contribution to the expectations of the least advantaged. Bensaid puts it thusly: "This hypothesis pertains to an ideology of growth commonly illustrated by the shares of the cake: so long as the cake gets bigger, the smallest share likewise continues to grow, even if the largest grows more quickly and the difference between them increases." The political conception of justice, be it Rawls or Habermas, doesn't hold in the face of real, existing inequality premised on the reproduction of the social relations of exploitation. The political theory of justice only makes sense in a world devoid of class conflict; in a world primarily driven by intersubjectivity and communicative rationality. Here, class relations and property relations are dissolved in a formal world of inter-individual juridical relations.

This viewpoint accepts a priori the despotism of the market; the whole question of production—and I would return you to the technical explanation of the labor theory of value in my previous question in which I start with Marx from production in order to ground reproduction—is displaced, in fact, is evaded. Let me quote Bensaid (2002) again, who writes: "Capitalist exploitation is unjust from the standpoint of the class that suffers it. There is thus no theory of justice in itself, only a justice relative to the mode of production that it proposes to improve and temper, sharing the old and false commonsensical view that it is pointless to redistribute the wealth of the rich, as opposed to helping them perform their wealth-creating role better, with a view to increasing the size of the common cake!" (p. 156). As long as you focus one-sidedly on distribution, you create a cover, an alibi in fact, for existing social relations of production, for the exploitation of workers by capitalists. Privatization, denationalization, and schools subjected to the guidelines of the private sector—promoted by the OECD, the World Bank, the World Trade Organization and the European Union—are the logical result of the logic of profit maximization that drives capitalism. There is talk now of developing a world market of education in the framework of the General Agreement on Trade of Services (GATS). The privatization of education is becoming generalized to the degree that it is being perceived as fundamental to democracy.

If you want to talk about the distribution of objects of consumption—and education certainly has become one of them—then I would, after Marx, urge you to talk about the distribution of the material *conditions of production*, and, of course, we could now enter into a conversation about NAFTA, and the World Bank, and the International Monetary Fund, and development and underdevelopment. But these arguments are now significantly established in the radical educational literature, so let's stop here.

KEN: Some have proposed a new paradigm for the left that is much more Darwinian in its approach to understanding and changing those conditions that afflict the poor, the oppressed, and the otherwise disadvantaged within society. It appears to maintain the core of those things that are and have been integral to a genuine left bearing (fighting unnecessary suffering of the weak and poor, of the exploited and the cheated), yet offers a Darwinian rationale for cooperation that takes seriously both competitive self-interest and altruism. Peter Singer's short, but provocative book dealing with this theme is a case in point, and it offers a kind of counter-narrative to Marxism. For those who profess education from a traditionally left perspective, but who recognize that a certain ennui and impotence has befallen the left in recent times, what is your take on the possibility of a revitalized cooperative left emanating from a more genuinely Darwinian perspective? Is there a real, and perhaps more realistic, alternative here to Marxist and neo-Marxist thinking, or will it just become the plaything for old-fashioned social Darwinist demagogues?

PETER: Well, you are referring here to the book, *A Darwinian Left*, by Peter Singer. I'm familiar with that book but not especially familiar with left Darwinism as a contemporary movement. Let's look at Singer's conception of left Darwinism for a moment. On the one hand, I like the fact that Singer condemns the dangers of a reactionary sociobiology but on the other hand, I seriously question Singer's notion of utilitarianism as the basis of the principle of human nature. Not to mention that Singer really has presented an underdeveloped and in many respects misguided critique of Marxism. His notion that Marx got it wrong because of the history of failed communist governments is puerile. It's too silly even to debate this notion. Singer also goes on to claim that Marx's most serious sin is his idea that there is no fixed human nature. Human nature supposedly changes with every change in the mode of production. And Marx supposedly committed another serious sin when he worked from the perspective of the perfectibility of humankind.

According to Singer, Marx and Engels claimed to have discovered the laws of human historical development that would lead to communist society and that according to these laws, the victory of the proletariat was ensured. Singer is critical of Marx's notion that social existence determines consciousness. Whereas a Darwinian sees greed, egotism, personal ambition and envy as a consequence of our nature, the Marxist would see these as the consequence of living in a society with private property and the private ownership of the means of production. Without these social arrangements, Singer believes that, according to Marx, the nature of people would be transformed such that people would no longer be concerned with their private interests. Darwinians believe that the way in which the mode of production influences our ideas, our politics, and our consciousness is through the specific features of our biological inheritance, and that if we want to reshape society, we need to modify our abstract ideals so that they suit our biological tendencies. According to the Darwininan perspective, all those who profess to be guided by motives other than self-profit—what Marx would call "gross materialism"—are the unwitting victims of an idealist illusion.

Prescinding from this enfeebling yet all-too-familiar interpretation of Marx, let's examine that famous sentence of Marx's (in Marx's Preface to *A Contribution to the Critique of Political Economy*) of which Singer is so critical: "It is not the consciousness of men that determines their existence, but their social existence that determines their consciousness." As far back as 1980, Jose Miranda pointed out that Marx's notion of determination must be understood in a way that is not deterministic because the German verb *bestimmen* is all too often translated as "to determine" and this verb means a lot of things unrelated to traditional conceptions of determinism. (Miranda notes that this major mistake in translation can be linked to translations into languages derived from Latin, where the basic word appears as a form of *determinaire*.) In

Marx's use of this term he in no way excludes the concept of human freedom or contingency; in fact, he uses the term dialectically. Marx makes a fuller explanation of what he meant by consciousness in *German Ideology*. Marx never forgot that just as circumstances help to form human beings, human beings also help to form circumstances. In contrast to what many critics of Marx claim, human beings for Marx are far from the passive actors of historical processes. Marx did not believe that there was no such thing as human nature. He argued that humans are biological, anatomical, physiological and psychological beings. He argued that an individual's human nature must be addressed but must also be understood in terms of how it has been modified in each historical epoch. In fact, Marx went so far as to contrast constant or fixed drives (such as hunger and the sexual urge) which are integral and can be changed only in form and cultural direction and the relative appetites (which are not an integral part of human nature and which owe their origin to conditions of production and communication). Humans were species—beings whose natures were clearly trans-historical and relatively unchanging in many respects (see Fromm, 2000). Marx distinguishes clearly between the laws of nature and the result of humans making a choice. Clearly, human beings produce their social relations just as they produce material goods; they are their own products as well as the products of history. And of history, it is quite clear that Marx did not view history mechanically, as if it was some wind-up sequence of causes and effects. Marx is interested in the laws of tendency within economics, not history's predictive capacity or laws of historical inevitability. History for Marx was always pregnant with possibility.

Marx did not reject the notion of human nature so much as a universal and timeless concept of human nature. Marx clearly could identify human characteristics that are universal and historically invariant and which set limits to the plasticity of human nature. This contrasts with the view of Rorty, who believes there are no biological or metaphysical limits on human plasticity. My friend Richard Litchman presciently notes, "the very notion of human nature as a *tabula rasa* is self-contradictory. Even a blank slate must have such properties as will permit the acceptance of the chalk, as the wax accepts the stylus, the inscribing tool. The issue is not whether there is a common nature, but what precisely that nature is" (cited in Sayers, 1998). When human beings make themselves their own creator by producing their own means of subsistence, then this signals the beginning of human history. The act of production creates new needs, something that Marx referred to as the first historical act. It is important to see Marx's understanding of human nature within the dialectical relationship of needs and productive powers. New needs are created through the productive activity we engage in to satisfy our universal needs, and this activity has to be seen in terms of the social relations which are themselves ultimately determined by such needs (Sayers, 1998). New forms of productive activity may result, and, indeed, new productive powers. Needs never arise in a vacuum. That is why in concrete conditions, human nature, in general, does not exist. Marx is interested in the social development of needs, beyond those necessary only for biological survival.

Singer's left Darwinism is not very helpful as a ground for social explanation without understanding, for instance, how jealousy, or selfishness has been realized in social individuals who are the products of a specific mode of production or a particular historical period. From a historical materialist point of view, nature is a precondition of human development and not an explanation of it. You can't explain the social in terms of the concept of the natural. The laws of natural evolution can't be transferred to social evolution. For Marx, social and moral developments are judged on how they impact on the growth of human nature in terms of the creation of powers and capacities. The stress in Marx is the development of new needs. As Sean Sayers notes: "Paradoxical as it at first seems, the ideal is the human being rich in needs. For on Marx's view this is equivalent to the development of human powers and capacities, the development of human nature" (1998, 164). True wealth, for Marx, lies precisely in the development of human nature. That is why I prefer Marx's Hegelian historicist approach to human nature over Singer's utilitarian and consequentialist approach to human nature. When Singer claims that the Russian revolution failed because the revolutionaries failed to consider the invariant need on the part of human beings for power and authority, such an argument is as specious as yak dung. Now what I like about Singer's work is his interest in the evolution of human co-operation. And he claims that most human beings won't co-operate unless it serves their own interests to do so. His notion of reciprocal altruism based on an evolutionary view of human psychology certainly is worth investigating. I like the fact that he wants a less anthropocentric view of our dominance over nature, and to cease our exploitation of non-human animals (something that appeals to my commitment to animal rights), and his commitment to stand on the side of the weak. My commitment is that the development of new and creative vital powers will be best served in the struggle for socialism.

KEN: I just finished a book on American Progressivism by Roberto Unger and Cornel West, and in it they make what might seem a few radical suggestions.

One is that voting should be made mandatory (much like jury duty) with the penalty of a fine to those who do not vote. The other is that the major commercial television networks should be required to grant ample and equal free time to candidates campaigning for office. This would be a condition of their licensing rather than a service paid for by taxpayers. Certainly, one might anticipate grumbling about protection of rights from the 50% plus of the population who presently do not vote, and from CEOs of the television networks who might deem such a measure unfair market interference. Is there a broader democratic good that might be served by enacting such measures, that might lead to more genuine education of and for the people?

PETER: At some level, ensuring that all the people will vote, that the entire *vox populi* will be heard, could be beneficial—I would like to think that if more Americans voted in the last election, that we wouldn't have the Bush administration. But of course, we have voter fraud in the United States, and what happened in Florida with the Bush mafia is a good example. What happened there—especially to ensure thousands of African-American votes would not be counted—was a shameful moment in U.S. history. But what good is voting—except as a mere formalist gesture—when the options are so perversely narrow? When you are really making a choice between a hard neo-liberalism and a harder neo-liberalism, between a benevolent imperialism and a more pernicious one under the imperial imperative of the Bush Doctrine of endless and boundless war. Tens of millions of protesters marched throughout the world, for example on February 15th, decrying the war on Iraq. It was the most unpopular war in history. And yet elected officials ignored the will of the people. It takes a fortune to win elections and they say the United States has the best democracy money can buy. It has the best media money can buy, too. And moneyed interests are linked to the military industrial complex—just take a look at who owns the major television stations and then see what else is produced by these companies—well, you can trace it all to the killing machines used to support the genocidal activities of Latin American dictators and of White House administrations who have carried out military strikes throughout the world fairly regularly, ever since the end of WWII. Of course, there are some real differences between the Republicans and the Democrats, and some important ones, such as a woman's right to choose, etc. And, yes, I don't want to trivialize that. So having two options I guess is better than having none, even though the two options you are given are still cut from the same imperialist cloth.

References

Bensaid, Daniel. (2002). *Marx for our times: Adventures and misadventures of a critique*. Translated by Gregory Elliott. London and New York: Verso.

Callinicos, Alex. (2003). War under attack. *Socialist workers party*, no. 273. Retrieved from http://www.swp.org.uk/SR/273/SR2.HTM.

Callinicos, Alex. (2002). Regroupment and the socialist Left today. Retrieved from http://www.dsp.org.au/links/ number 22.

Dussel, Enrique. (2001). *A commentary on the "Manuscripts of 1861–1863."* Translated by Yolanda Angulo. London: Routledge.

Fromm, Erich. (2000). *Marx's concept of Man*. New York: Continuum.

Hardt, Michael, & Negri, Antonio. (2001). *Empire*. Cambridge, MA: Harvard University Press.

Hobsbawn, Eric. (2003). After the winning of the war. *Le monde diplomatique*. Retrieved from http://mondediplo.com/2003/06/02hobsbawm.

Marx, Karl. (1970). *A contribution to the critique of political economy*. New York: International Publishers.

Marx, Karl, & Engels, Frederich. (1970). *The German ideology, part 1*. Edited by C.J. Arthur. New York: International Publishers.

Marx, Karl. (1976). *Capital* (Vol. 1). Translated by B. Fowkes, Harmondsworth: Penguin.

Mészáros, István. (2003). Militarism and the coming wars. *Monthly review, vol. 55*, no. 2, (June), 17–24.

Miranda, Jose. (1980). *Marx against the Marxists*. Maryknoll, NY: Orbis Books.

Sayers, Sean. (1998). *Marxism and human nature*. London and New York: Routledge.

Singer, Peter. (1999). *A Darwinian Left: Politics, evolution and cooperation*. New Haven and London: Yale University Press.

Wood, Ellen Meiksins. (2003). *Empire of capital*. London and New York: Verso.

"Traveling the Path of Most Resistance: Peter McLaren's Pedagogy of Dissent" by Ken McClelland was published in *Professing Education* (Society of Professors of Education). Part One was published in Fall, 2003; Part Two was published Winter, 2003. The entire interview (Parts One and Two) can also be found in *Correspondence*, (September 2003), Indian Institute of Marxist Studies (Delhi Chapter).

Interview 15

Peter McLaren and the Dialectic of Freedom

Michael Shaughnessy

Mike Shaughnessy contacted me when he learned that I had published a number of books this year. He wanted to do a report on the books for an Internet daily. Our email discussions led to this interview.

MICHAEL SHAUGHNESSY: One of your most recent books is *Capitalists and Conquerors: Critical Pedagogy Against Empire*. What are the top five points that you tried to make in this book?

PETER MCLAREN: Ever since writing *Life in Schools* and *Schooling as a Ritual Performance*, my books have mostly been collections of articles that I have previously published, sometimes modified to various degrees for the book I am putting together. So I don't set out to make certain points; I see what points are there after the book is put together. I produce a lot of written work, so much so that somebody once remarked that I have never had a thought go unpublished. Putting my articles together gives me a chance to revisit recent articles and make clarifications and to guide my thoughts to a precision they don't always have the first time around. And more recently

I have sought out students and young scholars to work with in a collaborative fashion, which I think is something sorely lacking among scholars—even leftist scholars—these days. But yes, there are always underlying themes to my books that can be traced back twenty years or more. In my work dating back to the mid-eighties, I have always tried to fathom the ways that capitalism functions in North American contexts, and more recently, in global contexts, with a special emphasis on Latin America. The structural crisis of capitalism in the 1970s was a watershed moment for world capitalism, and current developments such as neo-liberalism can be directly traced to this crisis. I want to underscore with a white heat that capitalism is not the best possible way to organize the social universe of human beings. In fact, it has transmogrified into a behemoth that, in a ferocious hunger for self-expansion, feeds off the commodification of social life that it creates. It is auto-copulatory. Worse, it ingests the detritus of humanity that it creates. More recently, since I began working from a Marxist humanist perspective in the late 1990s, I have tried to show the crucial role played by revolutionary social movements in the reclaiming of our humanity. At the same time I have been arguing that totalitarian regimes, such as the former Eastern Bloc police states, are not the necessary outcomes of Marxist revolutionary movements. Instead of retreating from Marx, educators need to rediscover the totality of his work. I have also exercised an uncompromising critique of liberal, centralist governments, such as the Clinton administration. In fact, I have tried to unpack the most central and ubiquitous contradictions at work within liberal democracies. I encourage educators to move beyond the liberal/conservative dyad and view the social universe of capital more critically. I am no more reluctant to critique a Democratic administration than a Republican one. I am not invested in favoring either one. I am invested in building a better society and I think it's time Americans stop exercising their possessive allegiance to one party or the other like they do their favorite sports team. It's time that educators especially invest in the fight against imperialist parasitism, poverty, war, and what my friend Henry Giroux calls "the terror of neo-liberalism."

I greatly value Marx's critique of political economy—in fact it is now central in my work—and know enough about Marx's work and the history of class struggle to be able to say that much that has happened in world history under his name has no doubt caused him to turn over many times in his grave. I also want to reveal, especially to my readers in the United States, that the history of the United States is far from unblemished. In fact, the United States has a bloody imperialist history of conquest, economic and military, that would shock most Americans if they knew it even in the most superficial sense. This bloody past, so full of presage, continues and goes on unchecked, especially now that the United States has achieved sole, world superpower status. But it is impossible for Americans to know about this bloody past unless they actively search for it outside the hegemonic precincts of the corporate media and visit the books, articles, and reports of dissident writers who publish outside of the mainstream. And this has been made very difficult since 9/11, because to do so puts curious Americans who have opened themselves up to the possibility that their country is the alpha-rogue nation among the main imperialist countries at serious risk of being labeled "America haters" and unpatriotic. I also try to encourage my readers to think "outside the box," not just in terms of social theory or political history but also in terms of how they would like to transform society. Do they want to continue the dream of bringing democracy via cluster bombs, attack helicopter gunships and fighter jets to countries that refuse to allow U.S.-dominated corporations to exploit them, or do they want to investigate the marriage of democracy to the beast of capital (the pro-imperialist state apparatus that also goes under the name of the military industrial complex), and what that might mean to the majority of human beings around the world struggling to eke out an existence with some measure of dignity? Or do they want to struggle for another world where racism, sexism, homophobia and all objectified and alienated social relations are abolished? I would say that the themes in *Capitalists and Conquerors* are more urgent than in any of my previous work. That is because the foreign and domestic policies of the United States have become more transparent; the bloodstains across the planet have become more visible to the naked eye, and our ability to trace crimes against humanity (not just to the White House but to the capitalist system itself that is the pilot light that keeps the engines of the military industrial complex grinding) has improved with the advent of alternative media, the Internet, etc. Our "militaristic messiah" has lost his clothes (including his shiny groin-enhancing flight suit with salacious diagonal straps), and we have been brought face-to-face with major political choices. The first choice is whether or not we are willing to look at the nakedness of our leaders, to stare directly at them in their unvarnished duplicity. And while there has been a significant ramp-up among those willing to criticize the Bush administration post-9/11, the majority of Americans still shield their eyes, refusing to hazard even a glance, lest their motivated amnesia grind to a halt and their world collapse. It is one thing to be a happy idiot or to soak up for hours on end the somniferous advice of television gurus, it is quite another to refuse actively to seek the truth, especially when it stands shivering before you. Instead of condemning their leaders, many Americans remain beholden to them; they rush to cover up their nakedness, to drape the quivering, shaking bodies of their Bible-thumping Ayatollahs in the flag. While they believe they are protecting their leaders from a vile liberal onslaught, an attack by ungodly secular humanists, they are only protecting themselves from seeing the truth. I am not just trying to "out" a shameful White House administration that is reviled by most populations around the world. That's too easy and it largely misses the point. My message is that while we challenge the Bush administration we have also to look beyond connecting examples of social dislocation to any one governmental administration and to see them as structurally rooted in the nature of global capitalism. I am trying to give readers some conceptual and theoretical armature that will help them to refocus their imaginations. I think it was Mark Twain who said something like: "You can't depend on your judgment when your imagination is out of focus." I am trying to exhort my American readers to look, to stare, and then to refocus through a new conceptual imaginary, to rethink the marriage of democracy to capital. Is there another bride, another bridesgroom more compatible for and less inimical to democracy? I think there is. It's called socialism. You can give it another name, so long as you mean the same thing. And finally (I am not sure here that I have talked about five points exactly), I am trying to develop a much more interesting style of presenting my ideas. I've even considered doing political film and theater in the future.

MICHAEL: After George Bush's term in office is up, what do you think will be the "legend of the Bush gang"?

PETER: The Bush gang—a term that my camarada and colleague Gregory Martin and I used in our chapter—refers to nothing short of a cabal of duplicitous thugs with corporate credentials and impressive political portfolios who will try to take credit for shifting the tectonic plates of the worlds political landscape, especially in the Middle East. They will sell it as bringing freedom and democracy to former sinkholes of human depravity. They know that many Americans will want to believe this. Of course, this is a reprehensible lie. But lies—the bigger the better—are what oil the right-wing propaganda machines, it's what steadies the ideological rudder and gives ballast to the reproductive function of the neo-liberal state, especially when the state tacks too far from the agenda of the neo-cons. I worry about the Bush legacy. Why? Look at Ronald Reagan. Under the cover of the Reagan Doctrine designed to stop communism from spreading (apparently domino-style beginning with Nicaragua's Sandinistas—a brazenly ludicrous assumption but it worked to conjure sufficient fear within the U.S. population, like the fictitious missile gap between the U.S. and the Soviets during the Cold War) to the doorsteps of the U.S.-Mexican border, the United States illegally supplied the Contra rebels in Nicaragua (who waylaid Sandinista supporters and attacked civilian farming cooperatives with 88-mm mortars and rocket-propelled grenades—even those populated by pacifists who refused to bear arms) and this clearly made the United States an accomplice in terrorism. Yet the U.S. media refused to castigate them. Remaining defiant in the face of the International Court of Justices (1986) condemnation of the United States for "unlawful use of force" and illegal economic warfare in its attacks on Nicaragua, the U.S. vetoed a UN Security Council resolution that called on all states to obey international law. The U.S. was determined to carry out the Reagan Doctrine and ignore both international law and opinion. And still Reagan is glorified in the national media upon his death as an indelible orator and avuncular leader who won the Cold War, and we haven't even touched on his domestic policies and his war against the poor people of the United States.

And now, under Bush, we have the ominous figure of John "Dirty Tricks" Negroponte, installed as the über-director of national intelligence. Negroponte is a career diplomat whose role in the dirty wars of Central America began when he was U.S. ambassador in Honduras between 1981 and 1985, during which time he took aim at the bogey-man of godless communism and coordinated the funding and training of the counterrevolutionary death squad known as the "Contras" in its illegal war against the Sandinista National Liberation Front. If there is ever a case to make that human beings are really a species of lizard that devour children and rule the world in order to harvest human flesh for their starving planet, it's Negroponte. While in Honduras, Negroponte turned a blind eye to the horrific crimes of a secret army intelligence unit—Battalion 316—that was trained and supported by the CIA and which led to an increase in human rights violations and tortures and missing leftwing critics of Honduran dictator, General Gustavo Alvarez Martinez. Critics of Negroponte now fear that the U.S. is more likely to be involved in extra-judicial killings in its ongoing war on terror.

For the United States backers of the Central American regimes responsible for such atrocities, it appears that communist dictatorships were always to be shunned whereas right-wing authoritarian dictatorships, in spite of their crimes against humanity, made strategic allies. For a time, Iraq's Saddam

Hussein was an ally of the U.S. until he served a more convenient role as the embodiment of evil. Many of the same war criminals that were part of the recently glorified Reagan years are now serving in their graying but no less gentler years in the current Bush Jr. administration.

And now we have Iraq. By some credible estimates, 120,000 Iraqis have been killed by U.S. and British air and ground strikes. There are few caesuras of tranquility in what has become for that country a symphony of death. Britain and America's reasons for escalating the bombing of Iraq in the ten months leading up to the war in Iraq were boldfaced lies, as official figures recently released by the British Ministry of Defense show. So, in effect, the war against Iraq began in earnest ten months before the actual invasion with thousands of bombing runs against command and control centers. In fact, it had begun much sooner than that, with the sanctions against Iraq, responsible for so many deaths of children, up to half a million by some estimates. At first the U.S. did not want to hold elections in Iraq, but pressure from the Shiite leadership caused the Bush administration to change its mind. Once the elections were held, the U.S. used them as a photo opportunity to help convince the world that victory for democracy was won (we all know that once the U.S. captured Baghdad, they staged the tearing down of the statue of Saddam amid a throng of cheering Iraqis and that they used the Jessica Lynch story to fuel its pro-war propaganda, even by Lynch's own recent admission). Of course, Iraq has been brought to the brink of civil war as the insurgency grows stronger. If the United States is so interested in democratic values why, when Iraqi interim government declared its intention to endorse the treaty on the International Criminal Court (ICC), did the transitional administration in Baghdad reverse its decision within a few days, presumably under unremitting pressure from Washington? The Bush cabal will never permit conditions to exist that could put its war criminals on trial or lead to real sovereignty for poor nations such as Iraq. Iraqi sovereignty, i.e. the Iraqi government's direct and real control over major economic decisions within its national borders, will never be permitted by the dominant capitalist states. Poor nations will never be allowed to retain government control over substantial capital flows in and out of their borders. Deregulation will always be imposed on these economies, wherever they exist. Political-economic sovereignty cannot be permitted within the laws of the capitalist universe, laws enforced by the dominant capitalist states, because such a move would defy the basic laws of capitalist accumulation and would give hope to the oppressed worldwide.

MICHAEL: You have posed the question: In his unconscious attempt to achieve "simplicity of the soul" over "duplicity of the soul" has Bush forsaken human reason? What led you to ask this question and how do you respond?

PETER: I think George Bush believes that he is an honest man, but he betrays no surfeit of scruples when he is conducting his presidential duties in concert with his intuitive feelings that he is God's envoy. He is the exception to the warrant that requires U.S. presidents to respect the separation of church and state when engaging in exigent issues involving national security. He is more like God's court jester, but the jokes are no longer funny (if they ever were) because they are drowned out by the shrieks of the dead and dying. Interesting to note the shift of the Vatican to the right, just as Reagan and Thatcher came into power. I would like to write something about this shift that culminated in the election of Benedict XVI, and how Benedict, when he was Cardinal Ratzinger, helped get Bush Junior elected by writing a letter to American bishops that condemned pro-choice political candidates (i.e, John Kerry). Look, I think Bush Jr. is using his "faith" in a destructive way. He sees himself as carrying out the will of God. According to some reports I have read, Bush believes that God wanted him to invade Iraq. I have no problem with religious faith. But as a materialist I believe that we need to employ reason to understand faith. I don't want to belittle faith; the more we explain faith does not mean that we need to take faith less seriously in our lives. Increasing our knowledge of faith can help us make faith work in the interest of social justice rather than employing faith in the service of what we perceive as some "otherworldly" command. In our quest to make the world a better place, we have to be cautious not to see ourselves as instruments of the divine that would cause us to stray into abstract utopian hinterlands too far removed from our analysis of the present barbarism wrought by capital. Our vision of the future must go beyond the present but still rooted in it, it must exist in the plane of immanence, not mystical transcendence. We cannot deny the presence of the possible in the contradictions that we live out daily in the messy realm of capital. We need to struggle for a concrete utopia where the subjunctive world of the "ought to be" can be wrought within the imperfect, partial, defective and finite world of the "what is." Any authentic future must be to some extent be connected to the material forces of the present. Our utopia must be born of the here and now since it exists in a potential state within the contradictions and conflicts that make up the present. Whereas Bush seeks an abstract utopia discontinuous with the present, one based on Biblical principles that are designed to serve the invisible forces of God on the basis of America's "providential history," I seek a concrete utopia based on hope and reason where feelings, beliefs and intuition can be rationally traced to their sources in the real world and where progressive change is brought about by class struggle, by anti-imperialist, gender-balanced, anti-racist pedagogies designed to bring about a social revolution.

MICHAEL: What are the main tenets in the age of neo-liberal globalization?

PETER: There was a time when the U.S. was a creditor nation; it is now a debtor nation. I don't have time to discuss all the historical reasons that led to this, but the era of neo-liberalism describes this shift. When you get down to it, the globalization of capitalism refers to the internationalization of capitalist relations of exploitation. It means the subjection of national capital by international capital. Its main concomitant is the astounding flexibility of capital and markets that makes it seemingly unassailable.

MICHAEL: With Ramin Farahmandpur, you have written *Teaching Against Global Capitalism and the New Imperialism: A Critical Pedagogy*. In it you discuss "contraband pedagogy." What exactly is "contraband pedagogy" and why is it important?

PETER: Contraband pedagogy is another name for revolutionary critical pedagogy. We wanted to emphasize its marginalized status as a dangerous weapon in the hands of the oppressed, as a pedagogy found mainly on the black market, like a rocket launcher that fires pencils instead of grenades, a pedagogy that, if seized, would be destroyed by the transnational capitalist class because they know that they are in its crosshairs. A pedagogy that cannot be named because it carries dangerous memories, subjugated knowledges of the dispossessed and the forgotten, the alienated and the exploited. I don't mean to romanticize this type of pedagogy, but I wanted a name that would evoke its essential complexion, its outsider status.

MICHAEL: Who should teach against globalization? When should we teach against the new imperialism? And why is it important that we do so?

PETER: We shouldn't teach against globalization. I have no problem with globalization per se but with the globalization of capitalism. We need to keep this distinction clear. Globalization is inevitable—the sharing of cultures, values, information, knowledges, etc., worldwide—but the globalization of capitalism is something else.

MICHAEL: In the socialist imagination, what type or format of educational policy would we see? What kinds of a "pedagogy of resistance" would be envisioned?

PETER: The policies would be very much directed at issues of scarcity and human needs, they would be focused on issues of regional development and achieved through class struggle by means of participatory modes of democratic decision-making.

MICHAEL: "We live in urgent times" is the first sentence of one of the chapters in *Teaching Against Global Capitalism*. What is the nature of these urgent times, and what do we have to address in these urgent times?

PETER: Clearly, capital, as a social relation, that is structuring most of life on the planet through neo-liberal policies and practices exercised by the transnational capitalist class is the central problem. The very soil in which capitalism rests is based on the overaccumulation of capital and the super-exploitation of rank-and-file wage laborers. These are irreversible contradictions and they are inherent within capitalist social and economic relations—those between capital and labor. They are taking us further away from democratic accountability and bringing us perilously close to what Rosa Luxemburg referred to as an age of "barbarism." Here in the U.S.—what I have called "las entrañas de la bestia" (the belly of the beast)—we are witnessing an attack by the religious right on gays, lesbians and women who are fighting for the right to control their bodies. Religious fundamentalists believe that this is divisive to American family values. But what is really destroying the American family, as well as families throughout the entire globe, is the exploitative nature of capitalism, its logic of commodification and its practice of surplus value extraction. As Marxist humanists will no doubt tell you, the major engine that drives the economic and ideological hegemony of capitalism is racism. Just examine the rates of poverty and unemployment among African Americans and Latinos. Class exploitation involves the buying and selling of human lives as commodities—the creation of what Marx called "wage slaves." We need wage slaves to keep capitalism in motion. In fact, wage slavery is a constitutive factor of our democracy. When you think about it, that's why wage slavery is camouflaged as a "voluntary contractual agreement," even though there is no alternative on the table. Well, there is an alternative: it's called unemployment, starvation, and death. The underdevelopment of the economies of the so-called Third World *has become a necessary condition* for the flourishing of the economies of the so-called First World. Marxists have long addressed this situation. There is a growing bipolarization and the over-accumulation of capital by a new breed of what I have described in previous interviews as "opulent gangster capitalists from reigning global mafiacracies." As a consequence, the odds of surviving hunger, poverty, malnutrition, famine, and disease are not very good for a growing segment of working-class men, women, and children throughout the world.

Check out the proliferation of *maquiladoras* along the U.S.-Mexican *frontera*, where the extortion of absolute surplus-value is increasing dramatically. It has to do with relative surplus value extortion through increasing the productivity of labor and reducing the value of labor-power. This is precisely how capitalism continues to hold living human labor hostage to the valorization process. How else is capitalism able to recast the world into its own image? Latin American educators don't have as much of a problem with Marxist analysis as do educators in North America—part of this has been the success of Cold World propaganda in linking Marxist analysis with totalitarianism and gulags—thats about like blaming the Christian crusades on the Sermon on the Mount.

MICHAEL: What led you to collaborate with Gustavo Fischman, Heinz Sunker and Colin Lankshear in your recent co-edited text, *Critical Theories, Radical Pedagogies and Global Contexts?*

PETER: I knew Gustavo as a doctoral student at UCLA and realized then that he was going to do brilliant and important work. He is a perfect example of an engaged and committed intellectual. Heinz Sunker is one of the leading critical theorists in education in Germany and fully engaged in the struggle for social justice in Europe and elsewhere. We have known each other for years and have collaborated on projects before. Colin Lankshear is somebody with whom I have worked on and off for fifteen years and one of the best authorities on literacy and the new technologies you can find anywhere. He's always one step ahead of most of us.

MICHAEL: Can you tell us about La Fundacíon McLaren de Pedagogía Crítica at the Universidad de Tijuana, which has recently been established in Mexico?

PETER: Yes, I was approached by scholars and activists in Northern Mexico familiar with my work, and they pitched the idea for an organization that would serve as a vehicle for critical pedagogy in Latin America, not only my work but work by other individuals as well. There is a website, a journal called

Aula Critica, and there are plans for conferences and seminars on contemporary issues, with the purposes of mobilizing educators for a social revolution, a revolution against capital.

MICHAEL: Are there other McLaren foundations planned?

PETER: There is a university in Cordoba, Argentina, that is establishing an Instituto Peter McLaren that is affiliated with a program in multiculturalism and migrations, and I have been approached with the idea of more Institutos in other countries in Latin America, but they have not been finalized so I don't think I should mention them yet.

MICHAEL: What do you make of these invitations to start foundations and institutes bearing your name?

PETER: I don't think they are about me as an individual as much as about the impact that critical pedagogy has made in general, which, of course, they associate with numerous educators worldwide. Which doesn't mean that they don't see some distinguishing characteristics in my work, such as the Marxist humanism that has become the cornerstone of my work over the last decade. The word "Marxism" is an alienating word to many North American educators, and it is less the case in Latin America. So-called Third World countries that exist at the periphery of the world capitalist system are overwhelmingly the low-wage areas, interest and profit-exporters (not importers), and they are prisoners of international financial institutions and dependent on limited overseas markets and export products. Haven't you noticed that there exists a strong relationship between the growth of international flows of capital and an increase in inequalities between states, and between Chief Executive Officers of Corporations (CEOs) and workers?

MICHAEL: *Red Seminars* is an exemplar of collective scholarship. It is now 2005. In retrospect, what is the legacy of Paulo Freire?

PETER: Freire's work is about establishing a critical relationship between pedagogy and politics, highlighting the political aspects of the pedagogical and drawing attention to the implicit and explicit domain of the pedagogical inscribed in the political. In writing a recent Preface to a new edition of Freire's book, *Teachers as Cultural Workers*, I had the opportunity to reflect upon Freire's enduring legacy. I mentioned that while Freire extolled the virtues of socialism and drew substantively from various Marxist traditions, he was also critical of dogmatic, doctrinaire Marxists whom he saw as intolerant and authoritarian. Freire argued that by refusing to take education seriously as a site of political transformation and by opposing socialism to democracy, the more mechanistic Marxists have, in effect, delayed the realization of socialism for our times.

Freire believed that the Left's cardinal mistake had to do with their absolute conviction of their certainties and had to do with their unfriendliness toward democracy—and this, Freire believed, played into the hands of the Right. At the same time, Freire never forgot that educators engage in politics when they educate, and that educators need to distinguish between repressive and emancipatory politics. To be a Freirean educator in these times requires a dauntless courage, a hopeful vision and a steadfast commitment. Recently, Nathalia Jaramillo and I were invited to speak in Venezuela about critical pedagogy, at the invitation of the Venezuelan government, who are undergoing a brave and important experiment with socialism. We were struck by how important Freire's work is in Venezuela, and how it is helping to contribute mightily to the Bolivarian revolution.

MICHAEL: Did you meet President Chavez?

PETER: Very briefly when he came to greet us in an office at Miraflores Palace. I am a great admirer of President Chavez and a staunch supporter of the Bolivarian revolution.

MICHAEL: What are you working on in the future?

PETER: I'm trying to develop further what's involved in creating a critical pedagogy grounded in Marxist humanism. As Peter Hudis has remarked, Marxist humanism is not the only approach to appreciate the importance of spontaneous self-activity or to argue that mass practice gives rise to new theory or that the experiences of resistance on the streets are expressions of theory. But Hudis does point out some very unique features of Marxist humanism that maintain, for instance, that the movement from practice is a form of theory, that theory is not the same as philosophy and that the philosophy that is needed in these very dangerous times, at this historical juncture, is Marx's philosophy of "revolution in permanence" developed to its next stage of dialectical development. Now these are very difficult conceptual, political and pedagogical issues and my task is to try to make sense of them for a revolution in education, one that is part of the larger revolution in permanence of which Marx speaks. To accomplish that, I will work on my own as well as collaboratively, and rely on the expertise of many of my mentors, and try to be worthy of the task at hand.

There is a lot we can do before the revolution, but we can't abandon it. If we realize that there can be no educational reform without a major transformation in human relations, and that this transformation is impossible without a major transformation in the means of production, then we will be focused solely on pedagogies based on deepening democracy, improving civil society, invigorating culture, bringing about equality of distribution of resources, and the like. Well, as admirable as these reform efforts are, and as important as they are for us to participate in, they still are structurally rooted in capitalist social relations, in the capitalist law of value and without transforming the economic structure of capitalism, educational transformation is too self-limiting to make enough of a difference.

"An Interview with Peter McLaren" by Professor Michael Shaughnessey is forthcoming in *The International Journal of Progressive Education*, in a special issue entitled, "Understanding Peter McLaren in the Age of Global Capitalism and the New Imperialism," in October, 2006.

Interview 16

critical pedagogy reloaded

Glenn Rikowski

This interview took place over email in July and August 2005.

GLENN RIKOWSKI: I would like to start off with the change of emphasis in some of your most recent books, principally *Capitalists and Conquerors* (2005) and *Teaching against Global Capitalism and the New Imperialism* (with Ramin Farahmandpur, 2005), where you have moved towards framing a critical pedagogy specifically *against empire*. Thus, compared to your earlier *Che Guevara, Paulo Freire and the Pedagogy of Revolution* (2000) it appears to be a kind of "critical pedagogy reloaded" with the sights set on the empire of capital in general and American imperialism in particular. In some respects, post-9/11 and after Iraq I guess this is not such a surprising shift. But I am intrigued as to how you see it, Peter.

PETER MCLAREN: It is gratifying for me to be having this chance to dialogue with you again, Glenn, only I wish it could be in person, either here in

Hollywood or in London (but I would argue for Hollywood if only because I have heard rumours that you havent been out of the U.K. in ages and so a visit with me is long overdue). I see that you've begun the questioning in sweeping Rikowski style, so let's see if I am up to the task. I agree with you that the shift toward a discussion of imperialism and empire is not so surprising, I suppose, for those that have been following the (often unwieldy) trajectory of my work, from a preoccupation with Deweyan critical pragmatism, the Frankfurt School (Horkeimer, Adorno, Benjamin, Fromm and, to a lesser extent, Habermas) post-structuralism (and some—perhaps even you, Glenn—have referred to this ersatz agglomeration as eclectic-chic) to a Marxist humanism. My recent book, *Red Seminars*, chronicles my collaborative work over the past fifteen years and you can detect the moments where it arches toward a Marxist humanism and still see where it is stuck in the morass of postmodern theory. So yes, I have joined the ranks of the Marxist educationalists (who number but a handful in the United States) and that shift has demonstrably marginalized my work even more (within the United States and Canada, but not within Europe and especially Latin America). This is partly because, in the larger scheme of educational critique in the United States, one does not see much discussion of empire and imperialism in the educational journals (although not surprisingly there is much more activity on this front in the sociology and political science journals, as well as the literary theory journals). There has not been much respite from ideological durance vile since 9/11, and critiques of Bush and his camarilla have been slow to materialize although you can find more and more of them of late coming from the academy. Whilst there has indeed been a ramp-up of generalized critique of the Bush administration, it hasn't led to—not yet at least—many book-length treatments of the U.S. militarism and empire by educationalists. But there is still no lack of postmodernist offerings. The constitutive iterability that structures the work of these absent guardians of pure contingency—their performative cross-dressing, their fashionable apostasy and back alley brigandism, their discursive prestidigitations—has given their politics an ambivalence that merely reconfirms their interdictions as they unwarrantedly assimilate the marriage of democracy to that of neo-liberal capital and its exalted glorification of profit. The disturbing tranquillity of such a politics, whose decidedly clever parlour games at this moment of historical dislocation are both elegant and devious, offers educationalists a backdrop against which to measure our absolute impoverishment. It appears that deconstructing the décor of their servitude trumps smashing the chains of capital that bind us to a life of exploitation.

Glenn, you asked me how I see things in my recent work. I characterize the era directly preceding our neo-liberal dispensation (just think of Thatcher and Reagan in cowboy chaps, on a pair of Palomino horses, silhouetted against the sun sinking beneath a cacti-laden horizon) as a time when the U.S. was a creditor nation—it is now a debtor nation. When you get right down to it (since I don't have time to trace with any detail the economic history), the globalization of capitalism marks the internationalization of capitalist relations of exploitation. It refers to the subjection of national capital by international capital. Its main concomitant is the astounding flexibility of capital and markets that makes it seemingly unassailable. However, the globalization of capital does have some new features that we can now index as part of a new stage of capitalist formation. I recall Bertell Ollman listing in a recent article some of these features that included the rise in influence of financial capital, the provocative new role played by banks and treasury ministries, the massive increase in personal debt that serves as a catapult for increased consumption, the restructuring and downsizing of the labour force and a fluid relocation of industries to developing countries in order to secure lower labour costs, the weakening of independent organs of the working class, the rapid flows of advertising, public relations and infotainment, the replacement of real goods as the main targets of investment with "financial instruments," such as national currencies, insurance, debts, and commodity futures, the increase in outsourcing and contract labour following the replacement of full-time jobs with temporary and part-time jobs, the privatization of public institutions and attacks on economic welfare and security reforms of the past century. What we are faced with—ultimately and overwhelmingly—is the subordination of social reproduction to the reproduction of capital, the deregulation of the labour market, the globalization of liquid capital, the outsourcing of production to cheap labour markets, and the transfer of local capital intended for social services into finance capital for global investment. Teresa Ebert and others have described the globalization of capital rather aptly as the continuous privatization of the means of production and the creation of expanding markets for capital and the creation of a limitless market of highly skilled and very cheap labour in order for capitalists to maintain their competitive rate of profit. The overall objective of American strategy in an age of "globalization" is deregulation combined with absolute minimal levels of expenditures on the part of governments. However, the global character of capitalism as an all-encompassing and indefatigable power that apparently no nation-state has the means to resist or oppose has been overdrawn. Capitalism still needs the protection of the nation-state and can be challenged by individuals and groups in transnational struggles. State power can be used in the interest of the working class. An interesting argument has been put forward by William Robinson of the University of Santa Barbara. Robinson argues that neo-liberal globalization is unifying the world into a single mode of production and bringing about the organic integration of different countries and regions into a single global economy through the logic of capital accumulation on a world scale. Non-market structures are disappearing as they are continually becoming penetrated and commodified by capitalist relations. There has been an accelerated division of the global class formation. The world is becoming effectively divided into a global bourgeoisie and a global proletariat. Dictatorship has been replaced by the neo-liberal state by the transnational capitalist elite. The nation state now performs the following functions: adopting fiscal and monetary policies that guarantee macro-economic stability; providing the necessary infrastructure for global capitalist circuitry and flows; and securing financial control for the transnational comprador elite as the nation-state moves more solidly in the camp of neo-liberalism, while maintaining the illusion of "national interests" and concerns with "foreign competition." In fact, the concept of "national interests" and the term "democracy" itself function as a "cloaking device" (for all you *Star Trek* fans) to enable authoritarian regimes to move with a relative lack of contestation towards a transformation into what Robinson has termed "elite polyarchies." Robinson's empirical research has made a convincing case for the appearance of a transnationalist capitalist class, but I don't have space to go into his research here. There are a number of theories of imperialism discussed or at least referenced in my recent books, as well, that emphasize imperialism by market power as opposed to territorial conquest. Ellen Meiksin Wood's concept of economic imperialism as reliant upon a territorially based nation-state system is one such theory; David Harvey's notion of economic imperialism via accumulation through dispossession is another, the work of Leo Panitch is yet another. I won't attempt to summarize them here. In my recent work, I don't attempt to resolve the differences among these and perspectives on imperialism as much as offer them—sometimes in a manner too scattershot—as theoretical weapons for educators to wield in their struggle to understand contemporary geopolitics in relation to the crisis of world capitalism. What I like about Robinson's work especially, is that it challenges the characterization of inter-imperialist rivalry of the sort that Lenin emphasized by arguing that the U.S. does not always act to defend its own capital and to exclude specifically national capitals. What I would like to emphasize is the role of the global elites who comprise the transnational capitalist class, a class that quite often relies upon the U.S. military in defending and stabilizing global capitalism in instances where one country or another refuses to play by the rules of the transnational elite. The U.S. plays the key leadership role on behalf of transnational capitalist interests—reinforcing structural adjustment programs, free trade agreements, etc.—and adopts the "alpha" role when it comes to "integrating" into the "free market" remaining socialist countries with military machinery unrivalled in destructive capabilities, trigger-happy military personnel who believe they are carrying out God's will in destroying the heathens, and vast stockpiles of cluster bombs, bunker-busting bombs, depleted uranium ordinances, and laser-guided missiles (it's called bringing "freedom and democracy" to rogue nations via "peacekeeping" and "humanitarian" interventions). Of course, in my books I don't adopt univocally one set explanation of imperialism but rather draw from a number of positions. That said, the fundamental task for us all remains unambiguous. As Fidel Castro once put it, "The anti-imperialist, socialist revolution could only be one single revolution, because there is only one revolution. That is the great dialectic truth of humanity: imperialism, and, standing against it, socialism."

GLENN: You have written a lot about the significance of class over the last five years or so, Peter, both in general for "life in capitalism," and specifically in relation to the U.S. What can critical pedagogy do to problematise and critique class relations, in your view, in research and writing but also in our work with students?

PETER: Well, one contribution that my work in critical pedagogy has tried to achieve has been to introduce your work to a wider North American audience—and, of course, that of Paula Allman, Dave Hill, and Mike Cole, and other British Marxist educationalists. Don't forget, the criticisms of my work by you and your camaradas in the 1980s and early 1990s were greatly responsible for overturning my orientation to postmodern theory and for my revisiting Marxist theory, leading to my eventual embrace of Marxist humanism (through the additional work of Peter Hudis and the News & Letters collective whose work revolves around the writings of Raya Dunayevskaya). It was your "scorched earth" writings, primarily in the mid-nineties, that helped to resurrect Marxist educational theory—a theory that had languished in a state of inertia since the early 1980s, or what you identify as its Classical Age (1976–1982). One contribution that your work, and those of your companera/os cited above, achieved, was to reveal the perils of the dominant Weberian conception of class (unfortunately one that still dominates educational research today but we are all working on changing that in due time!), a perspective that woefully reduces class to a "mode of social differentiation" or a feature of lifestyle or identity (i.e., race, gender, sexuality) in which "superstructural" differences are reified and reduced to social and political tensions or contradictions that exist largely at the level of culture and subjectivity. Critical educators who operate from a Weberian conceptualization of class are often driven by a politics that is necessarily gradualist and evolutionary and limited to reforming the polity through careful increments (more democratic decision-making, etc.) without fundamentally altering the market and commodity-exchange. Your work on education and the labour theory of value—particularly your discussion of the value aspect of labour power—was and continues to be a major breakthrough for the development of a distinctly Marxist educational theory. What I like about your current work on this is your emphasis on capital as a mode of being, as a unified social force that flows through our subjectivities, our bodies, our meaning-making capacities. Schools serve as a certain "habitus" or "pupa" that nourishes labour-power, a medium for its constitution or its social production, so that students whose labour power is incubated in capitalist schools are able to burst out of their chrysalises and spread their worker wings in the service of capital. But schools are more than this, they do more than nourish labour-power because all of capitalist society accomplishes that; in addition to producing capital-in-general, schools additionally *condition* labour-power in the interests of the marketplace through its emphasis on application for specific capitals, that is, through its emphasis on practical education and training that is related to both aspects of labour power and attributes of labour-power. You break this down even further, Glenn, to sectors of capital, national capital, fractions of capital, individual capital, and functions of capital. Schools trade in educating for these various capitals. But because labour-power is a living commodity, and a highly contradictory one at that, it can be re-educated and shaped in the interests of building socialism. Labour-power, as the capacity or potential to labour, doesn't have to serve its current master—capital. It only does this when it engages in *the act of labouring for a wage*. Because individuals can refuse to labour in the interests of capital accumulation, labour-power can therefore serve another cause—the cause of socialism. Critical pedagogy tries to find ways of wedging itself between the contradictory aspects of labour-power creation and, among students, creating different spaces where a de-reification, de-commodification, and decolonization of subjectivity can occur. And, at the same time, where the development of a leftist political subjectivity can occur (recognizing that there will always be socially and self-imposed constraints). Revolutionary critical pedagogy (a term coined by Paula Allman) is multifaceted in that it brings a Marxist humanist perspective to a wide range of policy and curriculum issues. The list of topics includes the globalization of capitalism, the marketisation of education, neo-liberalism and school reform, imperialism and capitalist schooling, and so on. Revolutionary critical pedagogy (as I am developing it) also offers an alternative interpretation of the history of capitalism and capitalist societies, with a particular emphasis on the United States.

It works within a socialist imaginary, that is, revolutionary critical pedagogy operates from an understanding that the basis of education is political and that spaces need to be created where students can imagine a different world outside of capitalist law of value, where alternatives to capitalism and capitalist institutions can be discussed and debated, and where dialogue can occur about why so many revolutions in past history turned into their opposite. It looks to create a world where social labour is no longer an indirect part of the total social labour but a direct part it, where a new mode of distribution can prevail not based on socially necessary labour time but on actual labour time, where alienated human relations are subsumed by authentically transparent ones, where freely associated individuals can successfully work towards a permanent revolution, where the division between mental and manual labour can be abolished, where patriarchal relations and other privileging hierarchies of oppression and exploitation can be ended, where we can truly exercise the principle "from each according to his or her ability and to each according to his or her need," where we can traverse the terrain of universal rights unburdened by necessity, moving sensuously and fluidly within that ontological space where subjectivity is exercised as a form of capacity-building and creative self-activity within and as a part of the social totality: a space where labour is no longer exploited and becomes a striving that will benefit all human beings, where labour refuses to be instrumentalized and commodified and ceases to be a compulsory activity, and where the full development of human capacity is encouraged. It also builds upon forms of self-organization that are part of the history of liberation struggles worldwide, such as those that developed during the civil rights, feminist and worker movements and those organizations of today that emphasize participatory democracy. Generally classrooms try to mirror in organization what students and teachers would collectively like to see in the world outside of schools—respect for everyone's ideas, tolerance of differences, a commitment to creativity and social and educational justice, the importance of working collectively, a willingness and desire to work hard for the betterment of humanity, a commitment to anti-racist, anti-sexist, and anti-homophobic practices, etc. Drawing upon a Hegelian-Marxist critique of political economy that underscores the fundamental importance of developing a *philosophy of praxis*, revolutionary critical pedagogy seeks forms of organization that best enable the pursuit of *doing critical philosophy as a way of life*. And that means finding time to read Marx, Hegel and other major thinkers, and developing a coherent way to live out our findings and discoveries and re-articulate them for the very specific times that we live in and for the unique struggles that lie ahead. I very much support the Bolivarian revolution in Venezuela, and this is one of the aspects that I am interested in: looking at Bolivarian pedagogical practices as a way of developing a broader philosophy of praxis. What are the specifics of this revolution, and how is it possible to develop a coherent revolutionary pedagogical approach? Obviously we can't transplant revolutionary critical pedagogy—North American style—in Venezuela, since it will emerge among the Bolivarian educators there with very distinct attributes and characteristics—as well with as a specific trajectory and tendency. But we can be part of a collective effort, and what we learn about pedagogical struggle there we can also introduce here so long as we are careful to reinvent—and restate—such pedagogical knowledge in the contextual specificity of our own struggle.

GLENN: "Race" has been another topic that you have written extensively on for many years. What are the special challenges that those on the Left face when teaching "race" in the U.S. today?

PETER: My frequent co-author, Valerie Scatamburlo-D'Annibale, and I just penned the following lines as an opening to an article we are writing:

> One of the most taken-for-granted features of contemporary social theory is the ritual and increasingly generic critique of Marxism in terms of its alleged failure to address forms of oppression other than that of "class." Marxism is considered to be theoretically bankrupt and intellectually passé, and class analysis is often savagely lampooned as a rusty weapon wielded clumsily by

> those mind-locked in the jejune factories of the nineteenth and twentieth centuries. When Marxist class analysis has not been distorted or equated with some crude version of "economic determinism," it has been attacked for diverting attention away from the categories of "difference"—including "race." Marxist analysis is often seen as hostile to race, as positing the reality of class as more important. This may be true for some versions of Marxism. But very often the hostility to Marxism from those whose priority is anti-racism or anti-sexism is a lack of understanding of the race/class/gender problematic that Marxists utilize in their understanding of the social totality of capitalism. Regrettably, to overcome the presumed inadequacies of Marxism, an entire discursive apparatus sometimes called "post-Marxism" has arisen to fill the void. Here in the United States, the majority of the educational left would define themselves as either non-Marxists or post-Marxists and it is therefore no surprise that they accept the relativism of the gender-race-class grid or triptych—also known as the much vaunted "intersectionality thesis"—that there is racism, classism, and sexism—and sometimes we are oppressed to varying degrees at various times and places by one or more of the phenomena. This conception is a major stumbling block for understanding class.

When we claim that class antagonism or struggle is one in a series of social antagonisms—race, class, gender, etc.—we often forget the fact that class sustains the conditions that produce and reproduce the other antagonisms, which is not to say that we can simply reduce race to class or reduce sexism to class. In other words, class struggle is the specific antagonism—the generative matrix—that helps to structure and shape the particularities of the other antagonisms, it over-determines the terrain upon which other struggles play out, it creates their conditions of possibility. But the unwillingness of many educators to understand this relationship (class as a social relation) has caused the educational left to, in effect, evacuate reference to historical structures of totality and universality. Class struggle is a determining force that structures "in advance" the very agnostic terrain in which other political antagonisms take place. I agree with Teresa Ebert that gender, sexuality and race become social differences only when they become part of the social division of labour. It is because of the divisions of labour and property that race, class and gender are sites of contestation and social struggle. In a world completely penetrated by capital, the most relevant social actor or historical agent is the "other" of capital—the wage labourer. Any counterhegemonic agency or human praxis that does not centre itself along this contradiction and this class antagonism will produce a faux-historical agency, a counterfeit agency that pacifies the bourgeois intellectual, but it will leave the current value form of labour and existing social practices untouched and intact.

This is why it is so important to bring educational reform movements into conversation with movements that speak to the larger totality of capitalist social relations and which challenge—to use a Rikowskian term—the very matter and anti-matter of capital's social universe. We need to keep our strategic focus on capitalist exploitation if we want to have effective anti-racist, anti-sexist, anti-homophobic struggles. We need to challenge global capitalism universally, which does not mean we ignore other social antagonisms, the horizon of which capitalism functions to sustain. Here I agree with Ellen Meiksins Wood, who argues that capitalism cannot be reduced to a particular oppression alongside many others but is a type of social torsion that imposes itself on the totality of our social relations. This does not mean that we have been discharged by history from our mission of grasping the "truth of the present" by interrogating all the existing structures of exploitation present within the capitalist system where, at the point of production, material relations characterize relations between people and social relations characterize relations between things. Rather, the critical educator must ask: How are individuals historically located in systematic structures of economic relations? How can these structures—these lawless laws of capital—be overcome and transformed through revolutionary praxis into acts of freely associated labour, "where the free development of each is the condition for the free development of all"?

Many post-Marxist anti-racists tend to assume that the principal political points of departure in the current "postmodern" world must necessarily be "cultural," and they gravitate towards a politics of "difference" which is largely premised on uncovering relations of power that reside in the arrangement and deployment of subjectivity in cultural and ideological practices—such a tendency is a reflection of the structural crisis of capitalism. Concepts of diversity rather than structures of dominance are what define the politics of difference in educational approaches to multiculturalism. If we examined the structures of power at work in the racialization of a social order, we would discover that the racial polity that defines the social order is structured in dominance by the founding contradiction within capitalist societies—the contradiction between labour and capital.

It is therefore imperative for critical social analysts committed to the struggle against all forms of oppression to move beyond the often obfuscating lens of "race" and concentrate more on how racism and capitalist exploitation are conjoined, on how they are mutually constitutive of each other. There is a tendency among multicultural educators to unwittingly reify race in a manner that prevents them from adequately grasping the interplay between the social relations of production and the complex process of racialization and its historical antecedents.

In no way am I suggesting that the lived realities of racial oppression be ignored—that would be simply foolish. I want to widen the lens of examining race and racism by focusing on the social relations of production which engender such constructions. So long as production is based on socially necessary labour time and abstract labour, the struggle to end racism and sexism will be seriously constrained. Which doesn't mean that we should simply wait for the revolution to occur and then think about attacking racism and sexism. No, of course not. We need to increase our participation in feminist struggle and anti-racist work. But we must at the same time deepen our understanding of the connection between race, class and gender antagonisms. Valerie and I have argued for a shift away from the concept of "race" to a pluralized conceptualization of "racisms" and their historical articulations with other ideologies and capitalist social relations. In our view, such a formulation would more accurately capture the historically specific nature of racism and the variety of meanings/connotations attributed to evaluations of "difference" and assessments of the "superiority" and/or "inferiority" of different groups. Here we take our cue from Marx, who perceptively recognized the way in which European and American capitalists promoted racial divisions within the working class. The categorization of people as inferior and subordinate was most often tied to their positions "in the labour market," and in this sense race becomes a modality of class oppression. I am more interested in the relationship between labour and the processes of racialization and the importance of understanding racist configurations contextually and in terms of *capitalist class relations*.

Some researchers have suggested that the Marxist foundations of critical pedagogy have led it to privilege issues of social class over race and other forms of "difference" while others have sweepingly declared that the entire enterprise of critical pedagogy is not only constrained by its "Marxist Eurocentricity" but that it is based on "white identity politics"—both positions which reveal a singular lack of understanding of the Marxist problematic of class with respect to race. In such narratives, Marxian theory itself is maligned as Eurocentric and racist. Contrary to those who advocate the abandonment of critical pedagogy's Marxist roots, we believe that Marx has become even more relevant in light of capitalist globalization and the imperial wars currently being waged on behalf of the transnationalist capitalist class. And we are very critical of those who would summarily dismiss Marxist theory as Eurocentric and racist.

One serious problem following from such an untutored grasp of the race/class dynamic within Marxist humanism has led to a pedagogy of multiculturalism that is seriously flawed at its root. E. San Juan's writings on multiculturalism have captured most of these flaws.

In San Juan's view, the multiculturalist problematic operates effectively as a form of "postmodern racism": a hegemonic scheme of peacefully managing the crisis of race, ethnicity, gender and labour in the developed North, a way of neutralizing the perennial conflicts in the system, a way of containing diversity in a common grid, a way of selling diversity as a means of preserving the ethnocentric paradigm of commodity relations that generate particularisms in the experience of life-worlds within globalizing capitalism. San Juan asserts that not only does postmodern racism reflect the inherent contradiction of the liberal democractic project, but it is the symptom of multiculturalist late capitalism whereby each local culture is refracted through an empty global position much the same way the way the colonizer treats colonized people as "natives" whose mores are to be carefully studied and "respected."

Multiculturalism from San Juan's perspective (and I am basically paraphrasing him here) becomes a disavowed, inverted, self-referential form of racism, a "racism with a distance"; it "respects" the identity of the "other," conceiving the "other" as a self-enclosed "authentic" community towards which he, the multiculturalist, maintains a strict distance rendered possible by his privileged universal position. Thus, dominant forms of liberal multiculturalism constitutes in some cases a form of indirect racism in so far as the dominant imperial white subject retains the position as the privileged empty point of universality from which one is able to appreciate (and depreciate) properly other particular cultures. Here, multiculturalists can fight for cultural differences while at the same time leaving the basic homogeneity of the capitalist world-system intact.

Again paraphrasing San Juan, culture as ethnic distinction reinforces the legitimacy of the racial polity. While we surely must recognize the integrity and value of people's cultures and life-forms, and for their collective right to exist and develop unimpeded, the key issue is how to universalize this multiplicity and autonomous singularities. This process of universalization cannot exist as long as the global logic of corporate accumulation determines the everyday life of people on this planet. The key is to abolish class divisions in a world where, as San Juan puts it, iniquitous property relations camouflaged by commodity-fetishism reify the entire basis of social life. That is, the solution to unravelling the antinomies and dilemmas of reification is abolishing the iniquitous social relations of production, the labour-capital contradiction.

Power relations are anchored in the iniquitous division of social labor which provides the edifice for an unequal distribution of wealth and devaluation of specific cultures. I also agree with theorists such as Teresa Ebert who argue that theories of racism, sexism and homophobia that relegate these antagonisms as effects of power fail to understand how power is derived from ownership of the means of production.

GLENN: How would you approach the general relation between learning for democracy and critical pedagogy? Is this a point where your work on Freire comes more to the fore?

PETER: Much of the work on democracy and education is grounded in a Deweyean, Rawlsian or Habermasian conception of social justice. I have tried to apply a Marxist critique to liberal and left-liberal conceptions of democracy, not in a systematic fashion, but as a way of inviting educators to think of the forces and relations of production. Here I have been influenced by the work of Daniel Bensaid, who does a good job of interpreting Marx's critique of the liberal-democratic consensus. Bensaid underscores what is essentially the irreconcilability of theories of justice—such as those by Rawls and Habermas—and Marx's critique of political economy. In the Rawlsian conception of the social contract, its conclusions are built into its premises since it never leaves the pristine world of inter-individual juridical relations. For instance, liberal theories of justice attempt to harmonize individual interests in the private sphere such that an injustice only occurs when the production of inequalities begins to affect the weakest members of that society. But Bensaid asks a crucial question: How can a society allocate the collective productivity of social labour individually? He concludes that the concept of cooperation and mutual agreement between individuals is a formalist fiction that excludes the messy world of class exploitation and the social division of labour. How is it possible to reduce social relations of exploitation to intersubjective relations, to dialogue, to participatory decision making at the level of the social contract, of civil society, of the public sphere? Here the concept of inequality is tied to the notion of creating *a fair equality of opportunity* and that these conditions of equal opportunity are to serve the greatest benefit to the least advantaged in society. Inequality is permitted to exist as long as such inequalities make a functional contribution to the expectations of the least advantaged. Bensaid likens this situation to a conception of economic growth commonly conceptualized as "shares of the cake." The idea is as follows: so long as the cake gets bigger, the smallest share, *pari passu*, continues to grow, even if the largest grows more quickly and the difference between them dramatically increases. This throws a bit of a wrench into the liberal theory of social justice, don't you think, Glenn? Such a conception of justice breaks down in the face of real, existing inequality premised on the reproduction of social relations of exploitation. This theory of social justice does have some sense to it, but only if we believe that we live in a harmonious world of decision-makers in which class conflict has ceased to exist. But look around you: we don't inhabit a world primarily driven by intersubjectivity and communicative rationality. There is an a priori acceptance of the despotism of the market in liberal theories of justice. Marxists don't accept this. Marx, after all, demonstrated how the formal equality of political rights can exist, hand in hand, with brute exploitation and suffering. The separation of economic rights and political rights is the very condition of the impossibility of democracy, a separation that the educational left has been stunningly unable to challenge in their discourses of reform. Marxists point to the constitutive impossibility of democracy in a society built upon property rights. This factor alone accounts for why democracy can be invoked against the democratic imperatives of the people in the name of the global imperium. Thus, Marxists would be sympathetic to Bensaid, who argues that capitalist exploitation is always unjust from the perspective of the class that has to endure it. Theories of justice are always relative to the mode of production that it proposes to control in the interests of all. Liberals view as pointless the idea of redistributing the wealth of the rich. They prefer helping the rich perform their wealth-creating role better, because this increases the size of the common cake. In fact, it echoes the famous words of George W. Bush: "Make the pie higher"! This perspective is landlocked on the side of distribution only. Because in this case the social relations of production and the exploitation of workers by capitalists has to be camouflaged, you leave all the public relations tasks to the private sector. And here, in the United States at least, there is never a discussion about economic rights. You can talk about human rights so long as you separate the notion of human rights from that of economic rights. You can't talk about the distribution of the conditions of production. Freire was very critical of militant Marxists who argued that little could be done to democratize education until class society was abolished. While Freire extolled the virtues of socialism, and drew substantively from various Marxist traditions, he never ceased to criticize dogmatic, doctrinaire Marxists whom he saw as intolerant and authoritarian. In fact, Freire argues that by refusing to take education seriously as a site of political transformation and by opposing socialism to democracy, the mechanistic Marxists have, in effect, delayed the realization of socialism for our times. This is a damning indictment, not of Marxism, but of a crude ultra-leftism that deserves to be held accountable for its economic reductionism. While I am frustrated sometimes with what appears to be an insufficient critique of political economy in his later work, I am a steadfast admirer of Freire. He is undoubtedly one of the most important influences in my work—he's as important for my pedagogical orientation as Moishe Postone is for your own theoretical orientation.

GLENN: Of course, your recent writings indicate that "all is not well" with American democracy (and indeed democracy in all of the most developed capitalist economies), and that critical educators have a particular responsibility regarding addressing the democratic deficit in their day-to-day work and lives. How do you see the role of "critical educator" in the struggle for democracy in school and the rest of social life today, Peter?

PETER: When Bush says that "the past is over," that "this is still a dangerous world" filled with "madmen and uncertainty and potential mental losses," he is speaking in apocalyptic terms that resonate with evangelical Christians who are not known for their appreciation of nuance and ambiguity. When he describes himself as "misunderestimated" we know that he is intent on following through on his plans. When he affirms that "families is where our nation finds hope, where our wings take dream" and when he exclaims that we must "Vulcanize society" or "make the pie higher" or when he assumes the role of the "education president" and asks, "Is our children learning?" we know that these malapropisms (if they are even recognized as such by his core constituency) help to endear him to potential voters in America's heartland. He has often been described as somebody most Americans would love to have a beer with in a local bar. So when his administration chooses to rule by the Big Lie, by carefully selecting bits of information to be disseminated by the media through speeches, interviews, and official statements to the press, and to make sure they are seen as "related," such as mentioning Iraq or Saddam Hussein in the same breath as 9/11, or just blatantly lying to the public about the real motives for the war in Iraq, these lies carry a great deal of credibility; they are, in fact, credible lies. It has been said that a lie can travel halfway around the world while the truth is still getting its boots on. This has always been the case with respect to the manufacturing of consent by means of the ideological state apparatuses in the United States, the corporate media in particular, but it has been ratcheted up considerably since 9/11. Bush, a born-again Christian who proclaims that he has a mandate from God, is the champion of evangelical Christians throughout the country, Christians who carry a lot of political clout. Some students at a nearby religious college see President Bush as an envoy of God whose very name, "Bush" (God appeared to Moses as a burning Bush) is viewed as providential. Teachers become an easily breached conduit for the official narratives of the state because they want to help their students develop a coherent worldview and provide them with an enduring stability, especially in times of crisis, of grave dislocation, of permanent war. The moral panic surrounding the meaning of patriotism in the post-9/11 United States has reverberated throughout the classrooms of the country. The anger and fear felt by teachers and students alike—proclivities easily leveraged by the Bush administration through the corporate media that amplify, echo, mirror and appease official government narratives at times of national crisis—have often intensified the feeling among Americans that they are under attack because they are responding to an apocalyptic calling by God to carry out the divine mission of salvation for all of humanity. We are confronted by a "national essentialism" or "millennialism" both secular and religious, or Judeo-Christian "triumphalism" on steroids, although it is fair to say that Americans historically have seen themselves as a self-designated Chosen People trying to create a new Jerusalem, a "holy utopia" modeled on what evangelicals believe God would like to see for the entire world. Accordingly, it is only those Americans who have accepted "Lord Jesus" into their lives who have the capacity, the will and the fortitude to redeem humankind. But faith in the unique moral destiny of the United States—the white man's burden writ in nuclear fission across the heavenly firmament—seems to increase during times of national crisis and along with it an intolerance of conflicting views, in this case those held by secular humanists, or Muslims, or atheists. So we have school boards in various states offering creationism or intelligent design as credible explanations of the origins of human life that they insist should be offered alongside scientific theories of evolution. In *Capitalists and Conquerors*, Nathalia Jaramillo and I write about this civil religion that serves to frame and define the Manichean Universe of good and evil—the moral universe within which George W. Bush and his "power puritans" love to operate.

The Christian Taliban that shapes the overall policy perspectives of the Bush administration feeds the determination of those who wish to transform the United States into a Christian theocracy. This has been a factor in stymieing efforts by the Left to take on the Bush administration.

There is a crazy resurgence of the "culture wars" in the U.S., most commonly associated with the 1980s during the Reagan presidency. Let me give you one example. Recently, former presidential candidate Pat Buchanan appeared on the popular right-wing television show *The O'Reilly Factor* (May 25, 2005), and accused Antonio Gramsci of being responsible for Paris Hilton's sexy television ads and for the corruption and decadence of U.S. culture in general. Whereas Buchanan maintained that the United States won the Cold War, he charged that "cultural Marxism" and "militant secularism" is winning the cultural wars in the United States as can be seen in the broken homes, delinquency and divorce rates. Buchanan said: "There was a communist known as Antonio Gramsci in Italy who argued that this is the only way that Marxism is going to win. And I have to say they are sure making progress and I think they're on the offensive." He added that "this is sort of, if you will, soft Marxism. And what its done is replaced Christianity. You know, a culture is a product of a cult. Western civilization is a product of Christianity. And Gramsci and the others realized they had to de-Christianize the culture. They had to change values. They had to make people think differently, and then the citadel of western civilization would collapse."

It is amazing, Glenn, how secular humanists have become the enemy. Any criticism of Bush by the Left is seen as the work of a Satanic force, or at the very least the work of weak-minded liberals who not only are responsible for the decline in America's moral values, but who also are unwilling and incapable of protecting the United States from terrorists who "hate our freedoms" and Christian values. Now couple this with the fact that educational leftists here in the United States are in the main reluctant to consider Marxist analyses of political economy in their research—mainly because of its immediate and overwhelming association with gulags and totalitarianism, and because, historically, their erstwhile support of state control of industry and nationalized property did not bear the socialist fruit that they had hoped—and now you have virtually no discussion of how to transform the capital relation itself in the educational literature. That is simply off limits.

The most that such left-liberal reformers can do is talk about how to reconstitute and revitalize the social contract, to deepen democratic decision-making and make it more participatory, and to struggle to make civil society more responsible in a bottom-up manner to the needs of the people. In short, you have the post-Marxist emphasis on radical democracy which is really a kind of damage control for capitalism. Because left liberals, or radical democrats, fail to recognize class as a matrix that generates the totality of social and political relations, the totality of social life as we experience it, the liberal-democratic horizon that provides the scope for their pedagogies permits no room to imagine a world outside of the capitalist law of value, outside of capital as a social relation and social force that invades the whole of our existence.

Reforms of this ilk seek, at best, a reassertion of productive capital over financial capital in the global economy (a return to a form of Keynesianism) or call for a global redistributive project, but rarely do they call for transcending the very value form of labour that gives life and lie to the social universe of capital. I am not a post-Marxist, I am a post-Marx Marxist. In this regard, I agree with William Robinson that we need theories of counter-hegemony that correspond to theories of capitalist hegemony. Robinson rehearses Gramsci's distinction between a *war of maneuver* (frontal attack) and a *war of position* (struggle of trench warfare, or of attrition). In so doing he convincingly argues that we must begin our anti-capitalist struggle with a strategic war of position, the exercise of resistance in the sphere of civil society by popular classes who are able to avoid co-optation and mediation by the nation state—and this means resistance at the points of accumulation, capitalist production and the process of social reproduction.

Robinson has established four fundamental requirements for an effective counter-hegemony that are worth repeating in this evaluation. First, he argues that we urgently need to build a political force upon a broader vision of social transformation that can link social movements and diverse oppositional forces. The resistance of popular classes needs to be unified through a broad and comprehensive strategy of opposition to those conditions that each social movement is opposing. How are the immediate conditions around which popular sectors are struggling linked to and derived from the larger totality of global capitalism and its social universe? The organizational forms of a renovated left must respect the autonomy of social movements, to social change from the bottom up rather than the top down, to democratic principles and practices within organizations themselves, and to an abandonment of the old verticalism in favor of non-hierarchical practices. The second requirement for an effective counter hegemony is building a viable socio-economic alternative to global capitalism. This is something that the Marxist humanists and groups such as Movement for a Socialist Future have been calling for in their publications and organizing over recent years. The third requirement is that popular classes need to transnationalize their struggles. Robinson here is talking about nothing less than the expanding of transnational civil society that serves as an effective counter-movement to global capitalism. His fourth requirement calls upon organic intellectuals to henceforth subordinate their work to and in the service of popular majorities and their struggles. Robinson importantly notes that fundamental change in a social order becomes possible when an organic crisis occurs, but that such an organic crisis of capitalism is no guarantee against social breakdown, authoritarianism or fascism. What is necessary is a viable alternative that is in hegemonic ascendance, a viable alternative to the existing social order that is perceived as preferable by a majority of society. So if we are going to carry this out, we have a lot of work ahead to educate Americans on the virtues of socialism over capitalism.

We need critical educators to help us confront the hydra-headed depredations of capitalism and to analyze how the social power of the popular classes is to be reconstructed. Such a reconstruction necessitates understanding intervention beyond simple forms of state intervention in the sphere of the circulation of capital. We need to extend to the state those very counter-hegemonic spaces of resistance that are occurring with social movements at the level of civil society. Further, social movements need to transnationalize those struggles. Here is where the progressives in the United States are at a stalemate. It's the same message, over and over, and it never urges us to leave the sphere of civil society or the public sphere. That is why I believe, along with Marxist humanists, that we need to become philosophers of praxis, that we need to build organizations that both reflect and serve as a medium for the construction of socialism.

While Minerva's owl only flies at dusk, that is, while we recognize only post-factum that the dialectics of negation moves the world inexorably forward, I don't believe that we, as philosophers of praxis, are destined always to arrive too late to effect any serious intervention. I believe that we can move the world forward. If I can be permitted to paraphrase Bertell Ollman's description of the Marxian dialectic and put it in pedagogical terms, we must learn to see the result of our own precondition as social agents as the precondition of what will become its result and its own negation. And in doing so we must become active agents willing and capable of intervening in such a history so that one day the capitalist exploitation currently driving humanity over the cliff of civilization will be seen as the prehistory of a socialist present. That's my vision, to one day see today's world of pain and suffering as the prehistory of a socialist present.

GLENN: You've spoken in Latin America regularly since the late-1980s, you've recently done work in Venezuela, met President Chavez, and have conducted seminars on critical pedagogy frequently in Mexico. Twenty years later, education scholars and activists have approached you in various Latin American countries and asked if they could set up foundations and institutes in your name centering on advancing critical pedagogy throughout Latin America. How do you see this development? Is it a final vindication of your work?

PETER: You are referring to the recent creation of La Fundacíon McLaren de Pedagogía Crítica in Tijuana Mexico, and the forthcoming Instituto Peter McLaren in Cordoba, Argentina, and others (that are still pending so I won't mention them). Yes, these were initiated by scholars and activists whom, I suspect, are drawn to the Marxist humanism that undergirds my work in critical pedagogy. But I would like to emphasize that these foundations and institutes are not about engaging my work in isolation from the work of other critical educators, but about developing cross-border collaborative work in the general field of critical pedagogy. If my work can serve as a flashpoint in this regard, and in developing a broader anti-imperialist pedagogical movement that is directed at creating socialism, then I look forward to a future of struggle on the streets as much as in the classrooms.

Interviewers

ANGELA CALABRESE BARTON is an associate professor of science education at Teachers College, Columbia University. Her areas of specialty include urban science education and critical/feminist perspectives on science education. She has published four books, the most recent *Re/Thinking Scientific Literacy* (with W.M. Roth) won the Exemplary Research Award from the American Association for Research in Science Teaching and Teacher Education Division. Her work has been published in *Educational Researcher, American Education Research Journal*, the *Journal of Research in Science Teaching, Science Education*, among other journals.

GUSTAVO FISCHMAN is an assistant professor in the Division of Curriculum and Instruction, at Arizona State University. His research interests are in the areas of comparative and international education, gender studies, and qualitative studies in education. Dr. Fischman is the author of two books and several articles on Latin American education, teacher education, cultural studies and education, and gender issues in education. He is associate editor for the online journals *Education Policy Analysis Archives* (EPAA) (http://epaa.asu.edu/) and *Education Review* (http://edrev.asu.edu/).

KRIS D. GUTIERREZ is professor of social research methodology in the Graduate School of Education and Information Studies at the University of California, Los Angeles. Professor Gutierrez is a national and international leader in cultural historical theories of learning and development. Her work addresses the relationship between literacy, culture and learning and centers around in the processes by which people, informed by their own personal and socio-cultural histories, negotiate meaning in culturally organized contexts, using language and literacies that are embedded within sociohistorical traditions. As director of a program for high school students from migrant farm-worker backgrounds, Professor Gutierrez's work brings critical and social theories together to help students acquire socio-critical literacies as a means of transformation.

JOE L. KINCHELOE is professor of education and Canada Research Chair at McGill University. He is the author of numerous books and articles about pedagogy, cultural studies, education and social justice, racism, class bias, and sexism, issues of cognition and cultural context. His most recent books are *Critical Pedagogy, A Primer* and *Classroom Teaching: An Introduction*. He is responsible for labeling Peter McLaren the poet laureate of the educational Left.

KEN MCCLELLAND is a doctoral candidate in education at Brock University in St. Catharines, Ontario, Canada. He is presently writing his dissertation on the confluence of the classical pragmatism of John Dewey with the neo-pragmatism of Richard Rorty. He is also the founding co-editor of *Professing Education*, a publication for the Society of Professors of Education.

MARCIA MORAES is a professor at Faculdade CCAA and Universidade do Estado do Rio de Janeiro. She is also a former associate professor at the University of St.Thomas-Minnesota. Her publications include diverse articles and chapters in education and the books *Bilingual Education: A Dialogue with the Bakhtin Circle* (U.S.:SUNY) and *Ser Humana: Quando a Mulher Está em Discussão* (Brazil: DP&A). She has also translated books into Portuguese including *Globalization, Education and the Crisis of Democracy* by Peter McLaren and Ramin Farahmandpur.

LUCÍA CORAL AGUIRRE MUÑOZ was born in Mexico City in 1954. She studied Sociology at the UNAM. She did interdisciplinary studies of social change at Nice, France. Her Masters degree and Ph.D. in the sciences of education were obtained in Baja California, México, where she has worked since 1982. She does research, teaching and administration at the Instituto de

Investigación y Desarrollo Educativo in the Universidad Autónoma de Baja California. Her main interest is in the field of Sociology of Education where she is engaged with critical humanism.

MIKE ALEXANDER POZO was a student at St. John's University in Jamaica Queens, New York. While at St. John's he was co-founder and co-editor of the *St. John's University Humanities Review.* His interviews have included among others E. San Juan Jr., Ngugi Wa Thiongo, Peter McLaren, Howard Zinn, Gregory Maertz and Henry Giroux. He is currently a doctoral student at UC San Diego.

GLENN RIKOWSKI is a senior lecturer in education studies in the School of Education at the University of Northampton, UK. He is author of *The Battle in Seattle: Its Significance for Education* (2001, The Tufnell Press). He lives in London. Contact: Rikowskigr@aol.com.

MASHHOOD RIZVI is the co-founder and editor-in-chief of Pakistan's first progressive magazine on education and development. *EDucate!* He has launched a series of ongoing dialogues on critical societal issues.

MITJA SARDOC is research assistant at the Educational Research Institute in Ljubljana, Slovenia, where he is currently engaged in research projects on citizenship education, human rights, school autonomy, inclusion and equal educational opportunities. He earned his MSc from the Ljubljana Graduate School of the Humanities and is doing his MPhil/PhD study at the Institute of Education, University of London, UK. His research focuses on political theory and philosophy of education with particular emphasis on citizenship education, equality, inclusion and diversity in public education. He has edited a number of journal special issues on citizenship education, social justice and has interviewed some of the most renowned contemporary political philosophers on the topic of education and political theory (e.g. Michael Walzer, Iris Marion Young, Martha C. Nussbaum, Stephen J. Macedo, Richard Dagger, Robert K. Fullinwider, Kenneth A. Strike, Eamonn Callan, et al.). He is executive editor of *Theory and Research in Education* published by SAGE, a correspondent for the *Politeia Newsletter* and member of the editorial board of the *Journal for Critical Education Policy Studies*.

MICHAEL F. SHAUGHNESSY is currently professor of education at Eastern New Mexico University in the Educational Studies Department. He has lectured in England, Africa, Finland, South Korea, Germany and Slovenia. He is on the Editorial Boards of *The International Journal of Theory and Research in Education, Educational Psychology Today and Gifted Education International*. He has been a social studies teacher in the South Bronx of New York City, has been a guidance counselor, school psychologist, and basketball coach. He has edited five books and published more than 500 articles.

DIANNE SMITH is the division chair and associate professor, Urban Leadership and Policy Studies in Education, at the University of Missouri-Kansas City. Her research interests include black girls and urban schooling; critical womanist/feminist pedagogy; and cultural diversity. She has lectured on critical pedagogy and womanist/feminist pedagogy at the University of Western Cape, Bellvue, South Africa; and the University of Port Elizabeth, Port Elizabeth, South Africa. She is past-president of the American Educational Studies Association (2004).

SHIRLEY R. STEINBERG is an associate professor at the McGill University Faculty of Education. She is the author and editor of numerous books and articles and co-edits several book series. She is also the founding editor of *Taboo: The Journal of Culture and Education*. Steinberg has recently finished editing *Teen Life in Europe*. She is the editor of *Multi/Intercultural Conversations: A Reader*. With Joe Kincheloe she has edited *What You Don't Know About Schools*, *Kinderculture: The Corporate Construction of Childhood*, and *The Miseducation of the West: How Schools and the Media Distort Our Understanding of the Islamic World*. She is co-author of *Changing Multiculturalism: New Times, New Curriculum*, and *Contextualizing Teaching* (with Joe Kincheloe). Her areas of expertise and research are in critical media literacy, social drama, and youth studies.

Index

A

I

S

V

W

Z

About the Title

RAGE AND HOPE is a website that was created as a project for Dr. James Scheurich's 1999 graduate course, Systems of Human Inquiry, at the University of Texas at Austin.

The site was developed by:

Cynthia Duda: doctoral student in curriculum studies
Responsible for collecting information on Henry Giroux

Ruben Garza: doctoral student in curriculum studies
Responsible for collecting information on Michael Apple

Linda Stacavich: doctoral student in educational administration
Responsible for information overview and reference section

Sing-Kwan Yang: doctoral student in policy and planning
Responsible for information on Peter McLaren

Laurie Williams: doctoral student in instructional technology
Responsible for information on Paulo Freire and web development

About the Author

PETER MCLAREN is an award-winning author, political activist and professor of education at the Graduate School of Education and Information Studies, University of California, Los Angeles. McLaren's contribution to the development of the field of critical pedagogy is well known worldwide. His writings have been translated into fifteen languages. He is the inaugural recipient of the Paulo Freire Social Justice Award, Chapman University. His classic book *Life in Schools* was judged by an international panel of experts to be among the top twelve books on education ever written. Recently, educators in North Mexico created the Fundación McLaren de Pedagogía Crítica to advance McLaren's work and the work of other critical educators throughout Mexico and the Americas. Professor McLaren is a member of the Industrial Workers of the World.

COUNTERPOINTS

Studies in the Postmodern Theory of Education

General Editors
Joe L. Kincheloe & Shirley R. Steinberg

Counterpoints publishes the most compelling and imaginative books being written in education today. Grounded on the theoretical advances in criticalism, feminism, and postmodernism in the last two decades of the twentieth century, Counterpoints engages the meaning of these innovations in various forms of educational expression. Committed to the proposition that theoretical literature should be accessible to a variety of audiences, the series insists that its authors avoid esoteric and jargonistic languages that transform educational scholarship into an elite discourse for the initiated. Scholarly work matters only to the degree it affects consciousness and practice at multiple sites. Counterpoints' editorial policy is based on these principles and the ability of scholars to break new ground, to open new conversations, to go where educators have never gone before.

For additional information about this series or for the submission of manuscripts, please contact:

Joe L. Kincheloe & Shirley R. Steinberg
c/o Peter Lang Publishing, Inc.
275 Seventh Avenue, 28th floor
New York, New York 10001

To order other books in this series, please contact our Customer Service Department:

(800) 770-LANG (within the U.S.)
(212) 647-7706 (outside the U.S.)
(212) 647-7707 FAX

Or browse online by series:

www.peterlangusa.com